The Complete Guide to

ADVERTISING

ADVERTISING

The Complete Guide To

ADVERTISING

Torin Douglas

**Consultant Editor
Barry Day**

M

A QED BOOK
First published 1984 by
MACMILLAN LONDON LIMITED
London and Basingstoke

Associated companies in Auckland, Dallas, Delhi,
Dublin, Hong Kong, Johannesburg, Lagos, Manzini,
Melbourne, Nairobi, New York, Singapore, Tokyo
Washington and Zaria

ISBN 0 333 38639 6

This book was designed and produced by
QED Publishing Ltd
32 Kingly Court
London W1

Editor Stephen Paul
Designers Tom Deas & Rita Wüthrich
Illustrator David Mallott
Picture Researcher Liz Sherriff
Art Director Alastair Campbell

Filmset by Text, Orpington, London
Origination by Hong Kong Graphic Arts Ltd
Hong Kong
Printed by Poligrafici Calderara S.P.A.
Bologna, Italy

CONTENTS

CONTENTS

FOREWORD

Someone once described advertising as 'the most fun you can have with your clothes on', causing many people to wonder what he had been doing with his adult life to date. But the remark is worthy of note on two levels at least. In the first place, the remark is shocking. You are meant to remember it and who said it. To that degree it is a form of *self-advertising*. (So, perversely, I shall refrain from mentioning its author.) Secondly, like all good advertising, it embodies and vitalizes a fundamental truth. Advertising *is* fun – otherwise grown men and women would not spend a professional lifetime dedicated to this frustrating art of the barely possible, not even for money. It is fun because it is a series of ever-changing communications conundrums that can only be solved if you understand society's ebb and flow, the nuances as well as the basics of the way we live now.

The people who make ads are dealing in people's dreams, hopes and fears, touching aspiration, providing reassurance and making as their contribution to this mad mosaic that is life (at least as depicted by the media), an offering of just about the only *good* news that is fit to print (to parody the famous banner-line from the *New York Times*).

The rationale for advertising lies woven in the fabric of the free enterprise socio-economic system, and if you embrace that, you take advertising with it as the most efficient – though, as yet unquantifiable – means of letting the maker of the product or provider of the service inform enough prospective users of what is available. Like the cuckoo clock, it works.

As to *how* it works, there are innumerable theories. Some people will tell you there are scientific rules. In fact, one of the first revered text books on the subject was Claude Hopkins' *Scientific Advertising*. Years later, David Ogilvy added his gloss to the same approach of 'How to . . .' advertising, by interpreting much of the quantitative teaching of the good Dr Gallup, the self-styled 'father of market research'. Here were the proven rules of layout, the tested ways to draw people into your headline, make your body-copy more readable and aid your brand-name recall.

All very sensible and proving one thing. Common-sense could help you produce an ad that came close to being fail-proof, if not totally foolproof. The 'rules' would help you avoid error. It still took a little thing called 'talent' to bring the rules to life.

Another approach – if not invented then at least popularized in the 1950s and 1960s by Bill Bernbach (of Doyle Dane Bernbach) – was all about the *attitude* an advertiser took towards its product. While advertising had traditionally from its brash, tub-thumping beginnings extolled the virtue of the brightest, biggest and loudest being the best, Bernbach saw things from another point of view. Anything of inherent quality that put its case candidly was worthy of consideration. Was it not possible that a man who admitted his imperfections and convinced you that he was trying to do something about them, was a more honest fellow, a more your-kind-of-fellow fellow than some of those nose-in-the-air

big boys? Bernbach brought a folksy freshness, not least to the *language* of advertising which had, even then, begun to atrophy into the soporific superlatives that are unfortunately still with us.

And then there were – and ever more will be – those other searches for the Holy Grail of advertising executional excellence, some magic formula that can be guaranteed to ring the bell. Perhaps every product had a USP (Unique Selling Proposition) within it waiting to be released, like a genie from the bottle? Perhaps there was some characteristic about every product that could be transformed with a touch of fantasy into memorable fairy-tale proportions? Hence the mnemonic (or memory-jogging) device that metaphorically and visually turned a kitchen cleaner into a White Tornado, or a laundry detergent strong enough to 'fight dirt' into a White Knight zapping stains with his lance.

Each and every attempt was quite comprehensible in its determination to fight the good fight against the sheer noise level and information pollution generated by *all* the media as we moved, somewhat stunned by it all, into the second half of the 20th century. Their crucial failing was the supposition that they could solve *all* the problems that arose. Sadly, far too often their glitter turned out to be no more than gold plate.

None of the pioneers was wrong. They just did not have the one and only exclusive solution and yet they thought they *should* have. After all, wasn't advertising about being No 1? In the last decade or so, I would say that advertising has groped its way towards a kind of post-pubertal pre-maturity, at least in this respect. The beginnings of a kind of wisdom have come from the realization that the only real No 1 is not the product devised by man, but the man or woman the product was devised to suit. That, together with a less arrogant appreciation of the supportive role advertising can play in the whole selling process. The nearest I can come to a definition of this process, is that advertising can *help create a relationship between a person and a product*. It can be an 'agent' or intermediary in that process, but its role is secondary not primary. If customer and manufacturer find each other through the common ground of the right product and the relationship lasts, then the advertising has done its work. Whatever advertising technique the advertiser uses to effect that all-important introduction is also, in the scheme of things, secondary. To think otherwise, I suggest, is to give advertising and the people who make it altogether too much importance.

Advertising is not an art, a craft, or anything *in its own right*. It is the application of certain artistic techniques, of various kinds of linguistic or filmic grammar *to the solution of a defined problem*. And that problem was defined by someone else when they decided what product to make or what service to offer. It is *their* problem. Whereas nobody, to my knowledge, *told* Shakespeare that he had to write a Sonnet to a Dark Lady. The only point of resemblance he had to the commercial imperative advertisers deal in daily, is that he only had 14 lines to say what he had to say.

Advertising has always been wreathed in metaphysical mists. From the time of the first medicine-man selling snake oil from the back of the stagecoach, to the self-induced hypnosis created by so-called 'subliminal' advertising, to the about-to-be wonders of global commercials via satellite, there has always been a need on the part of some people, at least, to believe in the talismanic properties of advertising and its supposed power to 'manipulate' its audience. The sort of examples I have mentioned are the kind people argue about the most, in tones ranging from a titillated *frisson* to total – almost religious – condemnation. With no Merlin to wave a magic wand and change our lives, perhaps the need to believe in miracles has taken this rather tame turn.

I have yet to see the evidence that advertising unsupported by product performance has ever had more than a temporary effect in persuading anyone to do anything against their own best interests. There is, however, a growing body of evidence that a *bad* product will be killed off quicker because of advertising – since more people will be aware of it sooner, try it and reject it.

It is now a permanent fact of contemporary advertising life, though, that the business is under attack for its 'failings'. In country after country, category after category of product advertising is being more and more severely restricted in terms of what can be said. Cigarettes, liquor, patent medicines, products aimed at children – the list grows daily. The concerns are legitimate, some of the restrictive measures more debatable. What is particularly interesting – and encouraging, if you believe in the essential vitality of the advertising process – is the way in which legal restrictions have led to imaginative and unexpected solutions to the newly-defined problems. Legislation as stimulation. Encouraging, too, is the way that different countries have set up self-regulatory bodies to monitor the veracity of their local advertising, in order to forestall government intervention and legal requirements. If there is one thing that advertising professionals agree on, irrespective of nation, it is that the people who understand advertising least are the politicians.

Ironic, then, that just about the most conspicuous new users of advertising these last couple of decades have been the *politicians*. Not merely in the use of paid advertising (where that is legally permitted), but in the use of the accepted techniques of the simplification or compression of information as a necessary means of conveying a complex point of view to a frequently apathetic consumer/voter. By and large, it is satisfying to relate, most politicians use advertising badly because they do not *believe* in it in a positive sense, but have come to accept it as a necessary evil in the modern electoral process. It always amuses me to see the expressions of entrapped indignation on the faces of politicians who have just been accused (usually on TV) of allowing themselves to be 'sold like a packet of detergent'! Naturally, it is meant as the ultimate insult, but if the average politician had their 'product story' put across as effectively and consistently as the average detergent, they should think themselves lucky.

What the politicians lack (as do all critics of advertising) is faith in the *process* of advertising – they fear that if it doesn't work overnight, it won't work at all. In fact, the history of advertising, brief as it is, would seem to suggest that the process works best slowly and continuously *over time*.

There is a world of difference between an *advertisement* and *advertising* – the act and the process. If that sounds too philosophical, think of the advertisers you grew up with who are still around and just as much a part of your personal scenery as ever – perhaps reassuringly more so in these troubled times. Coca-Cola, Kellogg's, Ford, Kodak, Heinz, Guinness, Martini, Esso and Shell . . . you name it – and you *could* name a hundred or more without any trouble, if you took the trouble. But you do not. You take them for granted – which is all most of them want, as long as you remember to ask for them by *name*!

The thing that all these household-name advertisers have in common is that they believe in advertising as part of the product. All of them have advertised continuously and consistently. Their customers have always known where they stood. Certainly, they have changed a little to allow for changing times, just as old friends do, but deep down they are still the same. Another thing they have done is to define what it is about them that makes them unique. It may be a distinctive style of advertising (like Coke). It may be a visual device (like the Esso Tiger), or an aspirational attitude (like Martini). Whatever form it takes, that distinctiveness becomes the *brand property* over time and a competitive advantage of incalculable value. That advantage, even when it is product – as opposed to perception – based, owes much of its success to the contribution of advertising in establishing, reinforcing and guiding the necessary evolution of the 'property'. It is, arguably, the most important single contribution advertising has made to date to the way we live now, this establishing of product touchstones.

When a previously successful and consistent advertiser fails, it is usually because they have lost the temper of the times. They have stopped listening to the echoes from the audience – the shuffling feet, the averted eye, the bored cough. They have also usually begun to take themselves too seriously. (Often their agency indulges or encourages them in this, but the fault remains squarely theirs.) Manner reigns over matter – style over content. The tone of the advertising alters subtly – talking *down* replaces talking *to*.

In the whole of advertising, there are few things so fascinating as to watch an advertising fad burn itself out with all the brilliance and longevity of a shooting star. It may be an individual style à la Ogilvy. We know what Ogilvy intended, but what many copyists took away was that a big picture, a long headline and lots of copy would suffice. Or Bernbach – another big picture. Less words and definitely *no* serifs – oh, and *insult* the product.

Lately, and particularly since TV, it has been a *look*. Lighting as substitute for insight. Get a famous film director to film your commercial and a good idea would inevitably emerge. All too often it didn't – with the result that the account moved to another famous film director whose distinctive look would inevitably . . . Even more latterly – and particularly since the permutations of video technology have revealed themselves to be just about endless – it has been a *technique*. As I write, the in-vogue is for computer animation that leaves Disney in the nursery. Here we are on dangerous ground, because the things the computer can do that we currently imagine for it to do are already staggering. If we can *think* of it, it can be done – no quibbles, no caveats and no one to blame but ourselves for not being able to think of anything better. What a sobering thought!

The only problem is that most of the time all we can think of is what has already *been* thought of – and then we try to put a quick contemporary shine on it. This particular quirk has always been a failing of the average human imagination – remember McLuhan's phrase about 'the rear-view mirror mentality'? We always move forward looking over our shoulder to see where we have been. But that was in relatively easier times when new possibilities seemed to be opening up sequentially. Now, with everything that has ever been still available and all these new toys to play with, the combinations are endless and the responsibilities awesome.

Technology – in so far as it affected advertising – developed in fits and starts until very recently, when all electronic hell began to break loose and flood us with possibilities and permutations. For most of the first half of the century there was only the printed word and picture to convey the commercial message. Radio only became important in America in the 1930s and TV not until after the Second World War, so – to all intents and purposes – several successive generations of 'Gutenberg Men' shaped the business of advertising in Western society.

But then, as each new medium joined the queue, particularly TV, a new dilemma was posed. Each *new* medium was immediately dealt with according to the rules of the preceding one. Thus, TV was obviously nothing more than a print ad that moved. That was how the United Kingdom, with its print heritage, reacted. (I know, I was there.) The United States, on the other hand, had a strong *radio* tradition by the time of TV, and early US TV commercials were much more like illustrated radio commercials. One further twist in the spiral to prove the point. Commercial radio arrived in the United Kingdom some 20 years *after* TV. So what did we do? We immediately wrote radio commercials that sounded like TV sound tracks . . .

And now we come to cable TV with its ability to *narrow*cast – as opposed to *broad*cast – its messages to highly selective and selected groups of people, so that careful targeting and specific creative execution will put us in at least a theoretical position to please some of the people all (or most) of the time. At the same time we have the possibility of beaming down from a satellite a cross-cultural, pan-national message that says something not too specific to *all* the people. In fact, any given advertiser will probably be doing both things at one and the same moment (which is where the investment in brand properties will pay off all over again). This is the new media pattern – at least for the time being. We shall have to improve on our historical performance in adapting to change, if we are to tap even a fraction of its potential.

The point is that there *are* no rules in the sense of immutable 'dos' and 'don'ts' – nothing that does not have to be continually questioned and reassessed in the light of a changing *total* pattern. Certainly, there are 'guidelines' – I prefer that expression to 'rules'. If you clutter a print layout with too many elements, it is likely to be visually confusing as well as aesthetically displeasing. Since the consumer does not *have* to read your ad, the chances are increased that they probably will not. Similarly, if you pack too many words into a TV commercial, especially if you are *saying* one thing while you are *showing* another, you are making your life more difficult than it need be. Those sort of obvious home truths I would call 'guidelines'. But the fallacy creeps in with the assumption – still held by many people – that media have some sort of boundaries of their own, that they are somehow self-contained and must be 'learned' separately and in isolation like subjects on a school curriculum.

To my eye and ear the evidence is overwhelmingly otherwise. The media *change* each other. The arrival of each new one pushes the others into different patterns and purposes. Sometimes the changes are small but always significant. The most obvious example is the way print has adapted to the 'TV Effect'. And let me add that this process had *nothing* to do with advertising and everything to do with the way the media work by their very nature.

The generations that used to receive their news about the outside world by reading it in the papers have now given way to a generation that relies on TV as its primary source of news and *then* turns to the newspaper to fill in the background, thus pushing it into a complementary but different role. Advertising is simply the main media story writ small.

Consumers who have been brought up as 'TV children' are now 'visually literate' as never before. You simply cannot watch 50 hours of TV a week (as the average American does), without being 'educated' by it. And let us ignore content for the moment. Just think of the learning of 'film grammar', the emotional meaning of a camera angle, the sense of pace in editing, the 'reality' of the street interview – all the tricks Hollywood ever dreamed of *plus* a whole new cornucopia made possible by videotape technology. And *all* of it happening subconsciously. None of these viewers *study* the TV medium as professionals do. They are simply *exposed* to it, and that combined exposure makes them look at life differently. They expect to have information presented to them TV-style – in motion, up close, dramatic. Other media, please copy or find a comparable mode.

Look at print advertising today with this in mind. It does not necessarily seek to replicate the TV image, but it is fashioned in the knowledge of the visual *expectations* created by the TV effect. When it stands perfectly still and demands the reflective study it could once upon a time have expected to receive as a matter of media right, it does so knowingly. It could be argued that that decision, too, is part of the 'Effect'. In the same way the coming of cable TV will affect the current TV establishment, which now tends to behave like print did at its unrivalled peak – as though to be 'state of the art' was enough.

Now that the domestic TV set is a receiver of electronic messages from a variety of sources – including the options the individual chooses to exercise in the viewing time available by way of video cassettes and discs, computer games and so on – mainstream TV is having to re-think its role for the future. If all of this sounds complicated – it *is*.

McLuhan once said that 'the ads of our time are the richest and most faithful daily reflections any society ever made of its whole range of activities'. I think he was right – I *know* he was right – and the reasons are fairly obvious. The reporting of *news* is a transitory thing. Today's news is tomorrow's history. For the time it is in front of you on the page or screen it may pass you passively by or it may reach out, grab you and change your life. But essentially it is there because it is there.

The reporting of a *product* is something very different in kind. If the product is not perceived as being sufficiently relevant to enough people, the product dies. So it is in the *commercial* instinct which shapes the message that the difference lies. The product must be seen to be relevant to the way people live, which means the communication must start from a common point of reference. Unless consumers believe that the advertiser *understands* them, there is little else to be said. Thus, the clues and cues, the minutiae of daily life – the little things that make up that life, the way people dress, talk, walk and behave – are all part of the communications vocabulary when an ad is put together. The best advertising craftsmen use them instinctively, not knowingly, as a kind of mirror held up to nature.

But not only must the observations be apt reflections of life and relevant to the product on offer – they must be *brief*. Advertising's need to tell much in little has also shaped a more general perception of how information is relayed and received – to the point where long-windedness becomes positively painful to the viewer. Miniaturization has become a legitimate form, and advertising's version of it just about the only remaining and satisfying example of beginning-middle-end narrative structure. And perhaps one more reason why good, well-constructed advertising is satisfying is that it makes the learning process palatable and painless.

Unlike so much contemporary 'art', striving to be different from all that has gone before, able to create new 'language' because specific meaning is not a necessary part of the mix, advertising presents the new in terms of the familiar. No new language because of the risk of confusion, which may lead to rejection. Instead, a well-developed sense of analogy and metaphor. This new thing is like this old thing but with this useful difference. Think of this dangerous new object called a 'motor car' as a 'horseless carriage'. One step at a time but you still end up safely where you have never *quite* been before. Advertising is part of the wallpaper of our lives and has been these many years, underlining the fundamental human values – often doing so too overtly for many tastes. Think, too, of the advertising lines which have entered the language as a kind of folk shorthand. That can only happen when a popular chord is struck. Nobody can buy or legislate for that kind of acceptance.

Advertising has always been and always will be controversial as a phenomenon. People want information so that they can make an informed choice. They also like certain advertisements as a form of folk art. At the same time, they are fearful of manipulation, which makes their attitude to advertising ambiguous. I imagine it will always be so. As I have tried to indicate, advertising is a means not an end, and, as such, it can be used badly or well. It is not good or bad in or of *itself*. That, I believe, is the crux of the argument.

Having rambled, somewhat randomly, around the subject that has occupied my professional life, I wondered how I might best sum up my interim conviction about the way it works. At which point, I came across something I had written a few years ago. I found I still agreed with myself – so for what it's worth, I would like to quote that Credo now:

'I BELIEVE that, while there may be effective individual advertisements, we are basically in the business of advertising that lasts. It is without question more difficult to produce an advertising campaign that works consistently over time, and adapts intelligently to social change during that time without losing its original identity.

'I BELIEVE in advertising that starts with the way people think and feel, and then finds a way to interpret whatever it happens to be selling to suit that context. That way an ad can hope to fit into someone's life and create a real relationship.

'I BELIEVE that all advertising must in some way reassure. It has to provide a point of reference. Advertising is not of itself innovation. In its use of language – and particularly in its attitude – it has to express even the new in terms of the familiar.

'I BELIEVE an ad should be a small reward. The reward can sometimes be the surprise of new and welcome information. It can equally well be the quiet confirmation of a long-held view from an old advertising friend – which is what brand-leader advertising is usually about.

'I BELIEVE that the great ad can – in its small way – crystallize the temper of the times. It can give shape to what people are thinking, often without even knowing it is doing it – so that the ad becomes a small but important thing to hang on to.

'I BELIEVE that when all of the above is truly observed then – and only then – does advertising technique become important. Then – and only then – does it matter that the product is the focus of the ad ... that the picture is sharp and clear ... the words touching and true ... the balance of the elements aesthetically pleasing. And then it matters one hell of a lot!'

And I still believe that that, as Walter Cronkite used to say, is the way it is ... The advertising is right there in the product. All we have to do is coax it out.

Barry Day

INTRODUCTION

WHAT IS IT?

Soap firms were among the first to discover the power of advertising in the 19th century, and one of the best-known names was that of Pears (*above*). This ad, entitled 'A pretty smile before the thrashing', is in the spirit of Millais' much-reproduced painting, 'Bubbles'.

The most powerful ads in the early years were posters, which offered advertisers colour illustration to help put across a desirable and dramatic image of their products (*far right*).

One of the most highly acclaimed television commercials in recent years showed a succession of embarrassing incidents, each of which was prompted by the sudden disappearance of a vital product. A car thudded to the ground as its tyres vanished; a farmer toppled backwards into the mud as his boots came off; a couple were thrown into each other's arms as the moving pavement they were on suddenly disappeared; and finally, an attractive blonde tennis player was seen looking first bemused and then horrified as her racquet disappeared, shortly to be followed by her tennis dress. 'You'd be surprised how much you'd miss Dunlop', said the voice-over.

An equally dramatic commercial could be made showing how much we would all miss advertising, though even the creative talents of Saatchi & Saatchi

Compton – the agency which made the Dunlop commercial – might find themselves hard pressed to convey all of the consequences.

The first few incidents would be easy. Posters and billboards would disappear, leaving the streets less colourful and the demolition sites bare. Most of the world's television stations would vanish – all of them in some countries – leaving people not only without TV commercials, but also without all the news, sport, entertainment and drama programmes they have come to expect. Many newspapers and magazines would cease to exist and those that remained would be much smaller and more expensive. Yet such deprivations would be nothing compared with the effect that the disappearance of advertising would have on the process of mass production and mass consumption, on the price and range of goods in the shops, on the economy and on employment. Without advertising, many products, companies and jobs would simply cease to exist.

If such claims seem far-fetched, a brief examination of the development of the advertising business since the 19th century may help to substantiate them. In order to do so, however, we have first to determine what we mean by the word 'advertisement'. This is harder than it looks, since, even within the advertising business, people disagree as to what counts as an advertisement. Much of what the general public would regard as advertising is relegated by many ad people into a category known as 'sales promotion', a term which covers most advertising material other than that placed in major media such as television, the press, radio and posters. This distinction can be confusing.

One of the most comprehensive, though rather unexciting, definitions of 'advertisement' is: 'any paid-for communication intended to inform and/or influence one or more people'. It was written by Jeremy Bullmore, the London chairman of a leading advertising agency, J. Walter Thompson, and the reason it is comprehensive is because it covers all the key elements.

Firstly, 'paid-for'. Free publicity, such as an interview on a radio station, or an article in a newspaper describing a product in glowing terms, is not an advertisement, even if it leads to a huge increase in sales. Payment for an ad is generally made in two ways – to the media owner, for the space or time in which the ad is displayed, and to the production company for the preparation of the ad itself, whether it is a TV commercial or a print ad. Even if no payment is made to the media owner – perhaps when a shop displays a poster for a local event free of charge – the material is arguably still an advertisement.

Secondly, 'communication'. Every advertisement is designed to convey a message to one or more people, and if there is no message there is no communication. To buy a poster site or a newspaper page and leave it blank, is not to advertise. There has to be a message, however brief, as well as a medium through which it is conveyed.

Thirdly, 'intended'. Advertisements do not always achieve their objectives. For example, a recruitment ad

FIAT 509

STAMPATO N° 1087 bis - 1925 - 25000 -   OFF. G. RICORDI & C. MILANO

TEEN + BEE = 365 Valentine's Days a year.
WOOLY I love you very much, wish I was at No. 66. Olly.
LITTLE LAW STUDENT I love you that much! Your very own Ghengis Khan.
RICH BITCH Thank you for another lovely year. Superstar and Legend.
THUNDERTHIGHS Love you with all my heart, hope we will always be together, and racing to the rock. Love E.S.B.
SEE 'COMMODORE GIRL+ Sid' and take a peek at a perfect program.
DEBORAH – All my love for ever. YRAC.
SPIKE – Love from me to you, but you don't know who, do you?
L L I have not forgot the 3d more but Im still saving up. Love you lots. PS Do like your hair?
TO CAROL great big chunks of Love from the Pig
WINNIE-THE-POO I send you "Double 88s" and "Pass the numbers to you", hope to "Eyeball" you – Pierrot.
BONNIE CHARLIE – Let's be friends. Solly and Cleo.
GEL – Ich lieber dich – Video Vic.
THE URGE IS STRONGER the nearer you get – can't wait to be with you. my pet! – to Pussy. Love Big Dog
JUNE, will love you for ever. – John
JUNE – All my love and may the foot improve to norm.–Peter.
AMLAJAN – still crazy after all these years – John (and Tigger).
YOGA PAT – the lbs may come, the lbs may go but I love you forever. J (and Tiger).
PEEPOM – I love your formats but regret that like you they do not work. – B.
KARDAMEINA peahen bride of the year fluffchick Julie. Love you forever. Martin.
ALISON – Hope you have a wonderful Valentine's Day. Thank you for a tremendous first year together. All my love, always – Simon x x x.
TO JANE. What can I say of that bewildering smile, enhancing every day. Nothing, only let it always be that way. Love John.
BOOPY. Love and kisses for all the happy times. Poopy.
MANDY, MANDY, Mandy. Mandy. Mandy. Mandy. Mandy. Mandy. Mandy. Mandy. Mandy. Mandy. Mandy. Mandy.
BOOBY BABY. You're the one that makes the world go round.
A PROPER CHARLIE You really are, just to see you I'd go far, you are my one and only heart, 'tis such a pity that we're apart.
BANDY COWMAN. (pure shining white) the Valentines Day Queen. From her grateful subjects.
CUDDLES – to let you know that I need them lots and lots forever. Roger.
GOOBIE BOOBIE Your adoring Weegie will love you always – love me too?
RUSHMA – Akkhi doonya ma rekha most beautiful aur pyari che.
IBRIS Take this alliance and complete my joy. The graduate.
SHEILA STEVENS is gorgeous. I should know – I married her!
KURT, Frölicher Valentinstag von dem gestreiften teufel.
EMMA PENGELI A gourmet dirt collector and best lover in both hemispheres.
LYNNE all my love and special thanks for B.P. Peter.
JEFFERS – remember! I will love you forever – always yours. Nimbus XXX.
BABY, I love you so much, in a grave condition. Irving Washington.
BEAR I will love you until the end of time. Love Paws.
DEAREST SUEE I love you more than chocolate you old sea dog.
EX PUBLICAN cuddles. Enjoying your holiday? All my love. Bubbles.
FRANCESA DE RIMINII – Thanks for two years – and many more. Love Pippy.
ALISON. – Stay silent frightened Prue. But I'll be semper eadem. Now get knotted. – Galalance.
ZIG sweetheart. Look in the bath. It's me! – Love Frances.
DARLING JIDDY you gorgeous creature. I love you more each Jemmie.
BINKIE BANKIE BONKY Binkie Bankie Bonkie Binkie Bankie I loves you.
GITA. – I adore you with all my heart and I know I'll love you forever. – Raj.
SHIRLEYBIRD. – I love you truly. You know I would not lie. – Plum.
CONVEY. – Lunch 20 20, if I'm still young enough to manage. – Po.
S.K. – Warm and lovely lady. I love you forever. – Bill.
LYNN. – Have loved you four years, will love you for years. – Baz.
SABBY darling you are still my champagne. I love you always. – Charles.
MY TRUE LOVE hath my heart and I have his. Red.
JOSEPHINE, from Russia and forever. with love. Wait for me. your Prince.
REALLY JO!!! Something about £60 from Atari would have been quite acceptable. (XXXX).
SUNRISE. Your happiness will always be my first concern. Always loving. S.S.
CHRISTINE. Henderson will always love you despite long absences and other interests.
MARY, You're in my heart, you're in my soul. Love Peter.
IF YOU'RE HAPPY JENNIFER, then I'm happy. Love Jonathan.
L.R. Loving greeting from Eeyore.
DOTTY TWOCHINS. There will never be anyone else. I love you terribly.
67831 TO 70523. 2692 Apart? Never! You'll always be closest to me.
D.J.H. All my love and energy is yours today and every day.
LITTLE POSSUM. – Lots of love and

may fail to attract a suitable applicant, but it is an advertisement nonetheless.

Fourthly, 'inform and/or influence'. The distinction between information and persuasion is almost impossible to define, and the vast majority of advertisements set out to achieve both. Even the most straightforward 'information' ad usually has elements in it designed to persuade, if only by the selection of the information given. 'Four-bedroom house, 100-foot garden' is undoubtedly informative, but the use of the terms 'four-bedroom' and '100-foot' is also intended to be persuasive.In contrast, some ads are designed solely to influence people, either in their attitude or their behaviour. Such ads may carry very little, if any, information.

Finally, 'one or more people'. Advertisements are rarely addressed to one person, for the simple reason that it is generally more sensible to write to someone individually, or ring them up, or even meet them in person. However, it does happen. On St Valentine's Day, the newspapers are full of small ads aimed at individuals ('Huggy Bear loves Minnie Mouse XXX'), while, on other occasions, advertisements are used to try to get in touch with a person whose address is not known. By and large, however, advertising is used to reach considerable numbers – often millions – of people.

Asked what is meant by the word 'advertising', most people will think of large companies selling products through television commercials and newspaper advertisements. Such advertising – sometimes known as 'manufacturers' consumer advertising' – now accounts for less than 40 per cent of advertising expenditure in the United Kingdom. The reason people think of such advertising first, is partly because large maufacturers are still among the largest spenders (though many governments now spend more on advertising than most manufacturers), and partly because it was manufacturing companies who developed the advertising process in the first place.

Advertising has been around for many centuries, and can be traced back to the days of ancient Greece, where historians have found the first clear evidence of the use of advertising for commercial purposes. The development of printing, in the second half of the 15th century, naturally offered a new dimension – the oldest surviving print advertisement in the United Kingdom was produced by Caxton in 1477, to promote his publication *The Pyes of Salisbury*. However, it was not until the end of the Industrial Revolution that advertising, as we would recognize it, really established itself.

During the 19th century, a number of factors combined to stimulate the growth of advertising. Of these, the most important was the development, in Britain, of large industrial companies, practising the mass-production theories of Adam Smith, and using economies of scale to turn out massive quantities of goods at a low unit price. In order to maintain the production of such large quantities of food, soap, clothing and other items, these firms needed to develop mass consumption as well as mass production – and the best way of doing this, since they could not afford enough salesmen to sell to the whole population in person, was by advertising.

Another important factor was the development, at around the same time, of the concept of mass retailing.

In the 1850s, encouraged by the Co-operative movement, grocery shops started selling basic products for working people; as the practice developed, these shops set up branches all over the United Kingdom. It was this combination of mass-production and multiple retailing that enabled manufacturers to start 'branding' their products. Firms such as Cadbury and Fry started packaging their products, not simply to protect them and preserve their quality, but also to *establish* their quality by the use of the company's own name. Instead of leaving it to the retailer to determine which company's products a customer would buy, they began to build their own relationship with the customer. They realized that, though they sold their goods to the retailer, it was the public that actually mattered.

By controlling the quality of their products, branding them with the company's own name and then advertising them to the public, manufacturers were able to build up their businesses dramatically; since that also increased the retailers' turnover, both sides of the business benefited. So too did the customers, since they had a wider choice of brands, and a stronger guarantee of the quality of the goods.

Advertising could not have developed, however, without another crucial factor, namely the growth of education and literacy in the second half of the 19th century. The Education Act of 1870 in Britain provided elementary education for all, and this, combined with the abolition of the tax on newspapers that had taken place 15 years before, led to a huge increase in the numbers of newspapers and magazines produced and sold. For the first time, advertisers had a mass-circulation press in which to promote their goods. Similar developments were taking place in the United States and in Western Europe and, by the end of the 19th century, advertising was established as a major element in the commercial life of the western world.

In those days, advertisements were largely confined to the media of press and posters, but, as breakthroughs in technology offered new developments in travel and entertainment, advertisers were quick to capitalize on them. Hot-air balloons were soon being used as mobile billboards, as were trams and buses, and shortly after the First World War the first cinema advertisements appeared. Radio advertising developed in the 1920s in the United States and most other countries, though not in the UK, which had to be content with commercials on stations beamed from abroad, such as Radio Normandie and Radio Luxembourg, until 1973. However, it was the arrival of television in the 1950s that revolutionized the advertising business. First in the United States and then in Europe, advertisers discovered the unique power of a medium which could broadcast sound and pictures into millions of homes. In the wake of this discovery followed the huge increase in advertising budgets that has turned the business into a multi-billion pound international industry.

The changes in the face of advertising during this century, however, have not been confined to the arrival of new media. One of the major developments has been the radical tightening up of the claims that companies can make about their products. Such controls have become more stringent throughout the years, and many

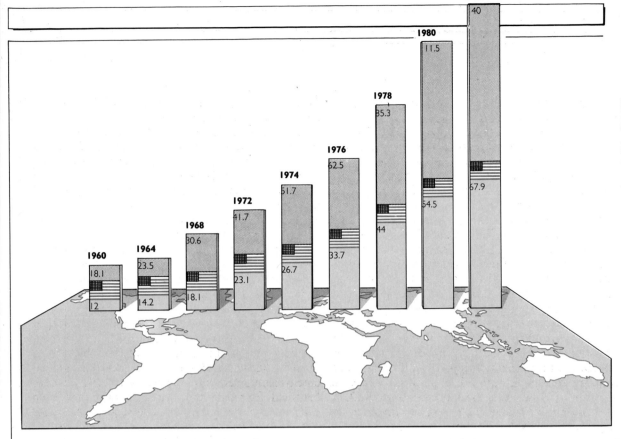

1982
40

1980
11.5

1978
35.3

1976
62.5

1974
51.7

1972
41.7

1968
30.6

1964
23.5

1960
18.1

12

14.2

18.1

23.1

26.7

33.7

44

54.5

67.9

Advertising expenditure has been growing consistently for the past 20 years throughout the world, according to International Advertising Association figures (*left*). That growth has speeded up in recent years. From 1960 to 1967, the annual compound growth rate was 6.8 per cent; from 1968 to 1974 it was 9.1 per cent; and from 1975 to 1982 it was 14.3 per cent. This chart also illustrates the predominance of the United States, which accounts for some 48 per cent of the world's advertising expenditure. Nevertheless, the US share is gradually declining: in 1960 it accounted for 66 per cent.

famous claims that were made as recently as the 1960s, such as 'Guinness Is Good For You', and 'Persil Washes Whiter', would not be acceptable today. Such claims, however, are as nothing compared with many of those made at the turn of the century.

Medical claims were a particular source of abuse. The Carbolic Smoke Ball Company announced that its product 'will positively cure coughs (cured in one week), cold in the head (cured in 12 hours), asthma (relieved in 10 minutes), bronchitis (cured in every case), influenza (cured in 24 hours), whooping cough (relieved the first application)' and a dozen other ailments. Unfortunately for the company's directors, the ad also offered a reward of £100 to any person contracting influenza after using the carbolic smoke ball. They were forced to pay up when a Mrs Carlill claimed the £100 and, on their refusal to pay, took out a civil action against the company. Other advertisers were slightly more subtle in their creative treatment. One poster showed the Pope drinking a cup of Bovril under the copy line, 'The two infallible powers – The Pope and Bovril'.

Gradually, thanks to a combination of legislation and voluntary self-regulation, such abuses became less common, until in most countries today, the substantiation required for advertising claims is extremely rigorous, and a number of products may not be advertised at all. Nevertheless, advertising throughout the century has been the target of much criticism, not simply on the grounds of misleading claims or spurious celebrity associations, but also on economic grounds. A number of academics have argued, variously, that advertising is a frivolous expense which can be cut at the first sign of economic trouble, in preference to other expenditure; that it encourages a wasteful increase in consumption; and that its enormous costs deter new competitors from entering a market. Such criticisms are still made, and in a number of countries there continue to be calls for the advertising of certain products – usually tobacco and alcohol – to be banned altogether, and for other advertis-

ing to be placed under greater legal controls. Some of these criticisms are justified. A number of advertisements still fail to meet the industry's requirement that they should be 'legal, decent, honest and truthful', and in less developed countries, there is evidence that manufacturers make wilder claims than they are allowed to elsewhere.

People in the advertising business are well aware that theirs will never be the most popular trade in the world. When Jacques Seguela, the man who devised President Mitterand's presidential advertising campaign, wrote his first book, he entitled it *Don't Tell My Mother I'm In Advertising – She Thinks I'm A Pianist In A Brothel*.

However, evidence has emerged in the last two or three years to counter some of the economic criticisms. A number of advertisers discovered that their sales were badly hit at the time of the 1974-75 recession, because they cut their advertising budgets and their competitors did not. Many firms learned their lesson, and the most recent recession has seen evidence of advertising being regarded as part of a company's capital investment in its products, to be removed at a firm's peril.

More politically significant is new evidence suggesting that advertising, far from putting up prices and deterring competition, actually keeps prices down by stimulating competition. Bodies such as the Federal Trade Commission in the United States and the Office of Fair Trading in the United Kingdom are now citing evidence to this effect, following the ending of advertising bans in the US on professions such as solicitors and opticians. Indeed, in the United Kingdom two consumers' bodies – the Consumers Association and the National Consumers Council – appear to agree with the OFT that bans on advertising act to the detriment of the public. This is a fresh view of advertising, in which the business that was once widely seen as wasteful and expensive is now being hailed as the consumers' friend.

Whatever people think about 'advertising', there is little doubt that they like advertisements – or, at any

Not all ads are aimed at large audiences. These personal ads, taken from *The Times*' Valentine's Day edition, are all presumably aimed at a particular individual (*far left*).

UNDERGROUND TO WOOD LANE

INTERNATIONAL
ADVERTISING EXHIBITION
AT THE WHITE CITY   NOV 29 TO DEC 4 1920

This London Transport poster for the 1920 Advertising Exhibition (*above*) shows many of the most famous advertising characters of the day: Johnnie Walker, Mr Punch, the Michelin Man, the 'His Master's Voice' dog and the Bisto Kids. These five are still famous today.

Through a combination of legislation and voluntary self-regulation the advertising industry has instigated a form of quality control (*far right*).

rate, some advertisements. One survey has shown that television commercials are more popular than the programmes. Another asked women if they would like their magazines to appear without ads, and the answer was a resounding 'no'. A third survey showed that people liked poster advertising, particularly in town centres, because it brightened up the buildings and hid derelict shops and building sites.

Advertising is a part of everyday life, as much so as the television programmes and newspaper articles among which it appears. Everyone has opinions on the ads they like and dislike, those they believe and those they distrust, even though few people will ever admit to being influenced by them. Advertising copy-lines have passed into everyday usage, songs from television commercials have topped the charts, and actors and models have become stars through their appearances in commercials and magazine ads. Many of today's top film directors learned their craft by making 30-second masterpieces, and still direct commercials in between their

feature films. Many of the world's top photographers and illustrators produce some of their best work for magazine advertisements and posters.

This book is about the process that brings such advertisements in front of the public; why companies advertise and where; who they want to reach and when; what they want to say and how – and whether the advertisements work. This process is described in detail in the second half of the book. First, however, we examine the three sides of the advertising business, and how they relate to each other. These three separate elements that make up the advertising triangle are: the advertisers themselves (who commission the advertising and pay the bills); the advertising agencies (who create the advertisements and buy the media space on the advertisers' behalf); and the media (who own the television stations, newspapers and magazines in which the advertisements appear). However, before embarking on this examination it is necessary to study the importance of the United States in the world of advertising.

Are you legal, decent, honest and truthful?

Advertisers have to be.

Enquiries to: The Advertising Standards Authority.
15/17 Ridgmount Street. London WC1E 7AW.

THE UNITED STATES

The undisputed home of advertising is the United States, where companies have a degree of freedom to advertise their goods and services unknown in most other countries. The United States dominates the advertising business in almost every way. It accounts for almost half of the world's advertising expenditure – $67.9 billion of the $140 billion spent on advertising throughout the world in 1982. It spends a higher proportion of its Gross National Product on advertising than any other country – around 1.6 per cent. And although it does not have the largest advertising agency in the world – that title is held by Dentsu, which has a phenomenal 25 per cent of the Japanese advertising market – the United States is the home of the largest agency group and no fewer than 17 of the world's top 20 agencies.

It has been said that all over the world admen look to Madison Avenue as Muslims look to Mecca. The New York street on which so many large agencies and media sales companies have their offices has become a synonym for the world of advertising in the United States, just as Wall Street has for finance. US agencies and advertisers control the vast majority of the money spent on advertising around the world, and a decision taken in New York can affect millions of dollars in billings, hundreds of admen's jobs, and the image and perception of a product in dozens of different countries.

In every country of the world except Japan US agencies and advertisers dominate the billings leagues, and it is not surprising that the all-time great men of advertising should have been American – albeit in one case by adoption rather than birth. These men helped shape the advertising business throughout the world, not just in the United States: men like Albert Lasker and Claude Hopkins of Lord & Thomas (later to become Foote Cone & Belding); Stanley Resor and James Webb Young of J. Walter Thompson; Raymond Rubicam of Young & Rubicam; Leo Burnett; Bill Bernbach of Doyle Dane Bernbach; Rosser Reeves of Ted Bates, who conceived the Unique Selling Proposition (USP); and David Ogilvy, who was born in England but founded a New York agency, Ogilvy & Mather.

Since it dominates the business in terms of billings, ownership and the great admen, it is not surprising that the United States has also tended to dominate the world in terms of the advertisements themselves: the style and techniques of US advertising have been adopted in many other countries, often through multinational advertisers such as Procter & Gamble, Coca-Cola and Johnson & Johnson adapting their US ads for use in the local market. Indeed, many campaigns conceived for the US market have run virtually unchanged all over the world.

For examples, one needs look no further than the three 'best ads or ad campaigns ever seen', as voted by 97 top US advertising men and women in 1976. *Advertising Age* conducted the poll as part of the United States' Bicentennial celebrations, and the top

three would almost certainly get on most ad people's lists. The overwhelming winner was Doyle Dane Bernbach's Volkswagen campaign, which received votes from no fewer than 60 of the 97 panellists. In second place was Leo Burnett's campaign for Marlboro and Marlboro Country, which took 28 votes. In third place with 24 votes was McCann-Erickson's 'Hilltop' commercial for Coca-Cola, featuring the song: 'I'd Like To Buy The World A Coke' (later to become a chart hit as: 'I'd Like To Teach The World To Sing', by the New Seekers).

All three have had an enormous influence on advertisers as well as a great impact on the general public. Each has spawned dozens of imitators but, more importantly, each has also had a more subtle influence on the face of advertising, by changing advertisers' perceptions of what is possible and what is the right way to put across a particular message. This is especially the case with the Volkswagen campaign, which was such a departure from the usual US car advertising that it had every agency in the country – and many abroad – reassessing the fundamental assumptions on which they had been basing their work in the past, and reappraising their plans for the future.

Influential as the United States is on the world's advertising, it does not have all the answers. Many advertising people – including a large number in the United States – would argue that in creative terms the United States has lagged behind some other countries in recent years, and this view has been borne out by the results at international advertising awards festivals. There is a widely held view that UK television commercials are the best in the world – a state of affairs which may owe something to the fact that in the United Kingdom it is accepted that people do not welcome a fast-talking salesman into their homes, and that commercials have to entertain as well as sell. This is no different an approach from that of Bill Bernbach's Volkswagen and Avis ads, but it may help to explain why in the United Kingdom the majority of television viewers say they like the commercials, while in the United States the same proportion maintains it dislikes commercials. It may also account for the fact that UK commercials' directors are now overwhelmed with work from the United States, making both commercials – Ridley Scott's '1984' Macintosh ad for Chiat/Day is one of the more spectacular examples – and feature films. *Chariots of Fire, Alien, Blade Runner, Flashdance, Fame* and *Shoot the Moon* were all directed by British directors who had started their careers directing commercials.

There is another reason why there is a limit to the influence of the United States on the world's advertising, namely the many differences of language, culture and laws that exist between countries, which have a profound influence on the way products and services are advertised. For example, the organization of the advertising media varies widely from country to country. Few countries have followed the example of the United States in having wholly commercial television

The Volkswagen campaign (*far right*) was a total departure from conventional car advertising in the United States and influenced advertisers and their agencies all over the world. Bill Bernbach showed that humour and wry self-effacement could be as effective as the 'hard sell'. The campaign was voted the 'best ever seen' by top US advertising executives in a 1976 *Advertising Age* poll.
Agency: Doyle Dane Bernbach.

Think small.

Our little car isn't so much of a novelty any more.

A couple of dozen college kids don't try to squeeze inside it.

The guy at the gas station doesn't ask where the gas goes.

Nobody even stares at our shape.

In fact, some people who drive our little flivver don't even think 32 miles to the gallon is going any great guns.

Or using five pints of oil instead of five quarts.

Or never needing anti-freeze.

Or racking up 40,000 miles on a set of tires.

That's because once you get used to some of our economies, you don't even think about them any more.

Except when you squeeze into a small parking spot. Or renew your small insurance. Or pay a small repair bill. Or trade in your old VW for a new one.

Think it over.

and radio systems (indeed, many have totally rejected commercial broadcasting on the basis of what they have seen in the United States), which means that in many countries TV advertising is either non-existent or severely restricted. Similarly, few countries have as wide a selection of national newspapers as the United Kingdom, and this affects the way advertisers plan and target their campaigns. In addition, the regulations governing the products that may be advertised and the claims that can be made about them also differ widely.

However, it is arguably the differences of language and culture that have the deepest effect, since it is only by understanding the needs and feelings of the target market that advertisers can produce the most effective advertising. For example, it took US car manufacturers many years to understand that there was a real need for smaller cars, because in the United States everyone was thought to yearn for ever-bigger cars. The success of the Volkswagen advertising campaign showed that this belief was not entirely justified, and is still doing so today.

Similarly, many campaigns that have been successful in one country cannot simply be transferred to other markets because they would not be understood, or have the same impact, in another culture: either the copy-line would not translate in any meaningful way or the concept itself would have no meaning. For example, neither baseball nor American football would generate much enthusiasm among audiences outside the United States.

Nevertheless, these barriers are gradually breaking down as the same television programmes and feature films are seen all over the world and a 'world-wide culture' becomes more of a reality. The coming of satellite television and data transmission may well mean that some of the media differences also break down, with more countries having TV advertising and national newspapers. As that happens, the dominance of US advertising may well become even more pronounced – whether that is a desirable state of affairs remains to be seen.

The Marlboro campaign has been running for 30 years and is now seen in most countries of the world (*above, right*). It is a prime example of US influence on world culture, since without the world-wide acceptance of Westerns on TV and in cinemas, the cowboy image would have no meaning. In the *Advertising Age* poll, it took second place behind Volkswagen as the 'best campaign ever seen'.
Agency: Leo Burnett.

The 'Hilltop' ad for Coca-Cola, with its chorus of children singing 'I'd like to buy the world a Coke', has been screened all over the world and is a rare example of a truly international commercial (*left*). In the *Advertising Age* poll it took third place.
Agency: McCann–Erickson.

Come to where the flavor is.

Marlboro Red or Longhorn 100's—
you get a lot to like.

© Philip Morris Inc. 1983

17 mg "tar," 1.1 mg nicotine av.
per cigarette, FTC Report Mar.'83

Section 1 –

THE ADVERT

THE ADVERTISERS

THE MEDIA

THE ADVERTISERS

KRONA

The Anglo-Dutch company Unilever is one of the world's biggest advertisers. Its subsidiaries make and sell a wide variety of products in many countries: household goods such as washing powder, lavatory cleaners and washing-up liquid; toiletries such as soap, shampoo and deodorants; and food such as ice cream, meat and frozen foods. One food item it sells in great quantities is margarine.

Unilever's UK margarine subsidiary, Van den Berghs, has recently had great success with a brand called Krona, which quickly became brand leader (in value terms) in the UK margarine market, and has since been launched in other markets around the world. Yet when Krona was launched, it could have been argued that the last thing the public needed was a new brand of margarine, since there were plenty on the market already. It could also have been argued that Van den Berghs itself had no need of a new product, since it owned most of the existing brands and had well over 50 per cent of the market.

The reason Van den Berghs launched Krona, and the way it went about it, explains a great deal about why and how companies market their products, and the role advertising plays in that process. It also goes some way to explaining how advertising works.

THE BIRTH OF A BRAND

Van den Berghs has been making margarine since the turn of the century, when it was developed to provide people with a cheap alternative to butter. Economy has always been a major reason for people choosing margarine rather than butter, but since the late 1960s other reasons for using margarine have come into play, such as ease of spreading, weight-watching and health concerns. Van den Berghs has responded to these new factors by tailoring brands to fit each sector. Blue Band was positioned as a margarine that was easy to spread and hence convenient; Flora, a margarine with a high level of polyunsaturated fats, was launched to meet the demand from the health-conscious; and Outline, a low-fat spread with half the calories of butter or margarine, was produced for those who were watching their weight.

By the early 1970s, therefore, the margarine market had become far more complex and price was no longer the sole factor in people's decision to buy margarine rather than butter. Sales of soft margarines in tubs were growing fast at the expense of the old-style packet margarines; the tub brands were largely used for spreading, while the packet products were increasingly being used mainly for cooking. Van den Berghs believed, however, that there was still an important and potentially large group of people whose need in this market had not been catered for. These were the people who remained attached to all the traditional properties of butter, but who were reluctant to pay the ever-increasing price. This was not a new phenomenon, of course. Throughout the 1950s and 1960s, Van den Berghs had positioned its largest-selling brand, Stork, as a margarine that tasted like butter, using the copy-line 'You can't tell Stork from butter'. In practice, it was debatable whether the Stork product really lived up to this claim, and Van den Berghs felt there was room for a new product that could be positioned as being closer to butter than margarine.

Developing such a product was easier said than done. As it happened, however, there was no immediate hurry. In 1974, when Van den Berghs had come to its conclusion that a butter-like margarine would find a market, the price of butter was very close to that of margarine, and it would have been just the wrong time to launch such a product. Butter in the United Kingdom at that stage was being heavily subsidized, and margarine's traditional advantage – that of price – had been totally eroded. Nevertheless, Van den Berghs was aware that this state of affairs could not last long. Britain had just joined the EEC and an inevitable result of this, under EEC competition rules, was that the price of butter would have to go up. No one knew exactly when this would happen but Van den Berghs was determined that, when it did, the new product must be ready. It therefore set up a major product and advertising development programme, designed to produce a margarine that in all respects would be judged by customers to match sweet cream butter.

Fortunately for Van den Berghs, a Unilever company in Australia, E.O.I., already produced a margarine called Fairy, which had many of the attributes of butter – in fact many people in Australia believed that it was really New Zealand butter, illegally imported, rewrapped and sold as margarine. Even more fortunately, one of Van den Berghs' UK executives, Paul Clark, had been in charge of E.O.I. at the time of Fairy's success, and so knew all about it. He decided to try the brand out on customers in the United Kingdom, to see whether they thought it tasted like butter too.

'When I went out to Australia, Fairy had 2 per cent of the market and was regarded as a cooking margarine,' says Clark. 'But when I tasted it, I discovered it was the nearest thing I had found to New Zealand butter. By the time I left, it had 30 per cent of the market and it was obvious that it had a future elsewhere.' Packets of Fairy, unlabelled, were left in a

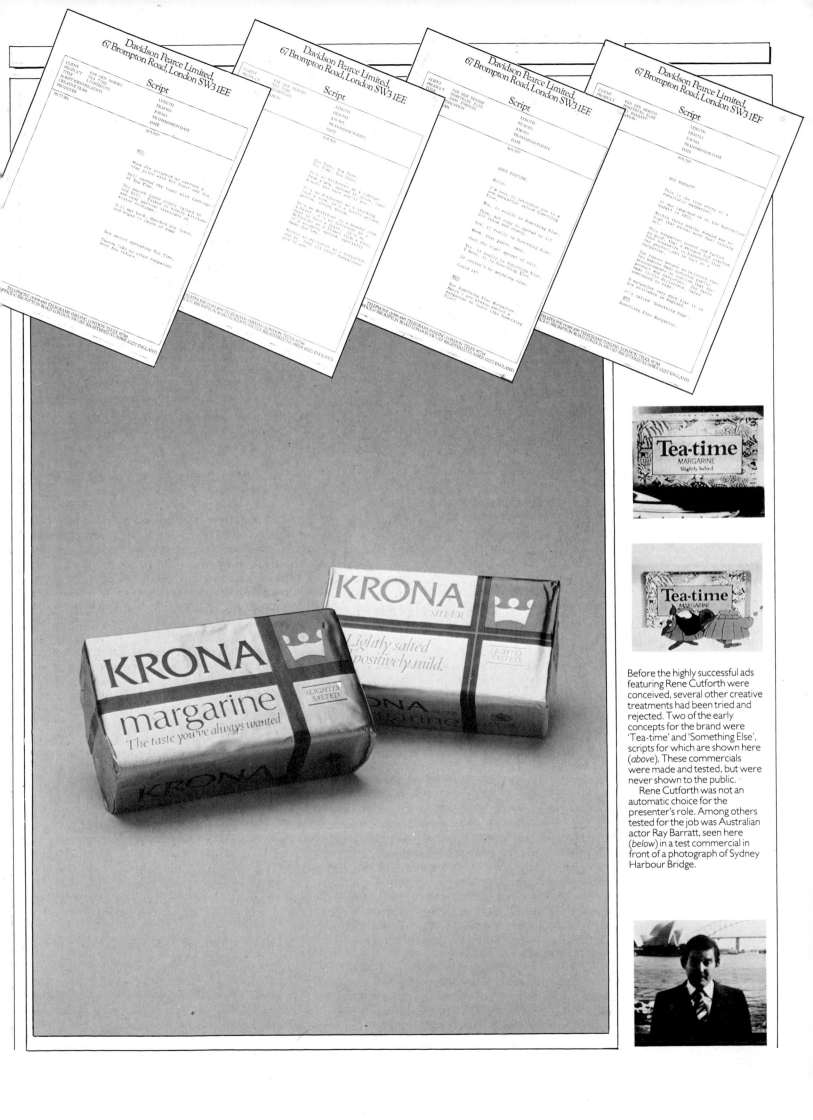

Before the highly successful ads featuring Rene Cutforth were conceived, several other creative treatments had been tried and rejected. Two of the early concepts for the brand were 'Tea-time' and 'Something Else', scripts for which are shown here (*above*). These commercials were made and tested, but were never shown to the public.

Rene Cutforth was not an automatic choice for the presenter's role. Among others tested for the job was Australian actor Ray Barratt, seen here (*below*) in a test commercial in front of a photograph of Sydney Harbour Bridge.

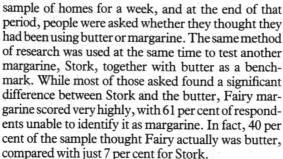

Bake them a slice of yesterday.

Van den Berghs had already marketed a brand on the premise that it tasted like butter. This was Stork (*above*), which throughout the 1950s and 1960s was advertised with the line, 'You can't tell Stork from butter'. In practice, it was debatable whether this claim was lived up to by the product. Doubts about the long-running Stork claim meant that a credibility gap existed in people's minds about any margarine claiming to taste like butter. An additional problem in the promotion of Krona was the fact that, largely because of the Stork campaign, the Government had introduced a set of Margarine Regulations which prevented margarines from being compared with butter in advertisements. Stork had to drop its old copy-line in favour of others like the one shown here (*below*).

Nothing makes flaky pastry flakier than packet margarine.

sample of homes for a week, and at the end of that period, people were asked whether they thought they had been using butter or margarine. The same method of research was used at the same time to test another margarine, Stork, together with butter as a benchmark. While most of those asked found a significant difference between Stork and the butter, Fairy margarine scored very highly, with 61 per cent of respondents unable to identify it as margarine. In fact, 40 per cent of the sample thought Fairy actually was butter, compared with just 7 per cent for Stork.

In the light of these results, Van den Berghs set about developing its own margarine, determined that this should not be launched until it had at least matched Fairy's rating with the public. During the next three years, the company tested 28 different products, finally producing one that matched Fairy on all the butter-like attributes. This was then tested in homes again, but this time clearly identified as margarine, with the positioning concept explained to the respondents. Over 85 per cent claimed that the product had at the very least lived up to their expectations and, when asked how much they thought it should cost, most put it well above the average price of margarine, at a level approximately two-thirds that of the average butter. The product, therefore, now seemed to be right.

In the meantime, throughout the three years spent developing the product, Van den Berghs had also been working on how best to communicate the benefits of the new product to potential customers. The product's brand name, pack design and advertising would all be key factors. The task was to communicate in a believable way the fact that the new product was very similar to butter in all respects, positioning it as an alternative both to butter and to other premium margarines. However, there were two major constraints on the way this could be done. The first was the credibility gap that existed, through the fault of Van den Berghs itself as much as anyone, in advertisements claiming that a margarine tasted like butter. Many customers now felt such claims were unbelievable. The second was the existence of the Government's Margarine Regulations, which prohibit any presentation or description of margarine that either explicitly or implicitly compares it to, likens it to, or even refers to, butter. There was no legal way, therefore, in which the product's basic benefits could be directly expressed to the customer.

The job of helping the company solve this problem went to an advertising agency called Davidson Pearce, which was appointed to handle the branding and advertising development of the product at a very early stage, several months before the first product tests had even started. For the next three years, while products were being tested, so too were advertising and branding concepts. One of the brand names tried was Tea Time, for which two totally different commercials were tested. One film was set in a lighthouse and could easily have been a butter ad, showing the product being spread thickly on hot toast – only the final line,

'Tastes like no other margarine ever has before', revealed what the product was. The other was a cartoon with a lively jingle, focusing on the word 'different', with lines such as 'It's as different as a cabbage from a pea', ending with the words 'Tastes as different as a margarine can be, from all other margarines you'll see'.

Another route depended entirely on the use of innuendo in the brand name, Something Else, and again several commercials were tried. One showed a man asking in a supermarket for Something Else and failing to make his meaning clear. Another showed actor John Fortune talking to the camera, spreading the margarine and tasting it: 'It really is Something Else,' he says, 'I mean, it is Something Else. It couldn't really be anything else. Could it?' The pay-off line came in a voice-over: 'Haven't you always wanted a margarine to taste like Something Else?' However, Van den Berghs and Davidson Pearce remained unsatisfied. It was not until more than three years after the product had begun to be developed, that someone thought of playing on the brand's origins – the extraordinary success of Fairy margarine in Australia and the rumour that it was not margarine at all, but something else illegally imported from New Zealand. Since the counterpart of Fairy had been developed for the UK market, the story of its success in Australia seemed a relevant and factual base on which to develop the advertising.

The style and presentation of the advertising – as well as the content – would be important in communicating the brand's benefits effectively, thus the choice of a suitable presenter was critical. A number of test tapes were made, with presenters standing in front of a photograph of Sydney Harbour Bridge. Each presenter read the same script which told 'the true story of a remarkable margarine', explaining about the rumours in Australia and how the product had been a runaway success. A margarine 'very much like it' was now available in England, said the script – it was called 'Something Else'. In the end the choice came down to two presenters – Australian actor Ray Barratt, well known in the United Kingdom from numerous TV series, and veteran television reporter Rene Cutforth. Even though research showed that housewives preferred Barratt, Van den Berghs and Davidson Pearce felt that Cutforth had a presence that was right for the brand, so they chose him.

Before Van den Berghs finally invested in shooting the commercial for real, however, it was having second thoughts about the choice of brand name. At this stage, the product was still being called 'Something Else', and the company was not convinced that this branding, with its tongue-in-cheek innuendo, was appropriate for the straightforward, documentary-style advertising approach that had been adopted. Van den Berghs decided to test several candidate brand names and pack designs in consumer research, though in the end it was the company's own judgement rather than the research that finally decided the issue. Though the Krona pack was not the winner in the

Davidson Pearce Limited,
67 Brompton Road, London SW3 1EF.

Script

CLIENT VAN DEN BERGHS   LENGTH
PRODUCT SOMETHING ELSE   FILM NO.
TITLE RENE CUTFORTH   JOB NO.
SCRIPT IDENTIFICATION   TRANSMISSION DATE
CREATIVE TEAM
PRODUCER   DATE

PICTURE   SOUND

RENE CUTFORTH:

This is the true story of a
remarkable margarine.

It was launched on to the Australian
market in 1970.

Within three months demand was
so high that stocks were running
out fast.

This margarine looked and tasted
so good, that a whisper had started
from housewife to housewife that
the product was in fact not a
margarine.

The rumour became so widely believed,
that the makers made numerous public
announcements to confirm that the
product was margarine. The facts
made little difference, sales
continued to rise.

The margarine very much like it
is now available in England.

It's called 'Something Else'.

MVO

Something Else Margarine.

TELEPHONE 01-589 4595 TELEGRAMS INKLING LONDON TELEX 917744
REGISTERED OFFICE 67 BROMPTON ROAD LONDON SW3 1EF REGISTERED NUMBER 102272 ENGLAND.

This was one of the first three commercials launching Krona in the south-west of England and Wales. It showed Rene Cutforth riding around Sydney in a taxi, stopping off at places like the New South Wales Parliament Building where questions had been asked about Krona's predecessor (*left*).

research preference scores, it was the most successful in conveying the concept of a high-quality product with clear butter-like qualities, as well as looking quite distinct from other margarines.

At this stage, it was decided to send a team of researchers and a film crew to New South Wales, Australia, on a fact-finding mission, where they established evidence proving that Fairy had been the subject of rumours claiming that it was not margarine, to the extent that questions had been asked in the New South Wales Parliament. Armed with Government records, old newspaper reports, and sworn statements from eye-witnesses – all of which would be required to verify the accuracy of the commercials for the UK's Independent Broadcasting Authority – they shot three commercials in Sydney featuring Rene Cutforth. These finished commercials were also tested, and it was established that the message that Krona would be very like butter had come across. There was a strong response to the content and to what was seen as the unusual documentary style of the commercial, and though there was a degree of scepticism about whether the product could actually live up to its claim, there was a very high level of willingness to try Krona.

By September 1978, butter prices had risen by 70 per cent in two years, and it was decided that the time was right to launch Krona into a test market. Two adjoining television regions in the south-west of England and Wales, the HTV and Westward regions, were chosen for the launch. Together they accounted for 10 per cent of the UK population, a sample judged to be large enough to provide a reasonable guide to the performance of the brand in the United Kingdom as a

whole, but small enough to minimize the capital investment. The area had a strong butter, but relatively poor margarine, market, so it was felt that if Krona achieved its target there, it was likely to be successful elsewhere.

Krona was launched in the test area at a price roughly two-thirds that of butter, thus giving customers an incentive to switch, while still emphasizing Krona's closeness to butter compared with other margarines. The marketing objective was to obtain a 5 per cent share of the market. The target market was designated as all housewives, on the grounds that demographic data such as age and class were of little importance in this instance. However, housewives currently using butter, but who were being forced to trade down because of the rise in price, were specified as the prime target group.

The advertising objective was to encourage trial of Krona by establishing it as the first margarine with a taste and texture indistinguishable from butter. In planning the advertising campaign, there had never been any doubt that television would be the medium used to launch the product; what was less predictable was the decision to concentrate on television alone, without any back-up from other media. However, it was decided that TV's various advantages outweighed the disadvantages of using it on its own.

The main reason for using television was that it was felt that the recommended creative approach would be less effective in any other medium. Also, television could ensure a high coverage – nearly 90 per cent – of the target audience, which had been defined as all housewives, while it also offered fast coverage. Television is regarded as an 'intrusive' medium, which is important when advertising a basic commodity such as margarine. It offers better regional facilities than other media for running test markets, and it gives considerable discounts to advertisers who are testing products. It is also regarded by the retail trade as a sign of marketing confidence, and it is possible to upweight the amount of advertising at short notice if necessary.

One disadvantage of television is that some housewives do not watch very often, and so a sizeable proportion of those in the target market might well see less of the advertising than they should. However, it was decided not to rob the television budget in the first year, since this would reduce the main impact of the TV campaign; in the second year it would be possible to use the press as a secondary medium.

To build up a high and rapid awareness of the new margarine, short heavy bursts of TV advertising were used. The target for the launch burst was to achieve 1,000 TVRs (television rating points) in four weeks, to ensure that light TV viewers saw the campaign, and that all three commercials were adequately aired. In addition to the television advertising, Van den Berghs also launched a heavy consumer promotion a week after the first TV ads had appeared, offering customers a full refund on their first purchase of Krona. Research later showed that well over 30 per cent of customers claimed that this promotion prompted them to purchase Krona for the first time. People were also encouraged to try Krona through tasting sessions in major stores, and over 20,000 such demonstrations have since been conducted.

The result of all this activity was a level of trial and awareness of Krona far higher than Van den Berghs had anticipated. The key question, however, was whether this initial success could be sustained, and that depended on the product itself. Would Krona fulfil the expectations that had been aroused by the advertising and promotion? Would people buy it more than once?

They did. Within three months of its launch, Krona had achieved a 10 per cent share of the market. Six months later, over 15 per cent of the households in the test area were still regularly purchasing Krona, and the brand continued to dominate the market with a share of over 10 per cent. Within a year it was brand leader. More than 50 per cent of Krona's volume sales were estimated to have come from butter – an important point, since Van den Berghs did not want Krona to succeed at the expense of its other margarine brands.

With the success of the test market, Krona was gradually extended into new areas of the country. By the time it was nationally available – two years after it first went on the market – Krona had a share of over 10 per cent of the national margarine market, compared with its target of 5 per cent.

How big a part did advertising play in the success of the launch of Krona? This is always difficult to determine, because sales are affected by many factors other than advertising, namely the quality of the product, its price and distribution, other forms of promotion, competitors' activity and more. However, there is a good deal of evidence to suggest that advertising played a crucial role in establishing the Krona concept in the public's mind.

A survey carried out in November 1978, the month after Krona's advertising first appeared, showed that 79 per cent of those asked were aware of the brand, and 24 per cent had tried it. This was an exceptional achievement within little over a month of the launch. Furthermore, 91 per cent of those aware of Krona were aware of its TV advertising.

A separate survey among Krona buyers showed that 66 per cent said that the TV advertising was the source of their awareness of the brand, compared with 13 per cent who heard of it from a coupon leaflet, 13 per cent who heard of it from a friend, and 11 per cent who saw it in the store. Of those who had not named TV as the source, 68 per cent had actually seen the ads, so that, in all, 89 per cent of Krona buyers within its first month on sale claimed to have seen the TV advertising. The agency, Davidson Pearce, points out that these figures should be seen in the context of the fact that customers are generally reluctant to admit that advertising is an influence on their behaviour.

Advertising was identified by customers as the primary influence on their initial purchase, and this is confirmed by the sales and attitude research. But *how* did the advertising work? An analysis by Davidson

Pearce, based on both the quantitative data taken in the months after the launch, and the qualitative research into the commercials, looks at the two elements of the advertising; communication and persuasion.

The communication of the idea that Krona was a margarine that looked and tasted like butter appears to have been successful. Qualitative studies showed that respondents saw the main message of the commercials as being, 'It's as good as butter', 'Closer to butter than other margarines', and 'Implying it was as good as butter', and this was confirmed by other research.

Persuading people that Krona really was like butter, despite the legacy of the incredibility of such claims, was also successful, as is shown by the high level of trial. The qualitative research shows that this persuasion was achieved in two ways – the style of the commercials, and their location. The novel 'documentary' style of the commercials was liked because it was different from other advertisements, particularly those for other margarines. The tone was serious, and it gave stature to the product. It was 'telling, not selling', leaving the choice to the customer and treating her as an adult, instead of talking down to her, and in particular, the personality of Rene Cutforth was important. All of these factors combined to give credibility to the product claims.

The agency, Davidson Pearce, suggest that the advertising also reinforces the Krona claim for those people who have tried and accepted it, because it confirms their own experience. They too have discovered that Krona tastes just like butter, and so the Australian experience was only to be expected. The intelligent tone of the advertising merely confirms their good sense in choosing Krona.

It could be argued, however, that, because the Krona product was right, and the timing was right in terms of the increasing price of butter, almost any advertising would have produced similar results. Davidson Pearce maintain that this was not the case. The problem was a formidable one. Conventionally, packet margarines were seen as cheap cooking items, yet Krona was a premium-priced brand. Previous claims comparing margarines with butter had proved unjustifiable, yet this was Krona's main claim. Regulations forbade explicit or implicit comparisons with butter, yet this brand's whole *raison d'être* was that it was indistinguishable from butter. In addition, there was a strong emotional aura surrounding butter, with its image of goodness, freshness and the countryside. Given that Krona's role was to be a cheap substitute for butter, it might well have been expected to appeal to the housewife's pocket but never to her heart. In fact, says the agency, there is evidence that Krona users were delighted with their 'discovery', and were keen to take on the role of evangelist, passing their knowledge on to their friends. The Institute of Practitioners in Advertising in the United Kingdom, appears to agree with the Davidson Pearce analysis. It awarded the Grand Prix in its Advertising Effectiveness Awards to the agency, for its work on the launch of Krona.

The Krona story is a classic example of the use of advertising, demonstrating how a campaign was conceived, the results it was designed to achieve, the way the campaign developed, and the effect it had on the customer and on sales. It illustrates many of the most important points about the role of advertising:

1. The fact that advertising is merely one of a number of elements that together make up what is known as the 'marketing mix', and that other factors – such as price, distribution, other forms of promotion, and the product itself – can be equally or more important.

2. The importance of creating the right brand image, and the way that the name, the price, the packaging, and the advertising must work in harmony.

3. The importance of defining a target market for the product and for the advertising campaign, and of selecting the right media to communicate with that market in the most powerful and cost-effective way.

4. The fact that advertising must not merely communicate and inform, but must persuade as well.

5. The importance of the relationship between the advertiser and the ad agency, with the agency virtually working as the off-shoot of the client's marketing department for several years before the product was even launched.

6. The importance of market research at all stages of the campaign – in the development of the product, the brand concept, the advertising, and in the measurement of the results of the campaign.

7. The strictness of the controls – some legal, some self-imposed – over the claims that may be made, and the creative treatments that may be used, in advertising.

8. That a new product does not need to be totally new in order to appeal to the customer, provided it offers a significant benefit.

9. That a manufacturer must not run the risk of 'cannibalizing' his other brands, by creating a product that merely takes sales from them without developing sufficient new customers.

But above all, it might be thought, the Krona story is a classic because it embodies what most people perceive as the main functions of the advertising – namely persuading people to try it.

To start with, most advertising is not devoted to telling people about new products, even though this is the most obvious function (some would say justification) of the advertising process. In fact, far more money is spent on advertising existing products and services. Secondly, advertising is not merely used to sell grocery products. Although these make up a significant share of the total expenditure on advertising, that share is declining in many countries, as categories such as retail, financial, leisure, transport and business advertising are developed. And finally, by no means all new products succeed, in fact the majority of those that get onto the market fail. While this is not necessarily the fault of the advertising (in most cases, research shows that it is the product itself that is to blame), it demonstrates that advertising does not always work.

Though there was never any doubt that television would be the main medium used for the launch of Krona, what was less predictable was that there should be no back-up from other media, especially since some housewives are light TV viewers. After the massive impact of the TV campaign in the first year, however, it was possible to use print ads as a back-up to TV (below).

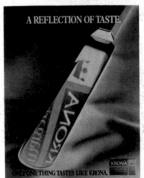

WHO AND WHY

NOT JUST SELLING SOAP POWDER

Whenever people want to belittle the practice of marketing and advertising (particularly when these skills are being applied to a business that has not traditionally used them, such as politics or finance), they often say that something is being sold like soap powder, or corn flakes, or margarine. Such jibes are based on the fact that the marketing and advertising business was developed by companies producing these basic commodities, but they no longer seem as relevant now that banks, building societies, computer firms, and government airlines are using exactly the same techniques.

The lessons of the soap powder and margarine firms have been passed on to organizations selling more complex and expensive products and services, and in the process, they have made these companies more efficient and competitive, more aware of their customers' needs and better able to meet those needs. Advertising is only one of the elements in the marketing mix from which these firms are benefiting, but it is an important one, not least because it is the one which generally absorbs most of the marketing budget.

A glance at the top advertiser lists in the United States and the United Kingdom gives a good indication as to the size of the sums invested by many companies in advertising. *Advertising Age* estimates that the biggest advertiser in the United States, Procter & Gamble, spent $726 million on advertising its toiletries, detergents and foods in 1982. In the United Kingdom, P & G was also the biggest single advertiser, spending £45 million at rate-card prices, according to figures from Media Expenditure Analysis Ltd. Thirty firms in the United States spent over $200 million each on advertising in 1982.

In second place was a retailer, Sears, Roebuck & Co – a prime example of the fact that in many countries it is now the retailer, rather than the manufacturer, who is calling the tune in marketing matters. In third place was General Motors, a manufacturer of consumer goods that, though fast-moving in one sense, are by no means the repeat-purchase items that people simply lift off the shelf.

In seventh place was American Telephone & Telegraph, another totally different type of organization, selling a service, rather than a product. Its market – like that of GM, but unlike those of P & G and Sears, Roebuck – is made up of both the general public and the business community, and its advertising strategy reflects this. In 11th place was Mobil, which advertises not merely to sell oil, but also to improve its corporate

The biggest advertisers in the United States and the United Kingdom (right).

Company	United States	Expenditure ($m)
1 Procter & Gamble		726.1
2 Sears, Roebuck & Co.		631.2
3 General Motors Corp.		549
4 R.J. Reynolds Industries		530.3
5 Philip Morris Inc.		501.7
6 General Foods Corp.		429.1
7 AT&T Co.		373.6
8 K mart Corp.		365.3
9 Nabisco Brands		335.2
10 American Home Products Corp.		325.4
11 Mobil Corp.		320
12 Ford Motor Co.		313.5
13 PepsiCo Inc.		305
14 Unilever US		304.6
15 Warner-Lambert Co.		294.7
16 Beatrice Foods Co.		271
17 Johnson & Johnson		270
18 Colgate-Palmolive		268
19 McDonald's Corp.		265.5
20 Coca-Cola Co.		255.3

Company	United Kingdom	Expenditure (£m)
1 Procter & Gamble		45.7
2 Mars		27.5
3 Imperial Tobacco		26.1
4 Cadbury		26
5 Kelloggs		24.5
6 Rowntree Mackintosh		21.8
7 General Foods		20.2
8 Electricity Council		19.6
9 Pedigree Petfoods		18.2
10 Nestle		17.3
11 Austin Rover		15.3
12 Lever Brothers		14.8
13 British Gas Corporation		14.7
14 Van Den Berghs and Jurgens		14.6
15 Gallaher		14.4
16 Birds Eye Walls		14.4
17 Ford Motor Co.		14.4
18 Co-operative Retail Societies		13.4
19 H.J. Heinz		13.3
20 Vauxhall Opel		13.2

Source: Campaign/MEAL

standing in the community, sponsoring high-quality television programmes – many of them made in Britain.

In 28th position was Mattel, the toy and electronics manufacturer, which has to appeal both to children *and* their parents in its advertising. And in 29th spot was the US Government, which in addition to using advertising to sell (the Mint markets gold and silver coins, including a commemorative 1984 Olympics coin), also uses ads to recruit people to the services, to improve road safety and to boost the postal service.

The top 30 UK advertisers demonstrated a similar diversity of products and services, though the upper reaches of the list were dominated by food, drink and cigarette firms. In 8th place was the Electricity Council, the publicly-owned organization that uses advertising to promote the use of electricity for cooking and heating, and to sell electric appliances such as fridges and cookers. In 13th place was its opposite number, the British Gas Corporation, another publicly-owned outfit, which does the same job for gas.

Three car firms featured in the UK list – one more than in the US top 30. Austin Rover, the volume car subsidiary of British Leyland, was in 11th place, Ford was 17th and Vauxhall-Opel, the General Motors subsidiary, was 20th. The top retailer on the list – the Co-operative Retail Societies – was only in 18th position, but three more made the top 30. Tesco, the supermarket chain, was in 25th place, MFI Furniture Centres was 28th and Boots, the toiletries and pharmaceuticals chain, was 29th.

It is interesting to note that the Government does not feature at all, but this is an indication of the different way in which the two tables are compiled. For example, the British Railways Board is in the table in 21st place, the Post Office is 23rd and British Telecommunications is 27th. In the US listings, Amtrak (the British Rail equivalent), and the US Postal Service (the Post Office equivalent), are both included in the US Government total. Were the telecommunications services in the United States publicly-owned, no doubt they too would be included in the Government total.

If one were to add together all the publicly-owned corporations in the United Kingdom – the Electricity Council, the British Gas Corporation, British Rail, the Post Office and British Telecom – and attribute their spending to Her Majesty's Government and all the spending by individual Government departments, the Government would be far and away the biggest advertiser in the United Kingdom. Even if one excludes all the publicly-owned corporations, however, on the grounds that their marketing and advertising activity is not directly controlled by the Government, spending by Government departments on campaigns for such purposes as to improve road safety, save energy, and recruit services personnel, would amount to over £30 million. In other words, a great many different organizations are using the techniques of selling soap powder for a great many different purposes. Since fast-moving consumer goods is the area in which it all began, since it still accounts for a large proportion of the spending, and since it still offers a great many lessons which can be applied to most other areas where marketing is used, it represents a suitable starting point.

FAST-MOVING CONSUMER GOODS

The Krona case history shows how a large and sophisticated marketing company sets about launching a new product. It might be thought that such an advertising campaign would be essential for any firm wanting people to try a new line, yet many new products are launched each year without being advertised to the public at all. They simply rely on people being able to find the item in the shops, hoping they will decide, on the basis of what they see on the pack, whether or not to buy it. Many such products – particularly those sold under a retailer's own name, rather than the manufacturer's – are very successful. So why do firms like Van den Berghs bother to advertise their new products?

The answer is that simply relying on a housewife happening to spot the new product in the supermarket can be somewhat risky, particularly if a company has spent many millions of pounds on developing and producing it. Suppose the customer does not happen to visit one of the shops where the product is on sale? Even if she does, suppose that, with all the hundreds of items on display, she does not happen to notice the new one? Even if she does see it, suppose that she cannot be bothered to read the details on the pack?

It makes more sense, given the amount of money a company will have invested in a new product, to make sure that the housewife is informed, so that she can either go in search of it, or, at the very least, be ready to look out for it the next time she goes shopping. Even if the manufacturer were prepared to take the risk of its potential customers not finding out about the new product, there is little chance these days that the retailer would let it. There are many more products available than most stores have room for, and there is stiff competition between manufacturers to get shelf space. If retailers are to risk giving up valuable shelf space to a new product (space that is currently devoted to an item that is already tried and tested), they want to be sure that the manufacturer is going to create demand for the new line. Often retailers will only accept a new product if they have been assured that it has sufficient advertising support. At the very least, if the company's budget will not stretch to advertising on TV or in the press, or even a door-to-door sampling operation, the use of display material at the point of sale – such as posters or leaflets – will ensure that the product is likely to be noticed by the store's regular shoppers.

The reason for promoting a new product is fairly obvious, but most advertising, as we have mentioned, is not for new products at all. Most of the money spent by Procter & Gamble, Unilever, Mars, General Foods and the other large advertisers, is used to promote products that have been around for many years. So why should firms still be having to advertise products such as Coca-Cola, Kleenex and Kellogg's Corn Flakes, which everyone has heard of and tried? It would be a truism to answer that these firms are satisfied that advertising boosts sales of their products (or that sales would suffer if they were not advertised, which is not quite the same thing), but companies such as P & G do not spend $700 million a year unless they believe they are deriving some

Confectionery firms like Mars (*right*) are among the biggest advertisers around. Even though almost everyone knows what a Mars bar is, advertising is still necessary to maintain and increase the level of sales.

benefit from it. They are not in the business of subsidizing advertising agencies, film production companies, TV stations and newspaper publishers. Nor are they in the business of getting the public to subsidize such companies through having to pay higher prices. Competition is so sharp in most markets that firms cannot afford to raise prices arbitrarily, and there is now strong evidence that the price of advertised goods tends to be lower than of those not advertised.

There are at least four reasons why advertising can boost or maintain the sales of established products. The first is that there are always new people coming into a market, ready to try products and services they did not want before. As people get older, their tastes and needs develop, and advertisers must constantly address themselves to these new potential customers.

A classic example is that of baby products. No one is interested in such things until they are about to have a baby of their own, whereupon they become the sole topic of conversation. People who have spent 20 years or more ignoring ads for nappies and prams suddenly become fascinated by them, and the same goes for many other products. Children start to become interested in sweets and soft drinks, teenagers in records and make-up, young men in beer and cars, and young couples in things for the home. A great deal of the money spent on advertising is aimed at such people, and in these ads, it is the customers that are new, rather than the products.

A second reason is that products are constantly being updated and improved to keep pace with changing tastes or technological developments. Canned foods give way to frozen foods, and frozen foods come in bigger packages as more homes have large freezers. Soap powders are replaced by detergents, which in turn are superseded by 'biological' powders, as fabrics and colours change, and the technology of washing machines develops. Some of these changes encourage manufacturers to launch completely new products – Krona margarine is a case in point – but other improvements are simply incorporated within existing products. Such alterations to a product have to be drawn to the attention of the public, just as completely new products do. The words 'new' and 'improved' may be the most overworked in the marketing man's vocabulary, but they are used quite legitimately in most cases. Manufacturers *are* genuinely improving their products in order to steal a march on their competitors.

The third reason for continuing to advertise products that are already well-known is perhaps the most fundamental – namely that people do forget about products unless they are constantly being reminded. They forget products in the short term, which is why advertisers like to jog their memory with posters near the shops or point-of-sale material inside, and they forget them in the long term. One reason why Coca-Cola, Kleenex and Kellogg's Corn Flakes are as well-known as they are is the fact that they have been advertised heavily and consistently over several decades. If these manufacturers stopped advertising, they might not notice any effect for a period of some months, but the chances are that once they *did* notice the effect, it would take a great deal more advertising to re-establish their products in the public's mind again.

One of the best-known examples of this phenomenon was the case of Delsey toilet tissue in the United Kingdom. In the early 1960s, Delsey, made by Kimberly-Clark, and Andrex, made by Bowater-Scott, were fighting – with some success – to build up the soft toilet paper market at the expense of the hard paper that had been used up till then. In the face of strong pressure from the retailers and the development of cheaper brands, both companies were forced to cut their margins, and hence their marketing budgets. However,

Del Monte
QUALITY

· INSIST ON DEL MONTE · THE HEART OF THE FRUIT ·
PINEAPPLE

The sun decides which pineapples will be the heart of the crop. It is their plumpness and juiciness that sets the standard for Del Monte pineapple. Only the fullest, roundest pineapple is delicious enough to be Del Monte pineapple. That's why families who grow up with a real love of pineapple, trust the Del Monte name. So, be firm – go right to Del Monte, the heart of the fruit.

Heinz is one of the biggest advertisers in the world, promoting a wide variety of products, among them baked beans (above).

The Best Loved Beans are Baked by Heinz.

while Bowater-Scott decided to maintain Andrex's advertising level, Kimberly-Clark diverted Delsey's marketing budget into discounting and consumer promotions, competing purely on price, with virtually no advertising at all. Within five years, Andrex's share of the market had risen substantially and Delsey's had fallen, and in addition, consumer research showed that the public's perception of Delsey as being soft and strong had fallen back while that of Andrex continued to grow. Now Andrex is one of the largest grocery brands in the United Kingdom with over a third of the toilet tissue market, while Delsey is no longer on sale.

The Andrex example also illustrates the fourth major reason for advertising products (both new and existing), namely to help build and maintain their brand image, and add to their value as perceived by the customer. This is a far more complex task, but it is central to much of the advertising that we see today, not merely in the field of fast-moving consumer goods, but also in many other areas.

Del Monte is one of the best-known brand names in the food advertising world. This ad (above) features a brand from a range of tinned fruit.

Heinz is also one of the best-known brands (above). Tony O'Reilly, President of Heinz, defines the acid test of a brand as 'whether a housewife intending to buy Heinz Tomato Ketchup in a store, finding it to be out of stock, will walk out of the store to buy it elsewhere, or switch to an alternative product'. The same goes for Heinz Baked Beans, advertised here by Young & Rubicam.

WHAT IS A BRAND?

The Yorkie bar became synonymous with lorry drivers as a result of the advertising campaign devised for the brand (*right*).
Agency: J. Walter Thompson.

The Andrex/Delsey case history first appeared in *What Is a Brand?* by Stephen King, director of planning and research at J. Walter Thompson, London. The question was posed again by Saatchi & Saatchi in a recent annual report, where it was answered by the heads of two major advertisers, as follows:

'A brand franchise is the very stuff of a brand. It is the unique sum of its taste and texture, flavour and smell, appearance and associations. A strong brand franchise reassures, gives confidence, and like an old friend, promises the certainty of pleasure. From all this comes the probability of long-term profits' – Kenneth Dixon, chairman, Rowntree Mackintosh.

'My acid test on the issue is whether a housewife intending to buy Heinz Tomato Ketchup in a store, finding it to be out of stock, will walk out of the store to buy it elsewhere, or switch to an alternative product' – Tony O'Reilly, President and CEO, H.J. Heinz.

The brand image – or personality or character – is made up of a combination of factors, both physical and emotional, which give it an aura that differentiates it from, and makes it more desirable than, other products of a basically similar nature. While the product must be of a high enough quality to stand comparison with the best of its competitors, it is as much the non-functional, emotional characteristics created by the name, the packaging, the advertising and the price that establish the value of a brand. It is such 'added values' that enable companies to justify a premium price for a product. That such values have a real effect on people's preferences was illustrated in two tests cited by King, in which products were tested against each other blind, and then named. When two household products, Brand K and Brand L, were tested against each other blind (ie without the respondents knowing what the brands were), 63 per cent preferred Brand L, and 37 per cent preferred Brand K. When the two brands were named, however, they came out almost even – 51 per cent to 49

per cent. When two food products (Brand A and Brand B) were compared, the blind test showed them to be virtually equal – Brand A 49 per cent, Brand B 51 per cent – whereas when the brands were named the preference for Brand B shot up to 67 per cent.

The blind tests show how the products perform on a purely physical and practical level, whereas the named test reveals the non-functional, added values that a brand possesses. Brands K and B have considerably more of these added values than their rivals, which gives them an extra advantage in marketing terms. In such qualitative research tests, brands are often referred to in terms of human characteristics, such as old-fashioned, sophisticated, friendly and cold. A major factor in the establishment of such emotions is undoubtedly the advertising, but the extent of the influence this will have on the overall personality of the brand depends on the product category. In some categories, as pointed out by Saatchi & Saatchi, rational factors tend to outweigh emotional ones, while in others it is the emotional values that count most.

In the case of the launch of Krona, the fundamental factor in the creation of the brand was the product itself, in that unless the margarine really looked and tasted sufficiently like butter, the whole rationale of the campaign would have failed. The only planned emotional factors – since the advertising campaign was deliberately stripped of emotion – lay in the shiny packaging and the name Krona, and these were only decided upon relatively late in the launch process. It later turned out that customers *had* found emotional values in the brand after all, stemming both from the Australian location of the commercials, and from their 'discovery' that Krona really did taste like butter (but these were regarded as an added bonus, rather than fundamental to the success of the brand). However, for many other products, the emotional elements of the brand have to carry a far greater weight than the functional ones. A good example of this is the launch of the Yorkie chocolate bar by

Rowntree and its agency, JWT, tried a number of concepts before arriving at Yorkie. Rations and Trek (*below*) were two of the many discarded on the way.

Rowntree Mackintosh.

Rowntree Mackintosh is one of the UK's biggest confectionery manufacturers, with major brands in almost every sector of the market. However, one market sector where it was weak was that of chocolate bars, where its own brand, Aero, had only a 9.7 per cent share, compared with Rowntree's 28.3 per cent of the chocolate confectionery market as a whole. The company therefore set out to launch a moulded chocolate bar that would take on the two biggest brands, Cadbury's Dairy Milk, and Galaxy, a Mars brand.

During its initial consumer research, Rowntree discovered that there was a desire among many people for a return to the traditional chunky, thick chocolate bar that had recently become a casualty of rising cocoa costs. In order to keep prices down and maintain the traditional shape and surface area of their bars, both Cadbury and Mars had reduced the thickness of their smaller bars, and Rowntree's research showed that customers were expressing disappointment. Rowntree researched a range of new products of its own, and one bar – a small solid milk chocolate block moulded in thick chunks – was particularly well received, with respondents expressing enthusiasm for chocolate 'as it used to be'.

It might be thought that this fundamental product benefit would have been sufficiently strong enough to support the brand on its own (being a rational factor like that of the taste and texture of Krona margarine), and would not have needed much in the way of emotional back-up to ensure the product was a success. However, there were a number of crucial differences between Yorkie and Krona that led Rowntree and its ad agency, J. Walter Thompson, to the conclusion that the 'thick versus thin' strategy would not be enough on its own. In the first place, Van den Berghs' main competitor for Krona was butter and not other margarines, and there was relatively little chance of anyone else producing a margarine that could compete on taste and texture with Krona.

By contrast, Rowntree faced two very vigorous competitors in Cadbury and Mars, both of whom would not find it difficult to produce their own bars in chunky form, if the Rowntree bar proved a success. Therefore Rowntree and JWT set about giving the chunky bar a complete brand personality, with a unique style and presentation which could be reflected in its name, its packaging and its advertising. They came up with a number of initial concepts, but all of them foundered at the consumer research stage, and all for very much the same reason.

The first concept that was tested was called Rations. It conveyed a strong outdoor image, but though the chunky, fulfilling nature of the bar was liked, the name was rejected because it did not convey much of a sense of enjoyment. The next concept to be tried was called Trek, and this one got to the film format stage, featuring outdoor activities such as mountaineering and potholing, but though the research showed Trek to be sustaining, nourishing, outdoor and rugged, it still seemed to be more austere than enjoyable. The problem was how to reconcile the need to convey the chunky, satisfying, sustaining nature of the product – which led to a rugged, rather austere, masculine presentation of the brand –

with the feeling of indulgence and enjoyment that people want from all confectionery products. The conflict was finally resolved by the introduction of the long-distance lorry driver, for whom the chunky bar would be the 'co-driver'. The imagery of the big lorry, the long day and the tough job would emphasize the sustaining qualities of the bar.

Various names were researched, including Quinn, O'Hara, Carter and Jones, but none was well received. However, two years earlier the name Yorkie had been the second choice after Trek, and this time the consumer research endorsed the concept. Qualitative research on two rough films suggested that the imagery was exactly right, particularly the background country and western music track which gave the film pace. However, the research also brought out the importance of the casting, in that the driver had to be clean-cut and appealing, and not too rough and sweaty, so that the enjoyability and 'niceness' of the product were suitably emphasized.

On the basis of the research, the launch commercial, 'Coast to Coast', was made. It featured an attractive lorry driver – played by actor Martin Fisk – driving all day, and the country and western music had a song added, telling of Yorkie's value as a sustaining companion on the road. There was a significant interlude when the driver stops at some road-works and waves on an attractive blonde in a sports car, enhancing his character and mitigating the apparent loneliness of the drive. The commercial ran for 45 seconds, on the basis that the need for impact and the opportunity to reinforce the power and substance of the imagery demanded a longer than average commercial.

Rowntree's decision that the 'thick versus thin' strategy would not be enough on its own to support the new brand turned out to be correct. The year after Yorkie was launched, Cadbury relaunched Dairy Milk and its other blocks in chunky form, and the following year Mars did the same with Galaxy. By that stage, however, Yorkie was firmly established with an image of its own, and was not dependent on the fact that it was thicker than other brands. Within two years of being on sale nationally, Yorkie was the fourth biggest line in the confectionery market, behind only the established favourites Kit Kat, Mars bar, and Cadbury's Dairy Milk. By that stage, it was already making Rowntree millions of pounds in profit. Four years after the launch, the company's share of the chocolate block market had grown from 10 per cent to 30 per cent.

There can be no doubt that the advertising had a major impact on the image of the brand and its sales success. Quite apart from the fact that research showed Yorkie selling better to heavy television viewers, the 'Coast to Coast' commercial made the brand famous and a part of popular culture. The actor Martin Fisk attracted a huge fan mail, and was voted the favourite pin-up in a newspaper poll ahead of such stars as Robert Redford. Lorry drivers wrote 'I hate Yorkies' in the dust on their trailers and people wrote in for details of the truck and the music. Without the advertising, Yorkie would have been just another chocolate bar – a chunkier one, it is true, but a mere block of chocolate just the same.

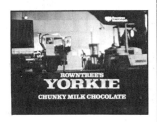

To emphasize the sustaining qualities of the Yorkie bar JWT created a role for it as the 'co-driver' for a long-distance lorry driver. Sitting on the seat beside the driver the chunky Yorkie bar is a welcome companion for the long journeys (above).

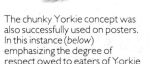

The chunky Yorkie concept was also successfully used on posters. In this instance (below) emphasizing the degree of respect owed to eaters of Yorkie bars!

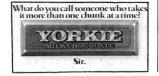

CONSUMER DURABLES

De uiterste grenzen van de ruimte. Audi 100. Auto van het Jaar 1983.

Advertising has helped car firms such as Volkswagen, BMW, Toyota and Audi break into many car markets and establish a significant share.
Agency: Ayer Barker.

Advertising a product that is relatively expensive and that will only be bought once every few years is a different proposition from advertising goods that are bought every week. To start with, it is unlikely, though not impossible, that the advertising will produce a sale on its own. Few people are likely to buy a car purely on the basis of a single newspaper ad or a television commercial they saw the night before. What they may well do, however, is go into their local dealer and ask for a test drive.

It is true that, for some products, advertising can actually provide a better demonstration or more detailed information than most shop assistants. A 30-second TV commercial may well convey a better impression of the capabilities of a food processor, such as the range of attachments and the way it slices vegetables, than a quarter of an hour in the company of the local electrical dealer. On the other hand, a commercial is unlikely to be an adequate substitute for a real-life demonstration in the case of a television set or hi-fi equipment, since it would be foolish to rely too much on one's own TV to convey the sound and picture quality of another make.

Because advertising generally produces less immediate results in the marketing of consumer durables than it does with packaged goods, it is sometimes regarded as a part of the marketing mix which can be dispensed with, or given a relatively low budget. Because each item is sold in thousands rather than millions, the huge economies in communication costs that advertising offers packaged goods firms, are less important to companies selling more expensive items. Whereas advertising can be seen as a vital part of the process that ensures economies of sale for companies producing fast-moving goods such as baked beans and detergents, it is possible to argue that more expensive goods can do without advertising at all. Yet this factor means that advetising can have a disproportionate influence on sales in such

markets, as some firms start to advertise heavily while their competitors continue to trade without advertising.

A good example of this situation is the UK car market. In the early 1970s, British car firms were reluctant to advertise heavily, particularly on television, preferring instead to rely on their dominance of the dealer outlets. There was even an unwritten embargo among the British companies that they would not advertise on television, except for the launch of a new car, or to clear stocks. Anxious to attract more car advertising, and faced with a flat rejection from the British firms, TV airtime salesmen approached importers such as Toyota, Volkswagen and BMW, who started regular, brand-building campaigns in the early 1970s. This stimulated the dealers and helped the importers build their dealer networks. The net result was that while importers had only a 27 per cent share of the UK car market in 1973, by 1979 their share had risen to 56 per cent. Naturally, this massive rise cannot be wholly attributed to the TV advertising, but there is little doubt that the campaigns played a significant part. That the importance of advertising is now recognized is demonstrated by the fact that the three major UK producers (two of which are subsidiaries of US firms), were all in the list of the top 20 advertisers in 1982.

The same thing has happened in a number of countries in many consumer durables markets – hi-fi, fridges, small electrical appliances, TVs and videos – where firms importing goods have used advertising to establish themselves. They have recognized that in order to increase their share of a market, they must first increase their share of the advertising in that market – their 'share of voice' as it is sometimes known. Saatchi & Saatchi cite one important consumer durable market in the United Kingdom, in which importers have consistently maintained a share of voice which is double their share of the market, with the result that the importers' market share rose from 10 per cent in 1968, to 55 per cent in 1980.

GENERIC

Not all product advertising is for named or branded products. In a number of cases, groups of manufacturers or producers decide to get together and fund a joint advertising campaign, promoting the product as a whole, rather than each marketing their own brand. This is particularly true of food producers, though it does happen in some manufacturing markets as well.

This type of advertising is known as 'generic' advertising, and such campaigns have been run for bread, milk, eggs, meat, mushrooms, poultry and a number of other foodstuffs. The main reason for doing generic advertising rather than brand advertising (which is the customary way of promoting food that has been processed in some way), is to make the funds go further. The producers believe that they can create a bigger impact by pooling their resources and having a single major campaign, than by each of them producing ads of their own. Another factor is the recognition that such foods' biggest competitors are not other producers of the same food, but different foods altogether. For example, the main rivals to milk are soft drinks such as Coca-Cola,

and the main rivals to eggs and meat are branded processed foods. The generic argument is that only by having advertising budgets that are on a par with the sums spent by such major brand advertisers can these foodstuffs compete.

Generic advertising is not confined to foods. The International Wool Secretariat promotes the concept of using wool, rather than specific wool products, using distinctive commercials featuring sheep. A group of gas central heating manufacturers recently came together to promote the use of gas rather than electricity for heating. The use of generic advertising does not necessarily preclude the use of brand advertising as well. In some cases, as in the case of the UK milk campaign, the advertising conveys many of the elements of a brand and is designed to change attitudes to milk, which was seen as traditional and boring, 'good for you' rather than satisfying. In other cases, the generic advertising works alongside brand advertising. For example, the bread campaign, designed to put across the nutritional value of bread, ran at the same time as advertising for brands such as Sunblest and Mother's Pride.

It is important to get some element of branding into a generic campaign, if only to stave off the advances of importers of the same commodity. For example, terms such as English, New Zealand, French, Danish and Dutch can become virtual brands in their own right – Danish bacon, Dutch butter and New Zealand lamb are examples of items which are regarded as brands in the UK market.

Willie Carson's favourite

Go smash an egg

Small electrical appliances (*above*) are another market in which importers can establish themselves through advertising.

Eggs are advertised on a generic basis because individual farmers can rarely muster sufficient resources for a brand advertising campaign (*left*). *Agency: McCann-Erickson.*

At Sainsbury's, you can move from a house to a château for just £1·60.

Our house claret sells for just £1.95. Bottled in France, it's the genuine article – designated "Appellation Bordeaux Supérieur Contrôlée".

Made from a blend of grapes, including Cabernet Sauvignon, it's a good, honest wine and perfect for everyday drinking.

Open an hour before serving and you'll find it soft and mellow with a fine balance of fruit and tannin.

At £3.55, our Château Barreyres is equally good value. (It's one of a range of thirty wines in our special Vintage Selection.)

From the heart of the Médoc, this fruity

claret is of medium weight and made with great care.

Some 30,000 cases are produced each year and most of the wine is swallowed up by the French themselves. (If you can resist the temptation to drink it now it will become even finer with a few years' bottle age.)

In all, Sainsbury's sell 7 clarets including a classic 1979 Château Grand Puy Ducasse at £7.45 and a good St Emilion at just £2.95.

The fact is, whether you want a house or château, no-one can accommodate you quite like Sainsbury's.

Good wine costs less at Sainsbury's.

Retailers now rank among the biggest advertisers in many countries. Sainsbury (*above*) demonstrates that grocery advertising can be stylish and effective.
Agency: Abbott Mead Vickers.

With many manufacturers spending huge sums on advertising their products, all of which – with the exception of mail order goods – have to be bought from shops, it might be thought that retailers had little need to advertise. Indeed, though there are a few product areas in which the manufacturers have traditionally left the advertising to the retailer – clothing and furniture are two examples – it was generally accepted until comparatively recently that it was the manufacturer, rather than the retailer, who did the advertising.

Why then are retailers such a dominant force in advertising today, to such an extent that in many countries they have been the fastest-growing spenders in the last 10 years? Why do many retailers now spend more on advertising their stores, than most manufacturers spend on promoting any one of their lines? If we analyse the list of the biggest UK advertisers not by manufacturer, but by product (eg by taking Ariel or Pampers, rather than Procter & Gamble, which makes them), the top 10 takes on a wholly new look. Seven of the top 10 'brands' are retailers – Tesco, the Co-op, MFI, Boots, Woolworth, Allied Carpets, and Asda. The word 'brand' is not inappropriate here. Many retailers are now using advertising and other elements in the marketing mix, to create a brand image for their companies every bit as powerful as those of Kellogg's and Heinz. In doing so, and in selling quality goods under their own name rather than those of the established branded goods manufacturers, they are posing a major challenge to the manufacturers.

The reason for these developments, is that competition between retailers, particularly on price, has been at least as fierce as it has among manufacturers, and as more and more trade has been concentrated within a handful of retailers, these companies have been able to use their power to get better terms. Not only have manufacturers found their own margins and marketing budgets squeezed, but they have also been made to put up funds to help pay for the retailers' own ads, thus strengthening the retailers' hand even further. These

developments have taken place not just in the grocery market, but in many other product categories, such as consumer durables, where the relatively high price of the goods means that large savings can be made. Most retail advertising, therefore, whether it is for groceries or hi-fi equipment, toys or furniture, it is heavily price-oriented, often consisting of full-page ads in newspapers crammed with the names of the products – occasionally a picture – and the prices. Even when retailers have set out to develop their own branding through their ads, they have preserved the strong price element in their campaigns.

Much retail advertising is also local in character. Even national retailers have local variations in prices and product ranges. For this reason, even if they use national newspapers and television, they will generally spend a large proportion of their budget in the local or regional press. Retail advertising (including operations such as car dealers) accounts for a major share of most local newspapers' advertising revenue.

Not all goods are bought from shops. A number of companies sell their goods by mail order, either through catalogues from which customers can choose any of a wide range of items, or from advertisements within newspapers or magazines, which will generally only be offering one or two lines.

The advantages of such a system are that the firm does not have to arrange distribution for its products, and that it cuts out the cost of the wholesalers' and retailers' overheads and profits. The disadvantages are that the customers cannot see the goods before they buy, and that they have to pay the cost of transport. It is particularly successful in regions where there are no major shopping centres, but even in major cities mail order items can be sold, particularly if the goods concerned are not available in the shops. Direct response advertising, as selling direct from advertisements is known, is the one area of the business where the effectiveness of an advertisement can be measured beyond any doubt. An ad either pulls in more orders than another for the same product, or it does not. Similarly an ad in one publication either pulls in more orders than the same ad in a different publication, or it does not. There is no need for elaborate research to attempt to equate the sales with the advertising – the link is direct. This is not to say that there is no place for research in direct response advertising, indeed, this area is as heavily researched as any other, for the simple reason that the research results can be applied directly. Creative treatments can be tested against each other, and so can media selection. The following day's post-bag will contain the results.

Direct response advertising is not used only to sell goods. Many companies use such ads to get people to write in for further literature, and the principle is exactly the same. The advertiser can tell from the number of coupons received whether the ad has worked. For some advertisers and agencies, the prospect of such an instant verdict on their work is extremely daunting, while others welcome it as the only true test of an ad's success.

SERVICES

A great deal of consumer advertising is not designed to persuade people to buy a product, but to spend money on a service, such as car hire, telephone rental, air travel, entertainment, or a meal out. In some of these cases, there is a tangible element – the airline ticket, the hire car itself, the McDonalds hamburger – but the 'product' that is being advertised is far more complex. It includes the elements of service such as speed, convenience, back-up and a smile, as well as the quality of the products through which that service is conveyed, for example, the efficiency of the car or plane.

Brand image is just as important a factor in the selling of services as it is in selling products – perhaps even more so. This is partly because there are so many opportunities in which to reinforce, or betray, that brand image, and partly because such services tend not only to be more expensive than packaged goods, but also more of a repeat purchase than most consumer durables.

The car hire firms and airlines are good examples. When Avis came out with its classic campaign – 'When you're only No. 2, you try harder. Or else.' – the advertising encapsulated the philosophy of service that the company was offering. Hertz eventually hit back with a campaign saying: 'For years, Avis has been telling you Hertz is No. 1. Now we're going to tell you why.'

Airlines have traditionally used air hostesses in their advertising to stress not just the element of service they are providing, but also to create a difference between them and their competitors in a field in which, until recently, there was hardly any price competition, and very little to choose between most companies. From the blatant 'I'm going to fly you to Miami like you've never been flown before', and, 'Fly me, I'm Marjie' of National Airlines, to the lengthy, soft-focus 'Singapore Girl' commercials for Singapore Airways, the air hostess has now become something of a cliché. In fact, so much so, that the small independent airline, British Caledonian, recently produced a parody of the genre with an adaptation of the Beach Boys hit, 'California Girls', entitled 'Caledonian Girls'.

However, not all services advertising is purely image-based. An element common to many services is the fact that they have fixed costs, no matter how many people are actually using them, and advertising is used to increase this usage. For example, airlines and rail services have to run every day, whether or not they are full, or even half-full. The postal services will be delivering letters down every street each day, whether there is one letter per household, or 10. Telephone companies will be having to pay off their huge capital investment in equipment whether or not people are making phone calls. Thus rail services will advertise cheap off-peak rates for travellers in order to boost their traffic and revenue. The postal services encourage people to use the post for paying bills and buying goods, because in that way they increase traffic and revenue. And telephone companies advertise to persuade people to use their phone during off-peak periods, at cheap rates. In all three cases, the extra income generated more than covers the cost of the advertising.

The Post Office advertises to persuade people to make more use of the existing service. *Agency:* McCann-Erickson.

By filling seats on trains that will be making the trip anyway railways can use advertising to increase their revenue (*above*).

Telephone services also advertise to increase usage of the existing service.

Will you be as fortunate finding a second career?

Heaven knows, you are going to need a second career more than this gentleman.

Compulsory retirement at 55 is on its way.

No matter how long your service, no matter how high your position, you could be out of a job, come your 55th birthday.

The company car will disappear.

The expense account will disappear. The private health insurance will disappear.

Sadly, your mortgage won't. You may well find yourself repaying that until you are 60 or 65.

Civil servants should be alright. They have indexed-linked pensions, courtesy of the poor old taxpayer.

Members of trade unions should make out too. They often have an army of negotiators to battle on their behalf.

No, it's the private sector business-man who will be in trouble.

His retirement age is going down, but his life expectancy is on the up and up. Today's 40 year olds can expect to reach 80. You could easily be faced with 25 years in retirement.

How will you manage?

That fixed company pension that looked oh-so-generous ten years ago, won't be worth much in another ten year's time, never mind twenty or thirty.

State pensions aren't famous for keeping up with inflation either.

Of course, with the two added together, you may just have enough to survive.

But is that all you want to do? Survive?

Wouldn't you prefer to do some-thing positive with the second half of your adult life?

Albany Life and the Inland Revenue can help you.

Start salting away a regular sum

each month. £15, £50, whatever you can spare.

We will bump up your contributions by claiming back from the taxman every last penny of tax relief we can.

We will then invest the total amount on your behalf.

We receive what is arguably the best investment advice there is. We retain Warburg Investment Management Ltd., a subsidiary of S. G. Warburg & Co Ltd., the merchant bank.

Start saving in your thirties or forties and you will amass a considerable sum, well before your 55th birthday.

When you are pensioned off, you will have a wad of tax-free money to cushion the blow.

Enough to set up shop in some sleepy Devon village.

Enough to pursue some half-forgotten craft, like working with cane or stained glass.

Enough to buy you a stake in some successful small business near your home.

Whatever you decide to do, you'll be better off mentally as well as financially. People vegetate if they have nothing but the garden to occupy their minds.

There is no reason why you shouldn't be active and working at 73, like Mr. Reagan here.

Though hopefully you won't have to carry the worries of the world on your shoulders.

To learn more about our plans send this coupon to Peter Kelly, Albany Life Assurance, FREEPOST, Potters Bar EN6 1BR.

Name
Address
                                    Tel:
Name of your Life Assurance Broker, if any

Albany Life

Many financial advertisers are now using consumer advertising techniques to sell their services to the general public. This ad for Albany Life Assurance (*above*) has won many awards, showing that financial advertising need not be dull.
Agency: Lowe Howard-Spink Campbell-Ewald.

Financial advertising comes in two distinct forms – campaigns aimed at the financial community, designed to raise funds, to report on company results or to assist or thwart a take-over bid, and campaigns aimed at the general public, to raise funds. The latter now rival many consumer products in the size of their advertising budgets, and the aggressive creative treatments they use.

Banks and other forms of savings institution, such as building societies and government savings schemes, now spend millions each year on developing their brand image and building their assets. Their conversion to the techniques of 'selling soap powder' has been among the quickest of all product sectors. In addition to heavy television campaigns, some banks have now teamed up with commercial manufacturers, such as Kellogg's and Procter & Gamble, to encourage young savers to collect tokens off cartons which the bank will redeem in the form of cash. Such advertising is no different from other consumer advertising, but traditional financial advertising is a far more specialized business, confined largely to the business pages of the quality press, where it will be read by stockbrokers, financial analysts and the rest of the business community.

However, even here consumer advertising techniques are making an appearance, most notably in advertising concerned with take-over bids. More companies are calling on the services of consumer advertising agencies – as opposed to the traditional financial specialists – to create campaigns designed to win a take-over battle. Full-page ads and double-page spreads have been used to explain the pros and cons of a take-over bid, in language simple enough for the ordinary shareholder to understand, and such campaigns have had a major impact. Research shows that the financial community itself dislikes and distrusts the practice, but if such advertising produces results (and like all campaigns, some are successful and some are not), companies will continue with it.

Such advertising, aimed at influencing share prices and the actions of shareholders, is similar in many ways to corporate advertising, and indeed a number of companies are being set up specifically to offer both services – financial and corporate communication – on the grounds that they are inextricably linked.

CORPORATE

A growing area of advertising by major companies is that of campaigns designed not specifically to sell products, but rather to convey a good image of the company itself. Corporate advertising, as this is called, may be aimed at a number of different target audiences – the company's customers, its suppliers, its work-force, its shareholders, local authorities, government, pressure groups and the media. It is designed to tell people what the company is doing behind the scenes, rather than in the market-place, and to explain how its operations are of benefit to the community. Many corporations these days are unknown to the general public, and while their products may be well-known the companies that make them (or the companies that own the companies that make them) are faceless. Other firms may be well-known, but the image they convey may not be favourable. In either case, the solution may be a corporate identity programme, which in a growing number of cases now includes an advertising campaign.

A case in point is that of the oil companies. Heavy advertisers before the oil crises of the 1970s, they had to cut back their advertising budgets when supplies were reduced and prices rose dramatically. While they no longer needed to persuade people to buy petrol, they did need to keep their name before the public, and in a favourable light. This was not least because in the new circumstances oil companies were regarded (like many other profitable multinational companies) with some suspicion, if not hostility.

The solution hit upon by most of the oil companies was corporate advertising campaigns featuring oil ex-

IBM is one of the biggest corporate advertisers in the world (*right*).
Agency: Saatchi & Saatchi.

Esso continues to use its tiger as a corporate symbol in many countries throughout the world even after it had dropped its 'Put a tiger in your tank' campaign. The tiger was used in commercials emphasizing Esso's role in exploration for oil in the North Sea and the use of its fuel in Concorde, and was later used for the direct advertising of products once again (*below*).
Agency: McCann-Erickson.

Exxon Solvents. Discover the power of purity.

Exxon now offers additional answers to your solvent questions. Whether your need is for a sensitive process or a critical formulation, our newly expanded line of solvents can offer some very pure choices.

Isopar® The Isopar line — nearly 100% branched-chain hydrocarbons, with only trace amounts of contaminants — is available in seven narrow-cut grades. Use Isopar when purity, selective solvency, low odour and low surface tension are important.

Norpar® This line combines purity and the virtual chemical inertness of straight-chain paraffins. Choose among C₁₂, C₁₃ and C₁₅

grades for applications where low reactivity and low solvency are important.

Essol® Hexane Our newest solvent has been specially tailored to give polyolefin makers and other chemical processing manufacturers another source of high-purity, reaction-diluent-grade hexane.

For more data on the high-purity Exxon solvent most appropriate for your particular application, write and tell us your needs. We'll send samples and technical literature. Contact Exxon Company, U.S.A., Room 2323, Box 2180, Houston, Texas 77001.

Please send literature on
☐ Isopar ☐ Norpar
☐ Essol Hexane
☐ Please send a sample in this distillation range:

NAME
COMPANY
ADDRESS
CITY
STATE   ZIP
PHONE

Exxon Company, U.S.A.
Room 2323 H, Box 2180,
Houston, Texas 77001

EXXON

Quality you can count on.

Two men were watching a mechanical excavator on a building site.

"If it wasn't for that machine," said one, "twelve men with shovels could be doing that job."

"Yes," replied the other, "and if it wasn't for your twelve shovels, two hundred men with teaspoons could be doing that job."

There are two ways to regard technological development. As a threat. Or as a promise.

Every invention from the wheel to the steam engine created the same dilemma.

But it's only by exploiting the promise of each that man has managed to improve his lot.

Computer technology has given man more time to create, and released him from the day-to-day tasks that limit his self-fulfilment.

We ourselves are very heavy users of this technology, ranging from golf-ball typewriters to ink-jet printers to small and large computers, so we're more aware than most of that age-old dilemma: threat or promise.

Yet during 27 years in the UK our workforce has increased from six to 15,000. And during those 27 years not a single person has been laid off, not a single day has been lost through strikes.

Throughout Britain, electronic technology has shortened queues. Streamlined efficiency. Boosted exports.

And kept British products competitive in an international market.

To treat technology as a threat would halt progress. As a promise, it makes tomorrow look a lot brighter.

IBM

IBM United Kingdom Limited, P.O. Box 41, North Harbour, Portsmouth PO6 3AU.

The French version of the Esso corporate symbol, the Esso tiger (*right*).

UNIFLO+ HUILE MOTEUR
+ Grande Protection
+ d'Economies

Mettez un plus dans votre moteur.

La nouvelle huile de l'Escale Technique. **ESSO**

---

ploration in the North Sea, Alaska and other treacherous locations. Esso continued to use its corporate symbol, the tiger, in its advertising; Shell used a stylish, but serious, animated commercial; and BP featured a number of humorous vignettes. All three companies used their North Sea exploration to emphasize the costs and the hazards they were undergoing in order to develop new sources of oil.

Evaluating the success of such campaigns is even more difficult than measuring the results of ads designed to sell products and services. Nevertheless, an extensive study of corporate advertising conducted for *Time* by Yankelovich, Skelly and White, suggests that corporate advertising can play an important role in creating a more favourable environment for those corporations that use it regularly. The research showed that among senior business executives, corporate advertisers enjoyed a 13 per cent higher awareness and a 34 per cent higher overall rating in terms of such qualities as good management, innovation, honesty and product quality, than non-corporate advertisers.

BUSINESS TO BUSINESS

By no means all advertising is aimed at the general public, or even at large sections of it. For example, financial advertising is a specialist business tailored to a specific market, but there is a far greater area of advertising that is similar in purpose. This is industrial advertising, otherwise known as business-to-business advertising.

Many companies never sell to the public at all, but instead produce goods and services that are required by other companies. Often, with a much smaller potential market than most consumer marketing firms, such companies can rely on their own salesmen to produce sales for them. Nevertheless, salesmen generally need the back-up of some form of advertising if they are to gain access to the people they must sell to, as a famous ad for the publishers, McGraw-Hill, once pointed out; '"I don't know who you are. I don't know your company... I don't know your company's reputation. Now – what was it you wanted to sell me?" Moral: Sales start before your salesman calls – with business publication advertising.'

Most business-to-business advertising appears in trade publications specifically aimed at particular industries. Such titles, never normally seen by the general public or by businessmen outside those fields, are often full of advertising and can be very profitable. The ads themselves, because they are aimed at a knowledgeable market, can use jargon in a way consumer ads cannot, and are often incomprehensible to the layman. Nevertheless, not all business-to-business advertising is confined to the trade papers. As with financial advertising, many companies are finding that consumer media, such as television and general interest magazines, can be used to sell their products to other businesses.

A pioneer in this area in the United Kingdom was Colt, an industrial heating and ventilation company. At one stage it was advertising in 47 different trade and technical publications. Realizing that this was reducing the impact of its campaign, Colt started advertising in the national press, not just in small spaces, but using full pages and double-page spreads. Using creative techniques (such as provocative headlines and dramatic photography) which were developed in consumer advertising, it attracted the attention of many company executives who may never have ploughed their way through the trade and technical papers. In 10 years, the company's business grew by nearly 600 per cent.

Another case in point is the growth of office equipment advertising on television, with firms such as IBM and Apple promoting their computers and word processors through TV commercials. Air and rail freight services are also using the consumer media more frequently, and there seems little doubt that this trend will continue.

This famous ad for McGraw-Hill (*top left*) has never been bettered as an argument for business-to-business advertising.

Computers and other business equipment (*left*) have become one of the fastest-growing advertising categories. *Agency: McCann-Erickson.*

CLASSIFIED AND RECRUITMENT

Another major sector of advertising which receives far less attention than the more glamorous consumer area is that of classified advertising. These 'small ads' are paid for by the line, and fill up page after page of some newspapers and, indeed, the whole of some titles. Such advertising accounts for over a third of all press advertising revenue in the United Kingdom, and the proportion is similar in many other countries throughout the world.

Many of these ads are placed and paid for by individuals, advertising their cars, houses or other items for sale. However, many others are placed by companies such as car dealers and estate agents, who use 'semi-display' spaces (a cross between the larger display ads and the small classified ads) to advertise a number of different houses and cars. Writing such ads is an artform in itself, not only in terms of the abbreviations that are used in order to cram in more details, but also in the style of writing designed to attract readers to the ad in the first place.

For many years, a regular feature of the UK classified property pages were the ads of London estate agent, Roy Brooks. These were so disparaging about many of his properties – in marked contrast to the high-flown claims of most estate agents – that many people were pleasantly surprised by the houses themselves. As Jeremy Bullmore, Chairman of J. Walter Thompson, said in *100 Great Advertisements*, 'by inventing and maintaining this style, I believe Brooks was the first person to "brand" an estate agent: to "add a value not in the product". And he did it in small, cheap, classified spaces, publication-set, with no pictures.'

Classified ads are not used simply to sell things. A substantial proportion of the money spent on classified advertising comes from firms who want to recruit staff. Such advertisements, though an often neglected area of the business, are not merely a major source of revenue to many publications – they are the financial base for many trade papers – but also provide a virtually indispensable service to many employers and employees. A number of specialist advertising agencies exist to handle such ads, highly skilled not just in writing recruitment copy, but also in selecting which publications will produce the most cost-effective results.

As in financial and industrial advertising, consumer techniques are often used in recruitment ads, and have been since the famous Uncle Sam and General Kitchener posters of the First World War. As was the case then, the major users of such techniques tend to be not commercial firms, but governments or public bodies. The simple reason is that such organizations generally need to recruit in larger numbers than most commercial companies.

However, advertising is not always needed. At times of high unemployment, the budgets for the recruitment of people into the police and the armed services are substantially reduced. The US and UK Governments have both produced dramatic and effective recruitment ads on television and in the press, but few commercial firms have done the same.

Ads such as these by the estate agent Roy Brooks became a regular feature of the classified property pages (*below*). In so doing, it has been said that he was the first estate agent to 'brand' his operation. They have often been compared with the Volkswagen ads in their 'warts and all' copy style.

£5,995 FHLD! Broken-down Battersea Bargain. Erected at end of long reign of increasingly warped moral & aesthetic values it's what you expect—hideous; redeemed only by the integrity of the plebs who built it—well. Originally a one skiv Victorian tower-middle class fmly res, it'll probably be snapped up by one of the new Communications Elite, who'll tart it up & flog it for 15 thou. 3 normal-sized bedrms & a 4th for an undemanding dwarf lodger. Bathrm. Big dble drawing rm. B'fast rm & kit. Nature has fought back in the gdn —& won. Call Sun 3-5 at 21 Surrey Lane, S.W.11. then Brooks.

Services recruitment advertising has come a long way since the famous Kitchener poster, 'Your country needs you'. Ads such as these for Army Officers (*below*) were highly effective and also acted as a 'corporate' image-building campaign for the services.
Agency: Collett Dickenson Pearce.

"So far as we are concerned, three years as an Army Officer can equal three years at university."

The driver of one of these cars was slightly injured.

The driver of the other car was killed. The cars were involved in a head-on collision with each other; they were virtually identical cars and they sustained very similar external damage.

The driver of the white car was wearing a seat belt and escaped with minor injuries.

The driver who was killed was not wearing a seat belt. And if you take a look at the interior photographs of the two cars, you can see the force of the impact where the driver without a seat belt was thrown forward against the wheel and steering column.

This was not a simulated crash. It actually happened on the A4 just outside Newbury. It happens all the time. Last year, it was estimated that 12,000 people were needlessly killed or seriously injured because they chose not to wear a seat belt.

If you don't wear a seat belt, you double your risk.

Wearing a seat belt reduces the risk of being killed or seriously injured by about half. This is not a theory. This is a figure produced from a meticulous study of road accidents in the U.K.

It is based, not just on statistics, but on painstaking analysis of the exact injuries of hospital patients, and of post-mortem examinations. And it is a figure which is supported by

the experience of many other countries round the world.

By not wearing a seat belt, you are deliberately doubling your risk of being killed or seriously injured.

Why don't more people wear seat belts?

More people wear seat belts today than they did, say, six years ago – but still only one in five regularly wears a belt. Why don't the others?

Well, there are a great many highly ingenious excuses. Doctors in hospital casualty departments have heard them all.

Some people fear being trapped in the event of the car catching fire. But fire is present in only an infinitesimal number of accidents – in fact only about 0.5% of serious casualties occur in such accidents.

And if you are involved in such an accident, and you're not wearing a belt, there is a very high risk of you being knocked unconscious. In that event, you certainly would not be able to free yourself. But that's only one of a familiar catalogue of excuses, none of which stands up to the facts.

The short journey fallacy.

By far the most common reason for not wearing a seat belt is the widely-held attitude that belts are unnecessary for short journeys round town.

Apart from the fact that over half of the total injuries to car users happen in built-up areas, there is no such thing as a 'safe' speed at which to have an accident. Without a seat belt you can be killed even at very slow speeds.

If you're involved in a head-on collision at 30 mph and you are not wearing a seat belt, the effect could be like falling head first from the roof of a 3-storey building. Is your steering wheel really the thing you'd most like to land on?

Unnecessary injury.

There are also people who choose not to wear a seat belt for no other reason than that they can't be bothered.

Some of them even resent being told the facts about seat belts.

They regard any form of persuasion as being an attempt to interfere with their personal liberty.

But the people who feel they should have the freedom to go through a car windscreen if they choose to, might consider this: have they really the right to occupy hospital beds unnecessarily when medical resources are already so stretched?

And have they the right to put the livelihood and happiness of their families at risk, simply because they themselves choose to ignore the simple cold facts?

CLUNK-CLICK
If you don't wear a seat belt, you double your risk.

ISSUED BY THE DEPARTMENT OF TRANSPORT, SCOTTISH DEVELOPMENT DEPARTMENT AND THE WELSH OFFICE

Government campaigns designed to change people's behaviour often go further in their use of shock and fear than commercial advertisers are allowed to. In this instance (*above*) the aim is to get people to wear seat-belts.
Agency: Young & Rubicam.

Although a large proportion of government advertising expenditure is devoted to recruitment, governments do run many other campaigns. These are generally designed either to change people's behaviour, to draw their attention to new legislation, or to attract business from tourists.

Some of the most dramatic government advertising is that designed to change people's behaviour, for example to warn people not to drink and drive, to wear seat-belts, to encourage children to cross roads safely, to prevent fires in the home or to prevent burglaries. In the United Kingdom it is accepted that television commercials for such purposes can go further in terms of their use of shock and fear, than commercial advertisers would be permitted to. For example, a long-running campaign to persuade people to wear seat-belts showed heavily scarred and disabled victims of road crashes. A fire prevention campaign used a far more emotive and harrowing treatment than would have been allowed in an ad for a commercial product, even one which would itself help

GOVERNMENT

prevent fires or reduce road casualties.

The results of such campaigns are monitored in great detail, and research has shown to the satisfaction of the Central Office of Information (the UK Government department that gives professional assistance to other departments) that there is a strong correlation between the advertising campaigns and people's actual or claimed behaviour. Fewer chip pan fires, more drivers wearing seat belts, less drinking and driving, wider observance of the Green Cross Code for children, and more TV licence fees paid are some of the results of such advertising.

In the United Kingdom and some other countries, such behaviour-changing advertising is paid for by the Government at normal commercial rates, both in terms of the production of the advertisement and the media space. However, in the United States and elsewhere, much of this activity is paid for on a charity basis by the ad industry itself. In the United States an organization called the Advertising Council supervises such campaigns for the Government. While this system has many benefits, the fact that both the production and the media space are being given free, means that the Government has far less control over the quality of the advertising and the amount of exposure it gets.

Other government advertising campaigns are aimed not at influencing social behaviour, but at informing industry or members of the public of benefits that are available to them, or of changes in the law. A recent campaign for the UK Department of Industry used television and press ads to tell small businesses of the Government grants that were available to them, inviting them to write in for a free guide to the various schemes. Some 60,000 firms were expected to respond – but in fact, 140,000 asked for the guide, and the campaign had to be halted before its planned run had ended.

The third main area of government advertising is that aimed at encouraging tourists to visit a particular country. The importance of the government's activity in this area varies greatly from country to country, but most nations have a government-funded tourist board which will advertise both overseas and internally. Such organizations may not always be seen as 'government' bodies, even though they are undoubtedly financed by the government. The definition of government advertising varies, and there are a number of organizations in many countries that are neither wholly government-run nor wholly commercial.

Although financed by the US Government, advertising by the US Army for recruitment purposes is not strictly speaking government advertising. However, this distinction need not be inviolable, and this recruitment ad for the US Army (*right*) is representative of the activities of the US Government.
Agency: Ayer Barker.

36 CHARLIE
TELEPHONE COMMUNICATIONS

Keep the Army's lines of communications open and open up an opportunity for yourself. "36 Charlie" is Army shorthand for an Army-trained telephone installer. Or choose to train in satellite, microwave, radio or signal communications, or one of over 300 other career training areas. If you qualify, we'll guarantee your choice. Which means you can serve your country in the way that best suits your talents. So if it's not 36 Charlie, it might be 31 Mike.*

ARMY.
BE ALL YOU CAN BE.

CHARITIES

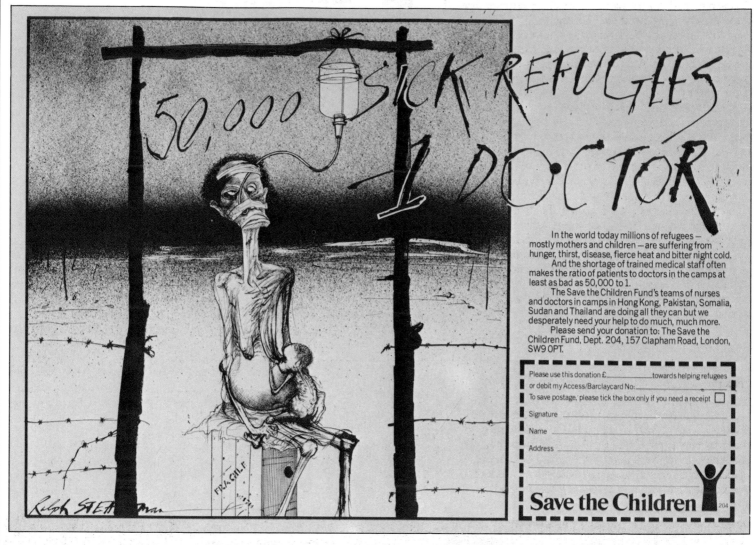

In the world today millions of refugees — mostly mothers and children — are suffering from hunger, thirst, disease, fierce heat and bitter night cold.

And the shortage of trained medical staff often makes the ratio of patients to doctors in the camps at least as bad as 50,000 to 1.

The Save the Children Fund's teams of nurses and doctors in camps in Hong Kong, Pakistan, Somalia, Sudan and Thailand are doing all they can but we desperately need your help to do much, much more.

Please send your donation to: The Save the Children Fund, Dept. 204, 157 Clapham Road, London, SW9 0PT.

Please use this donation £_____ towards helping refugees

or debit my Access/Barclaycard No:_____

To save postage, please tick the box only if you need a receipt ☐

Signature _____

Name _____

Address _____

_____

Save the Children

Charities have been quick to incorporate the creative experience of advertising agencies, as this ad (above) for 'Save the Children' (featuring a Ralph Steadman illustration) amply demonstrates. Agency: Ayer Barker.

If government campaigns designed to change people's behaviour are powerful, so too are campaigns for charities. Indeed, in the case of the United States, such government advertising is regarded very much as charity advertising. Yet true charity advertising is that designed to raise funds or other assistance for recognized charities, most of which have little money to spend on advertising. It is thus widely accepted that advertising agencies and production companies give their services free to charities, and in many cases the media space or time is donated as well.

Agencies like to do charity work not simply to salve their consciences, but because it is among the most creatively challenging work that can be done. Many of the most famous charity advertisements are remembered years after they were displayed. In some countries, however, there are strict regulations about what may or may not be said in charity advertising, particularly on television. In the United Kingdom, for example, the Independent Broadcasting Authority's advertising code states that 'no advertisement may give publicity to the needs or objects of any association or organization conducted for charitable or benevolent purposes', though it *is* permitted to give details of flag days, fêtes or other events organized by a charity. For this reason, most of the best charity advertising has appeared in newspapers or on posters.

POLITICAL

Like some government, corporate and charity advertising, political advertising is very close to what is sometimes termed propaganda. Many advertisements for political causes, figures or parties are among the most memorable campaigns ever devised, but whether they comply with the requirement that advertising should be 'legal, decent, honest and truthful' (as the International Advertising Association's code puts it) is often to be doubted. The advertising industry's control bodies have simply washed their hands of the responsibility for supervising political advertising.

In the United Kingdom, no advertising is permitted on television by any political body or to any political end. This prevents rich parties from taking advantage of their ability to outspend their opponents – as happens in the United States. However, political parties *are* given occasional free airtime, in proportion to the size of their following, and these 'party political broadcasts' are increasingly being produced as straightforward commercials. In the press and on posters, parties can buy as much space as they like, though some media owners endeavour (in the interests of impartiality) to impose restrictions on the amount of advertising they will take from one party.

The United States is the true home of political advertising, and many presidential campaigns have been brilliant, if less than honest, in their simplicity and power. However, in recent years the United Kingdom and other countries have seen some dramatic and effective political advertising, most notably, perhaps, in the campaigns for the Conservative Party by Saatchi & Saatchi which helped elect Margaret Thatcher in 1979, and re-elect her in 1983. However, political advertising is not merely concerned with getting politicians elected. Many political campaigns are run by pressure groups anxious to get legislation changed or preserved – the referenda in California and other American states provide numerous examples of this – or simply to change people's attitudes.

SUMMARY

The 13 categories of advertising referred to here, are by no means exclusive and watertight. Many campaigns would fit into two or three of these groups quite happily. Others do not quite fit in anywhere. For example, is an ad recruiting members for a union, such as the ASTMS ad 'The board and I don't like the colour of your eyes ', a recruitment ad or a political ad? What is the borderline between a packaged goods ad and a consumer durable

With the Conservatives, there are no 'blacks', no 'whites', just people.

Conservatives believe that treating minorities as equals encourages the majority to treat them as equals.

Yet the Labour Party aim to treat you as a 'special case,' as a group all on your own.

Is setting you apart from the rest of society a sensible way to overcome racial prejudice and social inequality?

The question is, should we really divide the British people instead of uniting them?

WHOSE PROMISES ARE YOU TO BELIEVE?

When Labour were in government, they promised to repeal Immigration Acts passed in 1962 and 1971. Both promises were broken.

This time, they are promising to throw out the British Nationality Act, which gives full and equal citizenship to everyone permanently settled in Britain.

But how do the Conservatives' promises compare?

We said that we'd abolish the 'SUS' law.

We kept our promise.

We said we'd recruit more coloured policemen, get the police back into the community, and train them for a better understanding of your needs.

We kept our promise.

PUTTING THE ECONOMY BACK ON ITS FEET.

The Conservatives have always said that the only long term answer to our economic problems was to conquer inflation.

Inflation is now lower than it's been for over a decade, keeping all prices stable, with the price of food now hardly rising at all.

Meanwhile, many businesses throughout Britain are recovering, leading to thousands of new jobs.

Firstly, in our traditional industries, but just as importantly in new technology areas such as microelectronics.

In other words, the medicine is working.

Yet Labour want to change everything, and put us back to square one.

They intend to increase taxation. They intend to increase the National Debt.

They promise import and export controls.

Cast your mind back to the last Labour government. Labour's methods didn't work then.

They won't work now.

A BETTER BRITAIN FOR ALL OF US.

The Conservatives believe that everyone wants to work hard and be rewarded for it.

Those rewards will only come about by creating a mood of equal opportunity for everyone in Britain, regardless of their race, creed or colour.

The difference you're voting for is this:

To the Labour Party, you're a black person.

To the Conservatives, you're a British Citizen.

Vote Conservative, and you vote for a more equal, more prosperous Britain.

LABOUR SAYS HE'S BLACK. TORIES SAY HE'S BRITISH.

CONSERVATIVE ☒

This campaign (*below*) by the Greater London Council against Government plans to abolish it, along with the other Metropolitan District Councils, helped marshal opposition to the proposals. Such ads would not have been acceptable on TV or radio in the UK.
Agency: Boase Massimi Pollitt.

Saatchi & Saatchi has consistently produced dramatic and effective political advertising for Margaret Thatcher's Tory Party. This poster (*above*) was one of a series that was instrumental in her general election victories of 1979 and 1983.

FROM NOW ON YOU HAVE NO SAY IN WHO RUNS LONDON.

Did you know Central Government intends to take away your right to vote in the GLC elections? **SAY NO TO NO SAY.**

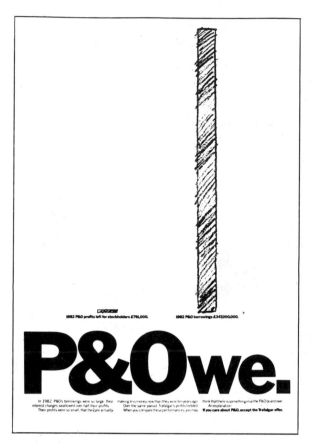

1982 P&O profits left for stockholders £791,000.   1982 P&O borrowings £342,000,000.

P&Owe.

In 1982, P&O's borrowings were so large, their interest charges swallowed over half their profits. Their profits were so small, that they are actually   making less money now than they were ten years ago. Over the same period, Trafalgar's profits trebled. When you compare these performances, you may   think that there is something else the P&O board owe. An explanation.

If you care about P&O, accept the Trafalgar offer.

ad? When does a corporate ad become financial or political?

In fact, it does not matter how one classifies each campaign. The point of splitting them up in this way is to demonstrate that advertising fulfils many functions other than the most obvious one of selling grocery products, and that it does so in many different ways. Nevertheless, the lessons of the Krona case history can be applied to any advertising and marketing campaign, whether it is for a soap powder, a TV set, an airline, a fire-prevention project or a presidential candidate. The product or service must be right; marketing objectives must be set; a target audience must be defined; advertising objectives must be laid down; and the campaign must be researched every step of the way, if advertising is to produce the results asked of it.

ORGANIZATION

Having looked at the various types of organizations that use advertising, and their different reasons for doing so, it is important to know who, within those organizations, actually takes responsibility for the campaign.

Ultimately, the chairman or chief executive of every organization will take the credit – or carry the can – for the advertising. Since an ad campaign represents the public face of the organization, it is how a company or body wishes itself and its products to be seen by the community. As the chairman of Harrods puts it, 'the chairman has to be responsible for his company's image'.

In practice, the person who takes the day-to-day

responsibility depends on the size of the organization. In a small company, the advertising will be planned and run from the top. Sometimes in such cases, the chief executive not merely acts as the advertising manager, but also appears in the advertisements. Airline operator Sir Freddie Laker, Remington boss Victor Kyam, and chicken farmer Frank Perdue are examples of this style of operation.

However, even small companies will have a department with some responsibility for the image of the organization, whether it is called the advertising or public relations department, whether it consists of one person or more, and whether it acts merely as a back-up to the line management or initiates and executes the policy itself.

Such an arrangement used to be the norm within the major marketing companies as well, but as marketing has become more sophisticated within the last 30 years or so, the advertising function has been integrated more closely with all the other elements of the marketing mix. Marketing managers and brand managers are now responsible for every aspect of their products, from the development of new lines, through their pricing, market positioning and packaging, to the advertising, and so in large companies there are a great many people with knowledge of, and responsibility for, the advertising function.

The number of people who have a say in the final decision on an advertising campaign, varies from company to company. Brand managers will liaise closely with their marketing manager and, in turn, with the marketing director before most campaigns are approved, but quite often the 'referring up' process does not stop there. In companies which produce comparatively few products – maybe only one – the advertising may require the approval of the board. In other cases, where a co-operative or generic campaign is being funded by a number of different companies or branches, the advertising may have to be approved by them all, or at least by a comfortable majority of the organizations involved.

However, the ever-increasing sophistication of the marketing management process does not mean that the role of the specialist advertising manager has gone forever. On the contrary, with the growing complexity of the media-buying process and the rise in costs, a number of companies now employ advertising managers or controllers in the same way as they use a research manager – to maintain a specialist knowledge of the advertising business, and to keep abreast of changes. This allows the brand managers to concentrate on the job of developing the marketing strategies of their brands.

One particularly important function such specialists provide is the co-ordination of media buying. Companies with many heavily advertised products are naturally valued customers of the media owners, and can thus negotiate considerable discounts if they organize themselves properly. If such companies only use a single advertising agency, this co-ordination can be done by the agency, but for firms that employ a number of agencies, such media co-ordination often warrants a small department of its own.

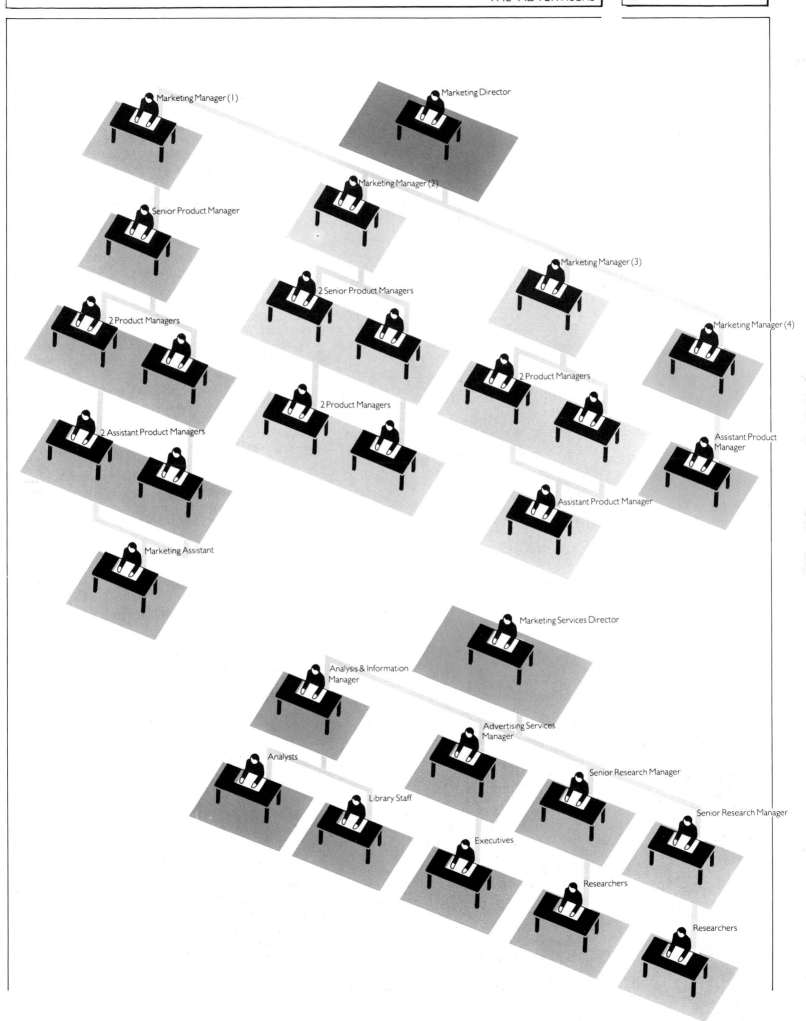

Marketing Manager (1)

Marketing Director

Senior Product Manager

Marketing Manager (2)

2 Product Managers

2 Senior Product Managers

Marketing Manager (3)

Marketing Manager (4)

2 Assistant Product Managers

2 Product Managers

2 Product Managers

Assistant Product Manager

Marketing Assistant

Assistant Product Manager

Marketing Services Director

Analysis & Information Manager

Advertising Services Manager

Analysts

Senior Research Manager

Library Staff

Senior Research Manager

Executives

Researchers

Researchers

2 THE AGENCIES

SAATCHI & SAATCHI

Saatchi & Saatchi Compton Worldwide is one of the world's top 10 advertising agencies. It has billings of well over $1,000 million, revenues of over $150 million, more than 70 offices in 40 countries and a client list that includes almost a quarter of the world's top 200 advertisers. Yet at the start of 1970, Saatchi & Saatchi did not exist.

An agency that gets from nowhere into the world's top 10 in 12 years cannot be regarded as typical, thus the Saatchi story is less of an object-lesson than the Krona case history. Nevertheless, the rise of the company does illustrate a number of points about the role and running of an advertising agency, not least of which is a continual striving for growth that is the hallmark of all successful agencies.

THE RISE OF AN ADVERTISING AGENCY

In 1970, Charles Saatchi (one of the two brothers who have built and given their name to the agency) was a partner in a London creative consultancy called Cramer Saatchi. A copy-writer in his mid-20s, he had made his name at Collett Dickenson Pearce, the outstanding creative agency of the time. His main claim to fame there had been an ad for Ford that was the first to make direct comparisons with named rivals – 'knocking copy', as it is known in the business. It was an ad which established his reputation for creating bold, innovative advertising that would get talked about – a skill which has paid dividends many times for the agency in its short career.

Saatchi had left Colletts with his art director Ross Cramer (now a successful commercials director) to set up a creative consultancy, producing creative work on a freelance basis for advertisers and for some of London's top agencies. The use of such outside creative teams is widespread, even though all agencies have their own creative departments. On some occasions it is because an agency's workload can suddenly – but briefly – escalate, while at others the agency may simply be seeking fresh minds and ideas for a particularly intractable problem.

Though a creative consultancy does produce advertisements, it is not an advertising agency. It does not get involved in the marketing strategy that lies behind a campaign, nor does it plan and buy the media space, both of which are functions fulfilled by the full-service advertising agency. In 1970, two of Cramer Saatchi's advertiser clients indicated that they would appoint the company as their advertising agency if it were to set itself up as a full-service agency. One was the Health Education Council, a Government-financed body set up to advise the public of the dangers of smoking, alcohol abuse and other health risks; the other was Jaffa, the Citrus Marketing Board of Israel. Charles Saatchi decided to accept the offer and set up as an advertising agency, but Ross Cramer decided against, and became a commercials' director instead. In Cramer's place came Charles' younger brother Maurice, a graduate of the London School of Economics, who had been an executive with a publisher of trade journals. Saatchi & Saatchi opened for business in September 1970 with around £1 million of billings.

Over the next five years, the agency produced some memorable and effective advertising, and won a number of blue-chip accounts. Probably the best known of these was an ad for the Health Education Council showing a picture of an apparently pregnant man, with the headline: 'Would you be more careful if it was you that got pregnant?' This ad received a great deal of editorial coverage in the national media. Indeed, rival agencies attributed much of the agency's success to Charles Saatchi's flair for generating such exposure, not just in the national press but in the trade papers too. The advertising trade press in the United Kingdom is particularly lively and competitive, with pages of stories each week revealing the accounts that are on the move and the agencies that have won them. Saatchi & Saatchi always seemed to be getting more than its fair share of such stories. Nevertheless, there could be no denying the fact that it was picking up such blue-chip advertisers as Dunlop, Great Universal Stores and British Leyland and producing excellent work for them. It was also expanding by buying other agencies, not just in the United Kingdom but in mainland Europe as well. The Saatchi brothers made no secret of their intention to grow fast and they put a number of noses out of joint in the process, not least by their habit – established at a remarkably early stage of their development – of writing regularly to other independent agencies in London offering to buy them out.

By 1975, Saatchi & Saatchi had made the top 20 in the United Kingdom, but was still some way off the top 10. By the end of that year, however, it had made its first great leap forward with the reverse take-over of the much larger, but stodgy agency, Garland-Compton, which was 49 per cent owned by Compton Advertising in New York. Despite the fact that Compton had supposedly taken over Saatchis, it was Saatchi executives who took all the key posts and the two brothers who took the largest share of the equity. The new agency was called Saatchi & Saatchi Garland-Compton, but in practice most people shortened this to Saatchi & Saatchi – after a few years this was officially recognized and the Garland name was dropped. (It is a commonplace in advertising that

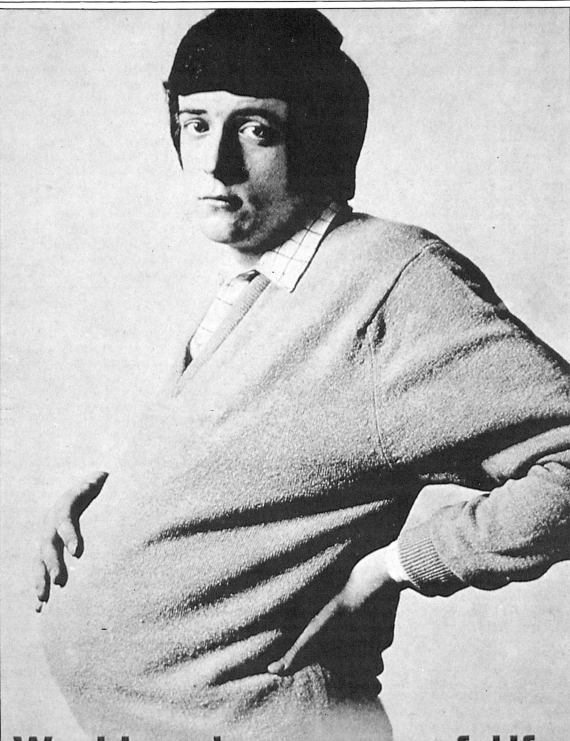

Would you be more careful if it was you that got pregnant?

Contraception is one of the facts of life.
Anyone married or single can get advice on contraception from the Family Planning Association.
Margaret Pyke House, 25-35 Mortimer Street, London W1 N 8BQ. Tel. 01-636 9135.

The famous 'Pregnant man' (*left*) poster for the Health Education Council, the first Saatchi & Saatchi ad to attract major attention.

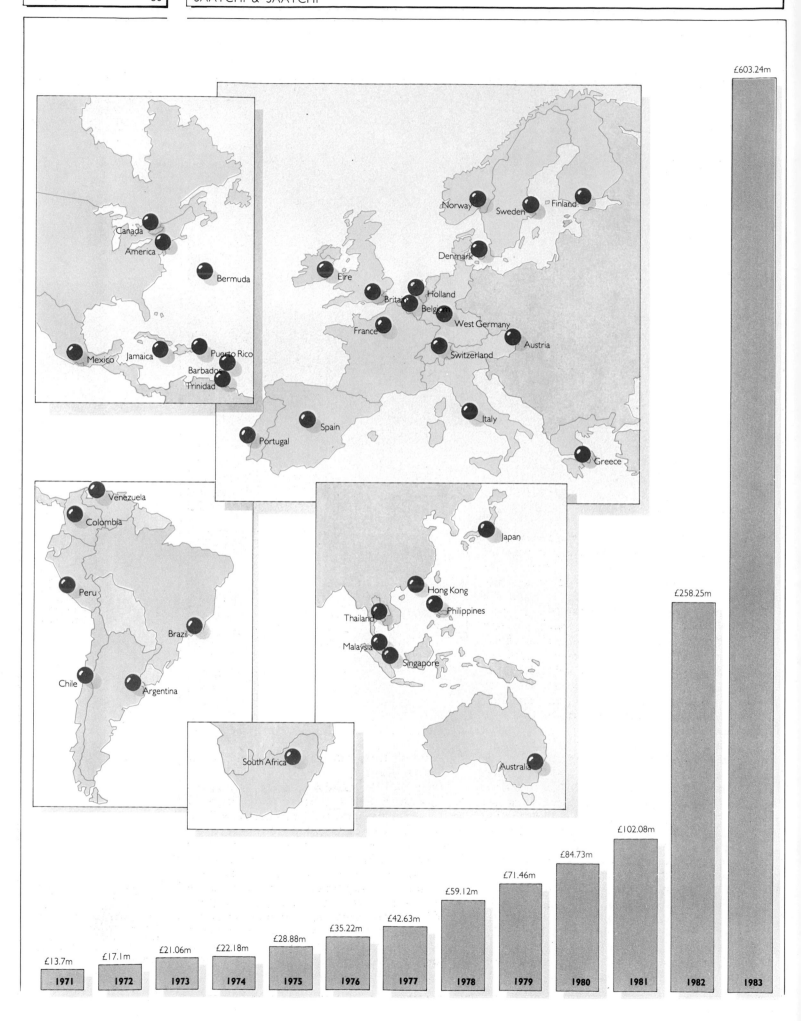

Canada
America
Bermuda
Mexico
Jamaica
Puerto Rico
Barbados
Trinidad

Norway
Sweden
Finland
Denmark
Eire
Britain
Holland
Belgium
France
West Germany
Austria
Switzerland
Spain
Portugal
Italy
Greece

Venezuela
Colombia
Peru
Brazil
Chile
Argentina

Japan
Hong Kong
Thailand
Philippines
Malaysia
Singapore
Australia

South Africa

£603.24m

£258.25m

£102.08m

£84.73m

£71.46m

£59.12m

£42.63m

£35.22m

£28.88m

£22.18m
£21.06m
£17.1m
£13.7m

| 1971 | 1972 | 1973 | 1974 | 1975 | 1976 | 1977 | 1978 | 1979 | 1980 | 1981 | 1982 | 1983 |

This 'Manhattan' commercial for British Airways ran in 35 countries and is a classic example of the agency's 'global marketing' theories (*left*). The ad purports to show the island of Manhattan being guided in to land at Heathrow airport, making the point that the airline flies more people across the Atlantic each year than the population of Manhattan.

disappeared. (It is a commonplace in advertising that all new – or newly merged – agencies have very long names, and that gradually common sense and usage reduce these either to initials, or to the first two names.)

The 1975 deal gave Saatchis a number of major benefits in addition to the financial ones. It put them among the top five agencies in the United Kingdom; it gave them a number of large blue-chip packaged goods clients such as Procter & Gamble, Rowntree Mackintosh and United Biscuits; and, almost by accident, it made them a public company, since Garland-Compton was already quoted on the Stock Exchange.

It was at this stage that the Saatchis' management abilities were first truly realized. Some of the earlier take-overs, in particular the first venture into Europe, had turned sour and everyone waited to see how the brash upstarts – as they were still seen in London – would fare with the likes of Procter & Gamble and Rowntree, who were used to a very solid, low-key agency. Would such clients stay? Some agency mergers are quickly followed by a mass exodus of clients unhappy about the way the new agency is operating, particularly if a number of the original agencies' own executives are leaving. Yet the Saatchi executives – by this time the two brothers had already moved out of the day-to-day running of the agency, onto a holding company board, though their personal influence was, and still is, strongly felt – showed themselves more than capable of running the new agency, which went

Charles (left) and Maurice Saatchi, despite their flare for publicity, are rarely photographed or quoted in the press. This is the most recent photograph (*left*) of the brothers, taken in 1984 for a profile in *Fortune* magazine headed, 'What makes Saatchi & Saatchi grow'.

from strength to strength. By 1979, it was top of the UK billings league.

Meanwhile, the holding company carried on buying agencies. In 1981, it bought another large UK agency group, the owners of the Dorland and Crawford agencies. This group was to be run as a second tier of agencies, entirely separate from the main Saatchi & Saatchi agency. One reason for not incorporating it into a new 'super-agency' was that most advertisers object to their agency handling business for any of their competitors, which means an agency can generally only handle one car account, one beer account and so on. By having two major agencies a greater overall growth is possible, since each agency can have, for example, its own car or beer account. (Some advertisers are sensitive even with such a separation of

Saatchi & Saatchi's remarkable growth is clearly illustrated by this chart of its annual turnover (*far left*). In particular the agency has grown in two years from around £100 million in 1981 to over £600 million in 1983, thanks mainly to the acquisition of the world's 14th largest agency, Compton Communications, in March 1982.

This poster (*above*) was one of a series produced for the Conservative Party during the 1979 general election. The first in the series, showing a long queue of unemployed and the headline, 'Labour Isn't Working', was run during the previous summer, and is credited with persuading Labour Prime Minister James Callaghan to delay the election.

agencies, and object to having a competitor handled *within the group*). The one country where such 'account conflicts' are not a problem is Japan, where the largest agency, Dentsu, accounts for a quarter of all billings while the second agency, Hakuhodo, accounts for 10 per cent. Each is run on a divisional basis – Dentsu 1, Dentsu 2 and so on – and each handles a number of apparently conflicting accounts.

The deal that took Saatchi & Saatchi into the world league took place in March 1982, when the company bought Compton Communications of New York (the world's 14th largest agency) for $55 million – the largest take-over in advertising history. Compton had part-owned Garland-Compton, the agency that had helped Saatchis into the big time, and now the Saatchi management was going to be given the opportunity to see if it could run an agency on an international scale.

In pursuit of still further growth, Saatchi & Saatchi has embraced the global marketing theories of Professor Theodore Levitt of the Harvard Business School, spreading the word through its annual reports which are shrewdly designed to educate the City of London in the ways of the advertising world – a world the City had always distrusted until the Saatchis demonstrated how it was possible for agencies to produce rapid, yet consistent growth in both turnover and profits.

This financial success does not explain, however, the fact that Saatchi & Saatchi is now a household

company name in the United Kingdom – the only advertising agency that any member of the general public is likely to have heard of. This fame is largely due to the fact that the agency handles the advertising for Margaret Thatcher's Conservative Party, advertising which made an important contribution to her election success in 1979. The Saatchi campaign for the Conservatives is also credited with having persuaded Labour Prime Minister Jim Callaghan not to call a general election in September 1978, as expected, but to delay it until the following Spring – a decision that arguably cost him victory. The ad that provoked this unfortunate decision was a poster showing a long line of unemployed people and the headline: 'Labour Isn't Working'. Later ads showed a blackboard on which was written: 'Educashun isn't wurking'; a long hospital queue with the line: 'Britain isn't getting any better'; and the simple statement: 'Cheer up! Labour can't hang on for ever.'

The outcry these ads caused in Parliament and on public platforms from Labour spokesmen gave the advertising extra exposure worth millions of pounds, since the ads were constantly reproduced in the news columns and on TV. Much of the abuse was heaped on the agency itself, which because of its unusual name quickly became famous, appearing frequently in newspaper headlines and cartoons. In advertising stories that had nothing to do with the Conservative

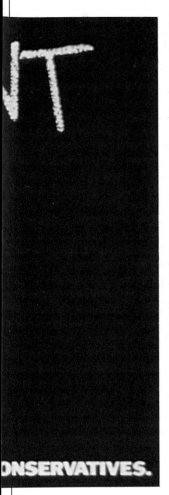

ONSERVATIVES.

This poster (*top right*) ran during the 1983 election, also won by Margaret Thatcher's Conservative Party, though the Saatchi contribution was probably less important this time. The ad created yet another storm of protest.

Party, the Saatchi name was sufficient to ensure they were given prominence.

The fame generated by the association with the Prime Minister did no harm to the agency's billings, and when British Airways, the national carrier, acquired a new chairman anxious to give it a new image, it was only natural that he should turn to the only UK agency with a world-wide network of offices and a place in the world's top 10. The service BA had received from the London office of its previous, US-owned agency, Foote Cone & Belding, had been excellent and the advertising much-admired, but now that there was a UK agency capable of handling the world-wide account it was seen as appropriate that it should handle the business. For Saatchi & Saatchi, this was the chance to demonstrate the global marketing theories they had been putting forward for several years, and when they launched their advertising, it was dramatic. The first commercial, called 'Manhattan', owed much to the film, *Close Encounters of the Third Kind*, and purported to show the island of Manhattan being guided in to land at Heathrow by air traffic controllers, in demonstration of the fact that the airline flies more people across the Atlantic each year than the entire population of Manhattan.

The award-winning commercial cost a fortune to make – several hundred thousand pounds – but this cost could be spread across no fewer than 35 markets around the world where the commercial was shown. Its sound-track was translated into 20 languages. For good measure, the commercial – and all the other ads in the campaign – trumpeted British Airways as 'the world's favourite airline', a global marketing statement if ever there was one!

It remains to be seen how far and how fast Saatchi & Saatchi can continue to grow, but it is worth examining what factors account for the agency's rapid success so far and what can be learned about the advertising agency business from its meteoric rise. *Fortune* magazine puts Saatchis' success down to a combination of 'advertising ingenuity, business shrewdness, and relentless self-promotion', together with the agency's highly aggressive drive for new accounts. The agency's own strategic goal has been, and still is, to combine high creativity with a world-wide, disciplined network. 'We have always aimed to create the one type of agency which has somehow eluded the grasp of those few men and women who have tried to achieve it', states the company. That elusive goal is: 'A large agency, certainly, with all the stability that gives to employees, and all the back-up that provides for clients – but one which at the same time also succeeds in being progressive, youthful and innovative in approach. The fact that this combination has so rarely been achieved in our industry increases the sense of purpose with which we continue to pursue it as our goal.' This strategy in itself says a lot about the agency business because it points up the traditional divide between the large, solid multinational agencies and the bright, creative agencies, whose work wins awards. This divide is gradually being bridged by some agen-

cies both in the United States and the United Kingdom, but for many others it will always exist.

The Saatchi success also demonstrates the importance of good business management, as well as advertising management, within agencies. The company has succeeded in increasing its profits every year for 13 years, and it is this factor that has given it the assets with which to buy larger agencies. Advertising agencies, by their nature, handle huge sums of money – albeit briefly – on their clients' behalf, and this money can be made to work financially if administered properly. The agency has been lucky, or clever, with its senior executives, almost all of whom have stayed with the agency right from the beginning. While long service in one agency is by no means unheard of in the advertising business, many executives these days are leaving to set up their own companies. The very success of Saatchis is, of course, an incentive to stay, not least because of the value of the company's shares.

The Saatchi story also points up other factors about the advertising world that many agencies now take for granted: the importance of publicity and being talked about within the business; the importance of 'bedding-in' clients after a merger, when business is at its most vulnerable; the problem of account conflicts and the need to set up a second-tier agency to maintain growth; the value of 'visible' advertising, if not on all an agency's accounts, at least on a select few; the importance of aggressively looking for new business, instead of fitting a job in in between work for existing clients; and not least, the importance of educating the financial world in the ways of the advertising business, so that finance is readily available for the company's expansion. Not the least surprising thing about Saatchi & Saatchi is that after decades in which advertising has been seen, certainly in the City of London, as an unstable business, without proper assets, and hence a poor investment, well over a third of the shares in the company are held by pension funds.

AGENCIES

Of the three sides of the advertising triangle, the agency is the only one which is not essential to the advertising process, and is the only one which depends entirely on advertising for its livelihood. Agencies these days – as they have always done – have to work hard for their living.

The advertising agency acts as the middle man in the advertising campaign. It creates the advertisements and books them into the media, performing a number of ancillary functions along the way. If the agency did not exist, the advertiser could create its own ads and negotiate with the media owners itself – and a number of companies do just that. In France, it has been estimated that almost half of all advertisers do without advertising agencies. If this suggests that the advertising agency is a relatively unimportant element of the business, however, nothing could be further from the truth. In most countries it is within the agencies (and the consultancies that perform some of the individual functions of the full-service advertising agency), that most of the real advertising expertise lies.

While it is true that the media owners employ full-time advertising staff to sell space and airtime, and though this requires a good knowledge of the way advertising works, it is not as complex a task as developing and executing an advertising campaign. Similarly, some advertisers have full-time advertising staff (as well as marketing and brand managers), but their role is generally that of commissioning and overseeing the advertising process, rather than the execution of it. Though individuals may move during the course of their career from an advertiser to an agency or from an agency to a media owner, the main repository of advertising skills is the advertising agency. It is no coincidence that all of the 'all-time greats' of advertising have been agency heads.

Agencies, like advertisers, come in all sizes and styles, and no agency will suit every advertiser. The largest international agencies, such as Dentsu, Young & Rubicam, J. Walter Thompson and McCann-Erickson, have billings of well over $2,000 million, and are amply equipped to handle huge multinational accounts, such as Coca-Cola, all over the world. Not all their accounts run into billions of dollars, or more than one market, but they are still unlikely to be the right agency for a small industrial advertiser, who wants to run a few ads in the technical press. Apart from anything else, their heavy overheads will mean neither side is likely to be able to afford the other.

At the other end of the scale there are a great many small agencies with billings of $2 million or less, that live perfectly happily off the budgets of small advertisers. In between, there is every size and type of agency that an advertiser could want. Some specialize in particular types of advertising, for financial, industrial, or pharmaceutical companies, or for advertisers wanting recruitment or direct response advertising. Other companies (perhaps not technically 'agencies') specialize in particular areas of a full-service agency's functions, like media planning and buying, or sales promotion campaigns. Even the full-service agencies that are in the market for most accounts – packaged goods, travel, consumer durables or whatever – differ widely from each other, not just in size but also in attitude and organization, and in the way they present themselves. The advertising agency business is highly competitive, and accounts worth millions of dollars switch agencies every year. Therefore, agencies have to position themselves in the market just as aggressively as they do their clients' products.

Some agencies are seen as highly marketing-oriented, with their eyes firmly on the sales figures, and with little time for supposedly 'creative' advertisements. Others are known for their entertaining, award-winning commercials. Ideally, most agencies would prefer to position themselves somewhere between these two poles of the advertising spectrum. However, whatever its size or positioning, a full-service agency will generally offer the following services to its clients whether it handles them itself or commissions them from outside firms – marketing and advertising planning, including the use of market research; creative work, including the writing and art direction of advertisements; the typesetting, illustration and photography of print ads; the production of TV, cinema and radio commercials; the selection and purchase of the media to be used; and the co-ordination of all these functions, ensuring that each stage of the campaign is executed correctly and on time.

THE GROWTH OF THE AGENCY

Advertising agencies started life providing a service not for the advertiser, but for the media owner. The first agencies were media brokers, who bought space from newspaper and magazine owners, and found advertisers to fill it, receiving in return a commission on sales of between 10 and 25 per cent. The nature of the agency business changed in the 19th century as competition between agencies grew, and as certain advertisers built up a close relationship with particular agencies. Originally simply advising advertisers on which publications they should use, the agencies then started to write the advertisements themselves, in the knowledge that the more effective the ads were, the more business they were likely to get. Gradually, the agencies' prime allegiance shifted from the media owner, who paid the commission, to the advertiser, who commanded the campaign budget. As this became the norm, agencies ceased to buy space speculatively and their 'broker' role came to an end (though there are still firms – known as advertisement representatives, or agents – who sell space on behalf of a number of media owners).

Some legacies of these original working procedures remained. Agencies continued to be paid by the media owner through a commission on the space sold, and this was eventually standardized at 15 per cent. Equally importantly, the agencies remained the financial 'prin-

World

Agency	Income ($m)
1 Dentsu	402.9
2 Young & Rubicam	376.6
3 Ted Bates Worldwide	356.1
4 J. Walter Thompson Co.	347.1
5 Ogilvy & Mather	315
6 McCann-Erickson Worldwide	276.1
7 BBDO International	238.3
8 Leo Burnett Co.	221.2
9 Saatchi & Saatchi Compton Worldwide	186.5
10 Foote, Cone & Belding	178.1

United States

Agency	Income ($m)
1 Young & Rubicam	246.7
2 Ted Bates Worldwide	233.4
3 Ogilvy & Mather	176.9
4 J. Walter Thompson	167.2
5 BBDO International	155
6 Leo Burnett Co.	136
7 Doyle Dane Bernbach	129
8 Foote, Cone & Belding	126.8
9 Grey Advertising	109
10 Dancer Fitzgerald Sample	86.4

Europe

Agency	Income ($m)
1 Saatchi & Saatchi Group UK	62.7
2 Publicis Conseil, Paris	35.4
3 J. Walter Thompson Group, London	33.7
4 D'Arcy-MacManus & Masius, London	30.5
5 Lintas, Hamburg	27.9
6 Havas Conseil, Paris	27
7 Team/BBDO, Dusseldorf	23.2
8 McCann-Erickson, Frankfurt	23
9 McCann Group, London	22.7
10 Charles Barker Group, London	22.4

Reprinted from *Advertising Age* March '83, June '83. © Crain Communications Inc. 1984.

cipals', responsible to the media owner for the payment of the bills even if their client failed to pay them. Because of this, an approval system of 'recognized' agencies developed, with agencies having to provide proof of their financial backing and stability. Only recognized agencies were eligible for the commission on sales.

This method of payment may seem curious in view of the fact that the agencies' main obligation was now seen to be towards the advertiser, rather than the media owner. In fact it made some sense in that the media owner was still benefiting from the agencies' operation. The increasing professionalism brought to the advertising business by the agencies boosted bookings. Better designed and written advertisements made the publications themselves look better. The advertisements tended to arrive on time and in the right form for reproduction, and the centralization of orders through agencies eased the media owners' administration. The fact that agencies acted as principals largely protected the media owner from the risk of taking ads from advertisers whose financial status was doubtful (though if the agency itself went into liquidation, the media owner could still lose considerable sums). The fact that agencies too had a living to make from advertising ensured that there was a growing wave of pressure on companies to advertise their goods and services. For all these reasons, the media owner was beholden to agencies, and this was recognized by the payment of the 15 per cent commission (generally 10 per cent in some minor media, such as trade publications). In fact, of course, since all the money spent on advertising actually

comes from the advertiser, and since it is the advertiser that is ultimately paying the agency, it is reasonable to assume that if the agencies' charges were not incorporated into the media rates, those rates could be reduced by 15 per cent.

As advertising agencies started to become major businesses, particularly in the United States, they began to expand overseas, initially at the behest of their biggest clients. J. Walter Thompson set up its first overseas office, in London, to service the General Motors business, and after that, as GM expanded its operation around the world, so too did JWT. The same happened with McCann-Erickson (which set up its offices to service Esso), and many of the other US agencies that are now multinational. Gradually, these agencies started picking up local business too, until today, American-owned agencies dominate most of the advertising markets around the world with the exception of Japan.

WHY USE AN AGENCY?

The fact that huge companies such as General Motors and Esso encouraged their advertising agencies to move into other countries with them, testifies to the value which major clients place on the service they receive from their agencies. But why should they bother to use an agency? Firms the size of GM and Esso have the resources to employ their own advertising department, not merely to supervise the campaign, but to actually write the copy and buy the space, just as an advertising

US-owned agencies dominate this list (*above*) of the world's top agencies in 1982, as compiled by *Advertising Age*. However, the world's biggest agency is Japanese – Dentsu – which has around a quarter of the total advertising market in Japan. This is unheard of in other countries, and is made possible by the fact that in Japan clients are not as concerned about account conflicts as they are elsewhere. The only other non-US agency in the top 10 is Saatchi & Saatchi Compton Worldwide.

agency does. Apart from the fact that a full-time employee is likely to know more about the firm's business than an outsider, there could also be cost savings, since a large firm would almost certainly be able to produce a campaign for less than the 15 per cent commission that the agency gets.

There are, however, a number of reasons why most companies prefer to use an agency. Perhaps the most important one is that most agencies can bring greater resources to an advertiser's campaign than the company itself could, since the biggest agencies, by and large, have bigger advertising billings than the biggest clients. For example, in the United States in 1982, the largest advertiser, Procter & Gamble, billed $726 million, while the largest agency, Young & Rubicam, billed $1,645 million. In the United Kingdom, the top advertiser, again P & G, billed £45 million, while the top agency, Saatchi & Saatchi, billed £114 million.

While size is not everything, it is an important factor in determining the quality of service an agency can provide. Agencies can offer the top advertising talent large accounts to work on in a wide variety of product fields, and this is as challenging to the account handlers and the media department as it is to the creative teams. It also gives the agency a wider breadth of knowledge about all aspects of the advertising business than any single client company is likely to get. Thus, in the case of all but the largest advertisers, most agencies will be able to attract people of higher calibre than their clients could, because they can deploy those people over a number of advertisers' business, throughout the year.

The media department of a major advertising agency will be negotiating with all the main media companies throughout the year, and will be in a good position to know the current state of the market and any developments that might affect its clients' business. Advertisers with products in just one category might only be dealing with one or two media, and even then only at certain times of the year. They will certainly have fewer media planners and buyers than an agency would.

Another element is the competition between agencies, both for accounts and for people. This keeps the adrenalin flowing, with each agency anxious to outperform its rivals. If a client is not satisfied with the people working on its account, it is possible – certainly in a large agency – to put a different team on the business. If a client is not satisfied with the agency itself, it is easy to change as there will be a great many others eager for the account.

Far from centralizing their advertising within their own company, many large clients use more than one agency, each working on a number of brands. This gives them the benefit of bringing even more minds onto the business, as well as providing a check as to how each of the agencies is performing in relation to the others. A final factor is that the advertiser's own staff can be too close to the problem – an outside firm can often put forward suggestions that an insider might flinch from.

AGENCY ORGANIZATION

Every agency tries to position itself differently from its competitors, and this is often reflected in the organiza-

tion of the company, with greater resources devoted to one department than another, or different reporting and planning structures. Despite such attempts at differentiation, however, most agencies are organized in more or less the same way. Big agencies will generally support more ancillary departments, such as research, information or sales promotion, but the key elements of each agency remain the same – account planning and management, the creative department, the media department, the traffic or progress department and the management of the agency itself.

In most agencies, this structure works in two ways – by functional department and by account group. From the agency's point of view, it is organized in a straightforward departmental form. The agency is headed by a chairman and managing director, with a board of directors, each of whom is responsible for a particular account or department. Occasionally, in agencies that have large, unwieldy boards, there is a two-tier board structure – a main board and, above that, an executive committee responsible for the day-to-day running of the agency. Not only does each client like to have its business run by a director of the agency, but both the creative and media departments often demand two or three directors as a recognition of their function's status within the agency.

From the client's point of view, however, an agency looks somewhat different, for in most cases agencies are also organized in the form of account groups, with each advertiser having one or more account groups to run its business. These account groups contain people from each relevant department – account planning and management, creative, media, and occasionally production – each of whom is responsible for their department's work on that business.

ACCOUNT MANAGEMENT AND PLANNING

These two functions may sound the same but they do not always coincide. Indeed, the term 'planning' has now become a somewhat technical one, and it is a fashionable debate as to what exactly the role of the account planner is, and where he or she fits into the account management structure. Individual agencies position themselves differently on the issue, and each attempts to persuade advertisers that its own structure is the one that produces the most effective advertising.

The account management role is far more clear cut. The account directors, supervisors, managers and executives are the equivalent – at various levels – of the client's marketing managers and brand managers, and are responsible for the running of the business. Indeed, account men (as they are often known, though some of the best these days are women), have often spent part of their career on the client side, and many marketing managers have worked in agencies. The account executive (titles vary in seniority from agency to agency) is responsible to the client for the running of its campaign, and co-ordinates the agency's activity on the account. As the agency's representative to the advertiser (indeed in J. Walter Thompson, account executives are known as 'reps'), the account executive has to try to keep both sides happy. It is not uncommon for the creative department in some agencies to feel that its work has been turned down because the account handler has 'undersold' it to the advertiser, and in turn, the client may feel the account man has failed to get the best work out of the creative department. The account executive will chair the agency's meetings on the business of the account and is responsible for producing the 'contact reports' or 'call reports', detailing any decisions taken, action in progress and so on, so that both the client and the agency have a written record of everything that is going on.

It has occasionally been suggested in supposedly progressive agencies that the account handling function is unnecessary, and that better work is produced if the client deals directly with the creative and media teams who work on its account. In principle this idea sounds attractive, and there was certainly a time when the account management people in some agencies did little more than take clients out to lunch, dinner, the races or more exotic forms of entertainment.

Those agencies that have tried to do without the account handling function, however, soon found that the co-ordination role was not as illusory as had been imagined. Apart from the fact that members of the creative department are not necessarily skilled in the other aspects of running an advertising campaign, client meetings take up a great deal of time – time that could often be better employed by such highly-paid people in producing more or better ads. Nevertheless, what some agencies *have* discovered is that they do not need as many account handlers as was once thought necessary, and that the role of some of them should be changed – hence the arrival of the account planner.

The account planner is trained in research techniques, and brings a more numerate and analytical mind than that of the conventional account man to the running of the account and the preparation of the campaign. The man generally credited with the development of the planning function in UK agencies was Stanley Pollitt of the Boase Massimi Pollitt agency, and he saw it as the closer integration of market research

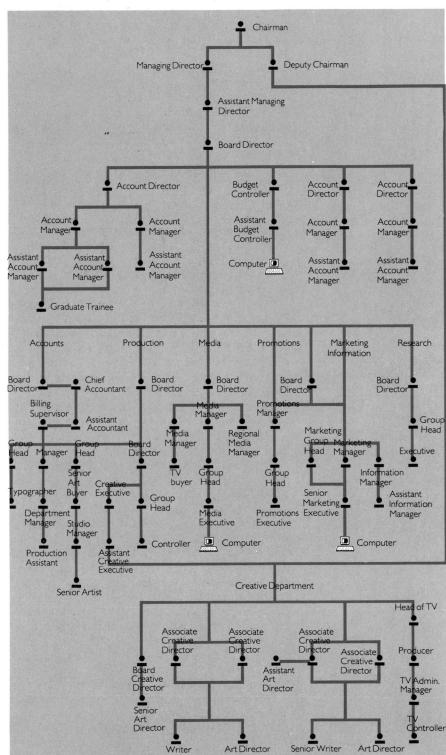

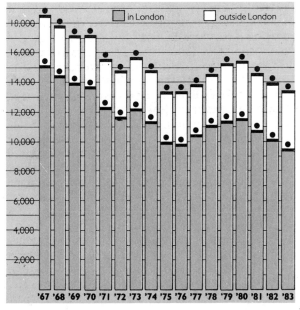

Though no two agencies are identical in their structure and organization, this chart (*above*) shows how one agency – Allen Brady & Marsh – handles the business of one of its largest clients. It demonstrates the wide range of jobs that have to be performed on the client's behalf, and the large number of people employed on a complex major account. Despite the numbers involved, however, employment within ad agencies as a whole has declined substantially in the last 20 years, as the chart (*left*) compiled by the Institute of Practitioners in Advertising on behalf of its agency members shows.

The creative department is arguably the most important in an agency, since it is strong creative work that attracts most clients. The creative team produces the basic concept for the ad, drawn as a 'rough' (*above*) and commissions the photographer who helps translate it into the finished ad (*far right*). The strip of photographs (*right*) are test shots, taken two hours before the shoot, to check the colour and the position of the model before she has her hair and make-up done.
Agency: Crawfords.

within the campaign planning process. 'I decided that a trained researcher should be put alongside the account man on every account,' wrote Pollitt in 1979. 'He should be there as of right, with equal status as a working partner. He was charged with ensuring that all data relevant to key advertising decisions should be properly analysed, complemented with new research, and brought to bear on judgements of the creative strategy and how the campaign should be appraised. Obviously, all this was decided in close consultation with account man and client.' The agency Pollitt founded, BMP, has certainly proved the effectiveness of this arrangement, producing advertising that wins creative awards and is effective in the market place.

Not all agencies employing planners use them in the same way as BMP, working as an equal partner with the account man, but the planner's function – to bring market research to bear more closely on the campaign thinking – is the same everywhere. For this reason, separate market research departments are now less common within agencies, though in some cases people who would be known as planners in one agency are called researchers in others.

THE CREATIVE DEPARTMENT

The creative department actually produces the advertisements, working to the brief that the account management and planners have produced. The department is run by the agency's creative director, who may or may not continue to create advertisements. The work involved in running the department, overseeing the work on each account, maintaining and improving quality and taking on staff, means that many people when they become creative director have little time to work on particular campaigns themselves.

At the core of the creative department is a series of creative teams, each consisting of a copy-writer and an art director, who work together to produce the advertising ideas, words and pictures, and see them through to their finished state. Often it is not entirely clear which of the two has come up with the idea, so closely do they work. For example, not all ads use words – or if they do it may simply be a copy-line that has been used for several years – but that does not mean the copy-writer has had no hand in the ad. Similarly, art directors can work on radio ads.

What happens next with the creative teams' work varies from agency to agency. Some creative departments have an art studio to produce finished artwork for the ads, while others have this done by outside studios. Some agencies have a typographer, to liaise with the typesetting houses where the copy is set, while in others this is done by the art director. Large agencies will have an art buyer, who commissions the illustrators and photographers, and occasionally a casting department, in charge of choosing actors and models for commercials. Some large agencies also have a television production department. Despite its name, this does not actually produce the commercials (which is done by an outside production company), but it supervises their production. The TV department liaises with the production

Say knickers to panties.

New, flattering 15 denier tights with knitted-in high cut briefs for longer looking legs.
The briefs have a cotton lined gusset and are made from a special fabric for a softer, more comfortable fit.
Choice of thirteen fashion shades. Three sizes. Around 99p.

Brief Secret
by
Aristoc

escalated and as the media world has become more complex (with new forms of television, more specialized publications and so on), clients have realized that enormous sums of money can be saved by better negotiation of space and airtime. In many countries this has led to the rise of specialist media buying companies, acting on behalf of advertisers.

The media department, headed by the media director, consists of media planners, who select the media to be used, and media buyers, who do the negotiations. This is another area of agency organization where there is some debate as to what is the most effective structure. Some agencies like to employ media staff as both planners and buyers, with each person planning the media schedule to be used, and then buying the newspaper or TV spot. The argument here is that the planner knows the overall objectives of the campaign and so can buy more effectively. Others separate the two functions, with the planner handing the schedule to the buyers, who then do the negotiation. The arguments here are that people who are good at planning a media schedule are not necessarily the best negotiators, and that space and time can be bought more cheaply by people who are negotiating in the market full-time, day in and day out. This is particularly the case with TV advertising in those countries where every spot is negotiable, and the price paid can fluctuate dramatically. Some agencies employ specialist media researchers. These are market researchers who can analyse the data about the audiences for each medium and their comparative costs, and provide back-up to the planners and buyers. In agencies without such full-time researchers, this job is done by the media planners.

TRAFFIC AND PRODUCTION

The traffic department (sometimes called the progress department) has to ensure that every stage of the campaign is properly co-ordinated, and that the ad reaches the right media owner at the right time and in the right form. In some agencies this final function is separate from that of the traffic department, and is performed by a production department (not to be confused with the TV production section of the creative department, though some of its work such as progress chasing and co-ordinating is the same).

The role of co-ordinating all these disparate elements is vital in a process as complex as that of putting an advertising campaign together. Not only do elements from a number of outside suppliers such as typographers and photographers have to be brought together, but in the case of print ads the department has to co-ordinate the production of the ads in different forms for different publications, because many have different page sizes and may also use different printing presses.

Individual publications may also require copy on different dates so that they can meet their own production deadlines. It is vital that the traffic and production department is in a position to send the relevant material to the publication in question so that all deadlines are met. Failure to do this could lead to the ad missing publication and could throw the whole campaign out of step.

companies, and its members have to be expert on commercial matters such as filming costs and trade union agreements, and on creative issues such as who are the up-and-coming directors, and which directors specialize in particular types of filming. In many agencies, however, there is no TV department as such, but simply a number of TV producers or co-ordinators working within the creative department who fulfil some of these functions, with support from outside freelances.

THE MEDIA DEPARTMENT

The media department is responsible for selecting the media in which the advertisements will appear, and for negotiating the best possible deal with the media owner. This function – sometimes known as the 'space-buying' department – was a relatively neglected one until about 10 years ago, but in recent years, as media costs have

Most large agencies have comfortable conference rooms (*right*) equipped with film projection, TV and video facilities.

Stewart Butterfield (*right*) is the Media Director at McCann-Erickson, London. He is responsible for the overall running of the department, and for policy decisions made by the department.

The media department's role is to contribute to the overall planning of the campaign and to negotiate with the media for space and airtime.

The media department (*right*) is headed by a media director, and consists of media planners and media buyers.

The traffic and production department (*right*) is responsible for ensuring that every stage of the campaign is properly co-ordinated.

AGENCY MANAGEMENT

The management of the agency itself is a separate function from account management, though account directors often end up running agencies and doing both jobs. The fact is, however, that unless an agency is run properly as a business, it will not prosper, no matter how effective its work is.

The peculiar nature of the agency business means that good financial management and strict accounting procedures are vital. Agencies deal in huge sums of money – millions of dollars a year – which they pass from their clients to the media owners. The media companies demand payment by a certain date each month and agencies have to comply, whether or not they have been paid by the advertiser. Agencies must therefore have efficient accountancy systems, ideally to ensure that they hold the advertiser's money in their account for as long as possible – the interest on such sums, even just overnight, is considerable – but mainly to ensure that they pay the media bills on time.

Cash flow can be a major problem for agencies. If an advertiser is late in paying the agency, the agency must have a sufficient balance or overdraft facility to pay the bills anyway, so that instead of gaining interest, it will be paying it. If an advertiser goes into liquidation, it can be the ruin of the agency, because, as principal, it is liable for the media bill. For this reason, many agencies take out insurance to cover the sums involved, though that in itself can substantially reduce the company's profit on an account.

A number of the largest agencies, particularly in the United States, are publicly-quoted companies, and in the last year or so there has been a growing trend in the United Kingdom for agencies to put some of their shares up for sale to the public. This in itself imposes added demands on the management of an agency and its accounts.

THE ACCOUNT GROUP

Having looked at each of the departments of the agency, it is now possible to see how they fit together for the client's purposes, through the account group. This group, run by one of the account management team, contains members from each of the major departments of the agency who are responsible for the department's work on that account. It is the embodiment of the concept of the full-service agency, incorporating the three main elements of any advertising campaign – the marketing, planning and strategy; the creative work; and the media side.

At its most basic, with a relatively small client and agency, the group will consist of the account man, a media person, the creative team, and a progress chaser, but for a more complex account it will be larger. For example, the account group at the London office of J. Walter Thompson on the Bowater Scott business consists of the following people: the account director, an account representative, an account planner, a creative supervisor, a copy-writer, an art director, a television

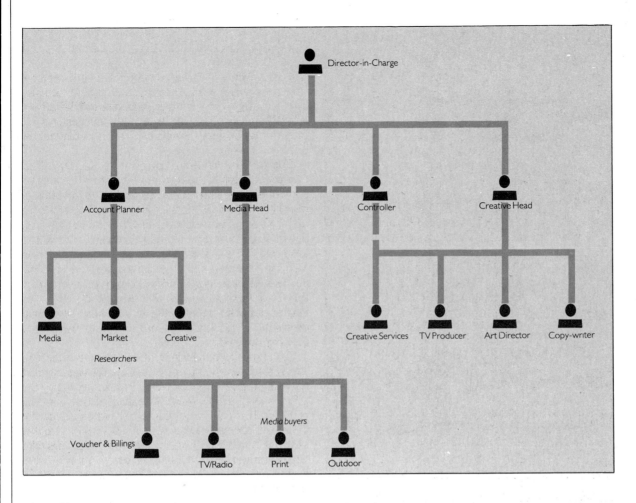

Director-in-Charge

Account Planner   Media Head   Controller   Creative Head

Media   Market   Creative

Researchers

Creative Services   TV Producer   Art Director   Copy-writer

Media buyers

Voucher & Billings

TV/Radio   Print   Outdoor

producer, a media supervisor, a television airtime buyer, a press planner/buyer and a production person. This group, or the key elements of it, will meet at least once a week, and considerably more often at crucial points of the campaign process. It is here that the advertising strategy is, if not decided, then certainly discussed from both a creative and media point of view. In particular, issues such as the 'inter-media' decision (whether television, press, radio or posters should be used) will be argued over, together with the size of the space, the use of colour and so on. This is where the media person can make 'creative' suggestions, pointing out that certain media are offering particular incentives and that, say, if the campaign were to use double-page spreads in certain newspapers, a particularly cost-effective deal could be negotiated. This is where the creative team can talk about media, suggesting that there are great creative possibilities on, say, posters and asking the media person whether it would reach the target market cost-effectively.

INTERNATIONAL

An extra dimension to the service offered by many agencies is that of international advertising. Many of the world's biggest advertising agencies built up their international networks in the wake of those of their clients, and a number of multinational companies use the same agency all over the world.

Nowadays, more and more large companies are looking for an international service from their agencies, and a number of firms have recently moved their accounts out of local agencies in order to have their business centralized internationally through a single agency. Such international alignment, as it is known, is the subject of some debate, with arguments both for and against the practice.

The issue surfaced recently, following a spate of internationally-led account moves. A few months before that, Cinzano's UK management had been forced to fire its agency, Collett Dickenson Pearce, despite a highly-acclaimed and successful campaign featuring Joan Collins and Leonard Rossiter, on the orders of head office in Italy. The account was moved to Foote Cone & Belding, which already held the business in 15 countries, on the grounds that the United Kingdom must be brought under the international corporate umbrella. The newspapers were full of the fact that Collins and Rossiter were being dropped – a rare tribute to the high awareness the campaign had generated – but ironically the campaign was brought back eight months later, through FCB, because no new campaign had yet been approved. Less than a year after the firing of Colletts, FCB lost the business to a creative consultancy, The Creative Business, and the Collins/Rossiter ads were run yet again.

A month before Colletts was fired by Cinzano, Parker Pens also fired its agency on the grounds of international alignment, again in spite of a highly-regarded cam-

The account group is run by one of the account management team – here (*above*) described as the account controller – who reports to the director in charge of the account. The controller co-ordinates the various elements of the account – media, creative and account planning – each of which is headed by a senior executive of the department concerned.

McCann-Erickson is probably the most experienced agency at handling world brands, with its work for Coca-Cola, Martini, Esso, Kodak and others. These Martini ads show how a basic style can be maintained in several countries, using the same artwork with the words translated into the relevant language.

paign. The agency in question was Lowe & Howard-Spink, a 'breakaway' from Colletts that has since become part of the Interpublic group of agencies. The stylish and distinctive Parker campaign had been conceived at Colletts and was continued at Lowe & Howard-Spink. What was interesting, was that when the business moved to Ogilvy & Mather, on international grounds, O & M maintained the same style and type-face in its ads for Parker, so that to the outside world the campaign remained the same.

But why should Parker have bothered to change its agency if it was going to maintain a similar campaign? The answer is that international alignment is not always motivated by a desire to run the same campaign all over the world. The mere fact of using a single agency, which can take on a good deal of the client's co-ordination work through its own international management network, is a strong enough reason for some advertisers. This does not alter the fact that, having appointed an international agency, an advertiser will almost certainly look at the possibility of running a single worldwide campaign. A strategy that has worked well in one market often works well in another, and if it is possible to share the production costs of a commercial between a number of countries the savings can be considerable.

One of the main proponents of the 'world brands' philosophy, in which products are sold under the same name, with the same packaging and the same advertising all over the world, is Saatchi & Saatchi Compton, which has taken up and promulgated the 'globalization of markets' theory of Professor Theodore Levitt, of the Harvard Business School. It maintains that a handful of worldwide agency networks will handle the bulk of an estimated $125 billion world advertising expenditure for major multinationals – world brands require world agencies. Nevertheless, perhaps the most experienced agency in handling world brands is McCann-Erickson, with Coca-Cola, Martini, Esso, Kodak and several other global clients. Despite the attractions of the global advertising philosophy, what is clear is that it cannot be the solution for the majority of brands or even for all multinational companies.

Another agency that has great experience of multinational advertising is Leo Burnett, which handles Marlboro, Seven-Up, Kellogg's and other accounts in many countries, and it maintains that each case must be examined on its merits. The agency's European co-ordination director, Lionel Godfrey, recently told a symposium on pan-European advertising, 'Many reasons are often quoted for running the same campaign in many countries. They include savings in production costs, savings in management time, the development of a unified image and the growth of international media, such as satellites.

'However, the only valid reason is if a global approach will sell more merchandise, more profitably, in total, than the sum of the different individual local approaches. If it will not, it is better not to begin.' Godfrey cited the different approaches of three of Leo Burnett's multinational clients, the most famous of which is Marlboro – along with Coca-Cola, one of the few undisputed world brands.

Marlboro uses a single advertising strategy, based on

the cowboy theme, which has been running for 30 years, and which has made the brand the largest-selling cigarette in the world. The campaign is said to have been conceived by Leo Burnett himself, and involved a radical repositioning of the brand, which had previously been aimed at women. The fact that the American West was one of the earliest examples of 'cultural convergence', being instantly recognizable the work over thanks to cinema and television, meant that the theme could be maintained throughout the world, even in China. However, though the advertising strategy is centralized, the creative work is executed locally, to account for local differences. In Nigeria, for example, the cowboy is black, while in Hong Kong he is not a cowboy but a ranch owner, thus acknowledging the importance of status in that market.

In contrast, another Burnett client, Seven-Up, not only uses a central advertising strategy but also produces its commercials centrally. This is necessary because the company lacks the local resources, but it also helps to maintain quality control and is more cost-effective. It means that the agency has to produce a wide range of commercials, since some will not be appropriate in certain countries. On the other hand Kellogg's, despite using Burnett in several countries, gives its local managers and agencies autonomy both on creative

strategy and execution, maintaining only an international right of veto, though it also provides central advice and the benefits of other countries' experience. 'Different eating habits make international food advertising hard to achieve and usually unrealistic,' says Godfrey.

Agencies that are structured to handle international business can theoretically offer benefits to advertisers even when the campaign used is not the same in all countries, by handling it in unprofitable markets as well as profitable ones. Nevertheless, it can be argued that this practice actually achieves the worst of both worlds, in that an agency network is bound to have weak offices in some markets. Many agencies argue that multinational clients are better off choosing a strong agency in each local market. One of the most highly-regarded agencies in London, Boase Massimi Pollitt, points out that two-thirds of its clients and three-quarters of its billings come from advertisers who advertise internationally, but that these firms do not seek to align their agencies purely for the sake of international neatness. 'Local conditions vary enormously,' says the agency's chairman, Martin Boase. 'People's habits aren't the same the world over, and if you try to impose a common stamp on a campaign it can lead to extremely bland advertising solutions.'

The Marlboro cowboy (*above*) is used all over the world, except where local ad restrictions prohibit the association of cigarettes with 'manliness', as in the United Kingdom. The cowboy is nevertheless adapted for local markets, as in this Nigerian ad (*top*).
Agency: Leo Burnett.

ALTERNATIVE SERVICES

Not every advertiser uses an advertising agency, and even those that do may not use their agency for all the elements of their campaign. Many find it cheaper and more effective (which is not necessarily the same thing) to use different suppliers for the separate functions of the advertising campaign. A few years ago, such practice was not merely frowned upon, but was forbidden in most countries by the rules of the trade bodies both of the media owners and of the advertising agencies. Such rules were not entirely logical, however, since advertising agencies themselves often use outside suppliers rather than trying to produce everything within the agency.

At the centre of the issue is the 15 per cent commission system under which agencies have traditionally been paid. For some large advertisers, spending millions of dollars each year on television airtime, 15 per cent is not only a great deal of money, it can also be a great deal more than it costs the agency to produce the campaign. Once the commercial has been made and paid for, the agency's only real work is through the media department, negotiating and buying the airtime. Yet under the commission system, it will continue to receive 15 per cent of the media cost every time the commercial runs. In such cases – and individual circumstances vary widely, depending on the number of different advertisements that have to be made, the amount of work that goes into them and so on – agencies might make a satisfactory profit from only 10 or 12 per cent commission, or, in some cases, even an 8 per cent commission. Yet the recognition rules of the media owners forbade agencies from passing any of the 15 per cent commission back to their clients. This was to prevent agencies from competing with each other on price, for fear, supposedly, that this would lead to a reduction in advertising standards.

Such recognition agreements have since been ruled restrictive practices in certain countries, and it is no longer a condition that the full 15 per cent must be kept by the agency. However, in practice certain clients had already been demanding *and* getting a percentage of the commission back for several years. One way in which this was achieved was by using specialist media-buying companies who worked for only 2 or 3 per cent of the campaign budget and handed the rest back to the client. The client could then get its commercial made, for a straight fee, by a creative consultancy. Sometimes it was not necessary to make a commercial at all, since some international advertisers already had a commercial that had been screened in other countries. The savings for a large spender on television could run into many thousands of dollars.

Quite apart from the issue of the saving on commission, however, such media specialists argued that they could also actually save money on the buying of airtime. By specializing in the media function, they could employ a few highly-paid staff who were experts at buying airtime without incurring the overheads of a full-service agency. Since these were the days when the media function was less highly valued and less highly paid – it is

the existence of the media specialists, as much as anything, that has changed this situation – a number of the best media directors and executives left to form their own companies.

The importance of the media specialist varies from country to country. In Sweden and France, for example, some are as large as the biggest agencies. In the United Kingdom, they account for about 10 per cent of television expenditure, and the biggest companies are just outside the top 20 agency rankings. Even before the media independents became established, creative consultancies existed to provide creative work for clients who did not need media campaigns, or to help agency creative departments in times of crisis.

Saatchi & Saatchi started life as a creative consultancy. Its early client, the Health Education Council, is a good example of an organization that uses striking creative work but has no need of media expenditure, since its posters appear in doctors' waiting-rooms and in hospitals (though it now uses paid-for media as well). The use of creative consultancies and media independents (sometimes known as the *à la carte system*), is still growing in most countries, and many of the world's biggest advertisers, such as Gillette, ITT and Carreras Rothman, use media independents in one or more countries.

The growth of such companies has forced agencies to relax their own attitudes to the way in which they will work. Some agencies with strong media departments handle media-only business themselves – just as the media independents do – while others have set up specialist media subsidiaries.

A number of agencies in the United Kingdom now work alongside media independents at the client's insistence, producing the creative work and the marketing and planning strategy, but using a media independent – instead of their own media department – to buy the space and time. Indeed, the new wave of agencies that have sprung up in the United Kingdom in the last four years owes much to the existence of the media independents, since in their early days when most of these bright, creatively-oriented agencies used specialist companies rather than creating their own media department, the media independents became the financial principals for the business.

Though the *à la carte* system has not displaced full-service agencies from their dominant position in most countries, it has resulted in many clients insisting on paying less than the 15 per cent commission to their agencies. Many advertisers now simply agree a fee with their agency each year, on the basis that the commission system is an arbitrary way of deciding how much to pay, and that it bears little relation to the amount of work involved. Others maintain that it is as good a system as any in a business where it is hard to work out on an hourly basis how much an agency should receive. For example, what is the value of a brilliant campaign a copy-writer thought up in the bath?

The flexibility now available to advertisers in the way they may put their campaigns together means that few companies now see any need to employ their own in-house advertising agency. Unilever, which was one of the first companies to have such an agency – Lintas, an acronym of Lever International Advertising Services – has gradually relaxed its hold on the company, allowing it to handle other accounts, placing some of its own business elsewhere and eventually selling it altogether. It does, however, still use it as a central media buying operation – a system that pre-dated the rise of the media independents by several decades.

SPECIALIST AGENCIES

There are other forms of specialization in the agency business. Several categories of advertising have developed their own specialist agencies because the requirements are different from those of general consumer advertising accounts, either in creative or media terms, or both. These include financial, industrial, direct response, recruitment and pharmaceutical advertising, all of which tend to be less glamorous and have smaller budgets than consumer advertising, but all of which require a great deal of specialist knowledge. In these cases, the conventional rule that agencies should not have more than one client in a particular area of business is turned on its head, and it seems to become a positive advantage to have a number of competing clients.

There are also a great many sales promotion companies. Most agencies would not regard these as advertising agencies at all, in that most of their output is not intended for the traditional media, such as press and TV, but for display in shops, bars, and on packs. Yet taking a wide definition of advertising, such companies are as much specialist agencies as any of the others in the specialist field.

Some of the specialist agencies are subsidiaries of major consumer agencies. One reason for this is that it allows such specialist companies to concentrate on their own area of activity, rather than simply being a small area of influence within a large agency. It also means that the overheads of the company can be tailored to the smaller budgets and different requirements of such advertisers.

Nevertheless, when they spot growth opportunities in such areas, big agencies are not afraid to take on accounts that would normally be thought of as the preserve of the specialists. Some major pharmaceutical accounts are handled by consumer goods agencies, and a growing number of financial advertising accounts are now moving to mainstream agencies. The largest recruitment accounts – such as those for government jobs like the police, nurses and the armed forces – are handled by consumer agencies. However, for the vast majority of advertisers in each of these categories, the smaller, specialist agencies still remain better able to handle such accounts.

BREAKAWAYS

Advertising is often described as a 'people business' – so is cannibalism, points out one agency chairman – and nowhere is this more true than within the agencies, whose main financial assets are their staff. A few agencies own their own building – indeed, in the early 1970s this led to a couple of publicly-quoted London agencies being bought for their property by asset-strippers – and though they may well have some valuable office equipment, computer hardware and software, by far the most important asset any agency has, is the talent of its people. This makes agencies very vulnerable, not only to the poaching by other agencies of individual members of staff, but also to complete 'breakaways' – new agencies set up by groups of key personnel, who have the personal allegiance of particular clients, and can take the business with them.

One of the most comprehensive breakaways of recent years was that from Collett Dickenson Pearce in London by its former managing director Frank Lowe and deputy managing director Geoff Howard-Spink. Lowe had been one of the architects of Colletts' success, and was highly regarded by several of the agency's biggest clients, including the brewer Whitbread, Parker Pens and Fiat, all of whom had benefited from superb creative work by Colletts. All three clients followed Lowe to his new agency, Lowe & Howard-Spink, which set up with billings of £9 million. It is a tribute to the staying power of Colletts that it withstood this blow, and though smaller, continued to win business and produce good advertising. Many agencies, given the personal and competitive nature of the ad business, never recover from such a blow and rapidly disappear from the advertising scene altogether.

Not all breakaways take business from the old agency, and many advertising people would eschew such behaviour. Indeed, there are doubts over the legality of it, depending on an agency's contracts with its staff and clients. Likewise it is not necessary for a new agency to be formed only by people who previously worked at the same agency. In the last four years, a 'new wave' of agencies has been launched very successfully in London by top creative and management people from a number of the largest international agencies. Most were set up by people from two or three separate agencies and few started with any accounts at all, but their track record in their previous – generally US-owned – agencies, and their wide contacts soon brought several of them success.

The ability simply to set up in business this way, in many cases starting with just a telephone and a hotel room, is an obvious attraction to many bright agency people and a matter of concern for all agency managements. These days it is even easier than it once was. The major problem for such new agencies used to be that of persuading the media to accept their ads, due to the stringent financial requirements placed on an agency by the media owners.

This problem has now been removed, in the United Kingdom and some other countries, by the arrival of the media independents, who have provided ready-made media departments – complete with media owner 'recognition' – for the new agencies. The media owners' concern that agencies should be financially sound is an understandable one, given that most of them rely on advertising revenue for a high proportion – if not all – of their income, and that their survival depends on the agencies' prompt payment of it.

Lowe rips £9m out of Colletts

by David O'Reilly

The shock waves caused by Lowe and Howard-Spink's breakaway from Collett Dickenson Pearce finally hit the agency this week as Frank Lowe moved out of Colletts for temporary offices in Covent Garden.

The £6 million Whitbread beer and lagers account and the £2 million Birds Eye business will both join Lowe and Howard-Spink, while the £3 million Fiat/Lancia account is to leave Colletts but has not decided definitely to follow Lowe. A further blow for the agency is its split with Walls Meat, which, in a move unrelated to Lowe's venture, is to move its £2 million business after disagreements about creative strategy. Walls expects to form a shortlist of three agencies.

So Colletts has lost £13 million in a week while Lowe and Howard-Spink is, with the £1 million Parker Pens account, billing £9 million only two weeks after announcing its existence. Colletts London billings are now £50 million.

As a first step in replacing the staff who have left, Colletts has hired Jonathan White, joint managing director of Kirkwoods, as a

Howard-Spink (left) and Lowe

senior account director. Colletts has also picked up £½ million of new product development work from Menley and James. Whitbread was expected to
Continued on Back Page

This is how the UK advertising paper *Campaign* broke the news that Lowe & Howard-Spink was taking £9m of business out of Collett Dickenson Pearce, one of the biggest 'breakaways' in recent years (*above*).

3 THE MEDIA

THE RISE OF THE SUN

Rupert Murdoch's News Corporation is one of the largest media companies in the world. It owns newspapers, magazines and television stations in the United States, the United Kingdom and Australia. Its biggest-selling and most profitable newspaper is the Sun, which is not only the United Kingdom's most popular daily newspaper, but also sells more copies than any other English-language daily in the world – over four million. The story of the rise of the Sun from the ashes of two ailing newspapers is as much a marketing and advertising case history as is the launch of Krona margarine, but it also provides an insight into the special problems and circumstances of media companies and their reliance on, and relationship with, their advertisers.

THE MAKING OF A MEDIUM

The *Sun* first appeared in its current tabloid format and under its current proprietor on Monday, November 17th 1969, but it was not the first new newspaper under that title and it was, in fact, the third paper in a line that stretched back unbroken – despite great financial difficulties throughout the period – to 1912.

It was in that year that the *Daily Herald* had been launched, as a paper for the Labour movement. By the 1920s, the Labour Party and the Trades Union Congress had formally taken over the publishing of the paper, and in 1929 a financial structure was set up which was to dictate the fortunes and policies of the paper for the next 40 years – until, in fact, it was taken over by Rupert Murdoch.

The 1929 deal left the TUC with 49 per cent of the *Daily Herald*, giving 51 per cent to Odhams (a successful publisher and printer of magazines) which set about trying to boost the circulation by a combination of cash incentives to party members who introduced new readers, and free gifts with the paper itself – a move which sparked off the incredible circulation and promotion battle of the 1930s.

Throughout that decade, four papers – the *Daily Herald*, the *Daily Express*, the *Daily Mail* and the *News Chronicle* – were fighting to achieve the largest circulation, largely by pouring money into incentives for readers, such as the works of Dickens and Shaw, insurance and pots and pans. The reason circulation became so important was to attract advertisers. Unlike most manufacturers, newspaper publishers derive their revenue from two separate – though partially linked – sources: readers, who pay the cover price for their copy, and advertisers, who pay for the privilege of reaching those readers with their advertising message. Very few publishers can rely solely on one or other of these sources (though free newspapers and magazines, deriving their income solely from advertising, are becoming increasingly common). Since the price of a newspaper does not cover the cost of producing it, the reason for increasing circulation was not to attract extra revenue from copy sales, but to get more money from advertisers. It can thus be seen that advertising plays a crucial role in the financing of newspapers, and that the needs of advertisers have to be taken account of by publishers.

Odhams was successful in its attempt to increase the *Daily Herald*'s circulation, passing first the one million mark and then – at the height of the free gift battles – exceeding two million, the first paper to do so. Then the war intervened and afterwards the paper's circulation started to decline, gradually but steadily, until by 1960 it had fallen below one and a half million at a time when some of its rivals, most notably the *Daily Express* and the *Daily Mirror*, were flourishing. What made the *Daily Herald*'s position worse was that those readers it did have were those of least interest to advertisers, being predominantly male, ageing and in the lower socio-economic groups, C2 and DE.

In 1961, Odhams was bought by the Mirror Group of newspapers, who in order to acquire the company – and its valuable magazine interests – gave a pledge to the Labour Party and the TUC (which still at that stage owned 49 per cent of the *Daily Herald*) to keep the paper going for seven years. It quickly became clear, however, that the *Daily Herald* had no real future. As Simon Jenkins says in his book, *Newspaper Money*: 'By the early 1960s, its traditional cloth-cap attitudes did not fit in at all with the image younger Labour voters were being offered by Harold Wilson, a garb more attractive to advertisers.'

The *Daily Herald*'s new owners commissioned research into the likely newspaper market over the next 10 years, research which suggested that as the population became younger (half the nation would be under 35 by the end of the 1960s), better educated and better off, the old political and class attitudes would be replaced by 'consumer politics' in which people would vote for whichever party was perceived to offer most. The conclusion reached was that there was room for a totally new type of newspaper, geared to the wants and needs of this new, better educated, more affluent consumer. The decision was taken that the *Daily Herald* should close and be immediately replaced by the *Sun* – a newspaper 'born of the age we live in', as the paper's sparkling launch advertising campaign proclaimed it.

The *Sun* was launched on September 15th 1964, a broadsheet like the *Daily Herald* had been, and it betrayed its heavily researched background in the front page story explaining what the new paper stood for. 'Look how life has changed. Our children are

The *Sun* has gone through several changes on the way to its present circulation. *(Opposite, top left)* the first paper entitled *The Sun*, launched in the 19th century; *(top right)* the forerunner of today's *Sun*, the *Daily Herald*, launched in 1912, which existed until September 14, 1964; *(middle right)* the first edition of the IPC *Sun*, launched on September 15, 1964; *(middle left)* the last edition of the broadsheet *Sun*, published on November 15, 1969; *(bottom)* the front cover and centre spread of the new tabloid *Sun*, launched by Rupert Murdoch on November 17, 1969.

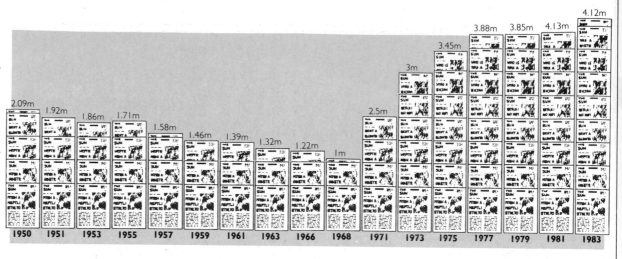

The *Daily Herald*'s circulation declined steadily from 2 million to 1.3 million in 1964, when it was relaunched by IPC as the *Sun*. Sales in the *Sun*'s first year increased, but after that the decline continued until 1969, when circulation barely reached one million. Following the take-over by Rupert Murdoch and the relaunch as a tabloid, sales rose dramatically, reaching a peak of 3.9 million in 1978. After circulation faltered and started declining in 1981, a price cut and the launch of bingo revived its fortunes and it broke the 4 million mark (*right*).

better educated. The mental horizons of their parents have widened through travel, higher living standards and TV. Five million Britons now holiday abroad every year. Half our population is under 35 years of age.

'Steaks, cars, houses, refrigerators, washing machines are no longer the prerogative of the "upper crust" but the right of all. People believe, and the *Sun* believes with them, that the division of Britain into social classes is happily out of date.'

Unhappily, despite the undoubted truth of these findings, the *Sun* did not strike a chord with the new consumers – it failed to reach its break even circulation. Advertisers had had high hopes of it – as indeed they might, considering that the whole paper had been conceived with them in mind – but without the required circulation it was no better placed to attract their money than the *Daily Herald* had been. There were plenty of other national newspapers – not to mention television – for advertisers to use.

The *Sun* limped on for five years, always losing money, with its circulation declining towards the one million level until finally, in the summer of 1969, the International Publishing Corporation (of which the Mirror papers had become part) announced that the paper would cease publication at the start of the following year. It was eight years since the Mirror Group had made its promise to keep the *Daily Herald* alive for at least seven years. Nevertheless, while closure had been considered, this announcement was mainly designed to attract a bidder for the title. The redundancy implications of closing a national newspaper – particularly one that had taken the place of the workers' *Daily Herald* – were daunting and a closure might have had repercussions for IPC's other Fleet Street publications, such as the *Daily Mirror*.

The first bidder was Robert Maxwell, who at the time ran Pergamon Press and has since built up the British Printing and Communications Corporation. He wanted to run the *Sun* as a Labour paper, controlled by a non-profit-making trust, but his scheme foundered through lack of support. It was then that Rupert Murdoch moved in. Murdoch already owned the United Kingdom's largest Sunday newspaper, the *News of the World*, and wanted a daily paper to make the most economic use of his printing presses. Had

IPC not sold him the *Sun* title, he would almost certainly have launched a tabloid daily of his own anyway. As a result he bought the *Sun* for a knock-down price, and in addition managed to secure more economical deals with the unions than other publishers were able to achieve. The new tabloid *Sun* was launched on November 17th 1969, and it quickly became clear that IPC's *Daily Mirror* (then Europe's biggest-selling daily paper with a circulation of well over four million) had a fight on its hands.

Though the now commonplace pictures of naked breasts did not start immediately – the first issue contained several photographs of naked women, but no nipples were visible – it was obvious that the new *Sun* was determined to be an unashamedly popular newspaper, in a way that its predecessor had never been. The *Daily Mirror*, which had quietly been pushing itself more up-market – particularly through an in-depth feature, looking at the background to the news, called Mirrorscope – was vulnerable to such an approach and it soon felt the consequences.

With its brash editorial approach majoring on sex and sport, and its even brasher television advertising campaigns, the new *Sun* quickly built up circulation in a way that the post-war *Daily Herald* and the first *Sun* had never been able to do. Its circulation soon passed the two million mark, reached three million in 1974 – five years after its launch – and almost reached four million in 1978. Even more significantly, however, in that year it passed the circulation of the *Daily Mirror*, which had been steadily declining throughout this period.

As the circulation increased, so did the advertising revenue. Advertisers are not particularly concerned with how a paper wins readers providing it does so: the fact that the *Sun*'s editorial quality was decried in many quarters did not alter the fact that as an advertising medium it had great value.

After a decade of success in which the paper produced large profits for the News Corporation – enabling it to fund many of its other ventures, particularly in its new market, the United States – the *Sun* showed signs of slipping from its pinnacle. The *Daily Mirror* had recovered from the blow to its esteem sustained when the *Sun* overtook its circulation, and had rebuilt

The present-day *Sun (left)* on the 40th anniversary of D-Day. The topless girl on page 3 is a regular feature and has had more than a passing influence on the paper's sales success.

its confidence while the *Sun* had lost some of its sparkle. By April 1981, the *Sun*'s circulation had slipped to just over three and a half million – less than 40,000 copies ahead of the *Daily Mirror*'s.

Had the *Daily Mirror* regained its former position as the United Kingdom's biggest-selling daily paper, the boost to its morale and market position – and the blow to the *Sun*'s – would have been enormous. Advertisers like to be associated with media that are doing well, and the emotional significance of the *Daily Mirror* overtaking the *Sun* – in addition to the mathematical one – would have brought big benefits for the former in advertising revenue. Rupert Murdoch took drastic action to stop this happening. In a move which took rival publishers completely by surprise, the *Sun* dropped its cover price by 2p for two months. This immediately boosted sales by 180,000 copies a day, and when the old price was restored the paper introduced a bingo game with big cash prizes for readers. At the same time, a new editor was brought in to liven up the content of the paper.

The net result was that the *Sun* increased its circulation by some 400,000 copies in the second half of 1981, but more importantly it widened the gap between itself and the *Daily Mirror* from 40,000 in April to no less than 700,000 copies by the end of the year. After that the gap continued to increase and in 1983 the *Sun*'s circulation topped 4 million, giving it a lead of more than a million copies over the *Daily Mirror*. Advertisers cannot ignore figures like that.

The success of the *Sun*, after the failure of its two predecessors, illustrates several points about the media and their relationship with advertisers. The first is that circulation is a crucial weapon in the battle for advertising revenue: the more readers a paper has, by and large, the more advertisers it will attract. However, the *type* of reader is important too. One reason why the *Daily Herald* was unsuccessful, even though it still had a circulation of one and a half million, was that its readers were not the sort that advertisers want to reach. By contrast, papers with considerably smaller circulations, such as the *Guardian* and the *Financial Times*, can make money because advertisers are keen to reach their up-market readers.

Another point this case history illustrates is that it is the newspaper itself rather than political beliefs or astute market research that attracts readers. The Murdoch *Sun* was born out of its proprietor's instinct that people would buy an entertaining paper heavy on sex and sport. By contrast, the *Daily Herald* was a paper that had allowed time to pass it by – largely, it must be said, because of an overwhelming awareness that it had to be a Labour paper with a conscience, standing up for the working man (while the *Daily Mirror* was proving that a Labour paper need not be dull). The original *Sun* simply did not have enough life, sparkle or character to attract readers: the research it was based on was perfectly valid, but the execution was weak.

However, the overwhelming point this case history illustrates is the ferocity of competition between the media, both for readers (or viewers) and advertisers. If there had been fewer other newspapers the *Daily Herald* would have made money even if its circulation had remained at one and a half million: it was the fact that there were other papers offering advertisers larger circulations and better quality readerships that meant it could not survive.

MEDIA

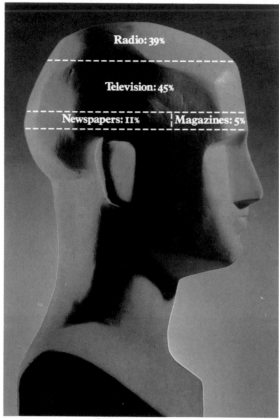

Radio is challenging television.

How Americans 18+ divide media time.
(Average 24-hour day, Monday to Friday.)
Source: R.H. Bruskin study.

Advertisers are faced with a wide choice of media, therefore publishers and TV and radio stations aggressively sell the strengths of their respective media with ads like these in the trade press. Here the US Radio Advertising Bureau puts its case against the giant medium, television (*above*).

of items such as posters or leaflets on display in shops, garages or other retail outlets; house-to-house deliveries of leaflets or free samples; and sponsorship of sports or artistic events. Such activity is generally known as sales promotion (or 'below-the-line' as opposed to 'above-the-line' advertising, which is paid-for space in the traditional media), but in its function of enabling advertisers to get their message across to the right audience, it is no different from a 60-second television commercial or a double-page magazine spread.

Each medium consists of individual businesses, for which advertising is an important – and in some cases the only – source of revenue. They range from huge communications companies such as News Corporation, CBS and Time, turning over millions of dollars, to local weekly newspaper publishers with only a few hundred readers. What they have in common is the need to persuade advertisers that their medium can provide the right audience at a reasonable price, and every media company has an advertisement sales department which is responsible for the firm's ad revenue.

THE MEDIA CHOICE

Every advertiser is thus faced with a wide range of options when setting out to run a campaign, with salesmen from each of the various media stressing the benefits of their own publication or television station, and the reasons it warrants a place on the campaign media schedule. So how does the advertiser decide which media to use?

Fortunately for many companies, some of the options rule themselves out straight away. There is little point in a local butcher with one shop advertising on television or in a national newspaper, even though most potential customers might see the ads. Even if a local butcher could afford it, the fact that most people who saw the advertising would live too far away to respond to it, would mean that the enormous audience it attracted would be largely wasted. The obvious medium for a local shop is the local newspaper or, if available, a local radio station.

The selection of the right medium is ultimately as important as the decision on what should actually be said in the advertisement. No matter how powerful or compelling the creative element of an ad, if it reaches the wrong people – or too few people – it cannot be effective. However, although the audience of each medium is a crucial consideration for an advertiser, there are two other important factors. The first is cost, and the second is the particular characteristics of a given medium, such as the creative opportunities it offers or the restrictions it imposes. All three factors have to be considered at two separate stages of the media planning process. The 'inter-media' decision has to be made first (ie television or newspapers or radio), followed by the 'intra-media' decision (NBC or Home Box Office, *The Times* or *The Daily Telegraph*, and so on).

Though the business of advertising could conceivably survive without advertising agencies, it could not exist without the media, for until an advertisement is actually communicating with its target audience it is not technically advertising. Without the television and radio stations, newspapers and magazines, posters and cinemas to disseminate the advertisers' message, no one would bother to create advertisements at all.

Though sky-writing is less fashionable than it once was, advertising now appears on balloons, parking meters, T-shirts, button badges, shopping trolleys, milk bottles and a host of other unlikely sales aids. More importantly, there are a number of other ways of communicating with the target audience that are taken very seriously by many major advertisers. These include direct mail, which is advertising material sent through the post; point-of-sale material, which consists

The increasing specialization of magazines means that advertisers can target their messages very specifically. Inc. (*above*) is aimed not at businessmen in general but at small to mid-sized firms.

Directories like the 'Yellow Pages' (*below*) are a major medium often overlooked by many advertisers.

Family Weekly sells itself to advertisers (*above*) with the help of Raquel Welch and the information that its readers spend more on furniture and home appliances than the traditionally high-spending Nielsen 'A' group.

Magazine publishers (*below*) take a dig at network television stations, whose share of the US audience is shrinking.

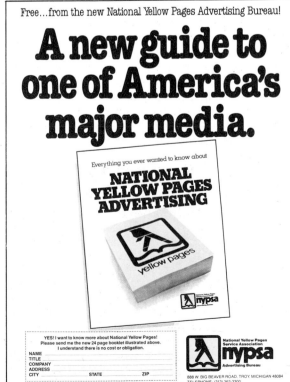

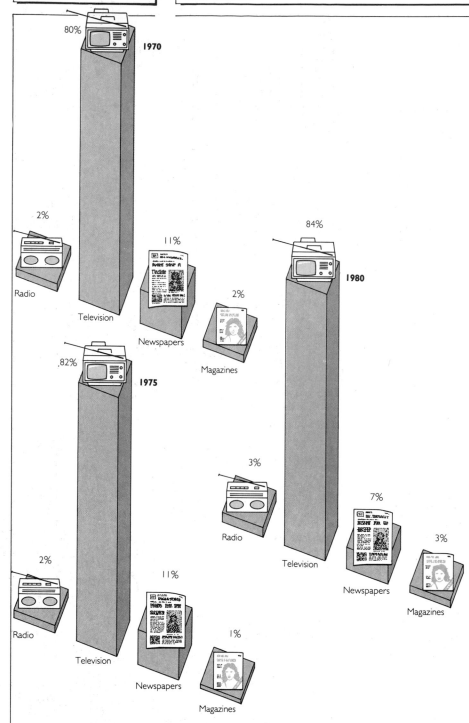

80%   1970
2%   Radio   Television   11%   Newspapers   2%   Magazines   84%   1980
.82%   1975
2%   Radio   Television   11%   Newspapers   1%   Magazines   3%   Radio   7%   Television   Newspapers   3%   Magazines

Research in the United States among 2,500 adults shows TV to be the most influential advertising medium (*above*). The research was carried out by R.H. Bruskin Associates for the TV industry, but Bruskin's other clients include many of the world's biggest agencies and advertisers.

AUDIENCE

The audience of any medium consists of the people who read a particular newspaper or magazine, watch a television programme or station, listen to a radio programme or station, walk or drive past a poster, and so on. The numbers and characteristics of such people are measured regularly, in varying degrees of detail.

Advertisers need to know not just how many people buy a publication regularly, but how many people *read* it and what sort of people they are. The circulation figures showing the numbers of copies sold are therefore supplemented by surveys designed to find out who reads each title. Similarly, advertisers do not simply want to know how many people watch television regularly, but how many people watch a particular programme and what sort of people they are.

The characteristics of the audience – age, sex, class, income, purchasing habits and so on – are important, because different advertisers want to reach different sorts of people. Most packaged goods advertisers want to reach housewives; beer advertisers want to reach young men; financial and office equipment advertisers want to reach businessmen. They must therefore know not merely how many people read a paper or watch a television programme, but how many *of their target audience* do so. The medium that is right for the soap-powder manufacturer is unlikely to be suitable for the investment company. Many advertisers have specific regional requirements because their markets are only in certain parts of the country. It is important for them to know the circulation area of a newspaper or the transmission area of a TV or radio station so they do not waste money by advertising outside their catchment area.

While the audience of a particular medium, in terms of size, characteristics and coverage area, is a limiting factor in the advertiser's media decision, the chances are that a number of different media will prove to be equally effective at reaching the target audience. The advertiser can therefore move on to the third consideration, the particular characteristics of each of the different media.

CHARACTERISTICS

The characteristics of a medium are often the crucial factor in deciding which an advertiser uses, simply because they dictate the sort of message that can be put across. They include physical features that affect the creative treatment; legal and other restrictions that affect what the advertiser is permitted to say; and factors of timing and editorial environment, that vary considerably from medium to medium.

Physical features include elements such as sound, colour and movement. A record advertiser ideally needs to use sound in its advertising, and so will be inclined, other things being equal, to use radio, television or cinema. Food looks much more appetizing when photographed in colour, so many food firms regard colour as a crucial consideration and would thus choose between television, cinema or magazines. Movement is an important requirement for products needing to be demon-

COST

Of the three basic considerations, cost is arguably the most important since it can rule out some media right from the start. A small company will probably not be able to afford to advertise on television or in national newspapers, however much it would welcome the business such increased exposure would give it.

Capital cost is thus the starting point in the decision-making process, so if the budget will not run to television, there is no point in considering any other factors. However, the budgets of most major advertisers are sufficiently large for them to be able to consider most, if not all, media. They can therefore move onto the next consideration, which is that of the audience.

strated, such as food processors or do-it-yourself equipment, and would suggest – again, all things being equal – a choice between television and cinema. However, as all other things are *not* equal, and the audience is an important requirement, cinema might well find itself out of the running for much of this advertising, for the characteristics of a medium must not be allowed to outweigh the basic audience requirements of a campaign.

Another physical factor that can be of importance is the amount of time or space available for a reasonable cost. A company that has a complicated message to put across, may feel that a 30-second television commercial is not enough in which to convey all the required information, yet the cost of using longer spots – say one or even two minutes – would mean reducing the coverage of the campaign dramatically. Such a firm would probably be more inclined to use the press, where even a half-page ad can carry considerably more information than a TV commercial. The permanence of the newspaper ad – it can be cut out and kept – is another factor of importance to many advertisers.

The practical issues of getting the advertisement in front of the audience are just as important. Some products and services are simply not permitted to be advertised in certain media. Cigarettes must not be advertised on television in many countries, while contraceptives and sanitary protection products are also widely banned from the screen. Such rules are not confined to the broadcast media, many publishers and editors also impose restrictions on the sort of advertisements they will carry, on the grounds that they do not want to offend their readers. In other cases, while the product category may not actually be banned from a medium, the advertiser may find the restrictions on what may be said so inhibiting that it is not worth using the medium at all. In the United Kingdom, charities and family planning services are both permitted to advertise on television, but the IBA imposes such strict copy requirements that few advertisers have availed themselves of the opportunity.

Time factors, such as the length of time it takes to create an advertisement and get it to the audience, or the need to ensure an ad appears on a particular day or at a specific time, can be crucial to some advertisers. Many, such as retailers (because of price changes), and financial organizations (because company results need to be published quickly), have to produce their ads very quickly. For such advertisers, newspapers and radio tend to be better than media that require copy a long time in advance.

Editorial environment is an element that influences some advertisers, and this applies not just to the press but also to television. Some companies feel that their advertisements are enhanced if they appear in 'quality' publications or programmes. Some airlines and prestige car firms like to run their commercials in news and current affairs programmes, not just because they are watched by a higher proportion of businessmen, but because they feel that the environment is more suitable than that of a comedy series or a soap opera. Other advertisers like the prestige that comes from advertising in *Vogue* or *The Times*.

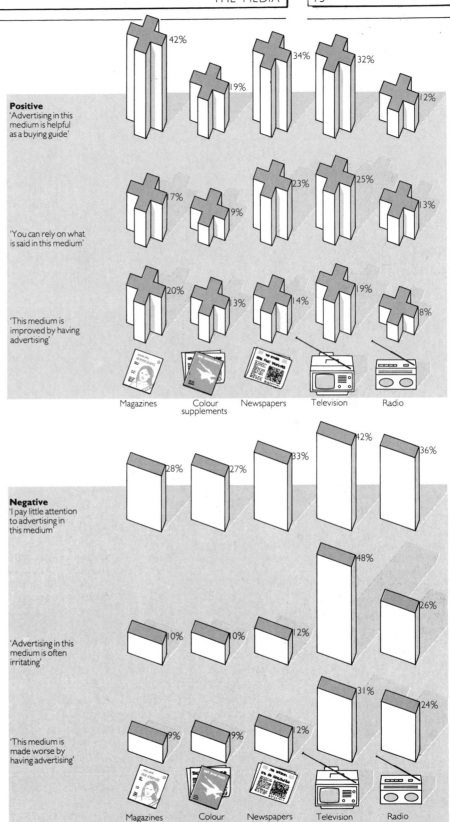

Positive
'Advertising in this medium is helpful as a buying guide'

'You can rely on what is said in this medium'

'This medium is improved by having advertising'

Magazines · Colour supplements · Newspapers · Television · Radio

Negative
'I pay little attention to advertising in this medium'

'Advertising in this medium is often irritating'

'This medium is made worse by having advertising'

Magazines · Colour supplements · Newspapers · Television · Radio

Many members of the public maintain that they pay little attention to advertisements, but the balance of their attitudes towards the various media differs significantly (*above*). Magazines emerge most favourably from this UK research – perhaps not surprisingly, since it was sponsored by the magazine industry – but other research, commissioned by rival media, has produced only subtly different findings.

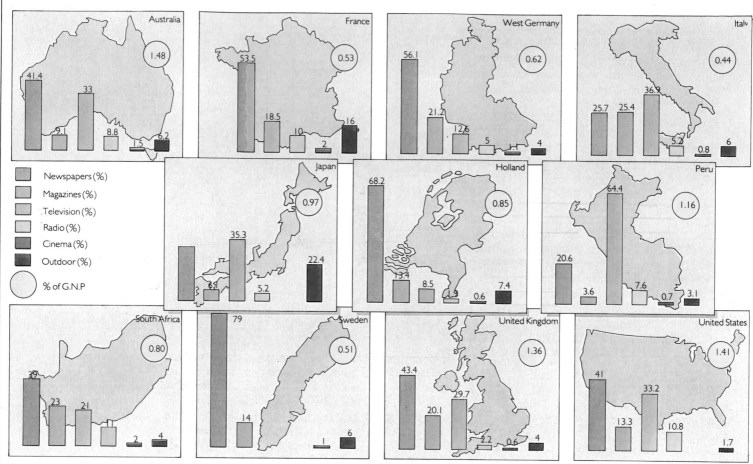

Australia 1.48
41.4 · 9.1 · 33 · 8.8 · 1.5 · 6.2

France 0.53
53.5 · 18.5 · 10 · 2 · 16

West Germany 0.62
56.1 · 21.2 · 12.6 · 5 · 1.1 · 4

Italy 0.44
25.7 · 25.4 · 36.9 · 5.2 · 0.8 · 6

Newspapers (%)
Magazines (%)
Television (%)
Radio (%)
Cinema (%)
Outdoor (%)
% of G.N.P

Japan 0.97
35.3 · 6.5 · 5.2 · 22.4

Holland 0.85
68.2 · 13.4 · 8.5 · 1.9 · 0.6 · 7.4

Peru 1.16
64.4 · 20.6 · 3.6 · 7.6 · 0.7 · 3.1

South Africa 0.80
39 · 23 · 21 · 2 · 4

Sweden 0.51
79 · 14 · 1 · 6

United Kingdom 1.36
43.4 · 20.1 · 29.7 · 2.2 · 0.6 · 4

United States 1.41
41 · 13.3 · 33.2 · 10.8 · 1.7

The share of advertising revenue taken by each medium varies widely from country to country, as this chart, based on figures from the JWT Unilever Co-ordination Group, illustrates (*above*).

WHO DECIDES?

All these considerations – cost, audience and the characteristics of the various media – will be taken into account before the media decision is taken. But who actually takes the media decision? Is it left simply to the media department of the agency to work out the numbers and decide which is the most cost-effective way of reaching the target audience? Presumably not, since the characteristics of each medium can be as important as the cost and the audience. How much say does the creative department have, since its people will actually be producing the advertisements? Are the media the creative people like to use given preference over less fashionable media? How much influence does the account team have in reconciling possibly conflicting views? Does the account director simply tell the creative and media departments to get on with it? And what about the advertiser who will actually be footing the bill?

Naturally there are elements of all these influences on the final outcome, but there are also two levels of media decision to be taken, and the influence of the parties varies in each. By and large, the media department has more influence over the second stage – the intra-media decision as to which titles or stations should be used – than it does over the inter-media decision between TV and the press, or radio and posters.

The advertiser, the account group and the creative department are all likely to have strong views on the inter-media decision, and while they will take advice from the media department on the overall cost and audience considerations of their decision, the media specialists' views will carry no greater weight than anyone else's, and often considerably less. The creative department, for example, has an indirect power of veto since it can suggest that no creative solution can be found for a medium its people are not keen on. This can be a dangerous tactic, however, for if the client is determined to use that medium it may well decide to find an agency that *can* find a creative solution.

Once the overall inter-media decision has been taken, it is generally left up to the media department to work out the detailed schedule, to decide which publications to use and when the commercials should be transmitted. The advertiser, account group or creative department may have views on the particular editorial environment of certain programmes, but after that it is the media department's job to plan and book the campaign.

THE SALES DEPARTMENT

None of these decisions gets taken in a vacuum. Every media company has an advertisement sales department whose job it is to pull in as much ad revenue as possible. In some cases, such as that of most commercial television and radio companies, advertising may account for the firm's entire income; for newspapers and magazines the proportion may be anything between 30 and 70 per cent; but whatever the proportion, advertising is vital to each company's commercial success.

Media companies cannot simply sit back and hope that advertisers will decide to put money in their magazine or newspaper, and so there is as much competition

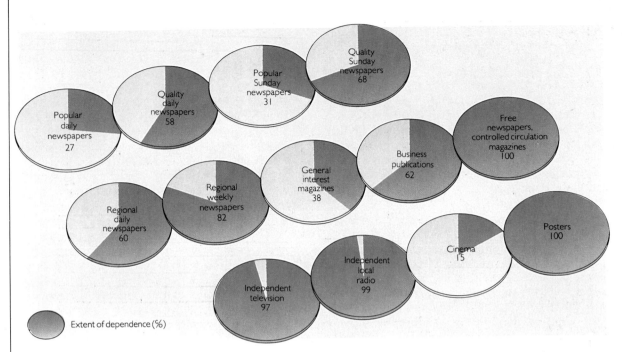

Popular
daily
newspapers
27

Quality
daily
newspapers
58

Popular
Sunday
newspapers
31

Quality
Sunday
newspapers
68

Free
newspapers,
controlled circulation
magazines
100

Regional
daily
newspapers
60

Regional
weekly
newspapers
82

General
interest
magazines
38

Business
publications
62

Independent
television
97

Independent
local
radio
99

Cinema
15

Posters
100

Extent of dependence (%)

Some media, for example BBC TV and Radio, survive without advertising revenue at all, being paid for by licence fee or by subscription. Others, like posters or free publications, are wholly dependent on advertising. Most media, however, rely on a combination of advertising and cover price revenue (*left*).

between the media owners to sell advertising as there is in any of their customers' markets. The size and structure of advertisement sales departments varies considerably depending on the size and nature of the company – a small publisher may have only one or two salesmen, a large newspaper or TV station might employ 100 or more. In general, however, the department will be headed by an advertisement director or manager, and will be divided into groups of people, each with specific responsibilities. These groups may be divided by advertising agency, with each group responsible for the clients of a number of agencies, or by advertiser, but whichever way they are organized their job is to get to know the people responsible for the media decision, and to ensure that they in turn know everything they need to about the medium.

Advertisement selling works on a number of different levels. The first obvious distinction is between the inter-media and intra-media decision. There is a great danger that if each individual publication or station sells only its own benefits rather than those of the medium it is part of, the overall selling of the medium will go by default. In other words, if all the magazine publishers sell their advertising space simply on the basis that they have a bigger readership or a cheaper cost-per-thousand than other magazine publishers, they are unlikely to pull many advertisers away from television. For this reason, some of the smaller media, such as radio, have set up centralized sales and marketing operations that can put the case for radio as a medium, selling on behalf of all radio stations. In Canada, this job is done by the Radio Advertising Bureau, while in the United Kingdom the job is split between the Radio Marketing Bureau, which promotes the medium but does not sell airtime, and a number of sales companies which sell time on behalf of regional groups of stations. Similar organizations include the Regional Newspaper Advertising Bureau, and the Direct Mail Sales Bureau. In other media, it is the job of the largest companies to make sure that the medium is

properly promoted, either through a concerted campaign run by their joint trade body – as is done by the Independent Television Companies Association in the UK – or, if companies find it hard to cooperate with their competitors for this purpose, by an individual firm. Mirror Group Newspapers has for many years promoted the cause of the newspaper advertising virtually single-handedly in the UK.

Quite apart from the inter-media selling, advertisement sales people have to operate on two levels, both servicing clients and selling to them. They must ensure that their advertisers – or potential advertisers – are kept informed of any developments affecting their medium (such as increases in audience, new features and programmes, and special advertising rates). And secondly, they must keep abreast of the campaigns their advertisers are planning, and make sure their medium is one of those being used. If it is not and it has a good claim to be, the advertisement manager will want to know why.

Much of this communication is done by telephone, but every so often a media salesman will make a presentation to the ad agencies. Traditionally, such presentations were made to the planners and buyers in the media department, and in most cases they still are. But such is the influence of the advertiser and the creative department on the inter-media decision, that many media owners are now putting their case direct to the clients and the creative people as well. They have realized that there is little point in arguing in terms of costs-per-thousand and ratings with the media department, if the creative department has already decided it does not like the medium. Large media companies will have research and marketing executives to help prepare such presentations, but in smaller firms, the sales executives will have to do the work themselves, alongside their normal selling activity. An important element of this activity is the negotiation of rates, for though most media companies have a rate-card, it is usually only the starting point for discussions.

TELEVISION

Television is generally regarded as the most powerful and persuasive of the media, but at the same time, it is not necessarily suitable for all advertisers. It offers large audiences and many of the media characteristics that advertisers want, but it is also expensive, and there are strict restrictions on what may be advertised. Indeed, in a number of countries, television advertising is simply not permitted, while in others the amount of advertising time is so limited that it is hard to put together a worthwhile campaign.

For those advertisers who can afford television and for whom the restrictions are not too severe, television is the most powerful medium available, and it has become the standard by which all other media measure themselves. Magazines, newspapers, radio stations and poster companies are forever comparing their performance with that of television and often claim that they are more cost-effective, or better at reaching motorists or businessmen than television. The reason for this is that most of the biggest national advertisers in the United States and the United Kingdom, put the bulk of their advertising budget on television. Eight out of the top 10 advertisers in the United Kingdom spend over 90 per cent of their advertising budget on television, including such firms as Procter & Gamble, Mars, Cadbury, Kellogg's, Rowntree Mackintosh, General Foods and Nestle. Most of the biggest spenders in the United States are similarly committed to television.

Nowadays it often seems as though television's best salesmen are in fact the manufacturers, retailers and ad agencies. Grocery retailers say that they are more likely to stock a new product if it is advertised on television, and many manufacturers give this as a major reason for using TV. In a recent survey, 71 per cent of grocery store buyers said that they thought television was the most effective medium for generating sales among their customers.

Advantages

The advantages of television lie both in the audience it reaches, and in the characteristics of the medium. In many countries, but particularly in the United States and the United Kingdom, television reaches virtually the whole population. With most people switching on for several hours every day, it is the number one leisure activity. In the United Kingdom, the average adult watches television for more than three hours a day, in the United States it is over four hours a day, and in most countries in Europe the figure is over two hours a day.

Though television is watched regularly by most sections of the population, it is particularly effective at reaching housewives, and this is one reason why it is so heavily-used by the manufacturers of packaged goods. A campaign on television rapidly builds up awareness of a product among a high proportion of the population. However, the main reason for its popularity with advertisers is the scope of the creative elements the medium offers. The combination of sound, movement and colour, gives it a creative advantage over all other media except cinema. Nothing can create a brand image more dramatically or sell more persuasively than film, with its use of such elements as music, emotion, humour, animation and personalities. Similarly, no medium can compete with it in terms of demonstrating how a product works or looks. But despite these undoubted advantages, television does not have things all its own way.

Disadvantages

Television advertising is expensive, both in terms of the cost of the airtime on the TV station (the transmission cost), and in terms of the cost of actually making the commercials (the production cost). Often the budget will not stretch sufficiently for the advertiser to run an effective campaign. Either the commercial is not transmitted frequently enough to build up a large enough audience or create a big enough impact, or the campaign can only run for three or four weeks in the year, which is likely to be too short for a major brand.

An added problem is that even though the commercial will be transmitted, there is no way of knowing whether there is anyone actually in front of the set at the time. It is a well-known fact that many viewers use the commercial break to put on the kettle – water consumption often jumps when the ad break starts in a popular programme – or for other purposes. This problem has been exacerbated by the introduction of the remote control switch, which allows viewers to switch from channel to channel during the commercial break to see

The power of television is amply illustrated by this 60-second commercial for Apple Computers (*right, far right*) based on George Orwell's *1984*. Directed by Ridley Scott for the agency Chiat/Day, it was shown once on network television in the United States during the Super Bowl game on January 22, 1984. Two days later, when the Apple Macintosh went on sale, 200,000 people queued up to see it, and within six hours they had bought $3,500,000 worth of Macintosh computers and left cash deposits for $1,000,000 more. The commercial received editorial coverage on the ABC, CBS and NBS network news, on BBC Television, on 27 local US TV stations and in virtually every major newspaper and news magazine.

Televisions's combination of
sound, movement and colour
give it a great creative advantage
over other media, as this
commercial for Martini shows
(*above*).
Agency: McCann-Erickson.

what other programmes are on.

Even if everyone watching the programme does stay to watch the commercial break, there is inevitably a high wastage factor. Many people who see the advertisement will not be in the market for that product or service, either because they are too old or too young, because they are the wrong sex or do not have a pet or a car, or because they do not live near enough to a particular shop. In addition, some groups of people tend to watch less television than others. These 'light viewers' (as they are known) include the AB social groups, businessmen and young adults. Commercials aimed at these people may suffer from particularly high wastage, or may not even reach a sufficient percentage of the target market at all.

Characteristics

Some of the characteristics of television carry inherent disadvantages for some advertisers. It is difficult to convey much information within the space of a 30-second ad, so advertisers with a complex message to put across may have to use another medium. In addition, there is no written record of what has appeared on the screen, so unless the viewer happens to remember everything that was said, much of the message may be wasted. While television may be good at conveying strong images or catchy jingles, it is less effective at putting across lengthy lists of prices or stockists. It is essentially a fleeting medium.

Time is another problem. It generally takes time to make a commercial, book the airtime and get the advertisement on the screen – at least three months in most cases. It can be done more quickly, but for advertisers who have to make changes to what they want to say, or who have an urgent message to get across, this factor may rule television out.

Another major problem with television – the major problem in some countries – is that it is the most restricted of all the media in terms of what products may be advertised, what may be said about them and how much advertising is permitted. In some countries, such as Norway, Sweden and Denmark, the question of television advertising hardly arises since none of these countries' TV stations carries any advertising (though the coming of satellite television may cause some changes). In France, Germany, Switzerland and Austria, no station may carry more than 20 minutes advertising a day, and in those countries most advertising is transmitted in lengthy 'blocks' of commercials between programmes, instead of being distributed fairly evenly throughout transmissions. This means that the advertising is less likely to be watched. Even in those countries like the United Kingdom, where advertising may take up six minutes of every hour of transmission (though only on the two commercial channels, not on the BBC), many products may not be advertised on television. In the UK, these include cigarettes, political organizations, religious bodies, matrimonial agencies and betting shops. In France, according to an analysis by J. Walter Thompson, the categories prohibited include jewellery, tourism, retail stores, building societies and computers (as well as alcohol and tobacco), and in Austria no advertising may be aimed at children.

Those products that are permitted to be advertised on television tend to be more heavily regulated than they are in other media. The regulations vary from country to country, but in the United Kingdom, for example, the Independent Broadcasting Authority has a strict code of advertising practice, with special sections on advertising and children, financial advertising and the advertising of medicines – all commercials have to be vetted before screening. Though other media in the United Kingdom have to abide by another code – that of the Advertising Standards Authority – it is less restrictive, and most ads are not pre-vetted.

All of these disadvantages mean that though, in theory, every advertiser might want to harness the power of television for its campaign, in practice this is just not possible for many companies. Given the medium's strengths and weaknesses, it might be thought that it would mainly be used for fast-moving consumer goods aimed at housewives. Indeed, in those countries where there are limits on the amount of advertising permitted, there is little time for any others. But in markets like the United States and the United Kingdom many other categories of advertising are finding their way onto the screen.

Airlines (whose advertising is predominantly aimed at businessmen) and car manufacturers were among the first to see that television was not just a medium for sausages, cereals and soap powder. Now there are commercials for airlines travelling to the Far East, for

The soundtrack for the Apple commercial is the voice of Big Brother, who speaks as follows: 'My friends… each of you is a single cell in the Great body of the State. And today, that great body has purged itself of parasites.

'We have triumphed over the unprincipled dissemination of facts. The thugs and wreckers have been cast out.

'And the poisonous weeds of disinformation have been consigned to the dustbin of history.

'Let each and every cell rejoice! For today we celebrate the first glorious anniversary of the Information Purification Directives. (cont. opposite)

This commercial for John Smith's Bitter also demonstrates the music, movement, colour and humour that are some of the strengths of television (*right*). It has won many creative awards around the world.
Agency: Boase Massimi Pollitt.

STAN: Like your new dog Arkwright. Here boy up up, down, sit, heel (whistle whistle). Doesn't do much does he?
ARKWRIGHT: Fancy a drop of John Smith's?
(*Hectic circus music*)
ARKWRIGHT. He just needs the right motivation.
VO: John Smith's Bitter. A tough act to follow.

'We have created, for the first time in all history, a garden of pure ideology, where each worker may blossom secure from the pests of contradictory and confusing truths.
'Our Unification of Thought is more powerful a weapon than any fleet or army on earth. We are one people. With one will. One resolve. One cause.

'Dallas' is a hit TV show all over the world as this selection of magazine front covers (*above*) shows, but advertisers are not always able to take advantage of its high audiences. In the United Kingdom it is shown on a BBC channel, which does not carry advertising. In many European countries TV advertising is either not permitted at all, or restricted to 'blocks' of advertising at certain times of the evening. In the United States and Australia, however, there are no such problems. In the US, in the second quarter of 1984, a 30-second network spot in 'Dallas' cost $200,000 and the audience was about 37 million.

'Our enemies shall talk themselves to death. And we will bury them with their own confusion.
'We shall prevail!'
Title and voice-over: 'On January 24, Apple Computers will introduce Macintosh. And you'll see why 1984 won't be like 1984.'

exclusive car manufacturers such as BMW and Audi, and for computer and office equipment firms such as IBM. In one month recently, the top 10 categories of advertiser on television in the United Kingdom included retail stores, wines and spirits, car hire, financial organizations, motor vehicles and travel. Many of these advertisers might be thought unlikely candidates for television, given that businessmen and members of the social group AB watch less television than average, and that people are unlikely to rush out and buy a BMW just because they saw it on television the night before. Nevertheless, television can be used successfully for such products, though not necessarily on its own. Such advertisers will use a combination of media, taking advantage of television's ability to show products in action and to create images, while backing this up with advertisements in newspapers or magazines. These provide the detailed information that television cannot, and will reach those ABs and businessmen who do not watch enough television. Such 'multi-media schedules' are becoming increasingly common, not only to overcome some of TV's basic weaknesses, but also to make the budget go further. In the United Kingdom in particular (where there is an increasingly heavy demand for, and limited supply of, airtime, and where there is not the competition between the stations that there is in the United States and Australia), the cost of advertising

on television has risen dramatically in recent years. This has resulted in many of the traditional packaged goods advertisers struggling to make their advertising budgets keep pace. Even in the United States, where competition between stations is virtually unlimited, TV costs have risen sharply.

Buying television airtime
Television airtime is generally sold in 'spots' of varying lengths. 30 seconds is by far the most common, though in most countries it is possible to buy spots of 10, 20, 30, 40, 50 or 60 seconds, or even longer. In the United Kingdom, where this facility became available some three years ago (before that the lengths were 7, 15, 30, 45 and 60 seconds), the dominance of the 30-second spot has been considerably reduced. An analysis by Saatchi & Saatchi shows that in 1978, 74 per cent of commercials screened in the London area were 30 seconds long, a further 15 per cent were 15 seconds long, and 7 per cent lasted 45 seconds. By the end of 1982, only 53 per cent of commercials were 30 seconds long.

The way airtime is bought varies greatly from country to country. In the United States, it can be bought nationally from the three network companies, CBS, ABC and NBC, or locally from individual stations or intermediate sales companies. (Sponsorship of programmes is also permitted.) In the United Kingdom, where there are 15 regional independent television companies each selling airtime in their own area, a national campaign has to be built up by buying time from each station individually, though the new breakfast TV station TV-am, does offer national advertising. In both countries, time can also be bought almost up to the last moment before transmission, though in practice most campaigns are booked well in advance.

By and large, advertisers measure the coverage of their TV campaigns in TVRs (television rating points) or GRPs (gross rating points). A rating point is the percentage of a particular market (ie households, adults, or housewives), that had the television tuned to the advertiser's channel when the commercial was broadcast. An advertiser may have a target of 400 housewife TVRs/GRPs, which means that it would have to transmit its commercial 10 times in programmes that each achieved 40 rating points, or 20 times in programmes achieving 20 rating points each, or any equivalent combination. Such ratings are determined by detailed audience research. In the United States, the United Kingdom and some other markets, sophisticated equipment is attached to the sets in a specially selected panel of homes to measure which channel the set is tuned to. The panel is chosen carefully so that it is a representative sample of the population as a whole, in terms of age, sex, social class, television viewing habits and other demographic indicators. To determine how many people are in front of the set at any one time (the meters on the set can only measure whether the TV is on and what it is tuned to, not whether anyone is watching), further research is done. This consists either of diaries which record every member of the household's viewing for the week, or of a recently invented piece of electronic equipment with which viewers can record their presence in front of the set.

The future of television

Television is currently undergoing many changes as a result of technological innovation, and these changes may well have a profound effect on its use as an advertising medium over the next few years. The introduction of new cable and satellite television channels is changing the face of television as it has been known since the 1950s, both by making it more international – satellite transmissions over Europe can be picked up in many countries – and more specifically targeted, as is already happening in the United States, through local and special-interest cable channels. In addition, teletext (a system that enables the printed word to be transmitted onto the television screen) means that some of the limitations of television are being overcome.

Satellites

Satellite television is viewed with great interest by many advertisers. In the United States, satellite 'super-stations' such as Ted Turner's WTBS in Atlanta are having an increasing impact on audiences and advertisers, with viewers receiving the service via cable. It is in Europe, however, that the most exciting possibilities exist for satellite at the moment, with many multinational advertisers seeing its arrival as a way of bringing TV advertising to those countries where at present it is severely limited or non-existent. Companies such as Kellogg's, Coca-Cola, Schweppes, Polaroid and British Airways have taken experimental spots through a UK company called Satellite Television, now owned by Rupert Murdoch. STV's Sky Channel can now be viewed via cable in the United Kingdom and a few other European countries, but the real potential lies in the possibility of transmitting signals direct to the home, since this could bypass local restrictions on TV advertising.

Oracle (*above*) is a videotex service designed to put text on the TV screen, but, as this version of the Esso tiger shows, it is being adapted to produce pictures too. *Agency:* McCann-Erickson.

The satellite channels that will transmit direct to the home are called Direct Broadcast Satellites (DBS for short), and the signals are picked up by special dish-shaped aerials, either on the roof or in the garden. It may well be, however, that those homes wired for cable will receive the DBS broadcasts as part of the cable service.

Cable TV

The basic technology for cable has been around for many years, during which time it has mainly been used to provide TV signals in those areas that cannot get a good broadcast signal. The advantage of the new optical fibre cables is that they can deliver a great many channels, 30 in some cases, and even more in some parts of the United States. This means that for the first time, it is possible to have cable channels specializing in certain subjects, as magazines do. In the United States there are channels devoted to the news, sport, rock music, the arts and even the weather. Each of these offers advertisers the opportunity of reaching particular sections of the population with their commercials, and a number of advertisers are now making commercials specifically for such channels.

Not all the cable channels in the United States show advertisements, since one of the selling-points when cable first started was that its programmes were not constantly being interrupted by commercials. This is particularly true of the film and entertainment cable channels like Home Box Office, though it is possible that advertising may appear on these too in time.

Videotex

The opportunities for advertisers offered by the capacity to put text on the TV screen are only just being appreciated. It is particularly useful for travel firms who want to give the prices or times of train or airline services, or for TV advertisers who want to give viewers further information. It also offers great potential for mail order advertisers.

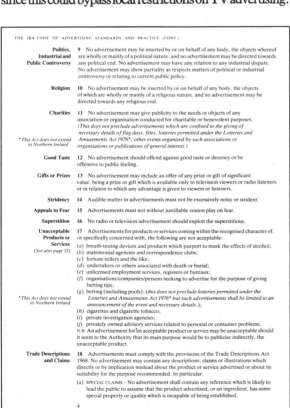

The Independent Broadcasting Authority's Code of Advertising Standards and Practice (*left*) places great restrictions on TV and radio advertising in the United Kingdom, as paragraphs 9 to 18 illustrate.

NEWSPAPERS

The World's Top Newspapers

Yomiuri Shimbun (Japan)	8.9m
Asahi Shimbun (Japan)	7.6m
Bild (Germany)	5.5m
Mainichi Shimbun (Japan)	4.4m
Sun (UK)	4.2m
Daily Mirror (UK)	3.4m
Sankei Shimbun (Japan)	2m
Wall Street Journal (US)	2m
Nihon Kezai Shimbun (Japan)	1.9m
Daily Express (UK)	1.9m

In most countries, more money is spent on advertising in newspapers than in any other medium. In the United States, newspapers account for 41 per cent of advertising expenditure, compared with television's 33 per cent. In the United Kingdom, the newspapers' share is 43 per cent, compared with television's 30 per cent. In Australia, newspapers take 41 per cent of all advertising money, in France 54 per cent, in Germany 56 per cent and in the Netherlands 68 per cent. Only in a few countries (among them Italy, Japan, Spain and a number of Latin American countries), is more money spent on television than in newspapers.

Given that television is accepted as the most powerful and effective medium, the dominance of newspapers in the expenditure tables may on the surface seem surprising, but it is accounted for by the fact that most countries have a great many more newspapers than television stations. In the United Kingdom alone there are nine national daily papers, eight national Sundays, almost 100 regional dailies, seven regional Sundays and around 1,500 regional weekly papers. In the United States, there are 1,700 daily papers and many more weeklies: none strictly qualifies as being a national newspaper, though attempts are being made to launch one. The United Kingdom is unusual in having so many national papers – a consequence of its having a large population in a relatively compact island, served by a comprehensive rail network. In most countries, the main newspaper markets are regional and local and there is often little competition. Some of the main advantages of newspapers are, therefore, only fully available to advertisers in countries where such national papers and such competition exists.

Advantages
One of the main strengths of newspapers as an advertising medium is that they can provide a wide variety of audiences in terms both of size and demographics. National newspapers, where they exist, can provide high circulations and coverage of the national market, and (where there is sufficient competition, as there is in the United Kingdom) quite specific types of reader. The people who read a 'popular' paper with a high circulation, like the *Sun* or the *Daily Mirror*, are likely to be very different from the people who read a 'quality' paper like *The Times* or the *Daily Telegraph*. For example, only 6 per cent of the *Sun's* readers are in the A and B socio-economic groupings, compared with 60 per cent of *The Times's* readers. Advertisers with upmarket products can use one paper, while mass-market advertisers can use the other.

In countries where there is less variety between papers, there is less of a difference between the types of reader. Even without that variety, however, newspapers can offer advertisers a great deal of choice in regional terms. Companies that have quite specific regional strengths – for example, retailers with branches in certain cities and towns – can isolate their customers with great accuracy by advertising in the local and regional press. Indeed, local retailers – including garages, gas showrooms, travel agents and all the other high street firms – account for the bulk of the regional newspapers' revenue. In addition, because newspaper advertising tends to be cheaper than advertising on television, a campaign in newspapers can last longer than a TV campaign, and can thus keep the brand in front of the customer for longer.

Characteristics
Unlike television, newspapers give the advertiser the chance to put across a great deal of information that the reader can keep for future reference. Many retailers use newspapers to advertise very detailed lists of prices. For example, Comet (a TV, radio and electrical chain of stores) takes double-page spreads crammed with 10 columns of prices.

Newspapers also enable firms to put coupons on their ads, either offering readers money off the product the next time they purchase it, or to encourage them to send off for further information. There is also a great deal of flexibility in terms of the size of ad that can be taken, and indeed in the size of the pages themselves. Some – generally quality papers – are 'broadsheet', while others are half that size, or 'tabloid'. There is no statutory definition of these terms, and some broadsheets are a good deal larger than others. Most newspapers base their charges on the single column centimetre, though in practice they only sell such small spaces to classified advertisers in the 'small ads' section.

Advertisers can buy virtually any size of space (and in

Newspapers are heavily sectionalized, particularly in the United States, and this enables advertisers to place their ads in those sections most likely to appeal to their audience (*below*).

Food Notes
Rating Guérard carryout, and a buy of the week. Page C7.

Art
Dutch paintings in Washington include happy surprises. Page C17.

Books
In 'The Journals of Sylvia Plath,' the woman herself. Page C21.

Television
Baryshnikov's tongue-in-cheek romping in Hollywood. Page C22.

WEDNESDAY, APRIL 21, 1982
Copyright © 1982 The New York Times

The Living Section

FOOD/STYLE/ENTERTAINMENT
C1

The New York Times

The Caffeine Conflict — Where Does It Stand?

By MARIAN BURROS

SEVEN-UP, once known as the Uncola, recently began an advertising campaign designed to convince the public that its lemon-and-lime-flavored beverage is preferable to other soft drinks because it does not contain caffeine. Understandably, this has upset the manufacturers of Coca-Cola, Pepsi-Cola and Dr Pepper, which do contain caffeine. They contend that 7 Up's advertising campaign is based on unsubstantiated health concerns. The dangers of caffeine, they argue, have never been proved.

This is the the latest in a series of controversies involving caffeine during the last few years that have changed the public perception of America's favorite wake-up beverage from a friendly, harmless substance to a potentially dangerous drug.

It began in 1978, when an advisory committee to the Food and Drug Administration reported that too much caffeine might have a deleterious effect on central nervous

Caffeine addiction: See the Personal Health column by Jane E. Brody, page C6.

system development. Since then, several studies have linked caffeine with birth defects, fibrocystic breast disease (a benign disorder) and pancreatic cancer.

There have been calls by consumer groups to ban caffeine as an additive in soft drinks or, at the very least, to require prominent labeling on products to which caffeine has been added. These have been countered by barrages of press releases from the soft-drink and coffee industries attempting to assuage public fears.

Between the pro- and anticaffeine forces stands the Food and Drug Administration, charged with sorting out the facts. But four years of debate and testing have not provided any clear answers. The issue of caffeine is still as muddy as a bad cup of coffee.

One thing that no one disputes, however, is the ability of this white, needlelike substance, which occurs naturally in coffee, tea, cocoa and chocolate and is added to soft drinks, drugs and food, to stimulate the central nervous system. Caffeine constricts the blood vessels, speeds up the heart and stimulates the brain, stomach, kidneys, ovaries and testes. On some people it acts like amphetamine, pepping

Continued on Page C8

This advertisement for the
Australian Newspaper
Advertising Bureau, designed to
sell newspaper advertising, puts
the case for newspapers very
powerfully (*right*).
Agency: Abbott Mead Vickers.

On April 24th, Argentina attacked Great Britain with one of the world's most sophisticated weapons.

It was a newspaper advertisement – aimed with pin-point accuracy at the most influential people in Britain.

It landed on their breakfast tables catching them totally unawares.

In some 1200 words it spelt out Argentina's claim to the Falkland Islands.

It went into great detail, much of it historical. (None of it hysterical.)

It was the kind of message that could not have run anywhere but in a newspaper.

Because only in a newspaper can you be sure of reaching the opinion leaders.

(John Nott, the British Minister of Defence won't be watching Knot's Landing when he's busy planning one of his own.)

Argentina may not know a lot about international law, but they're certainly no slouches when it comes to communication.

They know that in any campaign the surest shots are fired in newspapers.

Newspapers hit home in the homes that count.

some cases, virtually any shape), from a 'two centimetre double' (which is 2cm by 2 columns), to a double-page spread or more. The largest newspaper advertisements tend to be the highly complex offers of company shares which appear in the financial sections of the quality papers, and go on in minute print for five or six pages. Such financial ads illustrate two other strengths of newspapers, the first of which is timing. It is possible to get an advertisement into print very quickly in newspapers, because they print a new issue every day or week, and are relatively unrestricted as to how much advertising they take. If an advertiser wants to take several pages, many papers will simply run a bigger issue to accommodate the ad, and at peak advertising seasons such as pre-Christmas, most newspapers will be much fatter than at other times of the year.

The second strength is the newspapers' ability to offer advertisers specific sections of the paper in which to place their ads. Most companies want to have the ad announcing their financial results on the City pages rather than elsewhere in the paper. However, this is not always the case. Some large firms have put financial ads, suitably worded and designed, in the news section not just of the quality papers, but also of the populars, in order to communicate with their workforce and their customers. Holiday advertisers like to put their ads in the travel sections, fashion advertisers near the women's pages, and so on. In the United States, newspapers are heavily subdivided. The *Los Angeles Times*, for example, has seven separate sections every day.

There is one area of newspaper advertising where all the intrinsic advantages of newspapers come together, and that is the 'small ads'. The fact that newspapers come out every day, that they provide a permanent copy

which the reader can study, that they can put on extra pages in times of high advertising demand, and that they serve particular areas of the country, means that they attract a great deal of revenue from classified advertising. In fact, newspapers in the United Kingdom rely on classified ads for 35 per cent of their advertising revenue, and for regional papers this proportion is considerably higher.

Finally, newspapers have fewer restrictions on the types of advertising that can be accepted, and the content of the advertisements. Most newspapers still carry advertising for cigarettes and for other products which are not permitted on television. However, the editor does have the right to reject an ad and this sometimes happens, usually on the grounds that it might offend some readers. The Health Education Council had an award-winning ad promoting contraception turned down by several popular papers on these grounds, notwithstanding the fact that the papers in question were quite happy to print pictures of topless models and reports of lurid sex cases.

Disadvantages

One problem with newspapers is that in order to reach a large enough audience it is often necessary to advertise in a number of different papers, and this is particularly true of a national advertiser who wants to use regional newspapers. For example, a large grocery multiple like Tesco which puts ads in the regional papers covering each of its branches, has to produce a great many different ads with each one carrying a different store address. In addition, a copy of that advertisement – whether in block form or artwork, depending on the printing process used by the paper in question – has to be sent to every newspaper that will carry it. To try to reduce the complexity of this process, publishers in the United Kingdom have set up a Regional Newspaper Advertising Bureau, to simplify the planning and booking of such campaigns.

Another concern for some advertisers, is that the reader may never reach the advertisement if it is in the back half of the newspaper. Research on the reading and noting of advertisements suggests that this can be a real problem, so many advertisers try to insist on an early position in the paper.

Characteristics

The main disadvantages of newspapers are that they can offer advertisers no sound, no movement and very little colour – all factors which many companies regard as highly important. A few newspapers provide occasional colour pages (which benefit from a dramatic contrast with the rest of the paper), but these are few and far between. To counter this problem, a number of newspapers publish a weekly colour supplement on Sundays.

Without sound, movement and colour, newspapers are far less effective than television at creating images for products, or at demonstrating them in action. They also suffer from reproduction problems, since a great deal of work has to be put into the treatment of photographs and illustrations if they are to reproduce crisply on newsprint, which is never of a particularly high quality.

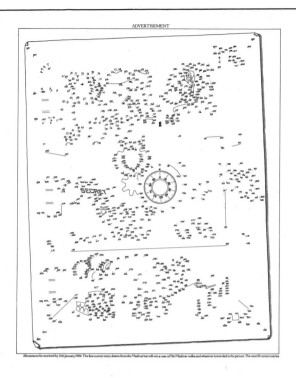

TOP DIPLOMAT'S CASE BAGGED!

Warrington connection revealed in customs swoop on Russian.

A team of customs men, acting on a Special Branch tip-off, detained the senior Russian vodka attaché at Heathrow yesterday evening.

He is still being questioned by members of the security forces, but it is understood that a number of important documents were found in his briefcase, and an apparent attempt to smuggle them out of the country to Moscow has failed.

The official is claiming diplomatic immunity, and the Russian Embassy has complained in strong terms to the Home Office. However, sources close to Downing Street say he is likely to be expelled or deported for 'activities incompatible with his status' – Whitehall jargon for spying – and an official protest has been lodged with his superiors at the Kremlin.

At the heart of the affair lie worries by both the Americans and the Europeans over the illegal export of Western technology to the Russians.

In this particular case, it would seem the Vladivar vodka distillery in Warrington is at the centre of the present rumpus. The papers in the diplomat's bag are said to relate to last month's break-in

at the vodka plant, but at the time it was never revealed whether the highly-prized Vladivar secret formula was stolen.

In a report* published yesterday, both the Foreign Office and the Ministry of Defence were dealt a broadside for failing to anticipate Russian determination to obtain the secret of Vladivar Vodka.

In particular, the MoD was heavily criticised for an 'appalling shortfall' in defending the strategic

Vladivar from Warrington. The Greatest Vodka in the World – and the secret documents.

Merseyside/Warrington area. It is claimed that for extensive periods, this area could only rely on a token force of 22 marines and an old WWII Bofors gun stationed on a barge in the Manchester Ship Canal.

Neighbouring Runcorn Borough Council responded immediately by declaring themselves a vodka-free zone. There are indications that other local councils will follow suit.

● The Russians at present lag about five years behind Vladivar in vodka technology. It is doubtful whether Vladivar would be able to remain the greatest vodka in the world if the Russians succeeded in stealing their formula.

Where will the Russians draw the line?

One of the diplomat's messages to Moscow has come into the possession of a national newspaper. Vladivar are asking anyone who can figure out what it reveals to get in touch with them on a post-card addressed to: Vladivar, P.O. Box Top Secret, Warrington WA4 6RD.

James Fighting Drinks, £9.95

All entries to be received by 11th January, 1984. The first correct entry drawn from the Vladivar hat will win a case of 70cl Vladivar vodka and whatever is revealed in the picture. The next 10 correct entries picked will receive a 70cl bottle of Vladivar each. A complete set of rules and regulations is available from the address given. All entrants must include their name and address, and be aged 18 or over.

This newspaper ad, always placed in weekend editions when readers have more time to study the paper, produced hundreds of replies from readers who had filled in the dots (left). Agency: Kirkwoods.

Buying a newspaper campaign

Newspaper ads can come in all shapes and sizes, and it is as much a creative decision as a media decision as to what size ads will be used. Selecting which newspapers to use is a matter of working out the coverage of the target market that will be achieved by a particular combination of papers, and the number of times the ad is to appear. All these decisions are influenced by research of the newspapers' audience, and this is done in two ways. The circulation is measured by auditing the sales of each publication, but this alone is insufficient for most advertisers since it does not tell them how many people read each copy, nor what sort of people they are. Readership research is therefore conducted to answer these secondary questions. Members of the public are shown a list of publications and asked whether they have read them recently, and if so, how frequently. They are also asked other questions to determine their age, their socio-economic classification and other details of interest to publishers and their advertisers.

Once the list of newspapers to be used has been agreed, the advertiser and the agency must decide where in those papers they want their ad to appear, and also when. Most newspapers charge a premium for special positions such as the front page, or a page 'facing matter' – ie facing an editorial page, thus theoretically ensuring that the page will stay open for longer and hopefully increasing the chances of the ad being read (though there is a counter-theory which suggests that if the editorial matter is too interesting, the ad will not get read at all).

Those advertisers who want to appear in the financial pages, the travel pages or the women's pages generally have to pay extra for the privilege, as do advertisers who want their ad to appear on a particular day or in a particular edition.

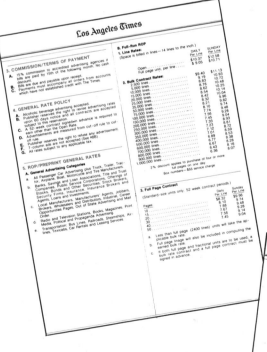

A typical newspaper rate-card (left, below) showing the prices of advertising per line, as well as the general conditions of acceptance, and also the sizes of the ads that will be accepted. These are just two pages from a 24-page rate-card.

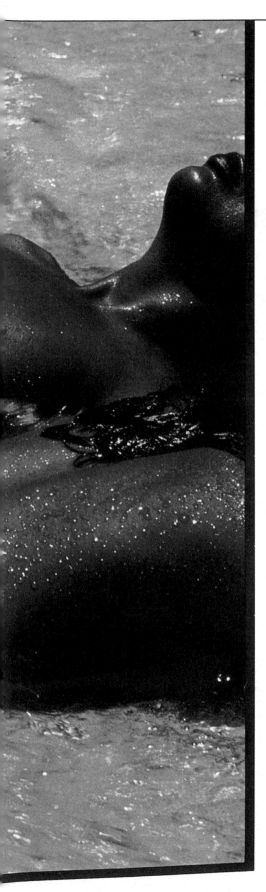

Aquasun. The sun tan lotion that stays on in the water.

It's water-resistant. So even as you're taking a cooling dip, you're turning brown.

A beautifully deep brown, too. It contains guanine, which allows your skin's natural colour to develop.

It also contains a vitamin based moisturiser.

So as you're drying off, it prevents you drying out.

There are three sun protection factors for all types of skin.

Once you put on Aquasun, you'll not only turn brown.

You'll be completely covered.

MAGAZINES

As an advertising medium, magazines have many of the advantages and disadvantages of newspapers, but there remain a great many differences between the two forms of press media. Magazines have many more colour pages, and can provide better reproduction than newspapers, but at the same time have longer copy deadlines and fewer regional editions, thus making them too inflexible for some advertisers. Their greatest asset is the diversity of their subject matter and the fact that they reach specific groups of people such as women, businessmen or hi-fi enthusiasts, and this makes them ideal for many advertisers. Their main drawback is that like newspapers they lack sound and movement.

The importance of magazines in the media market varies greatly from country to country, and they are particularly strong in markets which do not have much television advertising. In Belgium, for example, where television only accounts for 10 per cent of advertising expenditure, magazines account for 30 per cent, whereas in the United States, which spends 33 per cent of its advertising money on television, only 14 per cent goes into magazines.

The term 'magazine' covers a multitude of publications. Some, such as the Sunday colour supplements, the weekly women's magazines and the television programme papers have very high circulations, and these are mass-market media which can compete for many advertisers' budgets on an equal footing with both television and newspapers. Others, such as the women's monthly magazines, the home interest journals, and all the publications catering for hobbies and special interests, have smaller, but more closely defined, audiences. In addition to these consumer publications, there is also an enormous range of business magazines, some covering the business world in general, but many more devoted to specific trades. Virtually every business you can name has at least one trade paper if not more, each competing for a share of the available advertising revenue. Because of their comparatively small circulations but high coverage of the advertisers' target market, some of these trade publications can be extremely profitable.

Advantages
The strength of magazines in terms of audience, varies considerably depending on the type of title. The large circulation magazines offer a high coverage of the population as a whole (though women are particularly well served), and will carry advertisements for a broad cross-section of products and services. These offer advertisers a comparatively low cost-per-thousand. Those aimed at a particular group of people – whether consumer or trade publications – offer low circulations but high coverage of the most likely purchasers of the advertisers' goods, for which advertisers must pay a higher cost-per-thousand.

Many business publications are now delivered free of charge to executives in a particular line of work, in order to give advertisers the maximum coverage of their market, just as many local newspapers are. Often the

The World's Top Magazines
Reader's Digest (US)	17.9m
TV Guide (US)	17.3m
National Geographic (US)	10.3m
Better Homes & Gardens (US)	8m
Family Circle (US)	7.3m
Adac Motorwelt (Germany)	7.1m
Woman's Day (US)	6.9m
McCall's (US)	6.3m
Good Housekeeping (US)	5.4m
Ladies Home Journal (US)	5.2m

National Enquirer (US)	5.1m
Time (US)	4.5m
Playboy (US)	4.2m
Redbook (US)	3.9m
Star (US)	3.8m
Hor Zu (Germany)	3.6m
Penthouse (US)	3.4m
Radio Times (UK)	3.4m
TV Times (UK)	3.3m
Newsweek (US)	3m

Like newspapers, magazines
offer advertisers the chance to
include money-off coupons in
their ads (*right*).

This rate-card for *Time* magazine
(*below*) shows the varying rates
for separate international
editions. Rates also vary
according to the size of the ad
(left-hand column) and the
number of insertions.

TIME British Isles

Rate Base: 75,000
Circulation area: The United Kingdom and Ireland. **Advertising a**
cepted every week.

	1X	13X	17X	26X	39X	52X
Page B & W	$3,160	$3,035	$2,985	$2,905	$2,845	$2,7!
Page B & 1C	4,110	3,945	3,885	3,780	3,700	3,61
Page 4 Color	4,975	4,775	4,700	4,575	4,480	4,3!
2 cols B & W	2,400	2,305	2,270	2,210	2,160	2,11
2 cols B & 1C	3,000	2,880	2,835	2,760	2,700	2,64
2 cols 4 Color	3,965	3,805	3,745	3,650	3,570	3,4!
Dbl ¼ col B & W	1,960	1,880	1,850	1,805	1,765	1,72
Dbl ¼ col B & 1C	2,465	2,365	2,330	2,270	2,220	2,17
1 col B & W	1,295	1,245	1,225	1,190	1,165	1,14
1 col B & 1C	1,645	1,580	1,555	1,515	1,480	1,4!
¼ col B & W	1,045	1,005	990	960	940	9!
Dbl ¼ col B & W	790	760	745	725	710	6!
½ col B & W	725	695	685	665	655	64

TIME Scandinavia

Rate Base: 52,000
Circulation area: Denmark, Finland, Greenland, Iceland, Norway ar
Sweden. **Advertising accepted in Cycles A & C, check dates o**
page 3.

	1X	13X	17X	26X	39X	52X
Page B & W	$3,060	$2,940	$2,890	$2,815	$2,755	$2,6!
Page B & 1C	3,980	3,820	3,760	3,660	3,580	3,50
Page 4 Color	4,820	4,625	4,555	4,435	4,340	4,24
2 cols B & W	2,325	2,230	2,195	2,140	2,095	2,04
2 cols B & 1C	2,905	2,790	2,745	2,675	2,615	2,55
2 cols 4 Color	3,840	3,685	3,630	3,535	3,455	3,3!
Dbl ¼ col B & W	1,895	1,820	1,790	1,745	1,705	1,67
Dbl ¼ col B & 1C	2,385	2,290	2,255	2,195	2,145	2,10
1 col B & W	1,255	1,205	1,185	1,155	1,130	1,10
1 col B & 1C	1,590	1,525	1,505	1,465	1,430	1,40

TIME Israel

Rate Base: 15,000
Advertising accepted in Cycle A, check dates on page 3.

	1X	13X	17X	26X	39X	52X
Page B & W	$1,025	$985	$970	$945	$925	$9(
Page B & 1C	1,335	1,280	1,260	1,230	1,200	1,1;
Page 4 Color	1,745	1,675	1,650	1,605	1,570	1,5;
2 cols B & W	780	750	735	720	700	6!
2 cols B & 1C	975	935	920	895	880	8(
2 cols 4 Color	1,405	1,350	1,330	1,295	1,265	1,2;
Dbl ¼ col B & W	635	610	600	585	570	5(
Dbl ¼ col B & 1C	800	770	755	735	720	7(

editorial quality of such 'controlled circulation' papers is
as high, if not higher, than the magazines readers have to
pay for. However, many advertisers believe that a
magazine is more likely to be read by people who have
specifically ordered it, than by those to whom it has
come unbidden. For this reason, many controlled circulation magazines ask readers whether they want to
receive a copy, so that they can reassure advertisers that
copies of the magazine have been requested. In some
markets, like the United Kingdom, where there is a
strong network of wholesalers and retailers in the news
trade, most magazines – with the exception of the
controlled circulation ones – are supplied by news-
agents, but in the United States and some other
countries, many more magazines are bought on
subscription.

A major advantage shared by all magazines is that
they tend to be kept for a reasonable length of time and
be read by a number of different people. This means
that advertisers may be reaching a considerably larger
audience than the magazines' sales figures would suggest. It also means that people may well keep referring
back to the issue – often over many months – and thus
they will see the advertisements several times.

In a number of countries, where there are no national
newspapers, magazines are the only national press
medium, and this gives them a greater readership and
authority than most newspapers. This is particularly the
case with weekly news magazines such as *Time* and
Newsweek and, in Europe, general interest titles such as
Stern and *Paris Match*. In the United Kingdom, this role
is filled by the quality Sunday newspapers, which is one
reason why the attempt to launch *Now!* (a weekly news
magazine on the lines of the European and American
models) ended in failure.

Many such titles have a strong international circula-

tion. *Time*, *Newsweek* and the monthly *Readers' Digest*
have regional editions throughout the world, while
women's magazines such as *Vogue* and *Cosmopolitan*
publish entirely separate magazines – under the same
name and in the same style – in various markets. The
weekly UK business and news magazine, *The Economist*, sells more than half its copies outside the United
Kingdom. Such publications are of great value to international advertisers such as airlines, banks and the
tobacco and spirits firms, who create ads aimed largely
at the business community which can run in publications throughout the world.

Characteristics

The major advantage of most magazines is their editorial
environment and authority which stems from the fact
that they are reaching a specialist audience. This is less
true of the TV papers and the newspapers' colour
supplements, but for women's magazines and other
specialist titles there is often felt to be a great bond
between the reader and the magazine. Research shows
that many women like to see their weekly or monthly

magazine as a friend, and that they regard advertising in magazines as more believable, helpful and appealing than advertising on television.

The specialist nature of most magazines means that advertisers can tailor their advertisements specifically to the needs and knowledge of that audience, giving greater detail and talking in terms that those not interested in the product or service may well not understand. (Many advertisements in trade publications are quite incomprehensible to outsiders, but are much more powerful as a result.) In addition, magazines have many of the advantages of newspapers, and a few more. Like newspapers, they can carry a great deal of information, and can be kept for reference. They can also be used for coupons, either offering money off or further information (though with the more glossy magazines, many readers are less willing to spoil the page by cutting out a coupon). However, unlike most newspapers, their reproduction tends to be very good, and they carry a great deal of colour editorial and advertising.

The glossy nature of many magazines and the high proportion of colour are felt by many advertisers to add authority and appeal to their own advertisements, and they tend to ensure that their creative work comes up to the standard expected in a high quality magazine. The advertisements themselves then add to the appeal of the magazine. Many readers feel the advertising is an important part of the magazine 'package' and, indeed, in some magazines it is hard to tell what is advertising and what is editorial.

Disadvantages

The circulations of many of the largest magazines are in decline, and have been since the early days of television – indeed many have folded since then. It is becoming increasingly hard in many countries to run mass-market campaigns purely in magazines. However, as magazine publishers have adapted to these new circumstances, the circulation of the more specialist monthly titles has remained steady, and in some cases is increasing.

A major problem for magazine advertisers is that the most successful titles carry a great many pages of advertising at peak times of the year (particularly in the months before Christmas), and there is a danger that many ads will not be read. Some of the women's monthlies have 300 pages or more, and the weekly Sunday supplements can have well over 100 pages in November and December. The danger of an advertisement not being seen is particularly acute with the supplements, partly because they have not been paid for directly (they come as part of the Sunday newspaper package), and partly because there is so much other reading matter on a Sunday. It is also possible that a Sunday supplement will never actually be opened, which is extremely unlikely to be the case with a magazine for which the reader may have paid £1 or more. Nevertheless, advertisers are not totally logical. One of the paradoxes is that they would much prefer their advertisement to be in a healthy publication bulging with other ads (including many for their competitors) than to be one of the few ads in a less successful publication, even though it might have a better chance of being read.

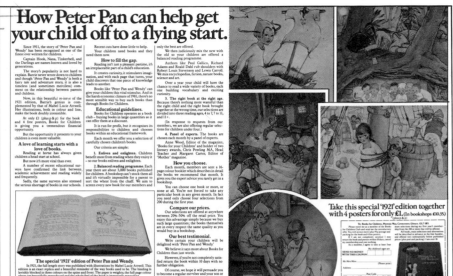

Characteristics

Because of their high colour content and their high quality reproduction, magazines have very long lead times, so advertising has to be booked and produced many months in advance. Though publishers are trying to shorten their copy dates, magazines are not a medium for advertisers who have to change copy – or even their total advertising plans – at the last minute.

Unlike newspapers, there is very little flexibility in magazines, and most campaigns have to run throughout the country, regardless of where the advertiser's main customers may live. Some magazines now offer limited regional sections, and such facilities are more common in some countries than others. The United States, because of its size, has more regional titles, but by and large magazines offer audiences targeted by subject matter rather than geography.

The biggest drawback for magazine advertisers, however, is the absence of sound and movement. Though colour puts them one up on newspapers in the battle with television for goods and services that require the creation of strong images and properties, it is still an unequal struggle. In addition, unlike television, a colour ad costs a good deal more than a black and white one.

Buying magazine advertising

Magazine advertising is bought in much the same way as newspaper advertising. Space is sold in a variety of sizes, though fewer small spaces are available and most major advertisers use half-pages, pages or double-page spreads. The audience is measured both in terms of circulation and readership, but the large number of titles makes it impossible for one survey to encompass the readership of them all, so many publishers conduct their own readership research. Unfortunately, because different publishers ask different questions (generally designed to show their magazine in the most favourable light), such research is often contradictory. Thus buying magazine advertising tends to be based more on hunch and the editorial environment of the publication than is the case with most other media.

This magazine ad (*above*) contains full-colour illustrations, a great deal of information (which can be read at leisure) and a coupon for the reader to send off for membership of Books for Children. No other medium offers this combination of strengths.
Agency: Abbott Mead Vickers.

Posters have been a favourite advertising medium with artists for many years. This classic 1927 Cassandre poster for Nord Express (*above*) still influences designers today, as does the German industrial poster (*far right*) which was produced in 1914.

A dramatic use of text and photography (*right*) makes this a powerful poster for Audi, but skilful media buying makes it even more powerful as the ad on page 95 illustrates.
Agency: Bartle Bogle Hegarty.

POSTERS

Outdoor advertising offers the simplest form of advertising there is – literally a message pasted to a wall. The wall comes in many forms – wooden hoardings, the inside and outside of buses and taxis, the inside of stations and airports, and purpose-built bus-shelters – but whatever the location, the simplicity of the concept remains.

People seeing posters have very little time to take them in (the one exception is in trains or on station platforms), so the message must be easily read and understood. This, combined with the fact that there is not the editorial or programme element there is with press and television, has led to it being called the purest form of advertising. However, it takes only a small share of advertising revenue – less than 5 per cent in most countries.

Advantages

In those countries with a substantial network of poster sites, outdoor advertising can give very high levels of coverage. Virtually everyone sees posters, whether or not they watch television or read a particular newspaper or magazine.

Poster advertising is relatively cheap, and so, provided the sites are available, most advertisers can afford to reach a large audience. Furthermore, posters are on display throughout the day and night, which means that they can be seen again and again. However, perhaps their biggest advantage is that they can be bought near shopping centres, and are thus an excellent 'reminder' medium for advertisers who want to reach shoppers just as they are about to make their purchases. They can also be bought on a local or regional basis, and it is also possible to buy a specific site. For example, a supermarket can buy sites on the nearest major roads, and put up posters directing drivers to the store. In a number of countries, posters advertising duty-free goods are sited on the roads and railway lines heading towards the airport.

The beginning of the end of the estate car.

The Audi Avant. Performs like a coupé. Works like an estate. AUDI

This dramatic and imaginative use of a single poster site in 1982 created hundreds of column inches of newspaper coverage for Araldite glue (*above*). The car was stuck to a metal bracket which was then screwed to the hoarding by the poster contractors, More O'Ferrall. *Agency:* FCO.

The following year, the agency, advertiser and contractor decided to go one better. They stuck the Ford Cortina back on the hoarding, with a punning reference to the previous year's poster (*left*).

A month later, a second car was added to the poster, with a new headline (*right*).

Finally, both cars were removed, leaving just a hole in the hoarding and another new headline (*below*).

A rate-card for Adshel, which
sells posters on specially built bus
shelters, offers different rates for
different towns (*above*).

Posters come in standard sizes
(*below*). In the United Kingdom
these are based on multiples of
4-sheets, though sizes in other
countries vary.

Characteristics

Posters have enormous impact, particularly the largest
ones, known as '48-sheets' and 'super sites'. They also
offer advertisers colour, and for these reasons the
medium is a great favourite with art directors, who love
to see their work dominating a street or a station, or
overlooking a square.

Disadvantages

In some countries there are too few sites or insufficient
co-ordination among poster contractors for advertisers
to be able to mount an effective campaign. Even in those
countries where posters are a strong medium, there may
be weaknesses in certain towns, or too many sites in poor
positions where they will not be seen by enough people.
In addition, posters are a very difficult medium to
measure in audience terms, though in the United Kingdom efforts are being made to rectify this problem.

Characteristics

Because posters have to be printed and then distributed
to each site, campaigns generally have to be planned a
long time in advance. It is also hard to have a campaign

put up on a specific day, and most campaigns have to be
booked for at least a month. However, efforts are being
made to improve the situation. In France, one poster
contractor, Avenir, caused a great stir with a campaign
designed to show that it could post a campaign on a
specific day. The original poster showed a girl in a bikini
stating that she would take her top off on September 2;
on that date it was replaced by one saying she would take
off the bottom of her bikini on September 4; on the 4th it
was replaced by one saying, 'Avenir – the poster company that keeps its promises.' In the United Kingdom,
London Weekend Television has run a much acclaimed
campaign that changes each week, while on the day of
the Austin Metro launch a poster advertising the new
car was put up throughout the country.

Other problems with posters are that they lack sound
and movement, that they can be damaged by the
weather or by vandals, and that in most cases they can
give very little information since people do not have time
to take in a complex message. The exception is in buses,
stations and trains, where people can often study the
posters for half an hour or more. All of this means that
posters tend to be used as a support medium, to back up
campaigns on television or in the press. However, if
planned properly they can be used to launch a product,
as was proved by the success of Perrier in the United
Kingdom.

A further problem for the outdoor medium is that it is
sometimes seen as a disfigurement of the environment.
In some countries this criticism is undoubtedly justified, but in those countries where poster advertising
has become more sophisticated, outdoor contractors
work closely with local authorities to ensure that poster
sites enhance the environment, by hiding eyesores such
as building sites or bomb-damaged areas, by funding
the erection of bus-shelters and by brightening up
shopping centres. In this way, by the creation of clean,
smart sites – often lit up at night – poster companies can
go some way to creating the right 'editorial' environment that advertisers often look for in other more
sophisticated media.

Buying a poster campaign

The sizes of posters and the lengths of campaigns vary
from country to country. In the United Kingdom, the
sizes range from 4-sheets (so-called because they were
originally made up from four separate sheets), which are
an upright rectangle usually sited near shops, through
16-sheets (the same shape, but four times the size), to
the horizontal 48-sheets. A recent innovation is the
12-sheet (a horizontal poster a quarter of the size of the
48-sheet), which is being introduced into shopping
precincts. In the United States, the most common size is
the horizontal 30-sheet. Some sites (usually hand-built
and hand-painted) are even larger than the 48-sheet, and
are available for one-off posters. These are most common in the United States, where this is one of the
standard forms of outdoor advertising.

Most campaigns have to be bought for a minimum of
one month, though some major poster advertisers hold
their sites on a yearly basis. These are known in the
United Kingdom as 'TC' sites, standing for 'till
countermanded'.

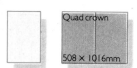

Quad crown
508 × 1016mm

Double crown
762 × 508mm

4 Sheet
1016 × 1524mm

12 Sheet
1524 × 3048mm

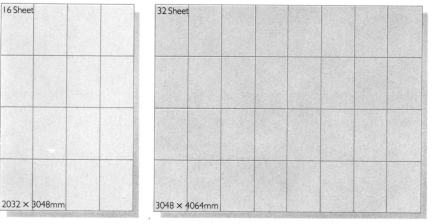

16 Sheet
2032 × 3048mm

32 Sheet
3048 × 4064mm

48 Sheet
3048 × 6096mm

MIDDLE TAR As defined by H.M.Government

DANGER: H. M. Government Health Departments' WARNING: THINK ABOUT THE HEALTH RISKS BEFORE SMOKING

Benson & Hedges (*above*) has been one of the most consistently successful users of posters.
Agency: Collett Dickenson Pearce.

4 Sheets

77,000

12 Sheets

1,500

16 Sheets

51,000

Some poster sizes are far more common than others. 12-sheets are comparatively rare because they are a recent innovation – a scaled-down 48-sheet that can be displayed in shopping precincts. 32-sheets are rare because they are being phased out.

32 Sheets

7,000

48 Sheets

37,000

Supersites

3,500

This poster for Audi (*left*) appeared in many towns on the hoarding next to the Audi ad shown on page 90 – a dramatic example of the creative and media teams working together. In fact, in this case, the sites were bought by a media independent, John Ayling & Associates, which acts as media department for the agency, Bartle Bogle Hegarty.

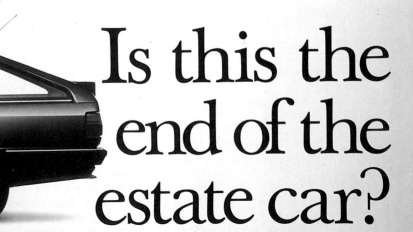

Is this the end of the estate car?

The Audi Avant. Performs like a coupé. Works like an estate. Audi

RADIO

CAPITAL NEWSLINE

RESEARCH SPECIAL · AUTUMN 1983

Colin Day and Carole Wilkins of Capital (below). Tony Twyman and Graham Woodham of RBL (above) presenting the paper 'The Psychology of Radio Listening' at the August ESOMAR Congress in Barcelona. The paper attracted a great deal of interest from many delegates involved in radio and advertising communiction from countries worldwide.

HOW RADIO ADVERTISING WORKS

Last year Capital launched a massive survey to explore radio listening and how radio communicates.

This was tagged **How Radio Works**. You may have seen this mentioned in earlier Newslines.

This Special Newsline gives a taste of the results and provides a reference point for future specialised papers.

Summary of Findings

1. Personal
Above all radio is a personal, human medium; it's live, immediate and topical, offering opportunities for listener interaction.

2. Affects mood
Radio affects moods and feelings in a wide range of ways, from arousing emotions, usually in the morning, through to calming them, especially during the evening. Radio's main function is seen as companionship, offering items which could inspire conversation, help neutralise sources of annoyance and simply fill in silences.

3. Friendly
Most people feel that they would genuinely miss radio if it were not available. It acts like a friend, providing company, entertainment and information without interfering with listeners' other activities or attention.

4. Sensitive
Programming and advertising are expected to be light-hearted, lively but gentle, identifying with, or at least recognising, listeners' needs.

5. Local
Independent Radio especially has a strong community orientation, and advertising can be enhanced by reflecting local identification.

6. People listen alone
Whilst TV viewing is usually a group activity, most radio listening is solitary, at home or when driving.

7. Not primary
People only rarely just sit and listen to the radio, hence attention must be gained and maintained over and above the interest in their other parallel activities.

8. Attention levels vary
Different types of radio programmes demand markedly different levels of concentration; music usually needs little concentration, talk programmes need continuous attention to the message.

9. Commercials less entertaining
Radio commercials are the poor relations of television commercials in terms of production values and entertainment. Radio attracts more criticism for poor presentation and repetition rather than variation and correspondingly appears to achieve lower brand recall than television.

10. Immediacy works
Of the radio ads perceived to be most successful, many use immediacy, topicality and localness to encourage or stimulate direct consumer action.

INSIDE

- Research method   p2
- Key conclusions   p3
- Specialist papers   p4

YOUR QUESTIONS ANSWERED — PAGES 2/3

Capital Radio, one of the two commercial radio stations in London, has a weekly audience of over four million listeners, making it one of the largest commercial stations in the world. In 1983, it launched a major survey into the way people listen to radio: this paper (*above*) summarized its findings for advertisers.

Ostensibly, radio might seem to have most of the disadvantages of television, with few of the advantages. It is a fleeting medium in which little detailed information can be given, and which gives the listener no permanent record of what has been said. Furthermore, it offers nothing visible at all – no colour, no movement, not even a picture of the product. Yet by way of compensation, radio has many other advantages. Of these, the most important are its power to tap the listener's imagination and the facility to reach listeners when they are involved in other activities, particularly activities which may involve the advertisers' products – such as shaving, driving and washing up.

Advantages

In most countries, radio is predominantly a local medium, but it is still possible to run a national campaign. Because radio is relatively cheap in terms of both airtime and the production of the commercial, the budget can go a long way. Though audiences for each

spot may be low, commercials can be played frequently and coverage built up over a period of time. The types of people who listen change at various points of the day, and advertisers can take advantage of this, for example by buying spots in 'drive time' in the morning and evening if they want to reach drivers and businessmen. In some countries, notably the United States and Canada, radio stations cater for specific types of audience, and this makes targeting very simple for advertisers (though the number of stations means audiences tend to be smaller). However, in other countries stations provide a mixture of programming, and advertisers who want to reach specific audiences have to do so either by buying airtime at particular times of day, or by buying spots in particular programmes.

Characteristics

Radio offers advertisers sound (the only medium to do so apart from TV and cinema), and this makes it a very powerful selling aid. Commercials can use music, humour, personalities and emotion, all of which are among some of the main strengths of television advertising. However, unlike most television sets, radio sets are portable and can be heard away from the home, or in every room in the house. In particular, they are listened to in circumstances in which watching television or reading a newspaper is impossible. (As radio salesmen are fond of pointing out, watching television while shaving or driving would be extremely dangerous!)

Radio is also quick to produce and to buy, which means that commercials can react to news events or to price changes. It is also, like television, an intrusive medium, in that it reaches people who may not be thinking of buying a certain product (and who might not therefore be reading the right publications), but who are in fact in the market for it. Recruitment advertising is a case in point. If people are not looking for a job, they will probably not read the recruitment pages in the newspaper, but they *might* be interested if the right job was drawn to their attention. People cannot flip past a radio commercial as they can flip over the page of a newspaper or a magazine, and because radio is a less formally-structured medium than television, people do not tend to leave the room when the commercial breaks come on thus the ads have a good chance of being heard.

Because of its relatively low cost-per-thousand and the fact that it offers sound, radio is often used as a support medium for television. Sometimes a complete TV soundtrack will work effectively on radio, while on other occasions the TV jingle can be used with a message specifically designed for radio.

Disadvantages

Listening figures for a particular station at any one time tend to be low – the main exception is in the morning, while people are getting up and having breakfast – so commercials have to be repeated a great deal to build up coverage. Consequently there is a danger that people will get tired of hearing a commercial too many times, thus it is usually necessary to make a number of ads which can be rotated throughout the day. Another problem is that, in some countries, there are towns and cities without a station, which makes it hard to achieve a

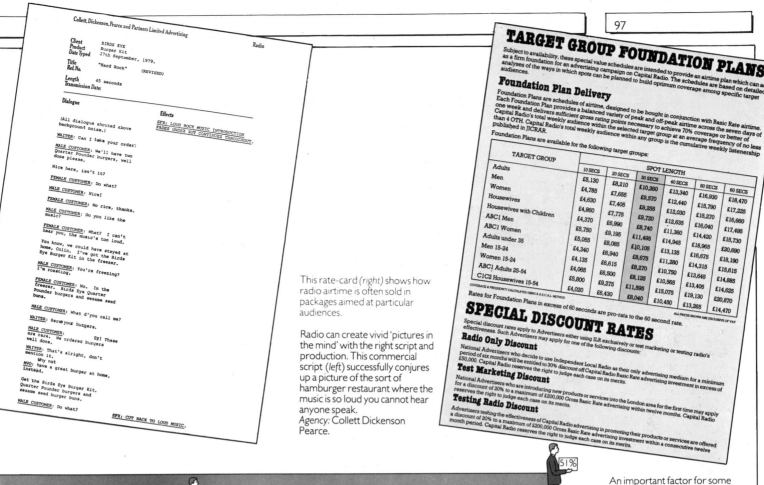

Collett, Dickenson, Pearce and Partners Limited Advertising

		Radio
Client	BIRDS EYE	
Product	Burger Kit	
Date Typed	27th September, 1979.	
Title	"Hard Rock" (REVISED)	
Ref.No.		
Length	45 seconds	
Transmission Date:		

Dialogue	Effects
(All dialogue shouted above background noise.)	SFX: LOUD ROCK MUSIC INTRODUCTION FADES UNDER BUT CONTINUES THROUGHOUT.
WAITER: Can I take your order!	
MALE CUSTOMER: We'll have two Quarter Pounder burgers, well done please.	
Nice here, isn't it?	
FEMALE CUSTOMER: Do what?	
MALE CUSTOMER: Nice!	
FEMALE CUSTOMER: No rice, thanks.	
MALE CUSTOMER: Do you like the music?	
FEMALE CUSTOMER: What? I can't hear you, the music's too loud.	
You know, we could have stayed at home, Colin. I've got the Birds Eye Burger Kit in the freezer.	
MALE CUSTOMER: You're freezing? I'm roasting.	
FEMALE CUSTOMER: No. In the freezer. Birds Eye Quarter Pounder burgers and sesame seed buns.	
MALE CUSTOMER: What d'you call me?	
WAITER: Here's your burgers.	
MALE CUSTOMER: Oy! These are rare. We ordered burgers well done.	
WAITER: That's alright, don't mention it.	
Why not	
MVO: have a great burger at home, instead.	
Get the Birds Eye Burger Kit. Quarter Pounder burgers and sesame seed burger buns.	
MALE CUSTOMER: Do what?	
	SFX: CUT BACK TO LOUD MUSIC.

This rate-card (right) shows how radio airtime is often sold in packages aimed at particular audiences.

Radio can create vivid 'pictures in the mind' with the right script and production. This commercial script (left) successfully conjures up a picture of the sort of hamburger restaurant where the music is so loud you cannot hear anyone speak.
Agency: Collett Dickenson Pearce.

TARGET GROUP FOUNDATION PLANS

Subject to availability, these special value schedules are intended to provide an airtime plan which can act as a firm foundation for an advertising campaign on Capital Radio. The schedules are based on detailed analyses of the ways in which spots can be planned to build optimum coverage among specific target audiences.

Foundation Plan Delivery

Foundation Plans are schedules of airtime, designed to be bought in conjunction with Basic Rate airtime. Each Foundation Plan provides a balanced variety of peak and off-peak airtime across the seven days of one week and delivers sufficient gross rating points necessary to achieve 70% coverage or better of Capital Radio's total weekly audience within the selected target group at an average frequency of no less than 4 OTH. Capital Radio's total weekly audience within any group is the cumulative weekly listenership published in JICRAR.

Foundation Plans are available for the following target groups:

TARGET GROUP	SPOT LENGTH					
	10 SECS	20 SECS	30 SECS	40 SECS	50 SECS	60 SECS
Adults	£5,130	£8,210	£10,260	£13,340	£16,930	£18,470
Men	£4,785	£7,655	£9,570	£12,440	£15,790	£17,225
Women	£4,630	£7,405	£9,255	£12,030	£15,270	£16,660
Housewives	£4,860	£7,775	£9,720	£12,635	£16,040	£17,495
Housewives with Children	£4,370	£6,990	£8,740	£11,360	£14,420	£15,730
ABC1 Men	£5,750	£9,195	£11,495	£14,945	£18,965	£20,690
ABC1 Women	£5,055	£8,085	£10,105	£13,135	£16,675	£18,190
Adults under 35	£4,340	£6,940	£8,675	£11,280	£14,315	£15,615
Men 15-24	£4,135	£6,615	£8,270	£10,750	£13,645	£14,885
Women 15-24	£4,065	£6,500	£8,125	£10,565	£13,405	£14,625
ABC1 Adults 25-54	£5,800	£9,275	£11,595	£15,075	£19,130	£20,870
C1C2 Housewives 15-54	£4,020	£6,430	£8,040	£10,450	£13,265	£14,470

COVERAGE & FREQUENCY CALCULATED USING R.A.S.C.AL METHOD

Rates for Foundation Plans in excess of 60 seconds are pro-rata to the 60 second rate.

ALL PRICES SHOWN ARE EXCLUSIVE OF VAT

SPECIAL DISCOUNT RATES

Special discount rates apply to Advertisers either using ILR exclusively or test marketing or testing radio's effectiveness. Such Advertisers may apply for one of the following discounts:

Radio Only Discount

National Advertisers who decide to use Independent Local Radio as their only advertising medium for a minimum period of six months will be entitled to 30% discount off Capital Radio Basic Rate advertising investment in excess of £50,000. Capital Radio reserves the right to judge each case on its merits.

Test Marketing Discount

National Advertisers who are introducing new products or services into the London area for the first time may apply for a discount of 20% to a maximum of £200,000 Gross Basic Rate advertising within twelve months. Capital Radio reserves the right to judge each case on its merits.

Testing Radio Discount

Advertisers testing the effectiveness of Capital Radio advertising in promoting their products or services are offered a discount of 20% to a maximum of £200,000 Gross Basic Rate advertising investment within a consecutive twelve month period. Capital Radio reserves the right to judge each case on its merits.

An important factor for some advertisers is the ability to reach customers as close as possible to the time of purchase. This research from the Radio Advertising Bureau in the United States shows how well radio performs in this respect (left). Significantly, however, it leaves out the medium that performs best of all in reaching customers close to the time of purchase – posters.

Per Cent Reached by Media Within One Hour of Day's Largest Purchase

Radio 51%
Radio 16%
Television 9%
Newspapers 6%

Time Elapsing Between Media Exposure and Day's Largest Purchase

Radio 1hr 57mins
Television 3hrs 24mins
Newspapers 3hrs 42mins
Magazines 4hrs

The table (below) is taken from Radio Facts, a promotional booklet produced by the Radio Advertising Bureau.

RADIO:
THE IMMEDIATE MEDIUM

56% Get Their First News In The Morning From Radio

Where People Get The News First, 6 AM-10 AM

	Radio	Tv	News-papers	Other	None
Persons 12 +	56%	21%	16%	1%	7%
Teens 12-17	56	23	13	—	7
Adults 18 +	56	20	16	1	7
Adults 18-34	62	19	12	1	6
Adults 25-54	57	18	18	1	6
College Grads.	56	15	23	—	6
Prof./Mgr. Males	56	16	24	1	4
Working Women	66	20	10	1	4

Radio Leads Other Media As First-News Source In Midday

Where People Get The News First, 10 AM-3 PM

	Radio	Tv	News-papers	Other	None
Persons 12+	38%	23%	13%	2%	25%
Teens 12-17	24	22	22	2	30
Adults 18+	40	23	12	2	24
Adults 18-34	50	20	12	2	17
Adults 25-54	41	18	13	2	27
College Grads.	43	9	16	1	32
Prof./Mgr. Males	41	5	16	4	34
Working Women	40	18	13	2	27

sufficient national coverage. However, in the United States, most cities have a great many radio stations, yet this too has its drawbacks, in that no one station has a very large share of the audience.

Characteristics

The lack of any visual image is a major disadvantage, and it is one that no other medium suffers from. While fashion and food advertisers may be able to do without movement and even, in extreme circumstances, without colour, it is hard for them to create interest without showing customers what they are offering. Nevertheless, it is not impossible provided copy-writers use their imagination. Even fashion stores and food advertisers have used radio successfully, though they have had to use other media as well. In addition, the lack of any chance for the customer to study the advertisement means that radio is weak at communicating complex messages or conveying much detail. Nevertheless, because ads are repeated frequently, it is possible to give information such as prices. Alternatively, a radio commercial may refer listeners to ads elsewhere.

Buying a radio campaign

Radio commercials tend to be made in the same lengths as TV commercials (though some stations are flexible and will negotiate a rate for any length of commercial). Campaigns can be bought on any number of stations, either directly, or, if several stations are to be used, through sales companies operating on behalf of a number of regional companies. Since audiences tend to be low, many advertisers buy 'packages' of, for example, 49 spots, to be broadcast either throughout the day or at certain key periods, such as 'drive time'.

The Levi's commercial, 'Rivets', shows just how powerful cinema advertising can be, with its beautiful photography and strong music track. The commercial is also shown on television, but loses much of its impact on the small screen. This was the film that preceded 'Stitching', the making of which is examined in detail on pages 148-153.

'Rivets' shows the making of the rivet on the front of the Levi jean, from the mining of the ore, through the stamping out of the metal, the transportation by truck to the jean itself.
Agency: Bartle Bogle Hegarty.

In terms of sheer visual power, cinema is the strongest medium of all, offering even greater impact than television. The combination of the large screen, multi-track sound and the absence of distractions means that almost every commercial looks and sounds better in the cinema than it does on television. The problem with cinema is that in most countries its audience is tiny compared with that of television. It does not matter how good the commercial is if it is not being watched by the right people in sufficient numbers. In addition, the cinema audience is largely made up of young people, which is fine for advertisers whose target market is young, but is a problem for many others. In most countries, cinema takes less than 2 per cent of the total advertising revenue.

Advantages

The cinema audience tends to be predominantly young (mainly 15- to 24-year-olds), and since this age group watches less television than average, it is a useful medium for products such as jeans, make-up, 'young' drinks, banks and goods bought by people setting up home. Campaigns can be bought locally or nationally, and a high proportion of the commercials are very local indeed – driving schools, restaurants, car dealers and so on. It is often possible to book commercials to run with a particular hit film as it goes round the country, or into a 'children's package' of Disney films.

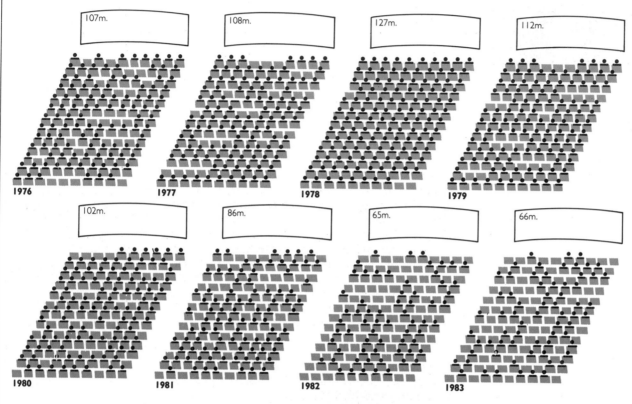

107m. 1976
108m. 1977
127m. 1978
112m. 1979
102m. 1980
86m. 1981
65m. 1982
66m. 1983

Cinema admissions have declined dramatically in the United Kingdom in recent years, according to figures from the Department of Trade and Industry (*above*).

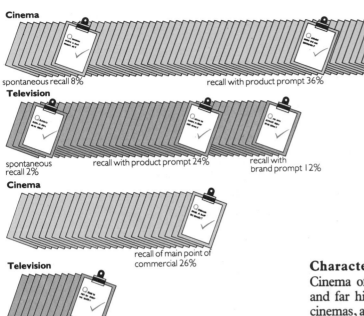

Cinema

spontaneous recall 8%   recall with product prompt 36%   recall with brand prompt 20%

Television

spontaneous recall 2%   recall with product prompt 24%   recall with brand prompt 12%

Cinema

recall of main point of commercial 26%

Television

recall of main point of commercial 9%

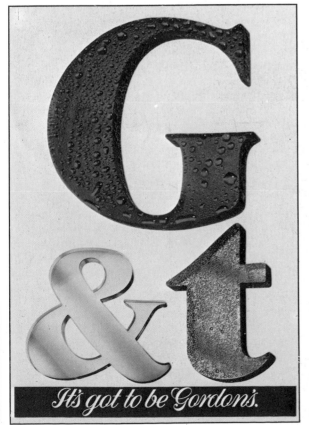

It's got to be Gordon's.

Advertising in cinemas has a greater impact than that on TV because of the larger screen, the better sound quality and the absence of distractions. In this research, Marplan tested the recall levels of the two media (*left*). A completely new commercial for a hitherto unknown product – a gas-powered hair-styling brush made by Braun – was transmitted for the first time on TV in London; the same night it was shown on 45 cinema screens in London. The following day, Marplan interviewed young women who had seen the commercial. Eight per cent of the cinema audience spontaneously recalled the brand name correctly, compared with 2 per cent of the TV audience.

After being prompted on the product group, another 36 per cent of cinema-goers and 24 per cent of the TV audience named Braun. When prompted on the brand name, a further 20 per cent of the cinema audience and 12 per cent of the TV viewers recalled the commercial, producing overall recall figures of 64 per cent for cinema and 38 per cent for TV. In addition, 26 per cent of the cinema audience recalled the main point of the commercial (the Braun curler is cordless because it is gas-powered) compared with 9 per cent of the TV viewers.

Characteristics

Cinema offers advertisers sound, colour, movement and far higher sound and picture quality – in some cinemas, at any rate – than television. Audiences get far more involved in films at the cinema than they do at home, and the same is true for commercials. Research in the United Kingdom shows that the recall of a commercial seen in the cinema is considerably higher than that of the same commercial shown on television, with audiences being more likely to remember not only the product and the name, but also the particular features covered in the commercial.

One advantage cinema has over television in most countries is that it is able to carry commercials for tobacco and alcoholic drinks. (However, they tend only to be shown with 'adult' films.)

Disadvantages

Cinema audiences in many countries have been declining as a result of television, and the coverage of adults over the age of 34 is particularly poor. Even the prime cinema-going audience – the 15- to 24-year-olds – do not visit cinemas that often, which means that coverage and frequency have to be built up over a period of time, and there is little chance of people seeing any commercial many times.

Characteristics

Cinema commercials are generally seen by a large number of people at once, which means that they can be a target for barracking or, simply, that the audience can be distracted by people talking, buying ice cream or just looking for their seats. Like television commercials, they are unable to convey much information.

Buying a cinema campaign

Cinema advertising can be bought in many ways – by individual cinema, by region or nationally – and for any length of time from a week upwards. Each commercial will be shown once every performance. An increasingly popular method of buying cinema is in packages linked to major films such as *Superman* or *Star Wars*, which are guaranteed to get big audiences. Similar packages, for children's products, can be bought with Disney films. There is very little audience research, other than admissions figures.

Gordon's Gin have consistently used dramatic cinema commercials, with beautiful photography (*far left*) emphasizing its green bottle and the bubbles of tonic water. Spirits firms are not permitted to advertise on television in the United Kingdom and, in any case, this ad would lose much of its impact on TV. The press ad (*left*) shows how the creative treatment is taken through into other media.
Agency: Foote Cone & Belding.

DIRECT MAIL

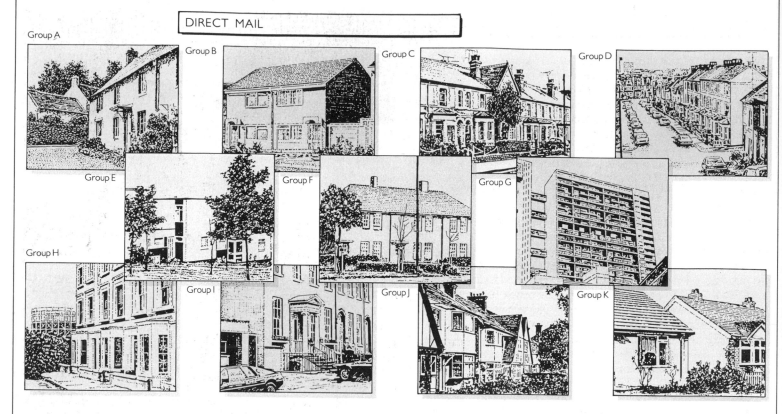

Group A Group B Group C Group D
Group E Group F Group G
Group H Group I Group J Group K

ACORN is a 'marketing segmentation system' which classifies consumers by the type of residential area in which they live (*above*). There are 11 ACORN neighbourhood groups: Group A – agricultural areas; Group B – modern family housing, higher incomes; Group C – older housing of intermediate status; Group D – poor quality older terraced housing; Group E – better-off council estates; Group F – less well-off council estates; Group G – poorest council estates; Group H – multi-racial areas; Group I – high status non-family areas; Group J – affluent suburban housing; Group K – better-off retirement areas.

The media discussed so far are those universally recognized as advertising media, the traditional 'above-the-line' media on which the vast majority of advertising budgets are spent. Yet several other methods of disseminating sales messages are used by commercial firms – most of which would be regarded by the general public as 'advertising' – and perhaps the most significant of these is direct mail. Indeed, more money is spent on direct mail in many countries, including the United States and the United Kingdom, than the traditionally accepted media of magazines, outdoor, cinema and radio, and there is some pressure for it to be seen as an 'above-the-line' medium. In the United States it accounts for some 15 per cent of advertising revenue, and in the United Kingdom it is exceeded only by spending on television and in the press.

Direct mail simply means sending advertising material through the post. It should not be confused with direct response advertising – which is designed to persuade the reader or viewer to respond directly to the advertisement, often by filling in a coupon – though they are both part of what is now known as direct marketing, and much direct mail is indeed intended to produce an immediate response.

The main advantage of direct mail is that it is far more selective than other media, in that, by the use of an appropriate list of names, it is possible for advertisers to send their sales message only to people likely to be interested in their product or service. Not only is there little wastage – in that those outside the target market are unlikely to see the advertising – but in addition the message can be tailored specifically to those people it is aimed at.

Creatively, there is little limit to the form in which the message can be sent. The advertiser can choose whether to send a letter or a brochure, in colour or black and white, one page or 20. With the advent of videos it is even possible to send TV messages directly to a specific market, and advertising agencies have been among the first to use this form of direct mail, sending prospective clients a video of their commercials.

However, direct mail is more expensive in terms of cost-per-thousand than other media. The cost of a campaign is made up of two elements – the production of the advertising material, and the postal charges – and the postage alone ensures a high cost-per-thousand. Nevertheless, for many firms direct mail still makes economic sense because of the high response rate it can generate, and because its results can be measured far more accurately than campaigns in most other media. It is also possible to test people's response to direct mail easily and cheaply, simply by writing to a small sample of the target audience.

The key to success in direct mail is the mailing list, and the compiling of lists of particular groups of people – linked either by their job or their purchasing habits – is a skilful business in itself. Building up a good list is more straightforward for industrial mail shots than for those aimed at consumers, but the latter is becoming more sophisticated thanks to new research systems such as ACORN (A Classification of Residential Neighbourhoods). This links people's address to their likely lifestyle and hence to their potential purchasing habits: the use of the electoral roll means that names and addresses can be produced for any given ACORN area.

The major problem with direct mail is that some people still dismiss it as 'junk mail', and throw it away unread. However, research shows that this proportion is comparatively low – 6 per cent for industrial mail shots and 18 per cent for consumer direct mail.

SPONSORSHIP

Like direct mail and point-of-sale, sponsorship is an area which borders closely on advertising without quite becoming part of it. Sponsorship takes many forms, but at its most basic it involves the sponsoring company paying to be associated with a particular event, usually in the field of sport or the arts. In return, the company may well get advertising rights at the event and this is the main reason why many firms get into sponsorship, particularly if the event is to be televised. In countries where cigarette advertising is not permitted on television, sponsorship is a way of getting the company's name – and in some cases those of its brands – onto television. For this reason, tobacco companies are among the biggest providers of sponsorship money.

Nevertheless, sponsorship is not a real substitute for advertising. There is no comparison between the value of a 30-second TV commercial and 30 seconds of a sponsor's name being seen on the screen. Advertising's function is the *direct* promotion of a company in time specifically bought for that purpose, whereas sponsorship is *indirect* promotion with the sponsor's name incidental to the main activity on the screen. While companies and their agencies do everything they can to enhance the value of their sponsorship in commercial terms, the basic difference still remains.

Yet there are advertisers who buy advertising space to perform exactly the same job of communication that other firms get by sponsorship. These are the companies who buy advertising space at sports grounds in the hope of getting television coverage. Like the sponsors, they can do little more than put their company name across, but because the price is far lower than that of TV advertising, they regard this as worthwhile. Increasingly, this advertising space is only being made available to firms who have sponsored the event. This is the case with the 1984 Los Angeles Olympics, where 32 companies in separate product fields have become official sponsors of the Olympics: no other products can be promoted in the various Olympic stadia. The enormous world-wide television audience for events such as the Olympics means that they are only worthwhile for companies whose name is known around the world, but on a national and local level many other companies become involved in sponsorship.

Direct advertising is only one element of the sponsorship package, even if it is the crucial one for many firms. Another important aspect is the fact of being associated with a particular type of event, in that the values of that activity – be it motor racing, opera or a marathon – can rub off on the product. This can then be used as the basis of advertising on TV or in the press. Naturally many automotive companies are associated with motor racing, since success in Formula One races can provide both direct and indirect benefits for car manufacturers, tyre and oil firms, but in addition the glamour and excitement of the sport means that firms marketing totally different products, such as cigarettes and toiletries, also want to be involved. The wide range of companies anxious to sponsor motor racing helps account for the fact that all racing cars these days are

mobile billboards, with their paintwork almost totally obscured by the names of half a dozen or more different companies. Another reason, of course, is that motor racing is very expensive, so a large number of firms are needed to pay the running costs of the teams. Furthermore, the fact that the TV cameras have to focus closely on the cars means there is the opportunity of sustained exposure on television for the sponsors of a car that is in the lead, as opposed to the fleeting glimpses of a name on a sign in the background.

One problem with sponsorship is that it is very difficult to measure the effectiveness of a particular venture with any degree of accuracy. A further problem is that it takes time to build up the public's awareness of the company's link with a particular event, especially if that event was well known in its own right before the sponsor became involved: there is evidence that when the sponsorship of an event is switched to a different company every year or so, no clear benefit accrues at all. Conversely, a company can become almost too well known for its sponsorship: Gillette stopped sponsoring English cricket's knock-out competition after almost 20 years, when it became clear that more people associated its name with cricket than with razor blades.

Tobacco companies are among the biggest providers of sponsorship money. Formula One motor racing is an obvious sport for an advertiser like Marlboro to sponsor, and they have been doing so very successfully for a number of years (*above*).

Hot-air balloons are probably
the most visually dramatic of
fringe media. In this instance
(*below*) the balloon has been
shaped to look like the product it
advertises – a spark plug!

FRINGE MEDIA

In addition to the major media and the below-the-line
activities, there are a great many other means by which
an advertiser can put across its message. These are often
lumped together under the somewhat disparaging
label, 'fringe media', but in the right circumstances, for
the right product, they can provide real benefits for
advertisers.

Fringe media include such things as hot-air balloons,
parking meters, supermarket trolleys and even milk
bottles. Much of this could, perhaps, be labelled outdoor or point-of-sale advertising, but what is interesting

is that it is advertising agencies, rather than sales promotion companies, who are taking the initiative in these
areas.

The fact that these media are regarded as being fringe
marketing activities does not mean there are no facts and
figures and rate-cards to back up their case. Indeed, in
the case of milk bottles, Kellogg's and its agency, J.
Walter Thompson, have research to show that the
advertising of Kellogg's Corn Flakes on milk bottles has
increased sales. (Milk bottles, of course, are a natural
medium for any breakfast cereal and the strong, colourful logo of the cockerel on the Kellogg's pack makes a
very powerful image, set against the whiteness of the
milk inside.)

POINT-OF-SALE

Point-of-sale material is generally regarded as 'sales
promotion' rather than advertising, but it is an important form of communication because it is the last chance
an advertiser has of reminding potential purchasers of
its product. It consists of any advertising material
displayed at the point of sale – in supermarkets, corner
shops, bars, fast-food outlets or petrol stations – such as
posters, display stands, leaflets, drip mats and ashtrays.

At one time, supermarkets were plastered from top to
bottom with such material, but these days most major
retail chains keep a much closer rein on promotional
activity within the store, only allowing one or two
tailor-made promotions at any one time, and making the
manufacturer pay heavily for the privilege. Such material is generally produced not by advertising agencies,
but by specialist sales promotion companies – though
some agencies have subsidiaries specializing in this area.
It is paid for not out of the advertising budget, but from
promotional funds, along with other forms of promotion such as competitions and money-off coupons.

Much point-of-sale advertising is akin to outdoor or
poster advertising, and indeed it is often unclear in
which category a particular item should be put. Technically the difference is that an outdoor site or hoarding
is owned by an outdoor advertising contractor, whereas
point-of-sale material is anything that appears in, or in
the immediate vicinity of, the shop or bar and for which
no payment has been made to the media owner. To the
general public, however, this is a matter of semantics,
since the same poster may often be displayed both on a
contractor's site *and* at the point of sale.

By and large, point-of-sale material is fairly straightforward. While it is true that leaflets can convey a good
deal of information, these are often designed to be taken
away and read at leisure. Most advertising at the point of
sale is simply designed to catch the eye and to get the
name of a particular product across – an extension of the
packaging, designed to ensure that it is the advertiser's
product that is selected and not that of its competitors.
While some is of a permanent nature – fascia boards,
display cases, ashtrays and so on – most is produced for
short-term use, to tie in with a particular advertising
campaign on TV or in the press, to promote a price
reduction or some other special offer, or simply to draw
attention to a new product line.

A promotion with a difference.

Our powerful new Benito Sherry promotion has that little extra difference – to arouse customer interest instantly and really send your sales climbing.

Each bottle of Benito Sherry will be wearing an attractive leaflet – promising your customers a beautiful rose to be sent to someone they care for.

The offer is absolutely free. For just two Benito bottle tops, an attractively packaged, freshly picked red rose is sent to the chosen person accompanied by a personal message written by the customer on the charming gift card incorporated in the neck leaflet.

Point of Sale

Naturally we are backing this unique promotion with impactful posters carrying the same theme. Eyecatching shelf strips will reinforce the message and further enhance the presentation of Benito Sherries.

A tasting too

Once your customers have tried Benito Sherry they'll be back for repeat purchases. Benito is a traditional Spanish sherry, blended exclusively for the Co-op, which compares excellently with heavily advertised national brands.

To prove it we are arranging in-store Benito Sherry tastings to take place during the offer period.

We'll send along a professional lady demonstrator with a special counter unit to spend two days in your store – enticing customers to sample the product. They'll be delighted with the taste and you'll be delighted with the response.

Announcement posters will be supplied in advance of the tasting event.

There are four sherries in the Benito range – Cream, Medium Dry, Pale Dry and Pale Cream. Make sure that your stock is adequate to meet demand – it would be a shame to miss out on this unusual and elegant promotion. Order now.

Most advertising at the point of sale is simply designed to catch the eye and put the product name across – a cross between posters and packaging (*this page*).

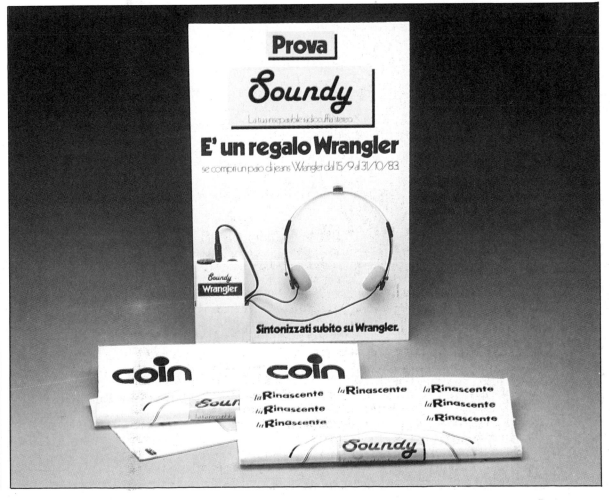

CREATING AND PRODUCING
THE ADS

Humour
Shock
Emotion
Demonstration
Celebrity Presenters
Comparative
Which Treatment?
Pre-testing

Levi Case History
Making a Commercial

PLANNING THE CAMPAIGN

TV Commercials

APPOINTING THE AGENCY

Beer Case History
John Smith's Bitter, Guinness, Fosters

BMW Case History
Making a Press ad

Woolworth Case History
The Winning of an Account

Planning
Product and Market Research
Campaign Objectives
Defining the Target Audience
Devising the Campaign Strategy
Setting the Budget

Press Ads
Posters
Radio

Appointing the Agency
Presenting for the Account
Making the Final Decision

THE CAMPAIGN

PLANNING AND BUYING
THE MEDIA

4 APPOINTING THE AGENCY

WOOLWORTH

F.W. Woolworth is one of the most famous retailing names in the world. In the United Kingdom, Woolworth is one of the half dozen biggest single advertising accounts, spending £8½ million a year on its TV and newspaper campaigns. In 1983, following a change of ownership and management intended to revive a company which had lost its way in the changing retail conditions of the 1970s, it became known that Woolworth was looking for a new agency. One of the agencies eager for the business was McCann-Erickson, and the way it set about trying to win the account (successfully, as it turned out) is a good demonstration of the various stages an agency generally has to go through in order to win new business.

THE WINNING OF AN ACCOUNT

On June 24th 1983, an article appeared on the front page of the advertising trade paper, *Campaign*, stating that Woolworth had parted company with its agency of eight years, Allen Brady & Marsh, and was looking around. Such stories always provide an opportunity for other agencies to make an approach to a client – even if the article states that the advertiser already knows which agencies it intends to visit – and on this occasion McCann-Erickson was one of those which took up the opportunity.

This was not the first time the agency had been in contact with Woolworth. Many advertisers make a point of visiting other advertising agencies even when they are not planning to make a change, simply to keep in touch with what is going on elsewhere: this is particularly the case with clients such as Woolworth, who only use one agency and thus have no opportunity for comparing agencies through their day-to-day handling of the business.

Woolworth's advertising director, David Collier, had visited McCann-Erickson a couple of years earlier, at the agency's invitation, to examine a market modelling technique called 'SCRIBE' which the agency had devised as a way of forecasting a product's performance in a variety of different circumstances. Such devices provide a neat opportunity for agencies to invite potential clients to visit them, without openly soliciting for their business. These contacts can then bear fruit several years later when the advertiser decides it is time for a change.

In this case, there was a particular reason why

Woolworth was one of those invited to see the SCRIBE system – McCann-Erickson was determined to win a major retail account. Three years before, the agency had lost the Tesco account despite having devised a highly successful change of image and strategy for Tesco, called 'Checkout'. The account had moved to an agency whose key personnel had all worked at McCann-Erickson, Grandfield Rork Collins. Despite the Tesco loss, many of the people who had worked on the account were still at McCann-Erickson. Since retail advertising is a specialist business, requiring many different advertisements and a particular understanding of the relationship between retailers and their manufacturers, retail advertising expertise is a valuable commodity and McCann-Erickson was determined to use it. Apart from any other consideration, retail is one of the fastest-growing areas of advertising: seven of the top 10 largest UK advertising accounts (as opposed to advertisers, many of whom have several separate brands) are retailers.

McCann-Erickson's new-business development team had been quietly wooing all the major retailers, including Woolworth, for several years. When the *Campaign* story broke, it was an opportunity that could not be ignored. The chief executive of McCann-Erickson's London office, Alban Lloyd, wrote to David Collier, saying that he had seen the trade press story and inviting him to visit the agency. A few days later, Lloyd received a telephone call from Collier, who said he was planning to look at a fairly large number of agencies, and that McCann-Erickson was one of those he would like to see. The intention was to reduce this list to two or three, who would then be invited to pitch formally for the business. McCann-Erickson naturally agreed to take part, and the first Woolworth visit to the agency was fixed for July 26th, almost one month ahead. The agency was not told which – or even how many – other agencies were being seen, though there was a good deal of unconfirmed speculation in the trade press. (It was reported that Woolworth visited nine agencies in all.)

The presentation an agency gives in attempting to get onto the short list for an account is sometimes called the 'credentials' presentation, since it largely consists of telling the prospective client about the agency itself and its existing work, rather than what the agency could do for the new client's business. Nevertheless, it is important to give a taste of the latter in order to whet the advertiser's appetite. 'It's a crucial balance', says Alban Lloyd. 'You can't tell the advertiser too much about its own area, because the advertiser will certainly know more about its own business at that stage than you will, and you may well be having to go on out-of-date information. In addition, you want to keep your powder dry for the main pitch. On the other hand, you don't want to keep so much to yourself that you don't get the chance to present for the account.'

Four Woolworth executives attended the credentials presentation on July 26th – Collier, two other executive directors and the sales and marketing manager. Six McCann-Erickson executives made the presentation – Lloyd, two account directors, a creative director, the media director and the research director. The brief to the agency for the presentation was very open. Woolworth had given no checklist of points that it wanted covered, as sometimes happens: the agency was simply asked to say what it wanted about itself in two hours, with half an hour left for questions.

Lloyd opened the proceedings, introducing the agency and stressing why McCann-Erickson particularly wanted to win a retail account. He suggested that if the agency was not appointed by Woolworth it would win another major retailer's business in the not too distant future. Each of the other directors then spoke in turn on a particular aspect of the agency's track record and organization, and on how they saw the possible development of the Woolworth business. Several case histories were given including, naturally, that of Tesco and the development of the group's move away from Green Shield stamps in favour of the Checkout price campaign. The SCRIBE model was explained, with particular reference to what it might do for Woolworth, and one director explained how the agency would actually manage a retail account (since a retail business account is more difficult to handle than most other advertising accounts).

Finally, the research director and one of the account directors discussed possible approaches to the marketing and advertising of Woolworth, based on visits to a dozen Woolworth stores, interviews with the public, and their own experience of the retail scene. 'We wanted to demonstrate that McCanns *understood* their business, that it was thinking about their business, and that on that basis we could develop the right advertising for them', says Lloyd.

A few days later, Lloyd received a phone call from Collier inviting the agency to pitch formally for the business. Lloyd naturally accepted, and on August 2nd he received a letter explaining how the presentation would be organized. McCann-Erickson would present on September 21st at 2.00 pm, giving the agency seven weeks to prepare. It would receive a detailed written brief before the end of the week along with a large package of research about the Woolworth business. In addition, a desk was being set up within the Woolworth building for any of the agencies involved to use for further research: the reason for this was not so much the question of security, but simply the sheer bulk of material available.

Nevertheless, security was an important consideration. McCann-Erickson was not told the names of the competing agencies – it later emerged that they were Foote Cone & Belding and Collett Dickenson Pearce – and was instructed not to reveal that it was pitching for the business. Such secrecy may seem strange – many advertisers are quite open about which agencies are presenting for their business – but it arises largely for reasons of commercial confidentiality. Many companies – rival retailers and manufacturers – would be keen to see the research Woolworth was showing the three competing agencies (only one of which, remember, would end up handling the business).

The brief, when it arrived, ran to 41 pages, together with six appendices and 10 attachments. It was highly

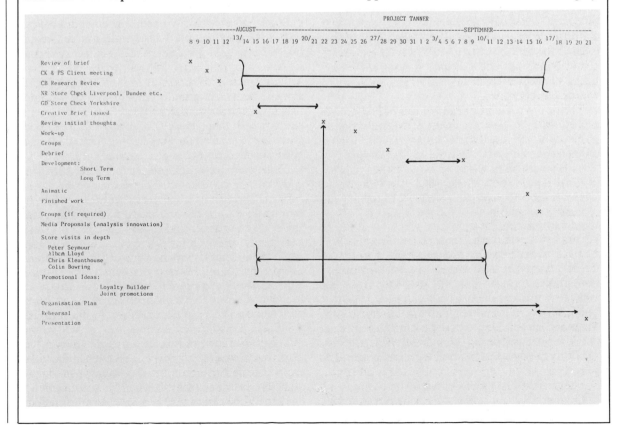

Agency pitches for major accounts are run on the lines of a military operation, amid great secrecy. This chart (*left*) shows the day-by-day preparations made by McCanns prior to the final presentation. The operation was always referred to by its code name, Project Tanner, so called after the colloquial name for a sixpence (Woolworth once having been known as 'the sixpenny store').

McCann-Erickson's chief executive, Alban Lloyd, was closely involved in the pitch, from the initial approach to Woolworth's advertising director to the final presentation and winning of the business.

confidential: only one copy was given to each agency and it had to be returned when the presentations were over. The importance of confidentiality meant that even within the agency no one ever referred to the fact that it was pitching for the Woolworth account. Instead there was a code name – Project Tanner, so called because of the colloquial name for a sixpence, Woolworth once being known as 'the sixpenny store'. (McCann-Erickson prides itself on its code names: when it was working on the Tesco account, the project was known as Operation Bookend, signifying the end of the Green Shield stamps book.)

A conference room was set aside exclusively for Project Tanner, and for the next seven weeks it was kept locked and only opened for those working on the pitch. Despite this, it was an open secret in the business that McCann-Erickson was one of the agencies pitching for the Woolworth account. Indeed, within the agency itself, no fewer than 30 people became involved in the preparation of the presentation at one stage or another, so the secret could not be restricted even to just board members.

The key executives on Project Tanner were those who had made the original presentation to Woolworth, and they ran it like a military operation. The first thing to be done was to find out everything they could about Woolworth: its sales performance, its public image, its standing in relation to its rivals and much more. On the first day that the desk in the Woolworth building was made available to the agencies, McCann-Erickson's research director, Colin Bowring, was there, pipping the other agencies to the post. David Collier made it clear that he and other Woolworth executives would be freely available to discuss any aspect of the business, and this offer was taken up many times by McCann-Erickson. One of the first things the agency asked for was a list of the most appropriate stores to visit to get a feel for the variety of problems and opportunities the company had. Everyone in the team was given a list of stores and a letter of introduction to the manager explaining the purpose of their visit. By the end of the seven weeks, McCann-Erickson executives had visited almost 150 stores.

The initial object of the research was to prepare a single-page brief for the creative teams so that they could start developing campaign ideas. Six creative teams – each consisting of an art director and a copy-writer – were put onto the project, though not full-time. Ten days after the agency had received its brief from the client, it had distilled the research into three separate single-page briefs for the creative teams, each brief being given to two teams. Each team found a room away from the agency – in hotels or elsewhere – to work on the project. They were given four weeks to come up with their solution, during which time they were reading the background research and visiting stores themselves, watching show-reels of competitors' commercials (these can be bought from a monitoring service) and generally immersing themselves in the subject.

Meanwhile, the agency was conducting its own qualitative research, holding group discussions with housewives to find out how they perceived Woolworth and its competitors in terms of price, value for money, store layout, variety of goods, quality of staff and so on. It was also preparing a staffing plan for the account, since Woolworth would need to be assured that the agency could actually manage the business on a day to day basis.

A fortnight before the presentation the agency started to pull the work together in earnest, and moved from the development of the strategy and the creative proposition to the production of a campaign. The creative teams produced three animatics and a fully-fledged commercial, together with no fewer than 50 print ads in the form of very highly finished roughs, made up from photographs and hand lettering. Most pitches would not require so many, but because of the breadth of retail advertising, the agency provided examples of various treatments, such as corporate style, ads for specific products, 'event' ads for Christmas, Easter and Mother's Day, and promotional ideas.

Three or four days before the presentation, the agency started a series of 'dummy runs', developing the form of the actual presentation – first deciding who would say what and in what order, and then polishing the whole operation. On September 21st, at 2.00 pm, nine Woolworth executives arrived at McCann-Erickson's offices for the presentation, including the chairman, John Beckett, the deputy chairman, Peter Firmston-Williams, and all the other members of the company's holding board. Since only four of the nine had seen the original credentials presentation, a certain amount of recapping had to be gone through to reaffirm the agency's own track record and its hunger for a retail account. The presentation was given by the same six McCann-Erickson executives as before, and Lloyd took the opportunity of stressing that all those present would be actively involved in the handling of the Woolworth business.

The presentation took three and a half hours. After Lloyd's introduction, one of the account directors explained the background to the agency's presentation: how the agency saw Woolworth's position in the market, its business problems and opportunities. The research director looked at the position from the

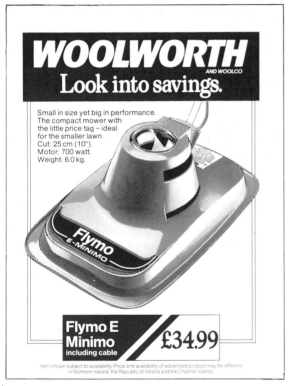

WOOLWORTH
AND WOOLCO
Look into savings.

Small in size yet big in performance.
The compact mower with
the little price tag – ideal
for the smaller lawn.
Cut: 25 cm (10").
Motor: 700 watt.
Weight: 6.0 kg.

Flymo
E-MINIMO

Flymo E
Minimo
including cable / £34.99

Item shown subject to availability. Price and availability of advertised product may be different
in Northern Ireland, the Republic of Ireland and the Channel Islands.

WOOLWORTH
HYBRID TEA or
FLORIBUNDA / 89p each

WOOLWORTH
AND WOOLCO
Offers subject to availability.

Gardening is one of
Woolworth's major product
categories, and this TV and
press campaign (*left*) was
among the first produced by
McCann-Erickson after winning
the business. The TV commercial
starts off with a family visiting
Kew Gardens and focuses on
several gardening products in
turn, among them the Flymo
lawnmower. Finally it switches to
the family's own garden, where
Dad is joking about charging
admission himself, only to
discover the dog doing some
digging of its own.

customer's point of view, and a fourth director explained how all this background thinking had been distilled into the single-page creative brief.

The creative director presented all the advertisements the agency had produced; the media director explained how the £8½ million would be split between the various media throughout the year; and an account director discussed the way the agency would organize the account internally, setting up a 'Woolworth unit' as an agency within an agency. Finally, Lloyd summed the presentation up and handed over a document containing everything that had been said, including pictures of the advertisements and the TV scripts. The presentation ended at 5.30 pm and the Woolworth executives departed, saying they would be in touch in a few days.

It was, in fact, a week later, on Wednesday September 28th that Lloyd received a phone call from Collier, inviting him to come round that evening to discuss the appointment in detail. At the meeting with Collier, all the details of the handling of the account were discussed: confirmation that the key directors would be working on the business, how many staff would be taken on, a full list of the services that would be provided and – most crucial of all – the financial terms on which the account would be handled. Finally, when everything had been agreed, all that remained was to decide how the appointment would be announced. Some advertisers are happy to leave this to the agency, or to issue a joint statement, but in this case Woolworth stated that it wanted to handle the announcement itself, which it did the following week.

McCann-Erickson officially took over the account on January 1st 1984, and the first ad appeared on February 28th, eight months after the search for the new agency had begun.

APPOINTING THE AGENCY

The starting point for every advertising campaign is the appointment of the advertising agency, or, to be more precise, the decision whether or not to appoint an advertising agency. It may be that the advertiser already has an agency, in which case it may just be re-appointed. Alternatively, the advertiser may decide to run its own campaign, without an agency at all. It may be that the advertiser wants to look at the alternative services available, and compare them with those of the conventional full-service agency. What is in no doubt is that, whatever the advertisers want, advertising agencies are always looking for new clients, and this has a profound effect on the way advertisers appoint agencies. Companies are bombarded with promotional material from prospective agencies throughout the year, and if there is the slightest whisper that they may be considering moving their account – and the advertising business and its trade press thrive on such whispers – they are bombarded with telephone calls and letters. As a result, the atmosphere within the ad business is one in which constant agency change is regarded as the norm, and that in itself fuels the desire on the part of both advertisers and agencies to seek new partners. Whether this impression of constant change is a true one, however, is a subject of some debate.

Saatchi & Saatchi Compton addressed itself to the issue in a recent annual report, maintaining that, as companies accorded a higher priority to their advertising expenditures, one result would be increased stability in the agency-client relationship. Clients like Kellogg's and Lever Brothers, it pointed out, had been with J. Walter Thompson for over 40 and 50 years respectively. Saatchi estimated that, on average, accounts worth between 5 and 8% of total advertising expenditure changed agencies each year in the United Kingdom, while in the United States the figure was said to be around 6 per cent. 'Why then do so many industry-watchers retain the *impression* of a constant merry-go-round of accounts?' asked the agency. 'Because 5 per cent of total advertising expenditure would represent over £100 million – in other words, £2-3 million of account changes every week. This is more than enough to provide substance for the industry's "musical chairs" image, yet it is still just a tiny proportion of the total.'

The reason Saatchi went out of its way to explain the 'musical chairs' image of the agency business is that as a publicly-quoted company it wishes to emphasize the stability of its own market. Some observers could not help pointing out, however, that the agency's own rapid growth was based on advertisers switching accounts, some of which – like British Airways – had been with their previous agency for several decades.

In 1983, according to the UK trade paper *Campaign*, accounts worth £372 million moved agency (including business transferred through agency mergers), representing some 10 per cent of total advertising expenditure. In the first nine months of 1983 in the United States, according to figures compiled by Doyle Dane Bernbach, 205 accounts worth over $1 million each switched agencies, making a total of $1,567 million. A large slice of the 1983 movement was accounted for by the world's biggest-ever account move, which produced a chain reaction that reverberated around the globe. It started when Procter & Gamble fired Young and Rubicam in the United States (though not in the rest of the world), because it believed it was taking on potentially conflicting business from P & G's rivals. The move was surprising in that P & G had a very close, long-standing relationship with its worldwide agencies and had worked with Y & R for 34 years. Within weeks, Y & R had resigned its P & G business elsewhere in the world, worth $60 million, to take on $120 million of accounts from one of P & G's rivals, Colgate-Palmolive. Colgate in turn had to drop two agencies to make room for Y & R, one of which – D'Arcy MacManus & Masius – it had worked with for 60 years. In a related move, Leo Burnett, which had been a Beecham agency for 20 years, suddenly became a P & G agency, taking on much of the business that Y & R had resigned.

Occasionally an advertiser changes agency not for advertising reasons, but to impress the outside world that there is a new broom sweeping through the company. Often such a decision is taken not by the firm's marketing management, but by a new chairman or chief executive, anxious to establish his or her presence. One of the quickest and easiest ways of changing a company's image overnight is by changing the advertising. When Guinness fired its UK agency, J. Walter Thompson, and appointed Allen Brady & Marsh, it not only made headline news in all the papers but the Guinness share price rose by 10p. The sacking was seen, rightly, as a demonstration that the new management was going to be more dynamic. The fact that the JWT advertising had been highly admired was neither here nor there. On other occasions, the 'new broom' is wielded by an incoming marketing director. The temptation to make one's mark by changing the agency is a natural one, but most large companies take great steps to resist it. Choosing a new agency is not only very time-consuming, but the 'bedding-in' process can be very disruptive as each side gets to know the other.

There is no doubt that a change of advertising can, on occasion, bring a company to life by changing its image and boosting its staff's morale. However, it should be possible for a company to change its advertising without changing its agency. Only if the agency has attempted and failed to come up with a new campaign to the client's liking should a change be considered.

At the centre of the multi-million dollar, multinational P & G and Colgate account moves lay the issue of account 'conflicts' – agencies handling competitive products – and the principle that agencies should not handle conflicting accounts lies at the heart of what many regard as the 'special relationship' between advertisers and their agencies. 'Many advertisers feel they work more intimately with their ad agencies than they do with other suppliers,' says Ken Miles, director of the Incorporated Society of British Advertisers. 'A great many advertisers see the agency as a partner, and a good agency/client relationship is certainly more than that of a supplier.

'The agency can be concerned with the very essence of the company's business, actually helping it create its

Seven ways a client can improve his agency in 1984.

1 Ask the agency to write down exactly what they expect the advertising to do.
An advertising agency is a machine for spending other people's money.

Before you part with yours, ask your agency exactly what they expect to come back with after they've spent it all.

Get a clear, precise objective out of them. Not a vague promise that the advertising will 'boost your image' or 'sell a lot of boxes'.

Ask for a more specific target. Like, 'The advertising will aim to increase by 10% the number of people who believe that your product is good value for money.'

This will focus both the minds and the resources in your agency on an agreed goal and, at the end of the year, both sides can judge how well the agency performed.

2 Insist on seeing one recommendation only.
The device of presenting clients with a raft of creative options is an old agency ruse to conceal mediocre work.

The theory is that a goose might be mistaken for a swan if you hide it in a flock of vultures.

But truly brilliant advertising solutions don't happen six at a time.

And if there really is a brilliant solution among the options on offer to you, why would any agency then make itself look foolish by showing you they're incapable of spotting it?

3 Ask to see the work they do for all their other clients.
Looking at your own agency's showreel achieves two things.

Firstly, it gives you an overall impression of the standard of their best work, which allows you to judge how good your advertising is by comparison.

Secondly, it provides a rare opportunity to discuss advertisements without the pressure of having to make decisions about them.

A surprising number of misunderstandings can be cleared up by talking about other people's advertising.

4 Telephone your agency's chief executive at unpredictable times.
Ask him how things are going on your account. Be specific, talk details.

If you get into the habit of doing this, you'll find that your account starts getting a greater share of senior management attention within the agency.

Since (with a few exceptions) the most senior people in agencies are also the most able, this can dramatically improve the quality of thinking on your business.

5 Write at least one unsolicited letter each year commending the agency team on a fine piece of work.
You may find it hard to believe, but the effect of such a letter can be galvanic.

Letters of praise from clients are circulated rapidly throughout the agency. People pin them up on their notice boards. Even creative people. It makes them feel good to work on your account.

But this gesture on your part will be far from altruistic.

The more popular an account is within an agency, the more it will attract the most able and talented people, who will even pull rank on some of their less gifted colleagues in order to work on an account where their efforts are recognised and rewarded.

Of course, if there is no piece of advertising during the course of a year which you feel warrants such praise, then a letter pointing this out will have a similarly galvanic effect.

it is now 3am precisely and our brand share in Tyne Tees is 7.8%.

This is much more effective than the six-monthly lunch, where there is sufficient warning for the agency man to get himself... thoroughly briefed and to give the impression that his finger is never off the pulse of your business.

6 Try to ensure that your agency makes a reasonable profit.
Agencies... businesses in a... are extremely... those resources... be finely calcu...

If an accou... able, an agenc... seek to reduce... costs are mos... bill, there is o... way to cut dow... cheaper peop... account and t... to devote less... time to it.

But if the... is making a... profit on yo... ness, this gv... right to dem... hours from...

7 Get in...
Assum... already,... to hear mo... out of your... other trick...

The... Chairman... Wilhite, D... number is...

Young...
Greater Lon...

Agencies are normally poor at advertising their own services – possibly because they have no client to blame if it goes wrong – but this ad by Young & Rubicam (*above*) tackles the problem very effectively.

Appendix II
Agency/Client Agreement

These draft provisions cover for the guidance of advertisers in preparing their agreements with agencies.

These provisions are merely suggestions and advertisers should ensure that from the beginning of their business relationship with an advertising agency, the respective rights, duties and procedures are understood and established to avoid misunderstandings that might damage the relationship.

The provisions that have been drafted cover the basic requirements that an advertiser should have in his agreement. Legal advice should be sought where special provisions need to be included to cover any special requirements that the advertiser may have.

SERVICES
The agency will provide the following services:–

1. Planning, preparing and placing of advertising on our behalf, checking, paying invoices and accounting for all such advertising placed on our behalf in all media.
2. Planning, preparing and supervising all display and other sales promotion material, activities and product publicity requested by us.
3. Planning and commissioning any research activity that we may require.

TERMS OF PAYMENT
The advertiser should make clear in his agreement the terms of payment, whether this be by fee, commission or combination of both. The following provision covers typical agreement for 15% commission of all work.

1. The charges on all advertising time and space purchased for us will be invoiced at the net cost to you plus agency commission of 17.65%.
2. *THE COST OF MECHANICAL PRODUCTION OF PRINT ADVERTISING* – type, composition production layouts, printing, engraving, block-making, art work, photography, model fees, etc. will be invoiced at the net cost to you plus agency commission of 17.65%.
3. *THE MECHANICAL PRODUCTION OF TELEVISION, CINEMA & RADIO ADVERTISING*
The costs of story-boards, artists, hire of studios, production houses, and other persons or organisations are charged at net cost to you plus 17.65%.
4. *CONFERENCES & TRADE PRESENTATIONS*
These will be charged to us at net cost plus 17.65% including the direct time of your executives engaged on such services and supervision.
5. *OTHER ACTIVITIES*
The cost of research commissioned on our behalf, design and copy content on all sales promotional material, packaging and the cost of all public relations activities undertaken on our behalf will be charged at cost plus a proportionate overhead, of the direct time of employees engaged thereon. The mechanical production and printing of all materials associated with these services will be charged to us at net cost plus 17.65%, unless otherwise agreed at time of briefing.

The Incorporate Society of British Advertisers has prepared a draft agreement for its members to use, if they wish, when appointing an ad agency (*above*).

---

products, which puts it in a different position even from professional advisers such as lawyers and accountants, who by and large deal with the external aspects of the business.'

The importance of agency confidentiality was epitomized by the case of the launch of Krona, in which the agency, Davidson Pearce, was working on the brand for some three years before it saw the light of day. It is for this reason that most big advertisers are extremely sensitive to the issue of account conflicts. When agencies merge, having been handling conflicting products, one of the accounts – usually the smaller – has to go. More difficult to assess is the situation in which an advertiser moves into a new product area which could bring it into conflict with one of its agency's other clients. Procter & Gamble is more sensitive to this particular issue than most advertisers, but on several occasions accounts have had to move because clients that were once seen not to conflict suddenly became competitors. Sometimes such a move in one relatively small country can put a whole world-wide account in jeopardy. In view of this special relationship between most advertisers and their agencies, the appointment of an advertising agency takes on a particular importance, and most clients go through a lengthy selection process before they make up their mind.

PRESENTING FOR THE ACCOUNT

Pitching for business is a skill in itself, and, though only loosely connected with the job of creating effective advertising, it is of crucial importance to all agencies. Winning new accounts is vital to the growth of an agency, not only bringing it increased billings and new challenges for the creative team, but also demonstrating to other advertisers and agencies that it is successful.

Winning several new accounts on the trot gives an agency momentum, and makes everyone in the company perform better. It also makes it easier to attract good staff and, in turn, win more business. Conversely, the agency that fails to win new accounts – even if it is growing through gaining extra business from its existing clients – can lose confidence in itself. Since all agencies lose accounts from time to time – often through no fault of their own – it is important that they are able to redress the balance.

For the agency, the new business pitch is arguably the most exciting part of advertising life, bringing to the fore all the competitive instincts that most ad people have in abundance. It is a game in which there are winners and losers, time is short and the stakes are high. For most accounts of any size, agencies treat the presentation like

Some months after losing the UK's best-known and most prestigious account, J. Walter Thompson put the experience to good use (*below*).

The bird that has flown is the toucan, a long-standing Guinness symbol that JWT had revived in its advertising.

Many observers of the advertising business have the impression that accounts are constantly changing hands – and, indeed, a number of major accounts do switch agencies each week. However, the fact that long-term business relationships are also possible in advertising is demonstrated by this chart showing how long the clients of J. Walter Thompson in London have been with the agency (*below*). Nearly a quarter of JWT's clients have worked with the agency since before 1960, and the average length of association is 14 years.

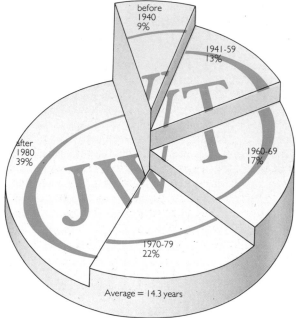

a military operation, drafting teams in to research the potential client's business, prepare strategies and, in a great many cases, to prepare creative work – occasionally, even going to the lengths of producing speculative commercials. However, for the advertiser, the presentation – and indeed the whole search for an agency – is less of a high spot. While the process may be instructive and even, on occasions, entertaining, the appointment of an agency involves a great deal of work on top of what is in any case a highly demanding job. In addition, of course, the advertiser is aware that all the effort being put into the new business pitch is at the expense of the agency's existing clients, in terms of both money and time. That is fine when the advertiser is the potential client, but not necessarily so satisfactory once the agency has been appointed.

In practice, most advertisers accept that their agencies are businesses which must be successful in their own right, and that this inevitably involves them in looking for new clients. Often they are delighted when an agency is winning new business, since it enables them to attract better people and to negotiate with the media owners from a stronger position. It also reflects well on their judgement. However, what advertisers do not like to see is the team that won the account for the agency whisked away to work on yet more new business pitches, leaving them with the second team.

To avoid this happening – and to avoid choosing an agency that lays on a highly impressive presentation but is less good at doing the real work – the advertiser must brief the agencies in some detail as to what it is looking for in the presentation. This in turn will depend on how many stages the advertiser is going through in its search for an agency.

It may be that the advertiser will ask half a dozen agencies to present their own credentials, including their work for existing clients, with no discussion of what they might do for the advertiser's business specifically. This has the advantage that none of them is told any confidential information about the company, its market performance and strategy – if there are five losing agencies, each of whom might later be pitching for a competitor's account, such information could be valuable. In such a case, the client would probably reduce these to a shortlist of two or three and give them a far more detailed brief, involving analysis of the market and the development of a possible strategy. Or, if the client has plenty of time to spare and is not worried about spreading its thinking too widely around the agency world, it may ask five or six agencies for a detailed presentation.

Such presentations will involve the agency in a great deal of work, conducting consumer research, pulling together sales figures and market trends, visiting stores and factories, and analysing the existing advertising of the client and its competitors. Having done this – usually at its own expense – the agency is in a position to make recommendations on the client's marketing and advertising strategy and objectives. It may also make creative strategy recommendations and even produce speculative creative work, although there is some controversy surrounding this practice. Some agencies have a strict policy of refusing to do speculative creative work, on the grounds that four to six weeks – which is often as long as an agency has to prepare its presentation – is insufficient time in which to get a real grounding in the client's business, let alone produce the campaign that is to solve its problems. Most will produce some work if asked, though usually only in a fairly rough state. However, agencies that wanted a large account badly enough have been known to produce a fully-fledged commercial costing many thousands of dollars. In cases where a client specifically asks for some creative work, a fee is usually agreed in advance, though it will certainly not cover the cost if an agency attempts anything elaborate.

There are other problems with speculative creative work. While in some cases the work that wins the account later becomes a highly successful campaign, in others that work has to be abandoned because research shows it to be the wrong strategy. Advertisers should not expect, therefore, to find the whole answer to their problems in the agencies' pitch for their business. While it may be that one agency comes up with the eventual solution straight away, perhaps more by luck than judgement, the advertiser should be looking more to the team as a whole and evidence of its strategic thinking and problem-solving ability, than to awarding the account purely on the basis of the most appealing creative work.

Other factors that may or may not influence a client include the whole style of the agency's operation and its presentation. Some agencies go for a full 'song and dance routine' – sometimes literally, acting out the commercial and singing the jingle – aimed at impressing the client with the agency's verve and razzmatazz. Others pull such stunts as having all their staff dress up in costumes appropriate for the client's business, or – in one case – reassembling a car on the second floor of the agency. One possibly apocryphal story had an agency keeping a client waiting in its reception area for half an hour, serving him coffee in a chipped cup, in order to bring home to him how his customers currently saw his operation.

There are no concrete rules as to how an advertiser should set about choosing a new agency, for so much depends on the advertiser's specific needs, and how much knowledge it has of the agency world before starting. The advertiser may be looking for an inspirational agency to give its business a totally new look and feel, in which case the style and atmosphere of the presentation and creative work may be the only evidence on which to make a decision. Other advertisers may be looking for much more of a marketing-based, problem-solving agency and, while they will not want the presentation to be dull, they will want plenty of evidence of research and sound strategic thinking. In either case, they will want to meet the team who will actually be working on their business, and not just the professional new-business getters.

MAKING THE FINAL DECISION

Making the final appointment is not always easy, even after the full agency presentations. Few agencies perform so outstandingly that there is no doubt in the client's mind as to which to choose. Often there is a great deal of discussion, with the agency's written proposals – often running into many thousands of words – being scrutinized in great detail. One agency may have scored the highest in one area, while being weak in another. Different members of the advertiser's team may have totally different opinions.

It is vital that the advertiser should decide at the outset who is going to make the decision – the advertising manager, the marketing director, the managing director, the chairman, or the whole board. Ideally, the selection team should be kept as small as possible. Sometimes the appointment is subject to a two-tier procedure. The marketing department makes its decision and then has to have it ratified by the board or the managing director, in which case the agency generally has to go through its whole presentation – or a shortened version of it – again.

There is one final factor that will often have a significant influence on which agency wins the business, especially these days, and that is the question of the agency's remuneration. For years agencies were not permitted to compete on price, so they won their business purely on the service they provided. Nowadays, restrictive practice legislation in many countries means that price is a significant factor in a client's decision. If an agency will handle the business for 12 per cent, as opposed to 15 per cent, the financial saving to the client can be so great – $300,000 on a $10 million account – that it is likely to outweigh most other factors.

However, while an advertiser would not go to a weak agency purely to save money, there are so many good agencies to choose from that price inevitably becomes a key factor. Remuneration is often, therefore, a significant element in the agencies' presentation.

Some agencies still make a point of adhering to the 15 per cent commission principle, arguing that only in this way can agencies offer the full service that they maintain produces the best advertising. One of the main champions of the 15 per cent commission is the chairman of the UK agency Allen Brady & Marsh, Peter Marsh, who took a four-page advertisement in the advertising press to explain his stand. This move was prompted by the fact that the Government – through its Central Office of Information – had decided to pay less than 15 per cent to some of its agencies. Though every agency likes to have Government business for the prestige it brings, ABM announced that 'when the COI mooted its revision to the remuneration system of agencies, ABM took it off the list of prospects with whom it would like to work'.

Eventually, having taken into account both price and performance, the advertiser will have made up its mind. At this stage, if the advertiser decides to move the account, it must terminate its contract with the existing agency and draw up a new one with the new agency. Most contracts state that the agreement can be terminated at 90 days' notice, but sometimes things move much faster. Some advertisers believe that once an agency knows that it is losing an account – and is thus eligible to work for its competitors – the sooner they part company the better.

5 PLANNING THE CAMPAIGN

The John Smith's Bitter commercials featured two characters from English pub signs – The Forester and The Cricketer – singing to the tune of 'Big John' (*right, far right*). Agency: Boase Massimi Pollitt.

The beer market is one in which advertising plays a vital role in the battle for brand supremacy. Every advertising agency wants to handle a beer account, partly because of the large budgets that beers tend to command, but also because of the opportunities they offer for strong creative work.

Because of its size and the fact that most beers are broadly similar – give or take differences in strength, colour and texture – the beer market represents a good framework within which to look at the advertising planning process, and in particular, to examine the different approaches taken by three companies whose products – and customers – might seem to be largely similar.

The UK beer market has a greater variety of types of beers than most other countries, with a large share taken by dark beers – bitters and stouts – as opposed to the light beers that dominate most other countries' beer drinking. There are also significant regional differences, with many brands only being sold in one part of the country. The three brands to be examined here reflect these differences.

One is Guinness, the largest-selling beer in the United Kingdom. Despite its position as brand leader, Guinness sales have been declining for many years as the stout sector of the beer market has diminished. Another is the Australian lager, Fosters, which had the most successful launch in the United Kingdom of any lager brand. (Lager is the fastest-growing sector in the market, increasing its share from 10 per cent to 30 per cent between 1971 and 1981.) The third is a regional bitter, John Smith's, which is brewed in Yorkshire. Though this is now available throughout the United Kingdom, with its Yorkshire origins being stressed in all aspects of its marketing, a separate campaign is required for the Yorkshire region since all the biggest-selling beers there are brewed locally.

All three beers faced marketing problems which required new advertising campaigns, and the planning that went into these campaigns offers an educational insight into the way most advertising campaigns are devised.

JOHN SMITH'S BITTER

Sales of John Smith's had started to decline at an alarming rate – dropping by 5.7 million pints in one year. The value of this lost trade was some £2 million, but there were knock-on effects as well: if fewer people were coming into John Smith's pubs to drink the bitter, less money was being spent on fruit machines, bar food and other drinks ordered by beer drinkers' wives and friends.

The brewers of John Smith's, Courage, looked at all the possible explanations for the decline, but failed to find an easy answer. The product had not been changed; the price had only risen in line with those of the competition; no change had taken place in the standards of the pubs themselves; there had been no reduction in the number of pubs; there had been no production problems, limiting the brand's availability; and no Courage brand had been promoted at the expense of John Smith's.

The problem, therefore, seemed likely to lie in the consumer's perception of the product, and so the advertising agency involved, Boase Massimi Pollitt, conducted a number of group discussions to find out how John Smith's was regarded by beer drinkers. The discussions were held in five separate Yorkshire towns and each group consisted of half a dozen beer drinkers, supervized by one of the agency's planners. It was discovered that John Smith's lacked character and did not arouse enthusiasm among its drinkers. This was particularly the case among the all-important younger age group.

'The importance of the younger drinkers is threefold', pointed out the agency. 'They tend to consume more bitter than older people; they go to more pubs and are more willing to try different drinks; and they represent the market's future and will retain, in later years, the tastes they now develop.'

The marketing objective for John Smith's was to increase volume sales and, though various options were examined (such as increasing the number of pubs), it was quickly decided that advertising was the most cost-effective way of achieving this, by revitalizing the brand in the eyes of consumers.

The main advertising objective was to restore the commitment of existing John Smith's drinkers to the brand, but a secondary objective was to attract lapsed drinkers. The way this was to be done was by improving the brand's image through the advertising, since image is an important factor in the choice of a beer, particularly among the under-30s. As the agency's planners said: 'Beer drinking is essentially social and group pressures can be strong. The public selection of a brand of beer reflects the buyer's self-image in the same way as choice of cigarettes, clothes or car. Buyers want to feel that they are making a sensible, defensible choice that reflects well on them as knowledgeable beer drinkers. This can override actual taste preference; the brewery adage that "people drink with their eyes" has been repeatedly confirmed by blind and

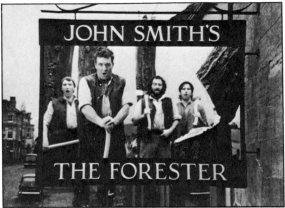

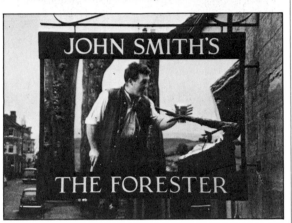

'I wish I could get down from chopping these trees, 'cause a John Smith's pub is below my knees.

'Now forestry is a worthy career, but stuck up on this sign I miss the big bitter beer that's Big John.

'(Chorus) Big John, Big John, Great Big John.

'Now don't get me wrong 'cause this job is OK... I like trees a lot if they fall the right way.

'There's advantages too with Big John Smith's beer – 'cause of the simple fact they've got branches everywhere.

'(Chorus) Big John, Big John, Big John (fades)'.

branded product tests, where the brand names can reverse the preferences expressed "blind".'

The target market for the advertising was defined as young bitter drinkers, between the ages of 18 and 20, in the socio-economic groups C1, C2 and D. However, the proviso was attached that the advertising should not alienate the brand's older drinkers.

Various strategies were investigated through group discussions, and it was concluded that the execution of the advertising had to be masculine, sociable, working-class and pub-based, with a contemporary tone that could rival lager advertising in its appeal to young drinkers.

The creative solution was a campaign based on the theme of 'Big John', derived from the fact that drinkers often asked for 'a pint of John's' at the bar. Using the old country-and-western song, *Big Bad John* (with suitably altered lyrics), one of the agency's creative teams came up with a character called Big John, who was depicted on the traditional signs that hang outside English pubs in the guise of 'The Forester' and 'The Cricketer' (both well-known pub names). In the commercials, Big John was seen to come to life, singing about the length of time he had been 'stuck up on this sign' and how much he missed 'the big bitter taste of Big John'. The 'Big John' theme referred both to the pint and to its drinker.

The commercials were given an extensive run in the Yorkshire region to re-establish the John Smith's name – in fact the campaign accounted for 34 per cent of all TV advertising expenditure for Yorkshire beers in the region, compared with 15 per cent the year before.

Qualitative research conducted by the agency after the commercials had appeared showed that the right message was getting across, both about the beer ('It's a big pint, it's good value with a good taste', said one Leeds drinker), and the drinkers ('It's drunk by big and manly chaps'). The research also showed that drinkers enjoyed the commercials and saw John Smith's in a new light. 'They're new and something different, not run of the mill adverts like the others', said one man. 'The Woodman one was brilliant. They're trendy and they're always bringing them up to date', said another.

These favourable responses were reflected in the sales figures, and the decline was immediately reversed. Sales of John Smith's in Yorkshire pubs rose by 4.8 per cent in the year after the ads first appeared, while the market as a whole declined by 7.7 per cent. More than 10 million extra pints were sold that year, with a value of £5 million.

To measure the effect of the new John Smith's Bitter advertising, Courage commissioned Marplan to measure drinkers' attitude to the beer, both in the Yorkshire region (where the campaign had appeared) and in the North West and Lancashire TV regions (where it had not). The chart (*below*) shows the improvement in attitudes in Yorkshire after the campaign (right of map) and the decline in attitudes in other regions.

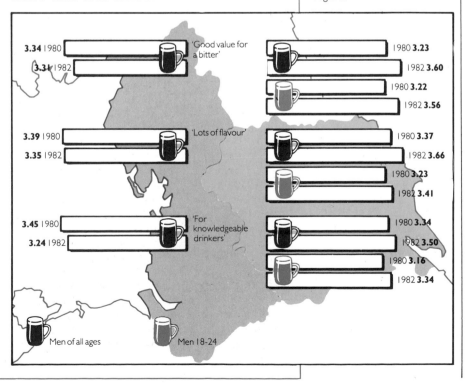

Guinness has an illustrious advertising heritage which makes it a much-coveted account and one in which wit and humour are vital. The Gilroy zoo (right) was a very popular campaign of the 1930s, while the anniversary of the Battle of Hastings in 1966 was made the occasion for a Guinness celebration (below).

GUINNESS

BATTLE OF HASTINGS 1066

BOTTLE OF GUINNESS 1966

If John Smith's had an image problem, Guinness had an even greater one! Though it still held almost 5 per cent of the total UK beer market and was the most widely available brand, its market share had been halved in 10 years as younger drinkers turned to lighter drinks, such as lager. Stout, with its heavy consistency and acquired taste was out of fashion, and it was widely believed that Guinness was a dying brand whose time had passed. If drinkers were rapidly forsaking bitters for lager, they were forsaking stout even faster.

Nevertheless, over the years Guinness had had an unrivalled reputation for its entertaining and witty advertising. Starting with the posters of the 1930s featuring the toucan and the Guinness zoo produced by Benson's (later to become part of Ogilvy & Mather), right up to the award-winning ads of the 1970s produced by J. Walter Thompson, Guinness advertising had established itself as the best-known and best-loved campaign in the United Kingdom.

Partly because of this – but also because of its massive budget and the fact that it had only had two advertising agencies in its history – Guinness had become the account that every agency wanted to win. There seemed little likelihood of the business moving, however, until the Guinness group – of which the brewing company was just one part – acquired a new chairman. J. Walter Thompson was abruptly fired and replaced by a rapidly growing UK agency, Allen

Brady & Marsh, well-known for its brash style and its irritatingly memorable jingles. Guinness advertising promptly disappeared for a period of 12 months, as Guinness and its new agency set about developing the strategy for a major new campaign that would lift the brand out of its long-term doldrums.

The core of the problem was that Guinness did not have the right image to attract the new, younger drinkers. Despite the fact that people had liked the witty advertising, it had not succeeded in encouraging them to drink Guinness. Many of the ads had emphasized the fact that Guinness has to be poured very carefully (to give it its 'head') and that it is an acquired taste (one award-winning poster said: 'I've never tried it because I don't like it'), almost turning Guinness-drinking into a time-honoured ritual.

The new management decided it was time to take the brand off this hallowed pedestal and bring it back to the mainstream drinkers' market, the young C2D men. As it happened, many people thought J. Walter Thompson had found just the strategy to achieve this – 'The Bottle of Guinness Supporters Club', which showed young men in pubs singing about how they had brought a new member into the club – but the campaign was never given long enough to see if it would do the trick.

When the new Guinness campaign was finally unveiled it was described by the firm as 'the most thoroughly researched campaign in the history of British advertising'. Not only market statisticians but sociologists and psychologists were called in, to look not just at the sales figures, but at how the brand was perceived both by regular drinkers and non-drinkers. 'Research told us who the target market must be', said one Guinness executive. '92 per cent of all beer is consumed by men and 79 per cent is consumed by draught drinkers. Among Guinness drinkers, 71 per cent is consumed by working people, the C2Ds. Half of all beer drinking is in the 18 to 34 age bracket and so we needed to lower the Guinness age profile.'

This broad target group, however, was too large to be reached effectively with one campaign, so the target market had then to be defined more specifically. 'We had three choices', said the agency account director. 'We could try to persuade heavy Guinness drinkers to consume even more, but since 8 per cent of our drinkers consume 35 per cent of our volume, this sector seemed unlikely to produce much further growth. We could try to attract new drinkers, but we believed this was unlikely to produce much benefit in the short term.

'However, nearly 70 per cent of those who drink Guinness drink it only occasionally, and they account for only 27 per cent of the volume of Guinness sold. About 1.7 million of these people are below the age of 35. If we could persuade each of these under-35s to drink just one extra pint of Guinness a week, we would sell an extra 300,000 barrels a year. And if every one of our occasional drinkers took an extra pint a week, the increase would be 750,000 barrels a year, doubling Guinness's present draught volume.'

After Allen Brady & Marsh won the Guinness account, it spent a year researching seven separate campaigns. This is one of the commercials from the winning campaign, involving a fictional caring group called 'The Friends of the Guinnless' (*left*).

SFX: Siren and squeal of tyres.
SFX: Door slamming.
SFX: Friendly pub sounds.
F.O.G. PRESENTER: Hi, I'm a Friend.
GIRLFRIEND: Oh, thank heavens. It's my Jimmy. He's come over all Guinnless.
JIMMY: Yeah. Y'know. My taste-buds are screaming...
F.O.G. PRESENTER: Guinness.
JIMMY: Yeah...But it keeps coming out 'Bitter'...'Bitter'.
F.O.G. PRESENTER: OK. Now I want you to take a deep breath and say 'Ness'.
JIMMY: Ness.
F.O.G. PRESENTER: Good. Now say 'Agin'.
JIMMY: Agin.
F.O.G. PRESENTER: Once more...
JIMMY: Ness – Agin.
F.O.G. PRESENTER: Faster.
JIMMY: Ness...Agin. Ness agin Ness aguinnessaguinness. A Guinness. A Guinness. A Guinness!
MVO: Thanks to the skill and dedication of Friends like Kevin, Jimmy made an immediate recovery.

No fewer than seven complete campaigns were prepared and tested, and the campaign that finally ran was pre-tested at five separate stages of its development. The strategy laid down that the campaign must offer no possibility of confusion with another beer; it must present Guinness more as a normal beer that might be enjoyed by anyone, but also as a beer with a unique character; it must challenge the drinker to reassess his or her drinking habits; it must make Guinness more 'top-of-the-mind' and memorable; and it must make it more approachable, a drink more 'for us' and less 'for them'.

The solution arrived at was to depict Guinness as the 'in' drink and to imply that non-Guinness drinkers were the 'out' group, through a humorous campaign centring on the 'Guinnless' – people who had gone too long without a Guinness. A fictitious organization, called the 'Friends of the Guinnless', was devised –

dedicated crusaders, always on hand to offer help, comfort and Guinness to the Guinnless. One TV commercial showed a man practising ordering a Guinness in front of a mirror, under the sympathetic tutelage of a Friend of the Guinnless.

Guinness put an astonishing £7 million behind the advertising campaign which ran in all the main media, and spent several more millions on public relations events, sponsorship and promotion at the point of sale. Despite an unenthusiastic reaction to the campaign within the UK advertising business (which generally felt that the ads fell below the high standards expected of Guinness advertising) awareness of the campaign proved very high, and when the company announced its first financial results after the campaign, it reported that volume sales had increased by almost 10 per cent. Whether the long-term sales decline has been halted, only time will tell.

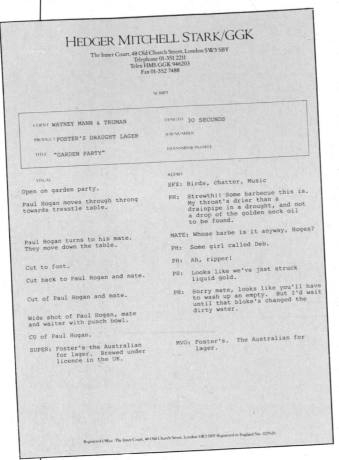

HEDGER MITCHELL STARK/GGK

The Inner Court, 48 Old Church Street, London SW3 5BY
Telephone 01-351 2211
Telex HMS GGK 946203
Fax 01-352 7488

SCRIPT

CLIENT WATNEY MANN & TRUMAN	LENGTH 30 SECONDS
PRODUCT FOSTER'S DRAUGHT LAGER	JOB NUMBER
TITLE "GARDEN PARTY"	TRANSMISSION DATE

VISUAL	AUDIO
Open on garden party.	SFX: Birds, chatter, Music
Paul Hogan moves through throng towards tresstle table.	PH: Strewth!! Some barbecue this is. My throat's drier than a drainpipe in a drought, and not a drop of the golden neck oil to be found.
	MATE: Whose barbe is it anyway, Hoges?
Paul Hogan turns to his mate. They move down the table.	PH: Some girl called Deb.
	PH: Ah, ripper!
Cut to font.	
Cut back to Paul Hogan and mate.	PH: Looks like we've just struck liquid gold.
Cut of Paul Hogan and mate.	PH: Sorry mate, looks like you'll have to wash up an empty. But I'd wait until that bloke's changed the dirty water.
Wide shot of Paul Hogan, mate and waiter with punch bowl.	
CU of Paul Hogan.	
SUPER: Foster's the Australian for lager. Brewed under licence in the UK.	MVO: Foster's. The Australian for lager.

Registered Office: The Inner Court, 48 Old Church Street, London SW3 5BY. Registered in England No. 1127620.

By using the Australian comedian Paul Hogan, Fosters instantly established itself as the Australian lager – and very different from the Continental-sounding brands. The fact that Fosters itself was already synonymous in the United Kingdom with Australian lager obviously helped.

In each commercial Hogan is seen observing British institutions, in this case the garden party, which he refers to as a 'barby' (*above right*).
Agency: Hedger Mitchell Stark.

FOSTERS

Compared with the problems facing John Smith's and Guinness, it might be thought that the marketing of Fosters lager was simple. The lager market was growing, after all, and had trebled its market share in 10 years. The Fosters name was already virtually a synonym for Australian beer in London, thanks to the many Australians who visited the city, for whom a number of pubs stocked specially imported cans. Nevertheless, the very success of the lager market was itself a problem, in that many brewers had launched several brands resulting in dozens of different lagers fighting for attention, most of them trading on their European (ie German, Scandinavian and Dutch) origins, with names beginning with 'Carl-', 'Heidel-' or 'Hof-'.

Watney Mann & Truman Brewers decided that, with all this European emphasis, there was probably room for an Australian lager, and they decided upon Fosters, which is brewed by Carlton and United Breweries of Melbourne. The tricky decision, however, was how to position the brand in the market place. Most firms would have decided that, as an imported lager from one of the less traditional lager countries, Fosters belonged at the premium end of the market where prices are higher but sales are lower, rather than

in the mass-volume draught lager sector. Apart from anything else, Watney Mann already had a successful brand in the volume sector – Carlsberg, which with 15 per cent of the market shared brand leadership – and there was a danger that Fosters might hit Carlsberg sales as much as those of competitors' brands.

Nevertheless, after a great deal of research into the potential of the brand, Watney Mann decided to brew Fosters under licence in the United Kingdom and position it as a standard lager, rather than in the

Here Hogan is introduced to the delights of the wine cellar (*left*). When the tasters all spit the wine out, he concludes he was right to stick to Fosters.

premium sector. In order to succeed with this approach, it required an advertising campaign that would give Fosters a strong Australian image which would appeal to young men – the same market as that for John Smith's and Guinness – but would not take it too down-market. There was a danger that the United Kingdom's conventional image of many Australians – as heavy drinking boors – might rub off on the brand, since Fosters was already seen as an integral part of the typical Australian.

Watney Mann and its agency, Hedger Mitchell Stark, cleverly avoided this by signing up the Australian comedian, Paul Hogan – then unknown to UK audiences – and giving him some very witty scripts in which he was seen observing strange British institutions such as hunting and the weather, with a wry Australian humour.

Fosters was launched on a test basis in the London region only. Within eight months it had captured 6 per cent of the London draught lager market – the long-established brand leaders only had 15 per cent each – and it was rapidly 'rolled out' to other parts of the country. Furthermore, far from reducing sales of Watney Mann's other brands, Fosters stimulated their sales: in those outlets where Fosters was available, the company saw a 12 per cent increase in its total lager sales.

HEDGER MITCHELL STARK/GGK

The Inner Court, 48 Old Church Street, London SW3 5BY
Telephone 01-351 2211
Telex HMS GGK 946203
Fax 01-352 7488

SCRIPT

CLIENT WATNEY MANN & TRUMAN	LENGTH 30 SECONDS
PRODUCT FOSTER'S DRAUGHT LAGER	JOB NUMBER
TITLE "WINE CELLAR"	TRANSMISSION DATE

VISUAL	AUDIO
Panning shot through wine cellar.	SFX: 1½ seconds silence. Contented buzz from wine tasters.
Close in on Paul Hogan who speaks to camera.	PH: G'day. When they invited me along to this turn out I took the precaution of bringing along enough of the amber nectar to go found.
	Looks.....
CU of wine taster sampling product.	....like I did the right thing too 'cos that stuff seems about as popular as a rattlesnake in a lucky dip.
Cut back to PH	
Medium shot of Paul Hogan and wine tasters.	Strewth! Must be worse than I thought.
SUPER: Foster's the Australian for lager. Brewed under licence in the UK.	MVO: Foster's. The Australian for lager.

Registered Office: The Inner Court, 48 Old Church Street, London SW3 5BY Registered in England No. 1127620

PLANNING

When a commercial appears for the first time on the TV screen, or a new poster is put up, the message it is putting across and the way it is executed may seem perfectly straightforward to the people it is aimed at. It may be trying to sell more baked beans, or persuade us to wear a seat belt, or to put our money into a particular bank. Yet behind almost every campaign lies a highly complicated planning process, incorporating a great deal of research, designed to lay down the advertiser's marketing objectives and strategy, and also its advertising objectives and strategy (which may sound the same thing, but are not).

The planning process must determine not only what the advertiser wants to say, but also when, where, how, and to whom it wants to say it (as well as how much money is available). Naturally there are slightly more sophisticated terms for each of these elements of the planning process: the 'who' element is called the target market or audience; the 'where' is the media strategy; the 'how' is the creative strategy; and the 'how much' is the budget.

PRODUCT AND MARKET RESEARCH

Every marketing and advertising exercise – even if it never gets to the stage of being translated into a campaign – has to start with research, because if the company concerned does not know how many customers it has, or what they think of its competitors, it is not likely to be able to deploy the techniques of marketing and advertising effectively. In practice, most organizations have a continuous programme of research, often stretching back many years, which is designed not solely for advertising purposes, but also to help them run their businesses properly.

The sorts of research that are used vary widely from organization to organization, but they come broadly in two forms: quantitative research, designed to find out how many people and what sort of people buy particular goods or like particular goods; and qualitative research, which is aimed at finding out why people buy or like particular goods, what they like most about them, or – often more importantly – what they don't like about them and why they don't buy them.

Quantitative research is done fairly continuously by most organizations, since the measurement of sales is the most basic indication a firm has as to how well it is doing. Companies need to know not only how many items they are selling and which items are doing best, but also how well their competitors and the market as a whole are doing, and whether items are selling better in one part of the country than another. If their sales are going down, they need to know whether this is because customers are buying their competitors' products or because they have stopped buying that item altogether. If the latter is the case, they need to know what the money is being spent on instead.

For grocery firms and companies in some other large markets, the A.C. Nielsen research company provides the most widely accepted sales data in most countries. It provides retail sales audits on many markets, measuring the volume of each product purchased by customers from shops. It uses a large and representative sample of retailers, who allow the Nielsen research executives to call on them every two months and analyse their stock, item by item. The resulting report gives not only the sales data for each firm, but also a great deal of other information such as the average price at which goods were being sold, the levels of stock in each outlet, and each product's market share. Over the next few years such data will become available much more quickly and more frequently, as laser-scanning devices at the check-out desk are used to feed product information directly into a computer.

An alternative method of compiling sales data is by researching the customers rather than the retailers, either by asking a representative sample to fill in diaries listing their purchases each week, or simply by providing them with a bag into which they put all the empty packs they have used. This not only gives the research company data on what sort of people are buying each product (as opposed to simply measuring the volume of sales), but it also takes account of products that are not sold through shops, or which are bought from retailers that do not allow the sales auditors into their stores (such as Boots, the UK's largest chemist). Most marketing companies regularly back up these sales data with research designed to find out how their products are perceived by the customers; how often they use them; how many packets they buy at a time; whether they ever buy the competitors' products as well; why they prefer one brand to another; and so on. For organizations that are not selling things, and thus have no sales data, such research is often the first measure they have of their performance.

All of this research is analysed by the advertiser and the agency in terms of trends in the market place, the level of competition and other factors affecting the sales of the product that need to be taken account of in the preparation of the advertising campaign. In practice, brand share, profit level and the overall performance of the market tend to be the key influences, but all the other factors can be taken into consideration when the marketing and advertising objectives and strategy are being set.

CAMPAIGN OBJECTIVES

Once the research has been analysed, the marketing objectives of a company may look very straightforward – to stop the sales slide, increase sales even faster, or whatever. In fact, when the marketing objective is formally stated, it will generally include specific targets to be achieved, in terms of brand share or actual sales increases. The marketing strategy (the method used to achieve these objectives) may or may not include advertising and, if it does, advertising may only be one of a number of elements in the marketing mix.

Nielsen research executives collect data from selected stores throughout the United Kingdom (*above*).

By and large, the advertising objectives will be different from the marketing objectives in that they will concentrate on the job that advertising has to do, rather than the overall result the marketing company wants to achieve. The advertising strategy will state, in both creative and media terms, how these objectives are to be met. For example, in the case of the launch of Krona, the marketing objective was 'to increase the company's share in the premium sector of the margarine market by securing for Krona a share of at least 5 per cent'. The advertising objective was 'to encourage trial of new Krona margarine by establishing that it is the first margarine with a taste and texture indistinguishable from butter'.

One reason why the advertising objective often has to be different from the marketing objective is that there is often no way of proving that it is the advertising that has increased sales of a product. It is now widely accepted that a great many other factors influence sales, among them price, distribution and competitive activity. For this reason, the advertising objective is often stated in terms that can be more closely linked to the advertising, such as customers' awareness and attitudes to the product, or encouraging trial of a new line. Both awareness and attitude can be measured by research. The effect of a campaign is recorded simply by measuring customers' awareness of and attitude to the product before it

begins, and then again at various stages during and after the campaign. Awareness is a fairly straightforward concept to measure, and is generally researched in two ways – 'spontaneous' and 'prompted'. In the case of spontaneous awareness research, customers are asked simply to name all the brands of, say, breakfast cereal they can remember. For prompted awareness, they are then shown a list of all the cereals on sale, and asked which they have heard of.

Awareness research was used during the launch of Krona and, as in the launch of any new product, it provided a very good measure of whether the advertising had been seen and registered. In the November research, a month after the brand was launched, Krona achieved a spontaneous awareness of 20 per cent and a prompted awareness of 79 per cent of those housewives interviewed. By February, spontaneous awareness was up to 22 per cent, and prompted up to 86 per cent.

Awareness research provides a less obvious measure in the case of a brand that has been on the market for some time, but it can still register significant changes as a result of an advertising campaign either for the brand itself, or for one of its competitors, since awareness of the competitive brands is often as significant for a manufacturer as that of its own. However, awareness on its own is of limited importance to an advertiser, since millions of people may be aware of a product and yet

MANAGEMENT SUMMARY REPORT CONTENTS:

CURRENT PERIOD TABLES: Great Britain tables showing the full range of Nielsen data.

BACK DATA TABLES: Great Britain tables showing consumer sales and market shares on a unit and sterling basis.

For the current period tables eight sets of information are arranged in columns. This range of data is provided for the total product class, the specified brands, sizes etc., and finally all other brands combined.

Here is the key to each column:

CONSUMER SALES £ AT R.S.P.	CONSUMER SALES	RETAILER PURCHASES	RETAILER STOCKS	MONTHS SUPPLY	DISTRIBUTION MAX OS OSF PUR MER % % % % %	AVERAGE STOCKS SALES/M	R.S.P. P
Sales made to consumers computed at retailer selling prices and expressed in sterling. The market shares are shown beneath as percentages.	Sales made to consumers expressed in the units specified by the client. The market shares are shown beneath as percentages.	Purchases made by retailers expressed in the units specified by the client. The market shares are shown beneath as percentages.	Stocks held by retailers in their shops and stockrooms expressed in the units specified by the client. The market shares are shown beneath as percentages.	The number of months retailers' stocks would last at the current rate of sale to consumers.	**SHOP DISTRIBUTION** The percentage of shops which: handled in the period (MAX): were out of stock (OS) or out of stock in the forward selling area (OSF) on the audit day: purchased during the period (PUR): and were giving display support on the audit day (MER) **STERLING DISTRIBUTION** A qualitative figure showing the percentage of total annual Grocery turnover accounted for by shops in each of the above categories.	The average number of units of stocks held by shops handling. The average number of units sold per month to consumers by shops handling.	The average price paid in pence by consumers calculated from the prices observed in self-service shops on the day of audit, and weighted by volume.

PAGE. 01   FOOD   PRODUCT CLASS Z   TOTAL GREAT BRITAIN

UNIT BASIS - TONS - AVERAGES & R.S.P. - LBS.
£ BASIS - THOUSANDS TO 1 D.P.

Nielsen Marketing Research

This report must be kept confidential. The client by contract has undertaken not to reproduce, divulge, or quote any part of it.

E3-JZ

	CONSUMER SALES £ AT R.S.P.	CONSUMER SALES	RETAILER PURCHASES	RETAILER STOCKS	MONTHS SUPPLY	SHOP AC PC MAX	OS	OSF	PUR	MER	AVERAGE STOCKS SALES/M WT.SALES/M	RSP P	FORWARD STOCKS
PRODUCT CLASS Z TOTAL ALL ITEMS	4,115.6 100.0%	1,713.9 100.0%	1,704.5 100.0%	91.9 100.0%	3.3	63 93 100	15 6 3	15 6 3	60 93 100		5.9 54.7 37.1	107.2	88.1 100.0%
BRAND A STANDARD	764.1 18.6%	307.2 17.9%	305.4 17.9%	13.9 15.1%	2.8	18 48 53	6 7 7	6 7 7	17 48 53		3.2 34.9 13.1	111.0	13.1 14.9%
EXTRA	710.5 17.3%	268.4 15.7%	267.6 15.7%	13.9 15.1%	3.2	12 49 55	4 8 10	4 9 10	12 48 53		4.6 44.7 10.9	118.1	13.5 15.3%
BRAND A CONS.	1,474.5 35.8%	575.6 33.6%	573.0 33.6%	27.8 30.3%	2.9	19 33 57	6 8 7	6 8 7	18 51 55	* 2 1	5.9 61.5 22.0	114.3	26.6 30.2%
BRAND B STANDARD	314.6 7.6%	127.7 7.5%	127.1 7.5%	8.0 8.7%	3.8	12 27 29	5 6 5	5 6 5	12 26 28		2.6 20.4 9.1	110.0	7.6 8.6%
EXTRA	373.3 9.1%	141.0 8.2%	140.1 8.2%	9.0 9.8%	3.9	9 36 41	4 7 6	4 7 7	8 34 40		4.1 32.1 8.0	118.1	8.9 10.1%
BRAND B CONS.	687.8 16.7%	268.7 15.7%	267.2 15.7%	17.0 18.5%	3.9	14 41 45	6 7 5	7 7 6	13 40 44	* 1	4.9 39.0 13.3	114.3	16.5 18.7%
ALL OTHERS STANDARD	1,269.8 30.8%	588.1 34.3%	585.4 34.3%	31.2 33.9%	3.2	44 54 62	11 8 6	11 8 6	40 52 61		2.9 27.0 22.0	96.4	29.6 33.6%
EXTRA	683.4 16.6%	281.5 16.4%	278.9 16.4%	15.9 17.3%	3.4	20 43 53	11 6 5	11 6 5	17 41 52		3.2 28.5 13.3	108.4	15.4 17.5%

Nielsen reports contain details of sales by brand and by market for different regions of the country, for individual types of shop and for the country as a whole (*above*). As such, they have become the marketing man's 'Bible' for manufacturers of a wide range of goods.

actively dislike it. People's attitude to the product is of crucial importance, and this too can be measured by research (though the process is less straightforward). At its most basic level, people are asked to rate the product and its competitors on a scale of one to ten, ranging from excellent to very bad. However, it is also possible to measure people's attitudes in other ways, either in terms of particular product qualities such as flavour, value for money and sophistication, or with questions bordering on the psychological, with products being defined in terms of human personalities.

In *What Is A Brand?*, Stephen King cites research in which people are asked to imagine brands as people. When asked about washing powders, this is how one housewife saw the personality of 'Mrs Ariel': 'I think she would be the sort of person who has got to get everything

done, though very well and very efficiently, to have a rather good social life at the same time.

'Very sparkling, she would be the sort who would also have a baby-sitter at the ready, to go out in the evening and take good care of herself; and who likes to keep young and follow trends.'

Thus an advertising campaign's objectives will generally be defined in terms of improving awareness of the product (or maintaining it in the case of a well-established brand leader), or changing people's attitudes towards it. Such forms of measurement cater for the two main tasks that advertising can accomplish – information and persuasion. But there can be other formal objectives for an advertising campaign, even if increasing sales – the most common marketing objective – is a difficult one to measure. One objective might be to encourage the trade to stock a product, or to give it greater shelf-space, since retailers are more likely to welcome a new product if it is being heavily advertised. Alternatively, if the product is sold by direct response rather than through retailers, the objective could be to achieve a specific sales target, since the results of the campaign can be measured quite specifically. In the case of campaigns not intended to sell goods, but to change behaviour – to save energy or wear seat belts, for example – awareness and attitude improvements naturally tend to be the main advertising objectives.

DEFINING THE TARGET AUDIENCE

Having decided what the advertising is designed to achieve, the next task is to work out how it should do it, and this involves producing a creative strategy and deciding which media to use. First, however, it is important to decide who the campaign should be aimed at, since this will affect not only the tone and message of the advertising, but also the media in which the ads are to appear.

Relatively few advertising campaigns are aimed at the whole population, simply because few products are bought equally by everyone, men and women, old and young, North and South. By deciding which sector of the population is most likely to be interested in the product or service, it is possible to produce a more effective campaign by concentrating the money and the message on those people instead of the population as a whole. This is not to say that those less interested or uninterested in the product will have no chance of seeing the advertising – any campaign run on national television will be seen by all sections of the population – but simply that, by knowing who are the most important people to reach, the campaign will have a greater chance of success.

There are several ways of defining a campaign's target market or audience: in terms of demographic factors, such as age, sex, social grade, region and the presence of children; in terms of heavy usage of particular products; and in terms of ownership of products on which the advertiser's product depends. Which factors are of most importance naturally varies from advertiser to advertiser. Some campaigns have a very broad target audience. The Krona launch is a case in point: the prime target market was defined as 'housewives currently spreading salted butter, who are being forced to trade down because of the increasing price of butter, but who do not wish to sacrifice the taste and texture of butter'. Since research showed that such housewives matched the profile of the UK as a whole, demographic factors such as age and class were not important, and the target market for media selection purposes was defined as 'all housewives'. (It is worth noting, by the way, that the term 'housewife' here does not necessarily refer to a married woman or, even, to a woman at all, but is in this context a technical term for anyone who does the household's grocery shopping. In practice, of course, the majority of such 'housewives' are married women.)

For other advertisers, more specific targeting is required. For some packaged goods companies, the target group will be only slightly more detailed than that for

THE NATIONAL READERSHIP SURVEY (UK)
Classification of Social Grades

Grade	%	Description
A	3%	Higher managerial administrative or professional
B	13%	Intermediate managerial administrative or professional
CI	22%	Supervisory or clerical and junior managerial administrative professional
C2	31%	Skilled manual
D	19%	Semi and unskilled manual
E	11%	Those at the lowest levels of subsistence: pensioners, widows casual workers, the unemployed

Socio-economic groupings are widely used in marketing and advertising to define target markets as accurately as possible. In the UK, the National Readership Survey's classification of the population is one of the most basic definitions of a target group (left).

Krona, for example '25- to 44-year-old housewives with children'. For others, social grade is an important factor, because of its use as an accurate guide to the purchasing habits and attitudes of different sections of the population.

Social grade is widely used in the United Kingdom as an element of market targeting, particularly for advertisers in the press, since the wide spectrum of national newspapers and magazines means that titles reach quite specific sections of the population that cannot be defined merely in terms of age or sex. While such grades are undoubtedly useful, as are the other demographic factors, in helping define a target market, how does an advertiser decide which of them to use? It might be thought that in many cases the answer was obvious – margarine will mainly be bought by housewives, beer by men, and so on – but in fact it usually comes back to more research. Not only do different brands of margarine and beer have different profiles of users, and need different creative strategies aimed at different types of people, but in many other markets it is by no means obvious who the main users or purchasers are, hence the need for yet more research.

Advertisers do not have to commission their own market research surveys to find out who their customers are, though many of them do. A great deal of information is available from continuous surveys conducted by research firms, who sell the findings to any company that wants them. One of the most important is the Target Group Index, which is available both in the United States and the United Kingdom, and which analyses a large number of product groups in terms of their users. The products covered include many of the major markets such as beers, cars, detergents, washing machines, soups and slimming products, and the analyses are in terms of the demographic profiles of the heavy, medium and light users, their reading and TV viewing habits (to help with media selection), and in several other ways. Alternatively, the manufacturers in a particular market will club together to pay for basic research, so as not to duplicate each other's efforts and expenditure. Naturally they will supplement these broad data with research of their own that will not be available to their competitors.

Having put together all the research that is available, the advertiser is in a position to define its target market for the campaign. It may be, however, that the exact definition of that target market will depend on the campaign strategy that is devised, in that one sector of the market may be deemed to be the most important for this particular campaign. In practice, therefore, the decision as to the target market is often taken as part of the process of devising the campaign strategy.

DEVISING THE CAMPAIGN STRATEGY

The advertiser now knows where its product stands in the market place. It has determined the marketing objectives (say, to increase volume sales by 5 per cent), and decided that advertising will be used as part of the marketing strategy. It has determined the advertising objectives (say, to increase awareness and trial of the brand among the new generation of adults), and decided, broadly, what the target market is. It must now decide on the creative strategy that will achieve these objectives.

There are a number of points to note at this stage. The first is that the advertising agency will already be closely involved in the planning process. Even if the agency has not been involved in the setting of the marketing objectives and strategy, it will almost certainly be concerned in the setting of the advertising objectives. The second point is that this stage-by-stage planning process does not need to be observed to the letter. Though it often helps to isolate each element, stage-by-stage, in some cases this structure is simply not appropriate. Quite apart from the fact that a good deal of 'post-rationalization' goes on to justify in marketing terms what seems like a good advertising idea, the advertising objectives and strategy can often be devised simultaneously.

Much, of course, depends on whether the agency was already handling the account before the campaign in question, and whether the brand is doing well or badly. For example, if a brand is on the slide or the client has decided for some other reason to change the agency, the advertising objectives may have been determined before the agencies even pitch for the account (though they can obviously attempt to change them if they disagree with them). The objective in that case may be to reposition the product, in which case the creative strategy will have to determine which elements about the product need to be changed or reinforced.

If an agency has handled a brand for 20 years, and it is the market leader, the positioning of the product will have been determined many years previously. The creative strategy for the new campaign will therefore involve more subtle questions of reinforcing the brand's already successful image. It is at this stage, therefore, that all the issues about developing the brand franchise come into play. The elements to be considered include the physical properties of the product, its consumer benefits (and any supporting evidence for these), and the existing positioning of the product and that of its competitors. In the case of Krona, for example, the consumer benefit was this: 'Krona has a taste and texture indistinguishable from butter.' The supporting evidence, as stated by the ad agency, was: 'When the counterpart of Krona was on sale in New South Wales, housewives could not believe it was margarine and a rumour that in fact it was New Zealand butter rewrapped as margarine spread round the State. The result was the brand became brand leader within weeks.' In the case of Yorkie, the basic consumer benefit was the chunky form of the product, but it was decided that this on its own was not enough to provide a sufficiently strong brand platform. The creative strategy was therefore to give the bar a complete personality of its own.

There are several different terms for the way a product is presented to the public – brand image, brand personality, positioning, promise – but they all come down to the selection of one element (occasionally more) of the product that is to be emphasized and built up. One such term that was favoured for many years was USP, standing for Unique Selling Proposition, a concept conceived by the Ted Bates agency. This stated that all ads should make a proposition to the customer that none of its competitors offered. It did not matter whether the product benefit selected was in fact unique, provided that no other brand was using that benefit in its own advertising.

Research is invariably undertaken at this stage of the planning process, to find out how people perceive a product and its competitors, and to test their reaction to alternative creative strategies. Finally, a strategy is decided upon, and it is this creative brief that is given to the agency creative department, and from which they must produce their campaign. Some creative strategies/briefs are quite complex. Others are quite short. Former copy-writer, Peter Mayle, summed up the creative strategy process in his book, *Thirsty Work – Ten Years of Heineken Advertising*, in which he revealed the creative brief given to the copy-writer for the Heineken campaign: 'The creative brief – which is advertising language for all the information that the marketing and research people can provide about the product and the market, plus consumer trends, documented findings, informed guesses, wild speculations, bazaar gossip, conjectures, projections, summaries, suppositions, recommendations and directions – in the end, the creative brief was precise, if a little short. It was, in fact, the very briefest of briefs, and consisted of one word: *refreshment*.'

SETTING THE BUDGET

There are various ways in which companies decide on their advertising budget. Some firms base their budget on sales figures, generally taking a standard percentage of sales revenue, either of the year just gone or of the projected figure for the year ahead. There is no accepted level, and advertising/sales ratios can vary dramatically between markets, and between companies within the same market. Another factor is the amount being spent by a company's competitors. Generally a company's share of its market's advertising expenditure should be roughly equivalent to its share of the market's sales. However, this will naturally be affected by the launch of new products, which usually require large budgets if they are going to establish themselves quickly. If there is a lot of new product activity in a particular market, the advertising-to-sales ratio can alter quite dramatically. Importers tend to spend more on advertising than their home-grown competitors, in order to establish themselves and their products in a new market.

However, the deciding factor when a budget is being finalized will be what a company can afford. If its margins are being squeezed by the retailers and the rising costs of raw materials, an advertiser may find it very hard to spend as much as it should on advertising – indeed, it may decide to stop advertising altogether and rely on cheap prices for sales.

Budgets are also affected by rising media rates. If the cost of television airtime is rising considerably faster than inflation (as it has been in the UK in recent years), advertisers have to decide whether to increase their budgets to keep pace, or simply to settle for less exposure on TV. In fact, the size of the budget may well depend on the medium to be used and the job to be done. While in some cases the budget will be determined right at the start of the planning process at the same time as the marketing objectives and strategy, in others it is not until the advertising objectives have been decided upon that the advertiser can determine the final campaign budget. In practice, however, the advertiser will know, at the time the advertising objectives are being drawn up, the likely overall budget limitations, so the objectives will have to be framed within those constraints. It may be that advertising can be given a greater share of the marketing budget than was originally envisaged.

The end result of all the research that goes into the devising of the campaign strategy is the creative brief. In the case of Heineken (*below*) the creative brief was itself brief – 'refreshment'. *Agency:* Collett Dickenson Pearce.

Consumer research is a key element in the planning of a campaign. Advertisers need to know how their product is perceived in the market-place, and one of the oldest methods of gaining this information is through consumer research conducted in the street (*above*).

BEFORE

AFTER

Heineken. Refreshes the parts other beers cannot reach.

CREATING AND PRODUCING THE ADS

INTRODUCTION

For most people, the next stage of the campaign process is the most exciting and, arguably, the most important, concerned as it is with the end product – the advertisements themselves. A great deal of work has already gone into the advertising campaign. All the marketing information has been analysed, and it has been decided who the target market is and what the role of the advertising must be. The creative strategy has been defined, and now the brief has been passed to the creative department. How does it get turned into advertisements?

This, of course, is the $64,000 question, and if there were a simple answer advertising agencies and their creative teams would not be as well paid as they are. The adage about genius being 1 per cent inspiration and 99 per cent perspiration largely holds true for the advertising business. Some of the best campaigns have their roots in the days and weeks of research that copy-writers can devote to getting to know the client's business

Many of the best ads are inspired by discoveries that copy-writers make when they are researching their clients' business. This famous 1970s poster for the Health Education Council came almost word for word from a Government pamphlet (*right*) *Agency:* Saatchi & Saatchi.

This is what happens when a fly lands on your food.

Flies can't eat solid food, so to soften it up they vomit on it. Then they stamp the vomit in until it's a liquid, usually stamping in a few germs for good measure. Then when it's good and runny they suck it all back again, probably dropping some excrement at the same time. And then, when they've finished eating, it's your turn.

Cover food. Cover eating and drinking utensils. Cover dustbins.

Heineken refreshes the parts other beers cannot reach.

before putting pen to paper, and some of the best copy has been lifted, virtually word for word, from existing literature. David Ogilvy maintains that, before he wrote his most famous ad for Rolls-Royce, he spent three weeks reading about the car and came across the statement that 'at sixty miles an hour, the loudest noise comes from the electric clock'. This became the headline.

Charles Saatchi found the text for his famous 'fly' poster for the Health Education Council almost word for word in a government pamphlet, according to John Webster of Boase Massimi Pollitt, who selected the ad for the book *100 Great Advertisements*. 'This is what happens when a fly lands on your food,' the ad began. 'Flies can't eat solid food, so to soften it up they vomit on it. Then they stamp the vomit in until it's a liquid, usually stamping in a few germs for good measure...'

The perspiration is not only the result of lengthy research and visits to the client's factory – sometimes it is brought on by weeks of thought and lack of inspiration. After eight weeks of such torment, copy-writer Terry Lovelock retreated to a hotel in Marrakesh, where he woke up at 3 o'clock in the morning and penned the immortal line, 'Heineken refreshes the parts other beers cannot reach.'

The problem is not simply one of thinking up a snappy line (or slogan, as people outside the ad business would say). The whole concept of the advertising has to be decided upon, and for any campaign there is a wide variety of possible creative treatments. Humour is one possibility, as in the case of Heineken. Shock is another, as in the HEC ad. Lengthy, reasoned argument is a third technique, as in the case of Rolls-Royce. Other recognized creative techniques include: the demonstration ad, which shows how a product works or looks; the comparative ad, which points out the advantages the product has over one or more named competitors; the testimonial ad, which relies on the endorsement of a satisfied user of the product.

Some ads use a celebrity or a cartoon character to add personality or credibility to their product. Others use mood, fantasy and emotion to persuade people, while still others use a 'slice-of-life' playlet. Not all of these treatments are appropriate for all advertisers. For example, lengthy rational argument is unlikely to be the right way to sell a beer, or any other product that relies heavily on brand image for its sales. Shock can only be used for a few campaigns, usually those which are trying to change people's behaviour rather than persuading them to buy things.

Many of the most famous advertising men have attempted to lay down formulae for successful ads, as if in tablets of stone. Rosser Reeves, with his 'USP', was one, David Ogilvy another. In fact, Ogilvy laid down dozens of rules in his classic book, *Confessions of an Advertising Man*, several of which have been disproved many times over, and some of which he himself now admits to reconsidering. Few advertising people these days would subscribe to the belief that there are rules to fit all occasions. 'If only there *were* a formula,' wrote John Webster in *100 Great Advertisements*. 'If only, for the next new product, all we had to do was a quick factory visit, a squared-up half-tone, a headline in lower case mentioning the brand name and the benefit, we could all get a lot more golf in.

'No, I'm afraid, like the elixir of life, one just doesn't exist. What works in some cases doesn't work in others. How can a solution for a car that does 50 mpg be the same as that for a jelly baby?

'Of course, there is something to be learned from all these accomplished people and all would-be advertisers would be well-advised to milk the benefit of their experience. But there will never be a substitute for original thinking.'

Many ads combine inspiration and perspiration in equal quantities. The famous Heineken line, 'Heineken refreshes the parts other beers cannot reach', was thought up in the middle of the night by a writer who had been wrestling with the problem for eight weeks (*above*).
Agency: Collett Dickenson Pearce.

James Cagney is perhaps an unlikely actor to find in a humorous commercial, as indeed are John Wayne, Humphrey Bogart and George Raft, but all four appear in a 1983 series of ads for Holsten Pils lager. The commercials (as their creators freely admit) were inspired by the feature film *Dead Men Don't Wear Plaid* in which clips from 1930s black and white movies were interspersed with fresh footage to produce a totally new film. In the Holsten commercials, British comedian Griff Rhys-Jones appears to be in conversation with each of the Hollywood stars – visiting Raft in jail; trapped on the ledge of a skyscraper pleading with Bogart to let him in; lending Wayne a bottle-opener in a wartime barracks; and, in this ad (*right*) having Cagney thrown out of a Western saloon, with the words; 'You dirty rat!'

The commercials, like the film, totally depend on the brilliant marrying of the old and new footage. The series has won many awards.
Agency: Gold Greenlees Trott.

HUMOUR

One of David Ogilvy's most famous rules – borrowed, as it happens, from Claude Hopkins – was that 'people don't buy from clowns', thus condemning all humorous advertising at a stroke. He has since modified this view, maintaining that it was true until recently, but that 'the latest wave of factor-analysis reveals that humour can now sell'. This came as something of a relief to him, he says, since he had always hated himself for rejecting the funny commercials submitted to him.

However, even in the mid-'60s, when Ogilvy wrote his book, there was plenty of evidence to suggest that humour, properly channelled, was a powerful sales weapon – and there is even more evidence today. This is particularly the case in the United Kingdom and some other countries, where there is a deep suspicion of salesmanship. In these countries it is accepted that ads for many products must entertain their audience if they are to hold their attention and win them over, as Guinness and Schweppes first demonstrated in the 1930s. Even in the United States, where people do not object so much to being sold to, witty advertising has had an enormous impact on many businesses. In the 1960s, most of these businesses seemed to be clients of Doyle Dane Bernbach, which under the guidance of Bill Bernbach virtually changed the face of advertising, not just in the US but all over the world. Campaigns such as those for Levy's Rye Bread ('You don't have to be Jewish to love Levy's' over a picture of a smiling Indian); for Avis ('When you're only No.2 you try harder. Or else.'); and most notably for Volkswagen, demonstrated that ads didn't have to be entirely serious to produce results.

It was not just their wit that made Doyle Dane's ads different – indeed many of the agency's campaigns were not humorous at all – but there is no doubt that the wry humour played a major part in getting readers and viewers to see companies differently, particularly when those companies had an image problem to overcome. For example, with a car that looked like the Beetle, a touch of wit in the advertising was vital! Likewise, the concept of making a virtue out of being No.2 rather than No.1 could only be accomplished with an element of humour. Neither campaign was designed to raise a belly laugh, but that they were humorous is not in doubt, and no one thought less of either company or its advertising because it didn't manage to keep a totally straight face.

Humour is almost certainly more widely used in advertising in the United Kingdom than it is in other countries and, indeed, to win a UK creative award for a TV or radio commercial these days the ad almost always has to be funny. The fact that a campaign wins awards and is funny does not mean that it is less effective than a hard-selling, strictly factual one, provided that in the pre-testing stage of the campaign it is shown that the message is actually getting across. Even P & G and General Foods, the most die-hard advocates of the hard-sell school of advertising, have recently won awards in the United Kingdom for humorous commercials.

It is often the humorous commercials that are named by the public as the ones they like best. The Cinzano

Long before her 'Dynasty' days, Joan Collins was starring in another highly successful series. Her unlikely partnership with actor Leonard Rossiter for the vermouth firm Cinzano began in the 1970s and is still running, despite a change of agency. The ads depend for their success on the audience knowing that the clumsy Rossiter character is invariably going to spill his Cinzano all over the cool Ms Collins (left).
Agency: Collett Dickenson Pearce.

series in which Leonard Rossiter invariably spills drink over Joan Collins was recently voted the best TV commercial by readers of *TV Times* magazine in the United Kingdom, and many other long-running humorous campaigns such as those for Heineken, PG Tips tea (with the chimps dressed up and drinking tea), and Hamlet cigars regularly feature in the popularity polls. However, while the commercials themselves may be memorable, it does not always follow that the product name is adequately communicated, and there is a very real danger that the humour can get in the way of the message. Many viewers who liked the Rossiter-Collins commercials had difficulty in naming the product (a large number thought it was for Campari, perhaps confusing it with another highly popular series of funny commercials, featuring Cockney actress-model, Lorraine Chase). It is possible to ensure that an advertisement fits the strategy, without necessarily losing the humour. Indeed, when Sony tried to drop John Cleese from its advertising, research showed that this would be a mistake and he was retained.

Hi-fi might be thought an unlikely area for humorous advertising, but in fact most product categories have shown themselves susceptible to humour. In the case of hi-fi, people were found to be very confused about what was available and the use of a comic like Cleese, putting across sales points in a simple way, was found to cut through this confusion. Indeed, another hi-fi firm, Philips, has used the comedians Mel Smith and Griff Rhys-Jones in a similar way. Cars too might have been thought too serious and expensive a subject for humour, but Volkswagen showed that this was not necessarily the case, and Volvo in the United Kingdom has helped prove the point, with extremely wry advertising on radio and in the press.

Humour softens the sales blow and puts the audience in a relaxed and warm frame of mind, in which it is more prepared to listen and accept what is being said. Nevertheless, it is rarely enough for an advertiser simply to amuse its target audience and hope to reap the sales benefit – this strategy is only acceptable if there is virtually nothing to say about the product. In most cases, humour – like music – must be linked to other creative techniques in order to have any effect, and it can be combined with many of the other treatments. It can even, at a certain level, be combined with shock.

The longest-running series of ads on British television is the chimps campaign for PG Tips tea, which has been running for over 25 years. The idea originally came from the Chimps tea parties held at London Zoo, though the chimps are now synonymous with PG Tips rather than tea in general. The 'Mr Shifter' commercial (below) has been screened more often than any other ad since it was made in 1971.
Agency: Davidson Pearce.

SHOCK

Shock and fear are two emotions that the advertising business is very wary of, because of their undoubted power to influence behaviour. Is it right for advertisers to attempt to shock or frighten people into taking some form of action? The answer, in most countries, is that it depends what that form of action is. For example, it is readily admitted in the United Kingdom that the Government is permitted to use creative treatments to persuade people to wear seat belts or observe road safety rules that commercial advertisers cannot.

Before the wearing of seat belts in the front seats of cars became compulsory in the United Kingdom, the Government's Central Office of Information ran an advertising campaign for several years showing the heavily-scarred victims of road crashes. In its pedestrian safety campaign, it showed a car about to hit a pedestrian, and then used the symbolic device of a hammer hitting a peach to convey the likely impact – few viewers could watch without wincing. Another commercial reconstructed the 'unforgettable journey' of a driver going through his windscreen, and subsequently into the operating theatre of a hospital, from the victim's point of view. 'We deliberately tried to create a nightmare,' says the creative man behind the campaign, Ken Dampier. 'We were saying "This isn't happening to somebody else, it's happening to you". Our research showed that most people wanted to wear seat belts, but that they often forgot or couldn't be bothered. A lot of people think it won't happen to them.'

Such techniques would not be permissible for use by commercial firms. The two UK advertising control bodies, the Independent Broadcasting Authority and the Advertising Standards Authority, have clauses in their codes of practice stating that 'advertisements must not without justifiable reason play on fear', the key phrase being 'without justifiable reason'. Fear is sometimes justified, they say, even if a commercial upsets some viewers, but in the case of commercial services or products far greater restraint is demanded.

Strangely enough, it is possible to combine shock and fear with humour, provided the subject matter is appropriate. It has been attempted with road safety advertising – the COI ran a campaign featuring dreadful drivers called 'The Blunders', which proved to be less effective than the straight 'shock, horror' technique – but it is more commonly used for issues of health, such as over-eating or contraception. The Health Education Council, with its agency Saatchi & Saatchi, has managed to produce 'shock' ads with a lightness of touch that, it believes, makes them more acceptable – and ultimately more effective. It ran a TV commercial showing a man stuffing himself with food from the cradle virtually to the grave. He was seen having a heart attack, ending up in hospital, where, in the payoff line, his wife asked him whether he was getting enough to eat.

Perhaps its two most famous ads were, however, for contraception. One was the 'pregnant man' ad which first brought the HEC – and Saatchis – to wide attention, and the second was one showing two pairs of feet and the 'thought bubbles' saying 'I hope he's careful' and 'I hope she's on the pill'. This was the one that was banned by some Fleet Street papers, who were nevertheless happy to carry daily pictures of topless girls. Such levity might not be thought appropriate for ads designed, say, to stop people drinking and driving, though even here puns have been used, for example in a poster showing a man waiting for the last bus, under the headline 'One Man Banned'.

One of the most powerful anti-drink and drive ads in the UK was run not by the Government but by one of the drink companies – Seagram – which ran a commercial in black and white showing the impact the loss of a husband has on a wife, simply by the camera moving through the house, focussing on all his clothes and possessions. The film set out not to shock but to move, through the use of emotion, and demonstrated the enormous impact that such emotional advertising can have.

That humour can successfully be combined with shock is amply demonstrated by this ad for the Health Education Council, promoting contraception (*below*). So shocking did some newspapers find it that they refused to carry it.
Agency: Saatchi & Saatchi.
This ad for the Scottish Health Education Unit (*far right*) also makes its point in a humorous, though shocking, way.
Agency: Hall's.

·Some hope!
Did you know an unplanned baby is born in Britain every few minutes?
The trouble is, it's a great deal easier to start a baby than you think, especially if you take chances.
A man takes a chance if he just hopes the girl is on the pill or is 'safe'.
A girl takes a desperate chance if she just hopes he'll withdraw. (A man sometimes promises to withdraw and then doesn't. And even if he does withdraw, you can still get pregnant).

If you're a man at least ask the girl if she's on the p and wear a contraceptive if she's not. You can buy them from chemists, barbers or slot machines.
If you're a girl you should never rely on a man. You can get advice and free contraceptives from doctors or Family Planning Clinics – whether you are married or not.
You'll find clinics listed in your telephone book.

The Health Education Council
78 New Oxford Street, London WC1A 1AH.

**WHY DO YOU THINK
EVERY PACKET CARRIES A GOVERNMENT HEALTH WARNING?**

Bowater-Scott unashamedly uses emotion to sell its Andrex toilet tissue, using not only Labrador puppies but young children and other animals as well so as to increase the 'aaah' factor (*above*).
Agency: J. Walter Thompson.

EMOTION

Playing on emotional values, usually through a combination of film and music, is one of the most basic and effective techniques in the creative man's repertoire. Many of the most famous campaigns – Coca-Cola, Marlboro, Martini, and almost all boxed chocolates commercials – rely almost entirely on stirring the desires and emotions of the target audience. Many other campaigns – such as those for washing powders – combine the technique with other types of creative treatment, such as a demonstration or a testimonial. Often there is a strong element of fantasy in such commercials.

The account group on the Andrex business at J. Walter Thompson measures the success of their own commercials by what they call the 'Aaah' factor. This is not 'aaah' as at the dentist or even 'aaah' as in Bisto, but the 'aaah' you get when people are watching an eight-week-old labrador puppy gambolling in the leaves with a squirrel, or sliding and falling over on a frozen pond. Andrex has been using the labrador puppy in its advertising for over 10 years, and when the commercials are being tested the number of 'aaahs' they get is seen as one significant measure of whether they are working. The fact that Andrex is a toilet paper shows that the product

itself does not need any intrinsic emotional values for it to use emotion in its advertising. The campaign also shows, however, that a heart-tugging ad can also convey real product benefits – in the case of Andrex this being that it is soft, strong, and very long. For most of the campaign's history, this has been demonstrated by the puppy running off with one end of the paper and unrolling it all round the house, or down to the bottom of the garden, or even along the side of a canal. The unrolling roll is regarded as a strong mnemonic device, and is instantly identified with the Andrex brand. The latest commercials forsake that particular device, but maintain the music, the puppy, and the 'soft, strong and very long' line. This is because the message about Andrex's length – it is longer than most brands on the market – is known to have got home, and there are other aspects of the brand, such as its range of colours, that the company wants to put across.

Advertising can play on a whole range of emotions. The desire for status, the desire to look good, the desire to be a good mother, the desire for things as they used to be. For a while, the last of these – nostalgia – was to be found everywhere, largely thanks to the Hovis brown bread commercials, directed by Ridley Scott, later of *The Duellists* and *Alien*. These soft-focus films, backed by an English horn playing a theme from Dvořák's *New*

All the ads shown here play on emotional values in various ways – fantasy in the case of Badedas (*below*) and Black Magic (*below right*), and love in the case of the Chivas ad written by copy-writer David Abbott.
Agency: Badedas – Allen Brady & Marsh; Chivas Regal – Abbott Mead Vickers; Black Magic – J. Walter Thompson.

Because I've known you all my life.

Because a red Rudge bicycle once made me the happiest boy on the street.

Because you let me play cricket on the lawn.

Because you used to dance in the kitchen with a tea-towel round your waist.

Because your cheque book was always busy on my behalf.

Because our house was always full of books and laughter.

Because of countless Saturday mornings you gave up to watch a small boy play rugby.

Because you never expected too much of me or let me get away with too little.

Because of all the nights you sat working at your desk while I lay sleeping in my bed.

Because you never embarrassed me by talking about the birds and the bees.

Because I know there's a faded newspaper clipping in your wallet about my scholarship.

Because you always made me polish the heels of my shoes as brightly as the toes.

Because you've always been there when I've needed you.

Because you still hug me when we meet.

Because you still buy my mother flowers.

Because you've more than your fair share of grey hairs

and I know who helped put them there.

Because you've remembered my birthday 38 times out of 38.

Because you're a marvellous grandfather.

Because you made my wife feel one of the family.

Because you wanted to go to McDonalds the last time I bought you lunch.

Because you let me make my own mistakes and never once said "I told you so."

Because you still pretend you only need glasses for reading.

Because I don't say thank you as often as I should.

Because it's Father's Day.

Because if you don't deserve Chivas Regal, who does?

World symphony, harked back to the days of the 1920s and 1930s, seen through the eyes of a Yorkshireman looking back to his boyhood. 'Hovis is as good for you as it's always been' was the message. Later Ovaltine, a product which people remembered from the 1940s, was revived with a nostalgic commercial that recreated a wartime street and home in loving detail.

Nostalgia does not have to be schmaltzy, as Boase Massimi Pollitt demonstrated in its series of commercials for Courage Best Bitter, which recreated 1920s pub scenes in black and white. The music is that of a pub piano, and the songs are full of humour. The final few frames, focussed on a pint of bitter, change from monochrome to colour as the voice-over says, 'Remember a pint of Best? Courage do.' Indeed, this element of humour can be vital to those products that are simply not seen as important enough by the public to have too many emotional values attributed to them by their advertising. Frozen peas are a good example of this situation. Birds Eye discovered that a cartoon with an animated pea called Cannonball, who was too big to be chosen by Birds Eye and who sings 'I keep on knocking but I can't get in', was more successful than the previous campaign which used a soft-focus, nostalgic film of a young girl in the countryside with a gently lyrical song entitled, 'Come home to Birds Eye country'.

DEMONSTRATION

In addition to such abstract creative elements as humour, shock and emotion there are several more specific techniques of advertising, the most widely used of which is probably the demonstration. Some creative directors maintain, almost as an inviolable rule, that if the product can be demonstrated and it is being advertised on television, then it *should* be demonstrated. Powerful though a demonstration is, it is rarely enough on its own to establish a brand, and it must usually be linked to other creative treatments to work successfully. It should also be noted that demonstration ads are not simply confined to television – it is possible, though less easy, to demonstrate products in the press too.

A product does not have to have moving parts to be demonstrated. Much demonstration advertising is designed to show how a product looks, rather than how it works. This is particularly the case with food advertising (where it is as important to give the product 'appetite appeal' as to show how easy it is to prepare), and fashion advertising. The posters and press ads for Pretty Polly tights, showing an expanse of elegant leg under headlines such as 'When was the last time a man said you had a great pair of jeans?', are arguably as much demonstration ads as the 30-second commercials showing how a food processor operates.

Often it is the consumer benefit offered by the product, as well as the product itself, that is demonstrated. When Lever Brothers launched Comfort, the first major fabric conditioner in the United Kingdom, it used the device of a glass-sided drawer full of woollen jumpers to show how much thicker and fluffier they became after being washed with Comfort.

All sorts of things can be demonstrated in advertising – the ease with which a margarine spreads, the length of a toilet roll, the amount of luggage a car can hold. The trick is to do the demonstration in a memorable way, as in the case of Andrex's unrolling roll, rather than by using a straight-forward presenter-to-camera technique – though even that, done with style, can have its place.

Demonstration ads are generally confined to television, but this Agfa ad (*right*) shows that print can also use the technique. The upside-down headline makes the point very effectively. *Agency:* SJIP/BBDO.

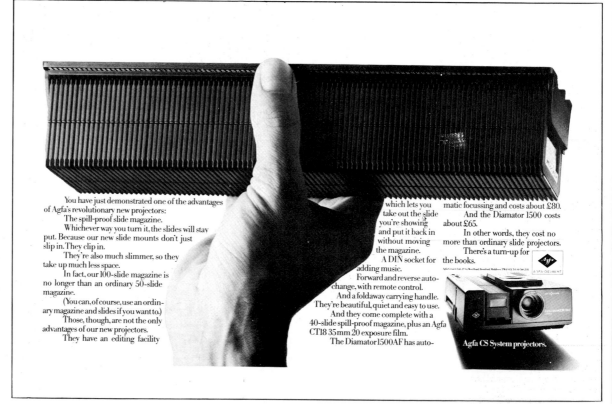

This Vauxhall commercial (*right, far right*) demonstrates just how much can be put into an estate car – four burly men and a marquee. Had viewers not seen it happen, they might not have believed it! *Agency:* Lowe Howard-Spink Campbell-Ewald.

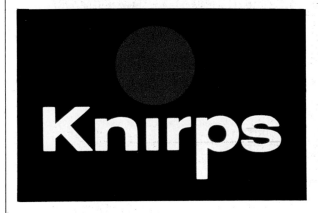

Looks like jeans are on their last legs.

Pretty Polly brings back lovely legs. **PP**

This is a classic demonstration commercial showing how much punishment a collapsible umbrella car take (*above*) — it can survive a car wash. 'You can break a brolley', says the ad, 'but you can't k-nacker a K-nirps.'
Agency: Gold Greenlees Trott.

This is not most people's idea of a demonstration ad (*above*) but in fact it shows the product in action just as dramatically as any TV commercial.
Agency: Collett Dickenson Pearce.

Heineken refreshes the parts other beers cannot reach.

J.R. Ewing is not a conventional presenter, but as a celebrity – albeit fictional – he has been much in demand by advertisers. A Dunlop commercial showed the 'Dallas' oil baron seething at the energy-saving qualities of a new brand of tyre. In this case (*above*) Heineken play on the fact that his face is instantly recognizable.
Agency: Collett Dickenson Pearce.

CELEBRITY PRESENTERS

The role of the presenter in advertisements can vary widely, depending on the job the ad is designed to do. He or she may be there to demonstrate the product, to interview satisfied users, or to give their own testimonial to the effect that they have used the product and found

Ted Turner, the man in the Hathaway shirt.

The classic 'Man in a Hathaway' shirt campaign, featuring a man with an eye patch, has been given a new lease of life by featuring successful men, in this case satellite TV entrepreneur Ted Turner (*right*).
Agency: Ogilvy and Mather.

that it worked. The presenter may be a celebrity, or an unknown – though the mere fact of being in a TV ad will confer recognition, if not stardom. Sometimes the presenter is a model, chosen for particular physical features, such as hair, teeth, or hands, while on other occasions a presenter is used as well as a model, to make the sales points that the model demonstrates. Sometimes the presenter is not seen at all, but merely heard as a 'voice-over'. On other occasions, the presenter is not a real person, but a puppet or cartoon character either created specifically for the brand or borrowed from a TV programme, a film, or a book. What they all have in common is the realization by the advertiser that the product on its own is not enough to make a compelling advertisement.

Normally a presenter is used as an alternative to a playlet, or 'slice-of-life' commercial, since the two types of advertisement tend to be mutually exclusive. Nevertheless, the edges can be blurred and there are commercials in which ordinary housewives are seen to bump into TV personalities in the supermarket, or in which a character in a playlet suddenly turns away and starts talking straight to the camera, as a presenter. The main difference between a presenter commercial and a playlet is the fact that in the former the commercial is talking directly to the audience, while in the latter there is generally no recognition that the audience is there at all, the selling being confined to the voice-over at the end.

Celebrities can be used in both forms of commercial, either as actors in playlets – as in the case of Leonard Rossiter and Joan Collins for Cinzano – or as presenters. There are a number of actors who are quite happy to appear in playlets but who would never accept a job as a presenter, on the grounds that they would be associated too directly with the product and would thus be seen to

Julie Walters' Ireland

IRISH HAND-CRAFT

Some places you go to, you just fall in love with. Head over heels. Ireland's like that. You go there. And you don't ever want to leave. You just feel at home.

It's like being a kid again. Like when I first went to the seaside with my Mum and Dad.

It's a bit to do with the way people in Ireland talk to you. The funny things they say. The way they look after you.

And the way the scenery looks all fresh and magic as if it's just been plonked down in the sea with the paint still wet.

You feel life's somehow really great again, like it always used to be. I'm not certain why they've snapped me in this woollen shop. I said – put me in a grand restaurant, or the theatre, or a dreamy medieval castle. Somewhere really nice.

But they fancied this woollen shop. Mind you, I bought a super jumper for my Mum while I was there. She'll like that.

The most interesting people go to Ireland.

🍀 **Ireland**

The Irish Tourist Board has been featuring celebrities in its ads, in this case *Educating Rita* star Julie Walters (*left*).
Agency: Ayer Barker.

A very powerful use of the celebrity presenter technique is the Goodyear series in which former police chief Sir Robert Mark endorses the safety benefits of the new Goodyear tyre (*above*). Mark's appearance added great credibility to the claims being made by the manufacturer.
Agency: Lowe & Howard-Spink Campbell-Ewald.

be endorsing it, even if they did not go so far as to give a testimonial for it. If the line between being a presenter and giving a testimonial seems a narrow one, it is there nonetheless. Terry Wogan can present an ad for Flora margarine, showing other people eating it, without necessarily saying he uses it himself. In many viewers' minds, the distinction may be too subtle in that as far as they are concerned he is 'advertising' Flora, but in the minds of the advertising control bodies the distinction between a testimonial and a straight presentation role is one of great importance.

The rules laid down in the United Kingdom for testimonial advertising are strict. All testimonials have to be genuine, and those giving testimony – whether celebrities or members of the public – have to sign a statement saying that their comments are true, and that they have not been 'fabricated in return for reward'. Even in the United Kingdom, however, where the regulations governing the content of TV advertising are stricter than in many other countries, there is confusion as to the extent to which a celebrity may be endorsing the product. Many people still believe that famous people who appear in ads 'are only doing it for the money' – which to some extent, of course, they are – without distinguishing between playlets or presenter ads, and commercials in which they are giving a genuine testimonial based on their own experience. However, whether this affects their perception of the product and the likelihood of their buying it is doubtful.

Many creative people maintain that the use of a famous personality is simply a substitute for a good idea. Nevertheless, there are obvious advantages such as: immediate impact; the endowment of the product with the stars' own perceived qualities; public relations and personal appearance opportunities; and, as one creative

director has put it, 'a bigness that can give an impression of really having arrived on a national scale'.

On the other hand, there is always the danger that the personality will be remembered at the expense of the product, or that a particular star will appear in commercials for a number of different advertisers, thus reducing their impact. At one time in the United Kingdom, John Cleese was in so many different commercials it was suggested that there should be a creative award 'for the best use of John Cleese', while in the United States it has been suggested that John Houseman is in similar danger. For this reason, advertisers who want to retain the impact of using a particular star will often 'buy him out' for a year, putting him or her on an exclusive contract for advertising appearances.

One of the best uses of a celebrity in recent years was that of the former Metropolitan Police Commissioner, Sir Robert Mark, by Goodyear in the United Kingdom. Goodyear had a new tyre that enabled cars to brake within a shorter distance and Mark, after seeing the tyre put through its paces, was prepared to appear in the commercial and say, 'I'm convinced it's a major contribution to road safety.' Nevertheless, the appearance of Sir Robert Mark on his own would not have been enough to convince viewers. As with most ads, a combination of creative techniques was used, and in this case Mark presented a demonstration of the tyre in action. In one ad, the width of a zebra crossing was used to show how the shorter braking distance could save lives, while in another a photoprint showed the amount of Goodyear tyre that would touch a wet road, compared with that of an ordinary tyre. In that particular case, the commercial combined the use of a presenter, a celebrity, a testimonial, a demonstration, and a certain amount of shock – though no emotion, fantasy, or humour.

In an effort to break Coca-Cola's dominance in many markets, Pepsi-Cola has been running 'The Pepsi Challenge' (*above*) (in which a member of the public is asked to choose blind the nicest tasting Cola). In the UK the 'taste tests' have been conducted by singer Joe Brown.
Agency: J. Walter Thompson

Volkswagen (*below*) compares the cost of a rail ticket to 40 destinations with the cost of driving in the VW Formel E Golf.
Agency: Doyle Dane Bernbach.

It's enough to drive you off the rails for good.

These costs are based on British Rail second class single tickets. And on the energy saving Volkswagen Formel E Golf which averages 54.3 m.p.g. at a steady 56 m.p.h., with the cost of petrol at £1.59 per gallon.

We appreciate you have to buy a Golf in the first place, but at least you can run it when you want, and take four more adults at no extra cost. Just try that with B.R.

Destination.	Miles.	🚆	VW
Aberdeen to London.	503	£39.00	£14.73
Aberystwyth to London.	211	£21.50	£6.18
Ayr to London.	390	£30.50	£11.42
Birmingham to London.	105	£11.30	£3.07
Bradford to London.	195	£19.60	£5.71
Bristol to London.	115	£11.70	£3.37
Cardiff to London.	167	£14.60	£4.89
Carlisle to London.	301	£27.00	£8.81
Coventry to London.	92	£9.50	£2.69
Derby to London.	123	£11.70	£3.60
Doncaster to London.	159	£16.10	£4.66
Dover to London.	71	£7.00	£2.08
Edinburgh to London.	378	£32.50	£11.07
Exeter to London.	172	£16.30	£5.04
Fishguard to London.	260	£25.50	£7.61
Fort William to London.	497	£39.00	£14.55
Glasgow to London.	397	£30.50	£11.62
Gloucester to London.	109	£10.30	£3.19
Holyhead to London.	268	£22.50	£7.85
Hull to London.	168	£19.10	£4.92
Inverness to London.	536	£40.00	£15.69
Kendal to London.	250	£23.50	£7.32
Leeds to London.	189	£19.10	£5.53
Lincoln to London.	131	£13.30	£3.84
Liverpool to London.	202	£18.90	£5.91
Manchester to London.	185	£18.90	£5.42
Newcastle to London.	274	£28.00	£8.02
Norwich to London.	114	£11.10	£3.34
Oxford to London.	57	£5.60	£1.67
Penzance to London.	281	£28.50	£8.23
Perth to London.	415	£34.50	£12.15
Plymouth to London.	217	£21.00	£6.35
Portsmouth to London.	70	£6.90	£2.05
Salisbury to London.	84	£7.90	£2.46
Sheffield to London.	160	£14.80	£4.69
Shrewsbury to London.	150	£14.50	£4.39
Southampton to London.	77	£7.50	£2.25
Stoke to London.	147	£14.50	£4.30
Worcester to London.	113	£10.30	£3.31
York to London.	193	£19.10	£5.65

Formel E Golf.

OFFICIAL FUEL CONSUMPTION FIGURES FOR THE GOLF FORMEL E - 40.9 M.P.G. (6.9 L/100KM) URBAN, 54.3 M.P.G. (5.2 L/100KM) AT A CONSTANT 56 M.P.H.
FOR MORE INFORMATION ON THE FORMEL E GOLF AND THE RANGE OF FORMEL E MODELS CONTACT: SALES ENQUIRIES, V.A.G. (UNITED KINGDOM) LTD, YEOMANS DRIVE, BLAKELANDS, MILTON KEYNES MK14 5AN.
TEL: MILTON KEYNES 679121. EXPORT & FLEET SALES, PERSONAL EXPORT SALES, 95 BAKER STREET, LONDON W1M 1FB. TEL: (01) 486 8411.

The 'Pepsi Challenge', as it is known, is a blind taste test in which people are invited to taste two colas and say which they prefer. In the United States, Pepsi can make it clear that the other cola is Coca-Cola, but in the United Kingdom, though the comparison is always with Coca-Cola, the ads may not say so, and even the phrase 'two leading colas' had to be dropped after complaints from Pepsi's competitor. Despite these limitations, the Pepsi Challenge has been a success in every country where it has been used. The Pepsi Challenge was designed for markets in which Pepsi has a low brand share, and where 'Coke' is seen as the generic name. It was started in 1975 after product tests in the United States showed that over half the population claimed to prefer the taste of Pepsi to that of Coke, even though sales of Coca-Cola were much higher. In Dallas, the first part of the United States to face the Challenge, Pepsi sales rose by 27 per cent within a year. In Canada, Pepsi sales went up by 58 per cent and in Spain by 30 per cent in the first year of the Challenge. In the United Kingdom, Pepsi's volume sales in the 'off trade' sector rose by no less than 72 per cent, and its market share by 20 per cent.

The campaign is adapted to suit the style and regulations of whichever country it is tried in, and in the United Kingdom, Pepsi's agency J. Walter Thompson decided to use a well-known entertainer, Joe Brown, to oversee the taste tests in the TV commercials. In addition to the TV advertising, Pepsi also conducts taste tests around the country, in stores, shows and exhibitions, so that the public can compare the two colas for itself.

The reason Pepsi cannot mention Coca-Cola in its UK television commercials is because the Independent Broadcasting Authority's regulations forbid the naming of competitors in taste comparisons, on the grounds, it says, that taste is almost entirely subjective. However, products for which factual comparisons can be made, such as cars, may name their competitors for comparison purposes, both on television and in the press. It will be recalled that one of Charles Saatchi's first claims to fame was writing the first 'knocking copy' ad in Britain, in which he compared the Ford Executive with 'grand cars' such as Jaguar, Rover and Mercedes simply by listing the features that each model offered. This technique is now commonplace among car advertisers. However, it is possible to be far more directly critical of a competitor, provided the ads do not unfairly attack or discredit other products. The IBA, which once insisted that no such naming could be permitted, relaxed its rules in the 1970s 'in the interest of vigorous competition and public information', but insists that its technical experts shall check all claims.

One of the best known 'knocking copy' battles in the United Kingdom recently has been that between two lawnmower manufacturers, Qualcast and Flymo, with both sides hurling technical reports and figures at each other as soon as each new ad appears. The battle was started by Qualcast, which makes the traditional cylinder mower, and was designed to halt the seemingly inexorable rise in sales of the rotary mowers, which 'hover' on a cushion of air. Only by naming its main

competitor and tackling it head-on in a performance test, did the agency, Wight Collins Rutherford Scott, feel it could win back the lost ground.

The agency's research showed that the hover was seen as being light and manoeuvrable – a sort of garden Hoover – which made it easy to use. Nevertheless, the research also showed that, when people had a chance to compare the hover with Qualcast's electric cylinder mower, they thought that the cylinder did a better job of cutting the lawn and was just as easy to use. In particular, it collected the clippings, which most hovers in those days did not.

It was decided to show a side-by-side demonstration of the two mowers, but instead of going for a serious approach, with a respected presenter to see fair play, Wight Collins opted for a playlet and a lightness of touch that was unusual for such advertising. The music chosen was 'An English Country Garden', and the jovial country voice of cricket commentator John Arlott provided the voice-over, which concluded with the words: 'The Qualcast Concorde. It's a lot less bovver than a hover.' Flymo immediately complained on several counts to the IBA, but its complaints were rejected. The Qualcast commercial, showing the Concorde leaving a beautiful striped finish and the Flymo leaving cuttings all over the lawn, was allowed to continue, and since then hard-hitting comparative ads have been a feature of

both firms' advertising at various stages.

The danger of such comparative advertising, with both sides making conflicting claims, is that, far from customers getting a clearer idea of the benefits of each product, they are left feeling totally confused. This has happened in the lawnmower market and also in the central heating market, where a particularly virulent outbreak of 'knocking copy' recently occurred between the electricity and gas systems.

After the Electricity Council ran ads stating that electric storage heating could be cheaper than a gas heating system, boosting its sales considerably, the gas heating manufacturers hit back with campaigns dismissing people who had bought electric storage heaters as 'Wallies'. 'Only a Wally thinks bigger is hotter' ran one headline. Another ad showed an electric flex tied in a noose, with the headline 'Gas central heating costs are nowhere near as painful'. People who had recently bought electric storage heaters were naturally upset at the implication that they had been conned.

It is arguable that such advertising does no one very much good, least of all the advertising business, which is trying to present itself as a responsible industry that enables fair competition to flourish and thus helps the consumer. On the other hand, comparative advertising which gives real information and does not rely merely on abuse can be of great value.

This Texas Instruments ad (*above*) gives the reader a side-by-side comparison of the display characteristics of an IBM computer (left) and a TI model. *Agency:* McCann-Erickson

The Gas Central Heating Group hit out at the cost of electric heating with this dramatic picture (*below*). *Agency:* Saatchi & Saatchi.

Gas central heating costs are nowhere near as painful.

Fashion has a major influence on the creative treatment an agency decides upon. The 'surrealist' campaign for Benson & Hedges (started in the 1970s) produced many imitators. This ad (*right*), showing the pack in a birdcage, was one of the earliest. *Agency:* Collett Dickenson Pearce.

MIDDLE T
EVERY PACKET CARRIES A

WHICH TREATMENT?

Faced with this wide range of creative options, many of which could be used for most campaigns, how do the copy-writer and art director know where to begin? What makes one advertiser use a humorous approach for a product when its direct competitors are being advertised in a straightforward factual way? Why does one campaign pile up emotional values on a product when its major rival is simply being presented by a celebrity? The fact is that there is no single 'right' answer. Even when a campaign is demonstrably a huge success, a different creative treatment might still have produced the same results. Nevertheless, there are a number of factors that will influence the type of creative treatment used, and thus narrow the choice down for the creative team. Not least of these is the advertising already being produced by the competitors, and this can work in two ways. If a rival campaign is proving a success, it may well be that the advertiser has discovered

something of crucial importance about the way the market is perceived, in which case all its competitors will have to react and focus on this particular point. In most cases, however, the opposite is true. A favourite phrase of agencies is that they must zig when others are zagging.

Another factor can be the agency's, or advertiser's, own house style. Procter & Gamble has a manual that lays down how its advertising is to be produced, though now it has started winning creative awards there are signs that not everyone is reading it (perhaps it has been updated). A third, highly influential factor is fashion. Ad agencies are just as susceptible to fashion as the general public, and when a particular style of ad catches on the screens and magazines are suddenly full of almost identical advertising. In the mid-1970s, the United Kingdom entered a phase of surrealist advertising, prompted by the highly original Benson & Hedges campaign devised by art director Alan Waldie, then of Collett Dickenson Pearce. The distinctive gold pack was depicted in a variety of unreal settings – in place of a

This Player's No. 6 ad (*top*) was one of a series which many people regarded as a pale imitation of the Benson & Hedges campaign.
Agency: Ogilvy & Mather.

Perhaps more successful, but still hardly original, was the Winston campaign depicting the pack as a skyscraper, thus emphasizing the brand's American origins (*above*).
Agency: KMP.

As defined by H.M.Government

ERNMENT HEALTH WARNING

parrot in a cage, a pyramid, an electric plug, a pen nib and a dozen other unlikely guises.

A variation of the surrealist technique then spread to television. A commercial for Foster Grants sun-glasses, directed by Nick Lewin, full of bright primary colours and quick cuts created a totally 'new look' in television advertising which lasted for several years, by the end of which time even such prosaic products as General Foods' Birds' Dream Topping had succumbed to the genre.

A fourth factor that may influence the creative team is psychological research, though this is far more common in the United States than other countries. While a great deal of motivational research goes into the planning stage of the campaign to determine the positioning and creative strategy for the product, it is mainly in the United States that such factors influence the treatment and execution of the ads. Vance Packard, in a 1981 epilogue to *The Hidden Persuaders*, runs through a number of the techniques apparently used in the United States: subliminal messages such as the word 'sex'

hidden in print ads (the shadows of the ice cubes in a gin ad could reasonably be perceived as spelling s-e-x); pupillometrics, the study of the pupil of the eye to show how intently people are responding to an ad; voice analysis, to show if people are telling the truth when they are asked to comment upon an advertisement; equipment to measure 'body clues', such as buttock movement, during the showing of commercials, to see whether people are bored or interested.

By and large such techniques are eschewed in the United Kingdom, where straightforward group discussions are favoured as the main way of assessing what the likely reaction to an advertisement will be. Such research is, of necessity, used largely as a 'responsive' element of the creative process, in that the creative team will have to produce its ads before the public can comment upon them. Where it can have an effect on the creative content of the advertisement is when the agency uses the results of the research to develop the campaign, rather than using it merely to see whether one ad works better than another.

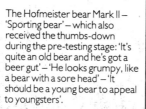

The Hofmeister bear Mark I – 'Sartorial Elegance' – designed to convey the fact that Hofmeister is the best lager. That the strategy did not work is revealed by the comments made during research: 'He looks like he's never been in a pub' – 'The advert's aimed at the higher class, but they drink wine – it's us yobs that drink lager!' – 'He's a snob'.

The Hofmeister bear Mark II – 'Sporting bear' – which also received the thumbs-down during the pre-testing stage: 'It's quite an old bear and he's got a beer gut' – 'He looks grumpy, like a bear with a sore head' – 'It should be a young bear to appeal to youngsters'.

The Hofmeister bear Mark III – 'George' – which proved a hit in research: 'It's the Fonz, a bit like a Flash Harry' – 'A cool dude' – 'Streetwise'.

George in action (*below*) on the pool table in one of the finished commercials.
Agency: Boase Massimi Pollitt.

PRE-TESTING

The creative team has been given its brief and has come up with its proposed campaign, which may include any number of the various creative elements we have discussed. Before anyone goes to the expense of having photographs taken, type set or a commercial filmed, most agencies will take the precaution of finding out what a few members of the public think of the idea.

A good deal of research will already have gone on during the planning stage of the campaign, aimed at finding out what people think of the product and what motivates them to buy it or one of its competitors. However, none of this will tell the agency whether or not the advertisements it has produced in the light of this research will actually get the desired message across – the fact that to the agency the message seems crystal clear does not mean it will be equally apparent to the general public. Sometimes an agency will test the advertising concept before showing it to the client, and while this is not essential it can be useful if the agency recognizes that what it is proposing is risky or breaking new ground. Indeed, if the agency is putting up creative work in a pitch for business, it will help if it can put forward research showing that it was well-received.

The first stage is to test the ad when it is still in the form of a 'rough' (in the case of a press ad), or a 'story-board' and script (in the case of a TV or cinema commercial). The degree of sophistication in the finished work can vary. For example, a press ad can be represented by a very rough drawing and a hand-written headline, or by a photograph and a printed headline. A TV commercial can use a hand-drawn story-board or photos for each frame of the story-board, or even an 'animatic', which is a video made from the drawings or photographs, complete with voice-over.

Sometimes an ad can be put through each of these stages, with research carried out on each occasion, in an effort to ensure that every element of the ad is right. A wide variety of questions can be asked. At the most basic level, respondents are asked to rate them in terms of whether they are interesting or uninteresting, clear or confusing, convincing or unconvincing, entertaining or boring. They can then be asked what they think the main message of the advertisement was, or who they think it was aimed at.

In a group discussion, it is possible to probe far more deeply into what people think of the ad and why. Indeed, Boase Massimi Pollitt, an agency that particularly favours this technique, has a great deal of evidence showing how campaigns have been radically altered by such pre-testing. One such case was that of the Hofmeister bear. Hofmeister is a lager of German origin, which has a picture of a brown bear on the label. A previous advertising campaign had used the bear, showing it drinking in a pub, but this strategy had subsequently been dropped. When BMP was asked to look at the problem, it did some research and discovered that, even though the bear campaign had not been successful, people still associated Hofmeister with the bear – a fact which suggested that it should be brought back. BMP proposed that, instead of the large, intimidating bear that had been used before, the bear should be turned into a cartoon-type character, with an aloof manner, a monocle, bow-tie and tails. The concept behind this characterization was that he had left the forest to learn about the best things in life, such as the opera, how to dress properly, and which was the best lager. The creative director particularly liked the concept, and so did the client, and it was on the basis of this proposal that the agency won the account. Unfortunately, when the concept was tested, it proved to be totally wrong. The groups shown an animatic of the ad thought the lager would be too special, up-market and expensive – but Hofmeister was not intended to be a premium lager.

Gradually, through a succession of animatics and group discussions, the bear was moved downmarket, until he acquired a sharp London accent and style, becoming 'one of the lads', an English version of 'the Fonz'. The fact that he started talking was also significant. In the early ads, there had been a presenter, explaining how the bear had left the jungle and come into society. The group discussions revealed that people were interested in the bear himself, and wanted him to be his own man – there was no need for an intermediary. The bear in its final form has been highly successful, increasing awareness of the brand and its sales significantly. Yet without the pre-testing stage BMP would have gone ahead with the bear in its original form, and the results could have been disastrous.

In another case, the pre-testing discussion groups reprieved John Cleese, who was about to be sacked after several years as the presenter of the Sony commercials in the United Kingdom. BMP won the account with the wrong campaign.

The Sony management had briefed agencies that it wanted to drop Cleese because he had been doing the job too long and was felt to be getting in the way of the product message. Instead, the company wanted to emphasize its position as technological innovators. BMP accepted the brief, and produced a campaign which won it the business. However, when they tested the animatics of this campaign (which the Sony management had been delighted with), the agency planners discovered that all the groups said that the new ads were not as good as those featuring John Cleese. When they probed further, they discovered that the public loved the way he put everything into layman's language. Most people are embarrassed when going into a hi-fi shop for fear of betraying their ignorance, yet Cleese was able to make them understand the benefits of Sony's systems. BMP then had to grit its teeth, and go back and tell the Sony management, including the managing director, that the strategy was wrong. It proposed a new campaign, using a robot version of John Cleese, complete with moustache and funny walk, to emphasize the technology of Sony.

This time the commercial tested perfectly, scoring high marks for entertainment and for getting across the message that Sony invented many products and that they were reliable. The Sony management, to its credit, accepted the change of strategy.

BMP maintains that researching commercials in this way means that more 'creative' – ie seemingly risky – work will be accepted by clients, since they have re-

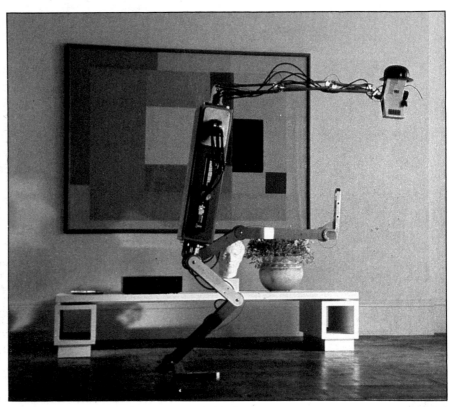

Sony wanted to drop John Cleese (who had been presenting its commercials for several years) and so a totally new campaign was devised. However, during research the public indicated that they felt the new ads were not as good as the Cleese ones. The agency therefore came up with this way (*above*) of meeting the client's brief – to emphasize its record of technological innovation – but still keeping Cleese. The Cleese voice, moustache, bowler hat and silly walk (from *Monty Python's Flying Circus*) make the robot instantly recognizable. *Agency: Boase Massimi Pollitt.*

JW/fs

Television Copy

FINAL SCRIPT

Client: SONY

Product: COMPACT DISC

Date: OCTOBER 17 1983

Producer: BARNABY SPURRIER

Title: "COCOA"

Job No: SON/50/5456

Length: 50 seconds

Colour–B/W:

Vision:

A modern room sparsely furnished but all expensive well-designed pieces. Could be a page out of an Interior Design magazine. The Sony compact disc player sits on a glass shelf.

The door opens, a slim computer enters and stops centre room. The top opens and a long jointed sort of electric arm mysteriously unfolds and hangs above it rather like a sick giraffe. On the end a tiny video camera peers about. Tiny lights flash intermittently with electronic noises.

In a closer shot we see just under the tiny lens is a human moustache. It 'looks' at us. Lights flash as it speaks.

From side panels two long spindly electronic 'legs' shoot out. The computer now walks up and down emulating the famous John Cleese funny walk.

The 'legs' snap back again an 'arm' emerges from higher up the computer. C/U of arm picking up Compact Disc. Arm throws disc onto player. Player 'tray' closes and starts playing. Show electronic counter.

Computer sits on sofa and picks up cup of cocoa and biscuit from small table. C/U of video camera 'head' as claws and small tube emerge to chew up biscuit and slurp cocoa.

Sound:

(Mysterious electronic music)

(FX Whirrs and bleeps)

Computer:
(John Cleese's voice)
Hello, remember me?
Yes you do, you know...

(FX electronic noises)

Well you know those Sony people – computerise everything

Take the new Compact Disc. One hour of Mozart out of a beer mat.
(FX compact disc tray closing)
(Dvorak)
Just listen to that. Pure sound played by laser.* No hisses and crackles of course –
but if you want that all you have to do is munch a biscuit and sip a cup of cocoa.

(FX crunch and slurp)

THE BOASE MASSIMI POLLITT PARTNERSHIP LIMITED
12 BISHOPS BRIDGE ROAD, LONDON W2 6AA 01-262 0011 01-258 3970

The Smash 'Martians' (*right*) were felt to be so outrageous that they were not put forward as a serious proposal. However, it was thought to be worthwhile to test the animatic along with the main campaign – they went down so well that the campaign was built round them.
Agency: Boase Massimi Pollitt.

search on which to base their judgements. A classic example of this is the 'tin men' who advertise Cadbury's instant mashed potato, Smash. One of the creative teams came up with the idea of having tin men from Mars deriving great amusement from the fact that people on Earth still went through the laborious process of peeling, boiling and then mashing potatoes. The idea was felt to be so outrageous that it was not put forward as the main campaign proposal; instead BMP simply asked the client if the animatic could be tacked onto the end of the other campaign when it was tested in group discussion. However, the tin men went down so well in research that there was no alternative but to build the campaign round them. Had the two campaigns not been tested, they would never have seen the light of day.

Not all campaigns are tested in advance, however. Some concepts are felt to be so 'different' that the agency maintains there is no point in researching them, since it will take time for the public to accept them. In other cases, campaigns have researched badly, and yet the client and agency have taken the plunge and gone ahead anyway. The famous surrealist campaign for Benson & Hedges was an example of the former, the famous Heineken campaign an example of the latter. Both

campaigns were produced by Collett Dickenson Pearce.

Once an ad has been completed, it is generally tested again to ensure that it is still on strategy (by this stage, of course, this is equivalent to checking the stable door after the horse has bolted, though it is still possible to make a few minor changes). Finished ads can be tested in more ways – and in more realistic situations – than roughs or animatics, because they can be directly compared with other finished ads. For example, rough ads are generally tested in the home or in the research company's offices, whether the method of research is a group discussion or individual interviews. Once an ad is in a finished state, it can actually be tested in the media, or in a public place such as a hall or a theatre, along with existing ads. A press ad can be pasted into a magazine, or actually printed in a small number of copies by publishers who offer advertisers this particular test facility. A television commercial can be played to a group of people in a hall along with programming and other commercials – later their recall of the ad can be tested and so, in some cases, can its effectiveness in sales terms.

TV commercials can now be tested on the air. In the United Kingdom, Granada Television runs a service called Talkback, using a panel of homes with interactive Viewdata sets. A questionnaire is shown on the TV screen, and by pressing numbered keys viewers can record their response to commercials shown during the course of the evening. Even more sophisticated technology in the United States means that specially-selected commercials can be substituted for alternative commercials in a sample of cable TV homes, without viewers knowing that their ads are different from other people's. By linking this facility to laser-scanning checkouts in local supermarkets, a firm called Behaviour Scan is testing the effect on sales of different commercials. Full-scale tests of advertisements can also be carried out by taking one region of the country and running the ad there, on a test market basis.

Commercials can now be tested on the air through the use of interactive Viewdata sets. Granada TV's Talkback service (*right*) uses an interactive Viewdata service, enabling viewers with special sets to answer questionnaires on the screen.

```
AGB CABLE & VIEWDATA          Page 10191a
              Talkback

Which two of these adjectives best
describe the Brand X commercial?
             Press                    Press
Amusing .....1     Useful.........6
Patronising..2     Boring........7
Informative..3     Run of the mill.8
Entertaining.4     Exciting.......9
Up to date...5     Persuasive.....0

1st answer < >        2nd answer < >
```

Coping with restrictions

A major influence on what sort of creative treatment to adopt can be the restrictions imposed by the codes of practice. This has been particularly the case with cigarette advertising, most notably in the UK, where the inability to say anything positive about the cigarettes themselves inspired the surrealist Benson & Hedges campaign. More recently, Winston – marketed, like B & H, by Gallaher – has come up with a new campaign that confronts the problem head-on (right). All the ads begin with the line, 'We're not allowed to tell you anything about Winston cigarettes, so here's...' *Agency: J. Walter Thompson.*

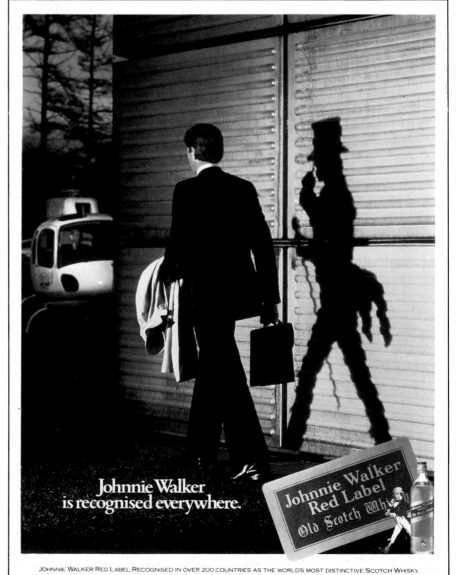

Brand properties

Every advertising agency wants to create a 'brand property' that will encapsulate the image of a product and ensure that extra mileage can be obtained out of the advertising over a period of several years. Naturally this is easier said than done, and there is no straightforward reason why some campaigns and characters should have caught the public's imagination better than others. Here are two of the most successful brand properties: the Esso Tiger (below) and the Johnnie Walker figure (right). The tiger, created by McCann-Erickson, symbolizes Esso all over the world and has appeared in several different guises over the years. At one stage he was a fun cartoon character, encouraging people to 'put a tiger in your tank'. Later, after the 1973 oil crisis, he became a more dignified, powerful beast. The cartoon was abandoned and footage of a real tiger was used in association with developments such as Concorde and exploring for North Sea oil.

The Johnnie Walker figure is a much older symbol of the brand, but is instantly recognizable all over the world, even in Communist countries. When Johnnie Walker Red Label was re-introduced into the UK after a gap of several years following an EEC pricing order, the re-launch ads simply used a picture of the Johnnie Walker figure and the headline, 'Guess who's come marching home?'

This end-frame from the commercial (*right*) pulls the whole strategy together – 'There's stitching. And there's Levi's stitching.' The film is effectively a 'torture-test' – a demonstration that it is possible to catch a marlin on the thread used in Levi's jeans.
Agency: Bartle Bogle Hegarty.

THERE'S STITCHING. AND THERE'S LEVI'S STITCHING.

It is often said that more work goes into the filming and production of a 30-second television commercial than goes into some of the programmes surrounding it. Occasionally, more work goes into the production of a cinema commercial than into the two and a half hours of feature film that follows. Certainly, the production of the 'Stitching' commercial for Levi jeans qualifies as an epic on several counts. The commercial lasts 60 seconds and has been shown in cinemas and on television in the United Kingdom and other countries in Levi's North Europe region, but it could be shown anywhere in the world and be readily understood, for there is no dialogue.

The commercial shows the battle between a deep sea fisherman and a marlin – the most prized catch in fishing. On the big cinema screen, accompanied by a 48-track musical score, it has an enormous impact – but then it had to, for it was the follow-up to the equally dramatic 'Rivets' commercial for Levi. 'Rivets' was the first commercial produced for Levi by a bright new UK agency, Bartle Bogle Hegarty. It showed the various stages in making rivets for the front of Levi jeans – mining the ore, smelting it down and stamping out the copper discs. It was very well received by the target market – 16- to 25-year-olds – and it was regularly applauded in cinemas. Furthermore, research showed that they understood the underlying message behind the commercial, namely that if Levi took this amount of care over a mere rivet, how much care must go into the rest of the jeans?

'Rivets' was always intended to be the first of a series of 'big' commercials designed to reinforce Levi's image as the brand leader, but because such commercials are very expensive – costing well over £100,000 to make – the agency could only afford to make one a year. Conceiving of a follow-up to 'Rivets' was never going to be easy, not least because the agency did not simply want to copy the technique of showing the making of another part of the jeans – nevertheless, 'Son of Rivets' was the working title for the new commercial during the early stages of its development.

The creative process began some three months after the launch of 'Rivets', which had taken place in the spring of 1983. The creative team, copy-writer Mike Cozens and art director Graham Watson, visited the Legler fabric mill in Italy to research ideas for the new commercial. During their visit they read in one of the company's research documents that the thread used for Levi stitching was so strong that it was possible to catch a shark on it. Here was a natural idea for a dramatic commercial – a 'torture test' showing a shark being caught on the Levi thread. Cozens and Watson returned to England and prepared a story-board showing the commercial as they visualized it. Despite the fact that there was to be no dialogue, the copy-writer still had a full part to play, since a shooting script had to be written. The only copy the public would see would be an adaptation of the punch line of the 'Rivets' commercial – 'There's stitching – and there's Levi's stitching.' When the story-board was completed, it was shown first to the agency creative director and then to the account team, who all approved it: it was then presented to the Levi marketing manager, who also liked the idea.

It had been decided that catching a marlin – a very fast type of bill-fish and a real prize for an angler – would be visually more dramatic than catching a shark, since marlin leap out of the water. The first task, therefore, was to discover where in the world it was possible to catch marlin in November, the month in which shooting would have to take place. Experts were consulted and a short list of locations was drawn up, all equally exotic – Panama, the Cayman Islands, the Great Barrier Reef, Kenya, Barbados and a place on the Pacific coast of Mexico, called Cabo St Lucas. Information about each of them – such as the weather, the prevalence of marlin and the clarity of the water (since much of the filming would be underwater) – was fed into a computer by an American firm that specializes in advising on film locations, and Cabo St Lucas was selected.

Meanwhile, the script had been sent for approval to the Independent Television Companies Association – the body which pre-vets all TV commercials. Approval is always sought at the script stage so that any difficulties can be ironed out before the agency goes to the expense of filming. In this case the agency had to provide substantiation of its claim that the Levi thread had a breaking strain of 10 lbs, sufficient to catch a 150 lb fish.

The agency took the precaution of hiring a game fishing expert, Graeme Pullen, as a consultant for the filming. The biggest fear was that having hired an expensive director and a complete film crew for the shoot, no marlin would be caught. The agency also had to find a production company to shoot the film. In practice, what often happens – especially in the case of a complex commercial – is that the agency selects a particular director and uses his or her production company. In this case, there was no question of

Six frames from the agency's story-board (*left*) show how the creative team visualized the commercial. It was on the basis of these illustrations and the script on page 152 that the client accepted the idea. Two of the marlin (*bottom*) caught during the filming of the commercial, with the film's fishing consultant, Graeme Pullen.

On the following two pages is the rough story-board drawn subsequently by the director, Tony Scott, in planning the shot-by-shot detail of the commercial.

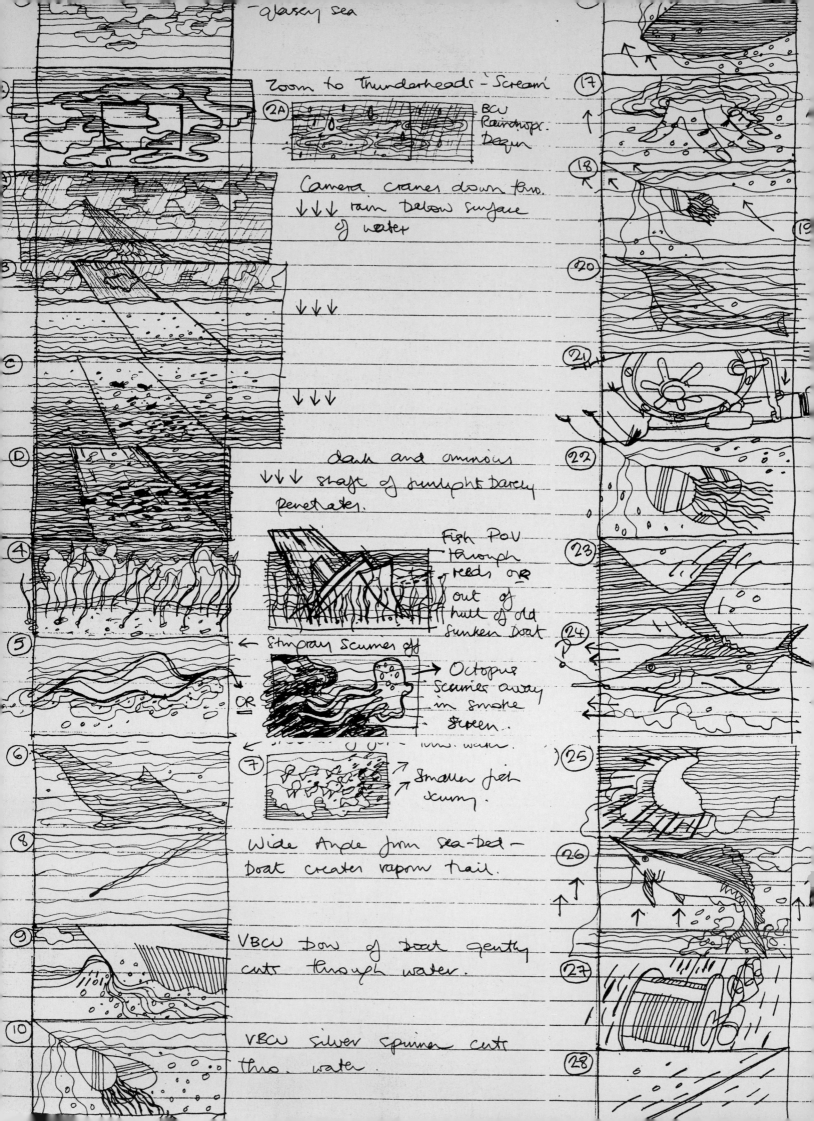

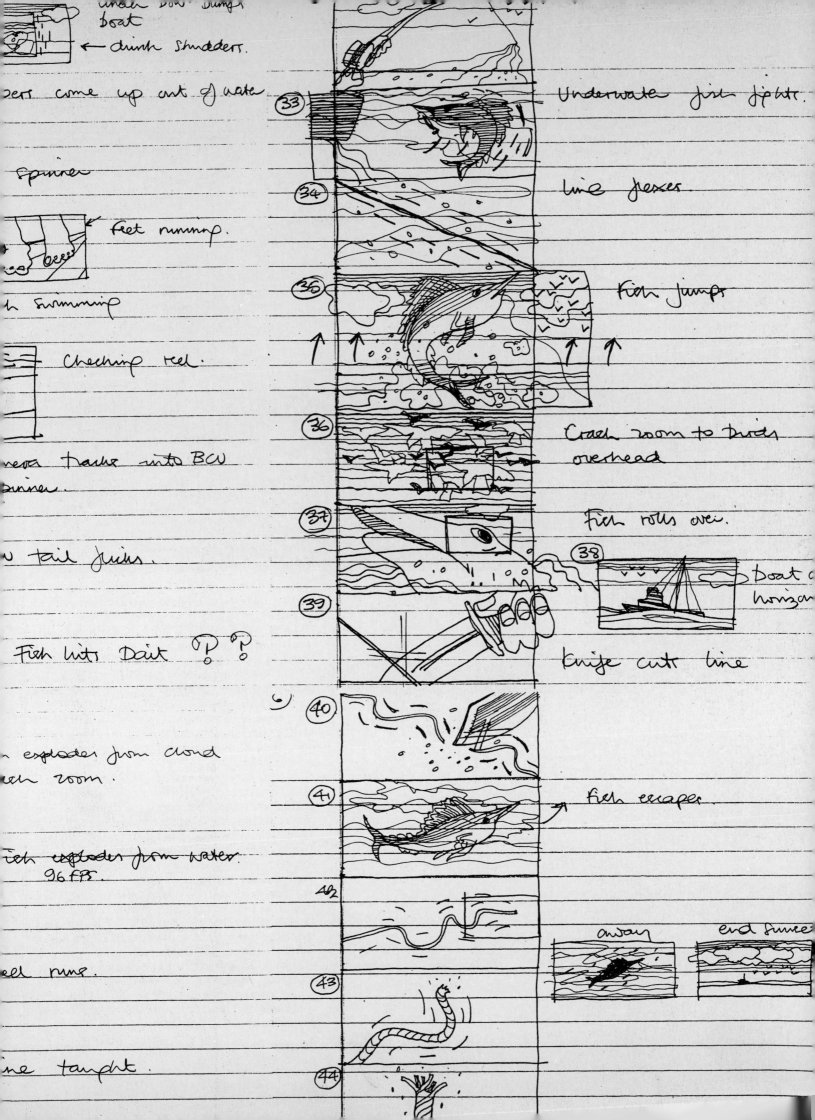

under bow jumps
boat
← drink shudders.

...ers come up out of water   ③③ Underwater fish fights.

spinner   ③④ Line presses.

feet running.

...h swimming   ③⑤ Fish jumps

Checking reel.   ③⑥ Crash zoom to birds overhead

...nera tracks into BCU
...pinner.   ③⑦ Fish rolls over.

...w tail flicks.   ③⑧ Boat / horizon

    ③⑨ Knife cuts line
Fish hits bait ?? ?

    ④⓪
...n explodes from cloud
...h zoom.   ④① fish escapes

...ish explodes from water.
    96 FPS   ④②

...el runs.   away   end scene

...ne taught.   ④③

    ④④

Four cameras were used for the Levi's shoot – three above the water's surface and an underwater camera (*right*). The script (*below*) begins with the camera moving from a shot of the tropical seascape to an underwater shot, in which the marlin is first glimpsed.

Bartle Bogle Hegarty
BARTLE BOGLE HEGARTY LIMITED

SCRIPT

Client	Levi Strauss (UK) Ltd
Product	Jeanswear
Date Typed	July 26th, 1983
Title	Stitching
Ref No.	1
Length	60 seconds

Transmission Date

Visual	Audio
	MUSIC THROUGHOUT.
Open on a Caribbean seascape	
Camera descends into water.	
Tranquil under water scene, various cutaways to tropical fish, plant life etc.	
Cut to a shadow of an ominous looking fish shape.	
The smaller fish disappear in a hurry.	
Cut to the larger fish, which is either a shark or a Marlin.	
Cut to a close up of a fishing reel.	
The fish takes the bait.	
Back to the reel as the line screams out, possible smoke from the friction.	
The rod bends and the line in the water tightens, small globules of water are thrown off in slow motion.	
The fight is on, various cut aways to hands on reel, feet digging in etc.	
Shots of line reaching maximum tension.	
The fish jumps out of the water.	
Cut to shot of the boat mast from very low point of view of the fish.	

putting the job out to several companies for quotations since the agency knew exactly who it wanted.

Their choice was Tony Scott, the brother of *Alien* and *Blade Runner* director Ridley Scott, and himself a noted director of feature films as well as commercials. 'He's a bit like Action Man', says Mike Cozens. 'He climbs mountains in his spare time and he has a reputation for being able to get things done. We knew it was going to be dangerous and difficult, with a lot of filming underwater, and that it had to be done in six days. He was the one we wanted, and fortunately he was available.'

A couple of days before the shooting was due to take place, an advance party flew to Cabo St Lucas to search out the best places for filming – and for marlin. This consisted of the director and the creative team, plus the agency producer (a freelance, David Trollope) and the fishing expert, Graeme Pullen. When filming began they were joined by the client's marketing manager, Peter Shilland; the agency account man, Tim Lindsay; a producer from the production company, Mike Hayes; and a freelance first assistant, Roger Lyons. Most of the film crew were American. They included a 'grip' who had worked on the filming of *Jaws*, and a lighting cameraman, Caleb Deschanel, who was nominated for an Oscar for the cinematography of *The Right Stuff*. In addition, there was the crew of the four boats (two of which were worth a million dollars each) which had been hired for the filming. In all, some 40 people were on hand during the shooting.

In these shots from the finished commercial we see the fisherman (*left*) clad in Levi's, and (*below*) a sequence showing his quarry battling to get away.

Four cameras were used for the shoot – one underwater and three above – and much of the film was shot at high speed so that some could be shown in slow motion for added impact. The cameras were filming simultaneously because it is impossible to tell in advance which part of the sea a marlin is going to emerge from. An enormous amount of film footage was shot in which nothing was seen except sea and sky. In the end the production team had close on 100,000 ft of film – reputedly more than for any commercial in history and, in fact, more than the entire footage shot for the feature film *Some Like It Hot*. (The average for a commercial is around 8,000 feet.) The rushes – the uncut footage – would have lasted 12 hours if shown at normal speed. In fact, the film was run through at high speed, and reduced to two hours of footage in which the marlin and the fisherman appeared.

The film was then cut down to two minutes by director Scott and the film editor back in London, Pam Power of The Film Editors, who then showed it to Cozens and Watson. At this stage, it had to be turned into a 'rough cut' of the actual 60-second commercial, with director, creative team and editor all contributing to the discussion as to which shots should be used and which discarded. When agreement had been reached, the rough cut was shown to the client, who also approved it. All that remained was to add the musical score. As it turned out, this element of the commercial proved to be almost as difficult as the filming – and certainly more time-consuming. Initial-ly two scores were tried – one by Ultravox (the UK rock group which had produced the 'Rivets' music), the other by a French composer, Olivier Bloclaine. Neither was entirely satisfactory, and so another UK rock group, Pink Floyd, were approached and were persuaded to adapt one of their existing tracks for the new film. In the end, however, it was music by Jeremy Healy, formerly of the UK rock group, Hazy Fantazy, that accompanied the commercial.

The main reason why none of the other tracks was used was that none of them performed well enough in research conducted before the commercial was shown publicly. This 'pre-testing' also resulted in some re-editing. For example, the fisherman used for the filming had been one of the crew members of the million-dollar camera-boats – an expert fisherman with a suitably rugged look. He had been filmed wearing a bright red baseball cap and reflecting sunglasses. Unfortunately, in research a number of the target audience felt that he looked too rich and too American, and consequently found it hard to identify with him. The agency decided as a result of the research to re-cut the film so that the fisherman's head would not be seen, thus concentrating the attention totally on the catching of the fish. Finally, the new music track and the re-edited film were married into the final print of the commercial.

'Stitching' received its première in London in the first week of April 1984, nine months after the idea had been conceived in the fabric mill in Italy.

TV COMMERCIALS

The process of creating the concept and pre-testing the advertisement is largely the same whichever medium the ad is intended for. Indeed, many campaigns run in a number of different media using the same basic strategy. For example, the 'Heineken refreshes the parts...' concept was conceived as a television campaign, but it had to be seen to work on posters as well if it was to be accepted, since posters in the United Kingdom are a major medium for beer advertisers. Later it was adapted for the press and for radio.

Nevertheless, some creative teams specialize in a particular medium. Writing a television script requires a very different technique from that needed for a press ad, and a radio script demands different skills again. A single clever copy-line may be equally appropriate for each medium, but turning that line into an advertisement is a separate process. While some copy-writers and art directors feel at home in many media, most teams have their preferences – and these days the main preference is television. This is not simply because television is considered by many people to be the most powerful selling medium, but also because it is one of the most glamorous. The creative scope is far greater on TV than it is in other media (with the obvious exception of cinema, which is even more glamorous). This is partly because of the combination of sound, movement and colour but also, it must be said, because of the opportunities occasionally afforded for filming on location in exotic places, or with well-known actors and actresses, or both. While there may not be much glamour in creating a hard-selling, kitchen-based TV commercial for a scouring product, there is certainly more glamour involved in it than there is in creating a press ad for the same product.

Writing the script

The script is not confined to the *words* used in a commercial – indeed, in some commercials there are virtually no words spoken at all. The script has to convey what is to happen in vision as well as on the soundtrack, complete with cuts, close-ups, music, sound effects and all the other elements that will affect the way the commercial looks, sounds and is made. For this reason, the art director is just as likely as the copy-writer to have a major hand in writing the television script. Most agencies pair their writers and art directors in creative teams, who work in the same room and bounce ideas off each other. Nevertheless, some writers prefer to work alone, subsequently handing their script to an art director who will then put his or her own visual stamp on it. This draft script will, in turn, be looked at by a creative group head (in a larger agency), or the creative director and the agency TV director, who may well have ideas about how it should be done. Finally, after it has been approved by the creative director, it will be shown to the account man, who may well have comments to make on it before it is presented to the client.

The script is divided into two halves, visual (or vision), and audio (or sound), and they are laid out alongside each other so that it is clear how the two marry together. Usually the art director will produce a rough story-board to go with it – a sequence of drawings representing still shots from the commercial – and by the time the script is presented to the client this will probably have been redrawn in more detail, to give a clearer impression of the look of the commercial.

The script has to be written with budgetary considerations in mind, since it is at this stage that £50,000 can be 'spent' at the stroke of a pen. 'Open on a Caribbean seascape', which is how the Levi 'Stitching' script begins, is one of the most expensive five-word sentences a copy-writer can come up with. Compare this with 'Open on interior of a garden shed', which is how the Qualcast script begins.

Thousands of pounds can be saved as well as added on at the script stage. When Alan Parker was working out how to film the Heineken 'Galley' commercial (a spoof 'demonstration' ad in which half of the slaves are given Heineken to drink, and the other half a selection of other beers), the pay-off was that the ship should be discovered to be going round in circles. How could this be filmed without taking all the actors out to the Mediterranean, constructing a floating galley and hiring a helicopter? The answer was very simple – they got someone to say, 'We're going round in circles.' However, there are some problems that cannot be solved that easily and cheaply. For example, in the Levi commercial, it would hardly have been possible to have done away with the fishing sequence, and simply have someone say, 'Catch any marlin today?'

As production costs have risen dramatically in recent years, with some UK commercials costing several hundred thousand pounds, a great deal of ingenuity has gone into creating commercials that do not cost an arm

Thousands of pounds were saved in the making of this commercial for Heineken (*below*) by changing the script. To convey the fact that the galley was going round in circles without having to hire a full-scale floating galley and a helicopter, the script was altered to have someone say; 'We're going round in circles.' *Agency*: Collett Dickenson Pearce.

Television Copy

Client: CADBURYS

Product: SMASH

Date: DECEMBER 2 1982

Producer: LYN GLYDE

SHOOTING SCRIPT

Title: PUMPING TIN

Job No: CAD/30/4730

Length: 30 seconds

Colour–B/W:

This is a typical shooting script (*left*). The vision instructions are on the left and the sound on the right. 'SFX' is shorthand for 'sound effects'.
Agency: Boase Massimi Pollitt.

Vision:	Sound:
Open on gymnasium. We pan past two Martian girls, one on a weight reducer, the other on an exercise bike and reveal Martian muscle man. He is about to lift bar of weights.	1½ seconds silence
Cut to close up of Martian as he jerks the bar over his head.	Anncr: There's nothing like a hard morning's workout...
Cut back to full length shot. He is standing upright but his arms (still holding bar) now reach the floor.	SFX: Martian straining SFX: Clank Anncr:....to build up an appetite.
Cut to door reading 'GYMNASIUM'. The Martian who is now exhausted comes through. Cut to kitchen with Martian taking Smash out of cupboard. C/U granules being poured. C/U Smash being whisked. C/U Smash and steak.	And for something quick and nutritious there's always Cadbury's Smash - real potato pieces that ripple with Vitamin C and soon mix into delicious mashed potato. SFX: Granules) SFX: Whisking) (under anncr.)
Cut to Martian at table. He beats his chest.	Martian: That was good. SFX: Clank! Clank!
Dissolve to Martian back in Gym. He walks on and commences to do a muscleman routine to the 'Wheels' cha cha rhythm.	Leaving you raring to go for your afternoon session. Music: Wheels cha cha. (fades)
Cut to pack shot.	Sung: For Mash get Smash.
Pack also does a muscleman routine TITLE	Music: Cha cha resumes.

THE BOASE MASSIMI POLLITT PARTNERSHIP LIMITED
12 BISHOP'S BRIDGE ROAD, LONDON W2 6AA. 01-262 0011/01-258 3979.

and a leg. This can be done by cutting out actors and exotic locations. It is far easier to cut costs at the script stage than it is once the production process has got under way.

Script approval

The regulatory system for TV advertising varies from country to country, but it is always best to get the script approved by the regulatory body before going to the expense of making the commercial, to ensure that it does not infringe the rules. In the United Kingdom, commercials have to be approved by the Independent Television Companies Association to see that they do not break the Broadcasting Act or the Independent Broadcasting Authority's Code of Advertising Standards and Practice.

The ITCA considers nearly 10,000 new television scripts each year, and has detailed discussions with the agencies on most of them. Many have to be amended, and a number are rejected altogether. Even if a script has been approved, it does not mean that the film itself will be – it may go further than the script indicated – but the ITCA will point out areas for concern at the filming stage. For example, no one associated with alcoholic drink in an advertisement 'should seem to be younger than about 25', according to the rules, and this is something that cannot be accounted for at the script stage.

This animatic for the Persil Automatic 'Showstopper' commercial (right) shows how close a film can come to the original drawings. In this case, the animatic was produced not for research purposes but rather to persuade a sceptical client that the commercial should be made. A full music track was recorded to go with the animatic, and the combination was enough to win the client's approval.
Agency: J. Walter Thompson.

Animatics

Agencies often make an 'animatic' of the commercial to help persuade the client to accept the idea, but it is generally produced for research purposes. Making animatics is a skill in itself, and there are certain artists who make a very good living by producing the drawings. These often require a great deal of character in the faces and detail in the locations, if they are to convey the impression of the finished commercial. Some animatics bear an astonishing resemblance to the shots in the commercial itself.

Nevertheless, an agency will sometimes not bother with an animatic on the grounds that all the impact of a particular commercial lies in the production values, which an animatic could not convey. This was the case with the Levi 'Stitching' commercial, which relied totally on action shots of a man battling with a 150 lb marlin.

Production companies

Once the script has been approved by the client and the regulatory bodies, and the animatic has been approved by the public, the commercial can move into the production stage. The agency's TV production department, together with the creative team, will select a production company and director to make the commercial. Quotes may be taken from two or three companies if the agency does not already know who it wants, but factors that will be taken into account include the company's 'show reel', any special skills required for the particular commercial, the agency's own experience of the firm and the cost.

If the agency does already know which production company it wants, it will give it a highly detailed briefing covering both the artistic and the budgetary elements of the production. This will cover the production techniques to be used, the casting, music, locations and so on. Much of this may be clear from the script and storyboard, but a great many detailed elements will have to be sorted out in discussions between the agency and the production company.

At the end of these discussions, with the full scope of the production clarified, the production company must come up with its estimate of the cost. The cost of commercials these days is frequently a matter of astonishment to many clients, who find it hard to understand how a 30-second commercial can be so expensive. A glance at the standard form used in the United Kingdom for a production quotation, which runs to six foolscap pages, gives a few clues. It is divided into 16 sections, including pre-production expenses, casting, production salaries, unit salaries, equipment costs, studio costs, location charges, recording and dubbing, film editing charges and videotape post-production charges. Each of these is also broken down into a great many separate elements. For example, the unit salaries section includes the following: production manager; assistant director/floor manager; second assistant director; lighting cameraman/lighting director; camera operator/s; focus puller; clapper loader; camera and crane grip/rigger driver; sound crew; make-up; hairdresser; continuity/videotape P.A.; carpenters on location; prop man; painters on location; stills cameraman and materials; home economist; vision mixer; and National Insurance (employer's contribution). While not all of these people will be required for every commercial, most of them will be needed for the majority. Such costs can escalate dramatically if a commercial takes longer to shoot than expected, so the production must be very tightly planned.

In view of these high costs, most advertisers are unwilling to let their agencies appoint a production company until they have estimates from two or three. There are two ways in which this can be done. The first is to give each company a detailed brief, including the script, the method of filming to be used, the location selected and the number of days' shooting required. In such cases, the estimates received back from each company will often be within a few hundred pounds of each other.

An alternative method is to give a very short brief to each company, consisting of the script and a little

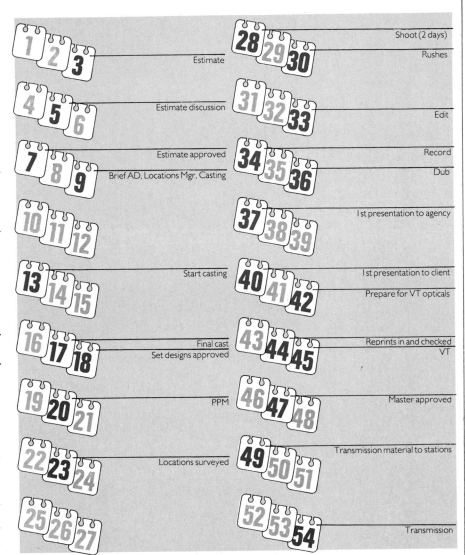

This chart (above) shows the ideal schedule for the preparation of a TV campaign, as recommended by Mike Gilmour, former head of TV at JWT and now managing director of the James Garrett production company. Very few commercials receive this amount of time. If the time is halved, as it often is, says Gilmour, the 'thinking time' is halved and costs increase. Every working week under 11 weeks (the 54 days in the chart) spent on the commercial can add 3 per cent to the bottom-line costs.

The standard production quotation form used by advertisers, agencies and production companies in the UK runs to six foolscap pages and is divided into 16 sections, each of which is further sub-divided (left). This gives a clue as to why commercials are as expensive as they are.

Directors like Ridley Scott and Hugh Hudson learned their craft in the advertising business before becoming successful feature film directors – Scott with *Alien* and *Blade Runner*, Hudson with *Chariots of Fire* and *Greystoke*. Other British commercials directors such as Alan Parker and Adrian Lyne have also been snapped up by Hollywood, so much so that creative directors have complained about the drain of the best talent. Nevertheless, most of these directors still make commercials when their schedules allow. Indeed, some of their commercials are mini-feature films in themselves, costing hundreds of thousands of pounds.

Hugh Hudson's spectacular cinema commercial for Benson & Hedges is a real epic. It shows what looks like an enormous obelisk (*above*) being dredged from the Thames: it turns out to be an enormous gold pack of Benson & Hedges which becomes the centre-piece of a Tutankhamen-style exhibition, generating long queues of sightseers.
Agency: Collett Dickenson Pearce.

Ridley Scott's commercial for Chanel (*right*) is dramatically shot and slightly surreal as piano keys, skyscrapers and formal gardens blend into one another.

background information about the effect the agency is trying to achieve, and then leave it up to each company to say how it would film the commercial and how much it would cost. Often this method can result in huge differences in the quotes put forward. J. Walter Thompson's head of television production, Mike Gilmour, used this technique when choosing a production company to make a commercial for Cockburn's Port. The commercial was to be set on a Russian submarine that had just picked up some British naval officers, and there needed to be shots of both the outside and inside of the vessel, including one of it cruising along on the surface of the water. JWT got three different quotes from production companies, each proposing a different location for the filming.

Company A had found the shell of a submarine in Malta which could be re-dressed for the purposes of the commercial. The outside shots would require an actual submarine and lifeboat. It reckoned it would need two days for travelling to Malta and back, one day to dress the submarine and set up everything for filming, two days' shooting in Malta and two days' shooting in a studio in London – making eight days in all.

Company B recommended using a British submarine, dressed to make it look Russian, which could be done in Portsmouth. It allowed for two days for shooting in Portsmouth, two for travelling there and back, and a further two for studio shooting – making six in all.

Company C suggested the film could be made entirely on Staines reservoir and in a studio at Barnes, both in London. The shooting would take two days, including a spare day as weather insurance. The exterior shot would be done with a 12-foot model, and the Staines skyline painted out at the post-production stage. The difference in cost was £25,000, and JWT plumped for company C. The commercial has since won a number of creative awards.

Another epic, this time shot by Ridley Scott, is the Apple Macintosh commercial (*above, right*) based on Orwell's 1984. It cost $400,000 to produce, and over 200 'extras' were used.
Agency: Chiat/Day.

This commercial for Cockburn's Port (*below*) was set on a Russian submarine, and was made in England. Another production company proposed to shoot the commercial in Malta, and quoted a sum £25,000 higher than that actually paid.
Agency: J. Walter Thompson.

Lyric A – "I'd Like to Buy the World a Coke"

I'd like to teach the world to sing
In perfect harmony
I'd like to buy the world a Coke
And keep it company
(That's the song I sing)
I'd like to teach the world to sing
And keep it company
I'd like to buy the world a Coke
And keep it company
(That's the song I sing)

© copyright 1971
by Shada Music Incorporated

Lyric B – "I'd Like to Teach the World to Sing"
(By Bill Backer, Billy Davis, Roger Cook & Roger Greenaway)

I'd like to build the world a home
And furnish it with love
Grow apple trees and honey bees
And snow white turtle doves
I'd like to teach the world to sing in
perfect harmony
I'd like to hold it in my arms
And keep it company.

I'd like to see the world for once
All standing hand in hand
And hear them echo through the hills
For peace throughout the land
That's the song I hear
(I'd like to teach the world to sing)
Like the world to sing today
(In perfect harmony)
A song of peace that echoes on
And never goes away.

© Copyright 1971
by Shada Music Incorporated

Perhaps the most successful advertising music of all time was the song 'I'd like to buy the world a coke' (above) from the 1971 Coca-Cola 'Hilltop' commercial, which became a world-wide hit as 'I'd like to teach the world to sing'. After that, every advertiser wanted to have a No. I hit. Agency: McCann-Erickson.

Casting

A few large agencies have their own casting department, but most rely on the TV producer or creative teams (often with the help of outside freelances) to select the actors, actresses and models for the commercial. Either way, correct casting is of crucial importance to the commercial's success.

If the commercial calls for the use of a celebrity, this may well have been specified in the script – indeed some scripts are built totally around the personality of a well-known character – but it is often the less well-known faces that are hardest to select. Many commercials call for 'typical' families, while others require people who have particularly photogenic teeth, hands or legs, depending on the product. Voices too have to be chosen very carefully.

If the commercial produced is intended to be the first of a long-running series, the actor or actress needs to be told, since, while a regular income will no doubt be very welcome, some people are worried about being type-cast in a particular advertising role which will then make it difficult for them to get other acting work.

Choosing locations

The first decision that must be taken here is whether the commercial can be shot in a studio, or whether an outside location is necessary. 'Outside' does not necessarily imply open-air – many commercials are shot inside real homes, partly because of the cost of building sets in a studio, and partly for greater realism. With the advent of lightweight and mobile filming and lighting equipment, this has become common practice.

An average studio set can take two days to build with a labour force of 10, while all the furniture and contents used have to be hired or bought. For one day's filming, a studio has to be hired for four days, to allow for the building and dismantling of the set.

Outdoor locations do not necessarily have to be in hot parts of the world, but they often are, simply because the weather is better and, with an expensive film crew on hand, it is more likely that the film will be completed on schedule. Nevertheless, this can backfire as J. Walter Thompson discovered when they went to California in August to shoot two 'typically English' outdoor commercials for Andrex, and encountered torrential rain for three days, which not only prevented filming but also flooded the location.

The complexity of choosing the right location was exemplified by the Levi commercial. The agency, Bartle Bogle Hegarty, and the production company, RSA, had to find the best area in the world for marlin fishing, since they could not afford to spend two weeks on location and not catch anything. They also required a very detailed weather report for the area, since much of the filming was underwater and would have been impossible in choppy seas. However, for less specialized requirements, there are companies that keep files on potential film locations.

Music

A third element – and one even more important to the final success of the commercial – is music. Like casting, this can be built into the script stage if the creative team already know a piece of music that they would like to use – indeed some commercials have been built round existing music, one of the earliest and best-known of which was the jingle 'The Esso sign means happy motoring', to a tune from *Carmen*.

It is more common for the music to be selected later, either from existing work or composed specifically for the commercial. The relationship between the music world and advertising works both ways, in that, while advertising often borrows existing tunes, a number of songs created for commercials have themselves become hits. Perhaps the best-known example of this was 'I'd like to buy the world a Coke', written by Roger Greenaway and Roger Cook, which later became a world-wide hit as 'I'd like to teach the world to sing'. Another example was 'Jeans On' by David Dundas, which topped the charts in the United Kingdom after being composed to promote Brutus Jeans.

After a while, it is sometimes hard to know which came first – the commercial or the hit song. This 'chicken and egg' situation has occurred with the Chas 'n' Dave music for Courage Best Bitter. Their first song 'Gertcha' was heard and adapted by creative director, John Webster, for the commercial, after which some songs were composed to order. In all cases, the words have to be changed before they can be released as records, to remove the advertising element.

Noel Coward's famous line about the potency of cheap music is nowhere truer than in the advertising business, though in many cases the music does not come cheap at all. It is possible to use recorded library music – and it has been done very successfully – but in most cases music will have to be specially recorded, either because it is newly-composed, or because it has been adapted, perhaps with new words or simply to fit into 30 seconds. Music is the most memorable element of many commercials, and for a number of advertisers it has become an integral part of the brand property. Barry Day, for example, maintains that Martini's brand property lies not in the slogan, 'The right one', but in the imaginative world created consistently in the advertising and evoked specifically by the Martini theme music.

Some advertisers simply use a jingle – a jolly combination of words and music, often quite short, that sticks in the brain, along with the brand name that is normally firmly built into it. Others use background music to convey a particular mood or emotion, and it is here that classical music tends most often to be borrowed. Dvořák's *New World* symphony now conveys the name Hovis to most people in the United Kingdom, while Bach's *Air on a G String* is totally linked in many people's minds with TV commercials featuring disastrous happenings, a shrug of the shoulders and the immortal line 'Happiness is a cigar called Hamlet'.

One advantage of classical music is that it is often out of copyright, and so can be borrowed and played about with as the agency or production company thinks fit. Agencies that have tried to adapt more recent 'classics' have found that some composers have placed very stringent restrictions on the use of their music for advertising purposes, often simply prohibiting it altogether. Even when the adaptation changes the order of the notes, but maintains the style of an original score, there can still be copyright problems, as many people found when the Vangelis music for the film, *Chariots of Fire*, became fashionable and versions of it started appearing in commercials.

The music will usually be put together after the filming has taken place, along with the rest of the soundtrack, as part of the post-production process.

Television Copy

Client: COURAGE

Product: Best Bitter

Date: 29th October 1981

Producer: Maggie Doyle

SHOOTING SCRIPT

Title: Margate

Job No: COU/40/4265

Length: 40 seconds

Colour-B/W:

Vision:	Sound:
Entire film shot 1930 period in black and white	Music by Chas and Dave based on tune of 'Massage Parlour'
Open on apparent still of outside of grocer's shop. Suddenly several assistants in long white aprons, appear like penguins busying in and out of shop. (Speeded up action).	Sung: Well I've been working hard to reach me target.
Cut to charabang full of people posing for photo. Zoom to see 3 young men (still).	To earn a few bob to take me down to Margate.
Cut to old picture of Margate pier. Quick cuts of men in bathing suits individually doing hand stands, being buried in sand etc on beach. (stills).	
Cut to still of 3 eating winkles with pins. Suddenly stills move as mouths chew frantically.	The winkles took some chewing
Cut to general shots of Margate in the rain (stills). Cut to 3 men about to enter pub. (still)	But the rain was nice and warm
3 heads turns to look off-screen L. Quick cuts of girl wiggling around in bathing costume (stills).	On the way to the pub I fell in love
Final shot of girl is live. Large daunting fully clothed mother walks on to join her daughter.	But I don't think much of your'n. No I don't reckon your one.
Cut to still of old man in party. paddling in sea, trousers rolled up	Roll up your trousers.
Cut to 3 pints being raised to music. Cut to C/U man drinking. (still) Cut to 3 drinking and talking (still).	Courage Best Mate.
Cut to C/U fishes head with mouth opening and closing.	wash out your gills and jellied eels are good for your brain.
Cut to jellied eel stall (still) Cut to hero feeding jellied eel girl from beach (live).	

THE BOASE M
12 BISHOPS BR

For Courage Best Bitter, the musical duo Chas and Dave adapt and play tunes of the 1920s and 1930s in a pub 'sing-song' style (*above, right*).
Agency: Boase Massimi Pollitt.

Hovis is a good example of an advertiser borrowing an existing classical 'hit' and making it its own. Dvořák's *New World* symphony is now firmly linked in British minds with the sepia-toned Hovis ads (*left*).
Agency: Collett Dickenson Pearce.

Nine frames from the Andrex 'Spring' commercial made on location in California (*right*). Getting the Labrador puppy to play with the rabbit instead of chasing it off the set was not an easy task!
Agency: J. Walter Thompson.

LOCATIONS

For many years, Bowater-Scott and its agency, J. Walter Thompson, have advertised Andrex toilet tissue by showing a Labrador puppy unrolling the paper around a garden, a house, or, on one occasion, along a canal. In this way they communicated the message that Andrex is 'soft, strong and very long'.

While reappraising the campaign, the agency decided that they wanted to increase the 'aaah factor' – the number of 'aaahs' from the audience when they see a puppy playing – and to do this they decided to show the Labrador puppy playing with other lovable animals in four commercials based on the four seasons of the year. The filming of the first three demonstrated many of the problems that can occur when making commercials.

The first two to be made were 'Spring', in which the puppy would be seen gambolling with a rabbit, and 'Autumn', in which its playmate would be a squirrel. Because of the uncertainties of the English climate, even in August, it was decided to film in California and re-create an 'English countryside' there.

When the agency and production team arrived in California it rained for three days, flooding the site chosen for filming. (There were other unforeseen disasters: one of the animal trainers was shot by his wife, and a truck carrying several members of the crew was involved in a road accident.)

Eventually the weather cleared up and the filming began. This involved 25 Labrador puppies, each aged between six and eight weeks, over 30 cases of Andrex toilet rolls (yellow for the Spring commercial, orange

The Andrex 'Autumn' commercial shot in a California dressed to look like England, required 2,000 plastic autumn leaves and a very patient film crew (*right, far right*). An additional hazard, not anticipated, was that a tree fell on one of the crew's trucks (*far right*).

The 'Spring' Andrex commercial involved the planting of 200 fake daffodils in order to create an English Spring scene in California (*left, below centre*).

Director David Thorpe tries to coax the Andrex puppy to gambol in the artificial snow (*right*). A selection of contact prints from the studio shoot shows the puppy's two co-stars (*far right*).

for the Autumn one) and 35 people, and all had to be transported to the site each day. It also required 200 fake daffodils, made of yellow silk, and 2,000 brown plastic leaves.

Predictably, there were problems with the animals. As soon as the puppy started gambolling with the rabbit (there were three rabbits in all) its natural instincts took over, with the unfortunate result that instead of sitting quite peacefully in front of the camera, looking soft and cuddly, the rabbit raced away terrified. Similarly, one of the two squirrels moved so fast that all that could be seen on the film was a grey streak. Nevertheless, at the end of two days' shooting, carefully supervised by animal handlers and vets, the agency reckoned it had sufficient material. It also had 35,000 ft of film – not much compared with the 'Stitching' commercial, perhaps, but still a great deal more than most commercials.

When it came to filming the 'Winter' commercial, which involved a great deal of snow, blue sky and a white duck, it was decided that to film on location was out of the question. Quite apart from the experience gained in California concerning the reliability of the weather, it was apparent that real snow and toilet tissue would result in a great deal of soggy paper, not to mention a cold and wet Labrador puppy. Even if these had not been sufficient problems, the fact that the puppy would leave footprints everywhere, thus necessitating moving the camera every few minutes, clin-

ched the issue. The commercial would have to be shot in a studio. How this was to be done was not clear, so JWT put the commission out to tender. Two directors, Tony May, who had directed 'Spring' and 'Autumn', and another experienced commercials' director, David Thorpe, were each asked to come up with a solution, and Thorpe's was chosen.

Thorpe suggested creating a garden in a studio with polystyrene and a special foam, using a thin layer of salt for the close-up shots. The blue sky would simply be a painted backcloth, the ice would be perspex. Vets were consulted to see if the artificial snow presented any risks to the puppies: they gave it the all-clear. Nevertheless, the client was not convinced that a studio shot could be made to look sufficiently realistic. A showing of another JWT commercial, for Crown Paints, also produced in a studio, swung the issue and permission was given for the production to go ahead.

The garden set was built at Shepperton studios, 4 ft off the ground for the convenience of the cameras. It took five days to build, and the shoot took three. As before, the puppies did not get on very well with their co-star, but nevertheless enough shots showing both the duck and the puppy were achieved. (The agency had originally wanted to use a robin, but wildlife protection regulations prevented this.)

In the end, the agency had 11,000 ft of film, of which some 5 per cent was worth considering for inclusion in the 30-second commercial.

The production gallery (above) is the heart of the whole post – production operation. Experienced technicians operate a bank of monitors so that every stage of the process can be supervised.

Post-production

After each day's shooting, the film is sent to the laboratory for processing and printing, coming back in the form of 'rushes' – prints of the entire day's material. The Andrex commercials generated 35,000 feet of film, lasting some 5 hours if shown non-stop, while the Levi shoot ended up 90,000 feet lasting 11 hours (much was shot at high speed, to produce slow motion effects). All this, remember, was for commercials that will last for, at most, 90 seconds. Few shoots produce as much film as these two, but even so most will produce an hour of material to be gone through and cut down to a minute or even less.

At this stage, the film is put in the hands of an editor who has to reduce it to the required length, working closely with the director and the agency's TV producer. In the meantime, work will be going on on the soundtrack. While any dialogue on the commercial will have been recorded at the shooting stage, other sound material (whether music or sound effects) will be added on afterwards. This process will go on at the same time as the film is being edited, since the visual and sound elements of the commercial must match exactly. This is known as the 'double-head' stage, with the two elements of the commercial – soundtrack and film – being run through in parallel and changed independently of each other. Eventually, the two parts are put together, along with the 'opticals' and other special effects that may have to be added to the commercial. Normally the client will be called in to approve the film before it is sent

back to the laboratory for this final stage to take place.

Optical effects include any lettering that is required on the screen, or switches from one scene to another, such as 'dissolves', which are designed to soften the effect of a straight cut. They involve taking a duplicate of those frames that need altering, and then working on them frame by frame to produce the desired effect. (Videotape, which is becoming increasingly prevalent in the production of commercials, can produce such effects almost instantaneously.) At this stage, the print also has to be 'graded' to ensure the colour quality is correct all the way through. Eventually, all these elements come together in the final print, with sound and vision perfectly married.

The commercial now has to be put into a form in which it can be transmitted by the television stations, and there are several ways in which this can be done. One is to produce 'bulk prints' of the commercial, which are then sent to each of the TV stations. In the United Kingdom, there are 16 TV contractors, each of whom stipulates that it requires six bulk prints, to arrive a week before scheduled transmission – since each print costs a fair amount to produce, this method is becoming much less common. However, it is still used for cinemas, and here the need is for many more bulk prints.

The alternative is to transfer the film onto videotape, and either put it onto a spool and physically send it to the TV station (which only needs one copy), or to have it piped direct to each station by landline, through one of the video facilities companies.

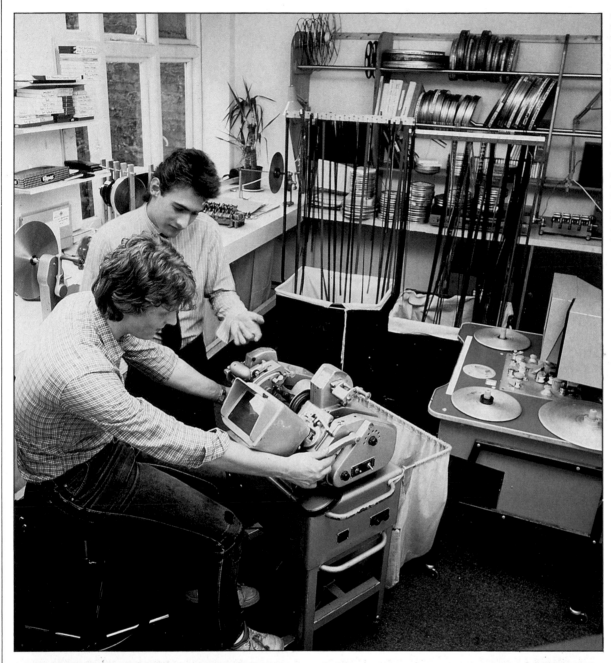

Once the shooting is completed, the director selects the best takes. These are then printed, and are known as 'rushes' or 'rush prints'. The rushes are transferred overnight to 35mm magnetic sound film. The picture and sound are then synchronized to make a double head (ie one projection head projects sound, the other head projects the picture). The director, producer, editor and agency producer then view the rushes in the editing room (*left*) to decide which takes to work with (the 'selected takes') and which to discard (the 'out takes'). The commercial is assembled from the selected takes. The editor puts together the best parts of the selected takes in the correct scripted order. This 'rough cut' is refined by the director and editor. The position and duration of the 'opticals' are then marked on the rough cut with a chinagraph pencil. Once a cut has been approved by the client it is transferred to videotape for completion. Dissolves, titles and special effects are added during videotape post production, possibly using digital effects (*bottom far left*) or computer graphics (*bottom left*) facilities.

Some animated commercials use existing cartoon characters like Yogi Bear, as Heinz did for its Big Soups ads (*right*).
Agency: Collett Dickenson Pearce.
Others create their own characters. These crows (*far right*) were devised specially for Shreddies and then featured on the pack.
Agency: McCann-Erickson.

This commercial, also for Shell, uses animation to convey the dangers involved in exploring for oil in the North Sea – something which would have been very hard to put across through the use of live footage (*right, far right*). Despite the beautiful colours and softness of the drawing, the full power of a storm at sea comes across.
Agency: Ogilvy & Mather.

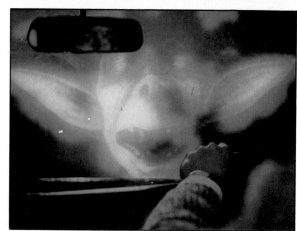

This commercial for Shell Suregrip road surface (*right, far right*) combines live action footage and hand-drawn animation. The live action was shot first, with the director making allowances for the position of the animation on screen. The creatures were then drawn to fit the movements in the live action, the two elements then being married together by matting on an aerial image camera.
Agency: Ogilvy & Mather.

Animation

Animation can be used either to produce commercials in the form of cartoons or to make models move, and many of the best-known and most effective commercials have used these techniques. Such commercials are produced by specialist animation companies.

Cartoons are often used for the creation of characters who can be strongly associated with the brand. The Spillers flour-graders, the Tetley tea-folk, the Esso tiger and Buzby, the bird from the British Telecom ads, are a handful of the characters that have become famous in the United Kingdom, and every other country has its own cartoon favourites. Sometimes, advertising takes cartoon characters who are already well-known, such as

Yogi Bear, and uses them for its own purposes.

In recent years, however, cartoon animation has been used not merely for the creation of humorous characters, but also to create mood and emotion. Richard Williams Animation has been particularly successful in this area, with commercials such as that for Ben Truman beer, based on a wood-cut style of drawing, or for Shell, in which the animator creates a North Sea gale swirling around an oil rig to produce an effect that live action filming could not match.

The other form of animation is model animation, in which puppets or other inanimate objects are made to move. One of the first characters on television, Speedy Alkaseltzer, was created by this technique, but the

The Smash Martians are an example of the imaginative way model animation can be used in commercials (*left*). Instead of cartoons, models are made to move by filming frame-by-frame. *Agency: Boase Massimi Pollit.*

animators' skills have moved on a good deal since then. The Cadbury Smash 'Martians' are one example of the imaginative way model animation has been used since then, while another is the Lego 'Kipper' commercial by TBWA, which won virtually all the world's creative awards. It showed Lego models being transformed, as if by magic, from a cat into a dragon, from a dog into a fire engine and from a ballistic missile into an elephant. Animation can be considerably cheaper than live action, particularly since actors' payments for commercials have increased so rapidly, but it depends on what sorts of commercial are being compared. Top quality animation tends to be cheaper than top quality live action, but it may well cost more than a low budget live action

commercial. Naturally the production technique differs greatly from that of live action commercials, in that it is drawings that are being filmed rather than people, and that they are being filmed one frame at a time. One of the main differences is that the soundtrack is generally recorded first, so that the animators can work to ensure that there is perfect lip synchronization.

One of the advantages of animation is that it offers greater creative freedom – cartoons can do things that humans cannot – but it also gives the agency and advertiser great control over the final commercial provided they approve the work at the crucial story-board and line test stages, which give a very clear indication of the way the final commercial will look.

Computer animation has added a completely new dimension to commercial production, as these examples for Wang and for Sensodyne toothbrushes show (*right, below*). Nevertheless the technique has become over-used in the last year as agencies and their clients have flocked to give their product the high-tech gloss of computer artistry.

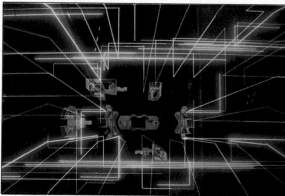

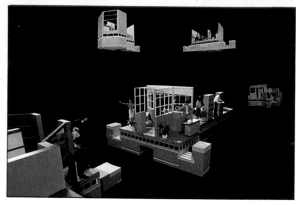

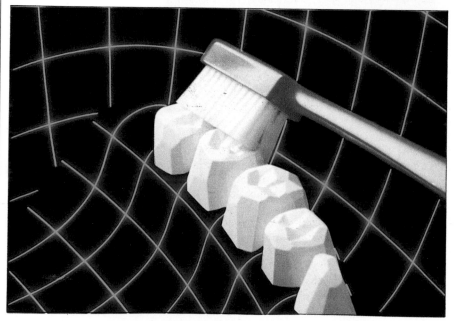

Film versus videotape

Animated commercials are always shot on film (but with advances in television technology this may not remain so for long) and so are commercials made for the cinema (the former because video does not lend itself easily to the hours of patient frame-by-frame work required, the latter because most cinemas still have no video projection facilities, and the picture quality is still not as good as that of film). Yet for most other commercials the question of whether to shoot on film or videotape can be a difficult one.

Videotape is simply the visual equivalent of magnetic recording tape – it does not require processing, as film does, but can instantly be played back. It is possible to shoot a commercial on video in the morning, and have it piped by landline to the TV stations for screening the same evening. This is how the newspapers produce TV commercials that incorporate material from the following day's paper (and it dents the argument that television is a medium that requires a long time for the ad production stage). It is generally slightly cheaper than

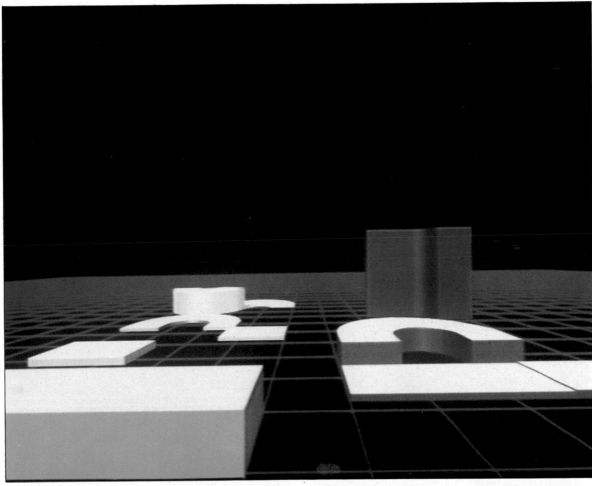

An example of animation produced entirely by computer (*left, below*). The dimensions of the letters were put into the computer by a digitizer. The programmer then instructed the computer to work out a smooth flying movement through the lettering and project it in line form onto a TV screen. When the animator was satisfied with the computer's flying movement, the programmer added colours and a light source to produce the finished job on tape.

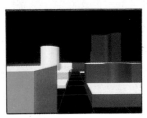
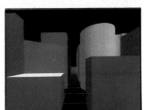
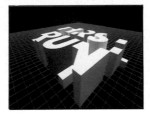
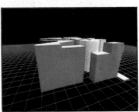

film (though not for location shooting, where the transportation of the sophisticated computer equipment needed can make it very much more expensive). However, the picture quality tends to be less good, though it is improving all the time. Perhaps the biggest disadvantage is the massive amount of electronic equipment required, which makes video far less mobile than film for reaching out-of-the-way locations.

Where video does score, however, apart from being quick and cheap to produce, is in the special effects it can generate. There is virtually no limit to the effects that video can achieve, from turning pictures upside down and revolving them, to changing their colour and halving their size, all thanks to computer technology. Optical effects that would take days to achieve on film can be generated very quickly on video. This in turn has led to the increasing use of computer animation – brilliant colours and futuristic digital effects in which letters and logos zoom towards the camera and away again, or technical drawings are traced out on the screen.

In many cases these days, agencies try to get the best

of both worlds, by shooting the commercial on film and then transferring it onto video for special effects at the post-production stage. However, though post-production work can be much quicker on video than on film, it can also be a great deal more expensive, because it has to be done in a studio manned by a full crew, whereas a film can be edited by a single person at an editing suite.

Is there a simpler way?

The advertiser who wants to be on television but who does not want to go through this complex and usually expensive method of production, has an alternative. At its most basic level, a TV commercial can consist simply of a slide, showing words and a picture, and a voice-over. Most television companies will produce such commercials for advertisers who do not want to go to the trouble of making their own ads.

The slide and voice-over route may be cheap and it will reach a large audience, but it does not take advantage of one of television's greatest strengths – movement – and it is unlikely to convey much atmosphere.

CREATING A PRESS AD

SHAKEN.

RIVAL 4 CYLINDER TWO LITRE ENGINE AT 2500 RPM.

A Martini may be improved by being shaken. But drivers seldom are.

So to smooth your way, BMW insist on using 6 cylinder engines even in their two litre cars.

Most other car companies settle on 4 or 5 cylinders, despite the laws of physics, which decree that engines with less than 6 cylinders can never be perfectly balanced.

You can see on the left the results of such imperfection.

And you can feel the difference yourself when you sit in the cars.

In the 4 cylinder car, you'd feel up to three times as many vibrations as in the BMW.

But in the BMW you'd feel even fewer vibrations than if you were sitting in an 8 cylinder car.

Hence the comment of 'Motor' that the 323i combines "rousing top end bite with smoothness unmatched this side of a V12."

Such a verdict reflects not only BMW's obedience to the laws of physics. But also that an individual counterweight is fitted for each

NOT STIRRED.

BMW 6 CYLINDER TWO LITRE ENGINE AT 2500 RPM.

cylinder (when others often have one balancing several cylinders).

The balance of BMW engines, happily, won't upset the balance in your bank.

For, with the help of fuel injection, the six cylinder engine uses no more petrol than many four cylinder engines of similar performance.

In the longer run, its engineering virtues are also reflected in the way the car holds its value.

For example, a 1981 six cylinder BMW 320 is now worth 25% more than a typical four cylinder rival of similar vintage.

The six cylinder BMW range starts at £9,180 for the 320i and £10,395 for the 520i.

In both cases, that's scarcely more than cars whose manufacturers have chosen to compromise on their engines.

And if they're prepared to compromise on the most important part of the car, where do you think those compromises will stop?

THE ULTIMATE DRIVING MACHINE

PRICES, AND INFORMATION, CORRECT AT TIME OF GOING TO PRESS INCLUDE CAR TAX AND VAT BUT NOT DELIVERY OR NUMBER PLATES. INCLUSIVE DELIVERY CHARGE INCORPORATING BMW EMERGENCY SERVICE AND INITIAL SERVICES £198 + VAT
MIDDLESEX OR TELEPHONE 01-897 6665 (LITERATURE REQUESTS ONLY). FOR TAX FREE SALES: 56 PARK LANE, LONDON W1. TELEPHONE 01-629 9277.

Producing a colour magazine ad such as this is a highly complicated process. The next four pages show how this ad and another in the same series were put together. *Agency:* Wight Collins Rutherford Scott.

date' of the publication in which it is to appear, which in the case of colour ads is likely to be at least six weeks (sometimes longer) before the date the ad will appear.

With the basic concept of each ad having already been approved, a further six weeks was allowed by Wight Collins for the production of the ad. Since the 'Shaken. Not stirred.' ad was due to run early in 1984, detailed preparation of the ad had to begin some 12 weeks before, at the end of September. The first requirement was to sort out the budget for the production of the ad and to commission a photographer (illustration was obviously out of the question). In this case, the photography was relatively straightforward.

The art director, Cathy Heng, commissioned a well-known advertising photographer, Stak, to do the job. He had not worked on the BMW account before because he did not specialize in taking shots of cars (an area in which particular expertise is required). This, however, was not a conventional picture of a car but a 'still life' of an engine and cocktail glasses. The shoot took a single day, in Stak's own studio. The photographs, taken on 10in by 8in stock, were not re-touched, except that the logo identifying the rival engine was removed. The contrast between the ripples in one glass and the stillness of the other was exactly as photographed. The photographs were shown to the BMW marketing department and approved.

Meanwhile, the 'body copy' of the ad was being written by Wight. In most cases, a brief would be given to the creative team before the ad was put together, but in this case, because Wight had been to the factory as part of the management team and knew the thinking behind the ad, no brief was deemed necessary. Once the copy had been approved, it was passed to the agency typographer for setting and he, in turn, commissioned an outside type house to set the copy, subsequently cutting it up and laying it down on the artwork himself.

The photographs were then sent to a processing house to be turned into colour separations – one sheet each for the blue, yellow, red and black elements – and proofs, or progressives, of each colour were run off to show the relevant publications how each element was to look. The agency then sent a set of separations and progressives to each publication in which the ad was to appear.

The layout for the ad was based on the mechanical artwork, which consists of a black and white print of the two colour photographs laid out in position above the type, overlaid with a sheet of tracing paper on which the headline – to appear on the photographs themselves – is set. The black separation sheet incorporates everything on the mechanical artwork – picture and type – and thus a set of separations is all that is needed to reproduce the ad.

At Wight Collins, the agency insists on receiving proofs before printing begins so that it can advise on whether one colour or another needs to be given more weight, and so that it can check that everything is exactly in position. Every proof – one for each publication – and the mechanical artwork has to be approved by a number of different people, including the creative director, the art director, the account director and the typographer, and a stamp for their signatures is placed on the back of each one.

Normally the agency likes to have a week to get the photographs taken, a further two weeks to get the copy approved and set and the artwork laid out and approved, and a final week to produce the separations. Occasionally, however, the photographs require a good deal more work than that needed for the 'Shaken. Not Stirred.' ad. This was the case with another ad for BMW which majored on the other theme of the campaign – the speed and efficiency of BMW's servicing.

One of the creative teams, copy-writer Derek Day and art director Mick Devito, came up with the idea of using the Parmalat Brabham-BMW Formula One racing car in which Nelson Piquet won the world championship. The car had a BMW engine and the mechanics could do a pit-stop change in a record time of 9.2 seconds. Day and Devito produced a rough showing the team in the customary 'arms-up' position at the end of the pit-stop, with the headline: 'Of course, servicing your BMW will take longer, but not much longer.'

The ad was shown to BMW for approval of the concept. They pointed out that the headline was going to have to be changed – even if the service took twice as long as the Brabham team's, it would only take 18 seconds, and BMW owners would naturally expect a slightly longer service than that! The headline eventually ran: 'We've also found ways of servicing your BMW faster.'

Once it had been approved, the agency had to take a photograph of the Brabham mechanics in action, and this proved to be easier said than done. The team refused to do a 'dummy run' for the purpose of the ad, and though they initially permitted an approved photographer to attend their practice session for the British Grand Prix, the time of the practice was changed without the photographer being informed, so he missed it! In the end, the agency approached all the official race photographers on the day after the Grand Prix asking if they had any shots of the Brabham team in the pits.

They eventually found one photographer, David Winter, who had taken a set of shots during the 10-second pit-stop, but unfortunately none was quite suitable. Each one was spoiled by the presence of a man in a white shirt standing in the forefront of the picture. However, since they were the only photographs available, the agency had to make the best of them. Art director Mick Devito had the 35 mm transparencies blown up to colour prints and then cut them up, taking the best bits from each photograph to form one composite that matched the original rough drawing. He then stuck the bits together with sticky tape and handed them to Parkway, a professional photocomposition studio, together with the original transparencies. They produced the photograph subsequently used in the ad.

OF COURSE, SERVICING YOUR BMW WILL TAKE LONGER, BUT NOT MUCH LONGER.

The agency 'rough' as presented to the client (*left*) and the finished ad (*bottom*). (Note the change in the headline.)

The finished ad is made up of seven or eight photographs, cut up and stuck together. This was necessary because no single photo was good enough to use. These three photographs (*above*) show why: a man in a white shirt appears in every shot and had to be cut out of the picture. A professional photocomposition house ensures that the final picture looks totally natural. However, one of the mechanics appears in the picture twice!

WE'VE ALSO FOUND WAYS OF SERVICING YOUR BMW FASTER.

When Nelson Piquet steers his Parmalat Brabham-BMW into the pits, he can expect to be roaring out again within a matter of seconds.
After all, the team holds the record for the fastest pit stop ever: 9.2 seconds precisely.

This level of efficiency isn't something that's reserved for the race track, however.
Indeed, your local BMW dealer has, as part of his team, something even Piquet doesn't have: a computerised service tester.

It can put your BMW through 192 separate tests in a matter of minutes, instead of hours.
Which means a full service on, say, a 525i now takes 20% less time than before.
And time, as the saying goes, is money.

As well as making services faster, BMW have also succeeded in making them rarer.
And once again, computer technology plays a part. Under the bonnet of every BMW is a micro-circuit that memorises exactly how every

mile has been driven. It then uses this information to calculate the optimum moment for a service.
With a normal driving style it can increase the mileage between services by an average of 40%.
This unique level of high technology in both

car and dealership means a BMW now spends more time where a BMW belongs: on the road.
Or, if it happens to be a Parmalat Brabham-BMW, on the way to the World Championship.

THE ULTIMATE DRIVING MACHINE

Press ads make their point with both words and pictures. In this Heineken press ad (*right*) the only copy is the long-running line; 'Heineken refreshes the parts other beers cannot reach', and the picture has to do all the work. This ad was a highly topical one and only appeared once, the day after British news-reader Anna Ford threw a glass of wine over the man who had sacked her from the breakfast TV station TV-AM, Timothy Aitken. *Agency:* Lowe & Howard-Spink Campbell-Ewald.

HEINEKEN REFRESHES THE PARTIES OTHER BEERS CANNOT REACH.

PRESS ADS

Creating a press advertisement seems, on the surface, a good deal simpler than creating a TV commercial, and it is true that the overall process is much less complex. Yet creating a good press ad is at least as hard as creating a good TV commercial, and most people in the business feel that there are comparatively few really good press ads around these days.

The confinements imposed by the printed page, compared with the opportunities to use sound, movement and glossy production values as offered by television, makes great demands on the creative team. It is very easy to flick straight past a press ad, or to concentrate on the editorial matter next to it, so a press ad has to grab the reader's attention and then hold it for as long as it takes to get the message across.

Nevertheless, there are compensations. It is possible to impart a great deal more information – and hence sales points – in a press ad than on television or radio. It is also possible to aim an ad more specifically at one group of people and so, in many cases, press ads can operate at a more detailed and intellectual level than most TV commercials.

All of the creative treatments, such as humour and testimonials, can be used in the press, though some are less well-suited to this medium than they are to television. For instance, it is much harder to harness the power of emotion on the printed page than it is with the help of music and film, but as any novelist will know it is not impossible – the difficulty for the copy-writer is to get the reader absorbed enough in the ad to become involved in it. Everything therefore depends on the headline, the pictures and their layout. Only if these are sufficiently dramatic will the body-copy have a chance of being read. Here we come back to the question of 'rules', since all the main rules that have been laid down

over the years have been about press advertising, largely because the great men who devised them made their names before the arrival of television.

David Ogilvy, basing most of his theories on the research of Gallup and the Starch Readership Service, maintains that five times as many people, on average, read the headlines as read the body-copy, so that unless the headline sells the product the vast proportion of the advertiser's money has been wasted. He goes on to say that the headlines that work best are those which promise the reader a benefit – like a whiter wash or more miles per gallon. Headlines with news in, he says, are recalled by 22 per cent more people than those without news. Headlines in lower-case type work better than those in capitals.

Many such rules are simply common-sense, but as John Webster points out no rule will fit every occasion and many ads that have broken the rules have been enormously successful, while many others that have followed the rules have failed.

Writing the copy

Writing copy for press is far more challenging than writing for TV. To start with, most copy written for television never communicates directly with the public, since it is describing what is to be seen in the commercial rather than what is to be said. Even those words that will be heard by the public will be heavily influenced by the way – and by whom – they are delivered. By contrast, no one gets between the press copy-writer and the audience. Every word will be displayed for the public to see – whether or not the public reads them depends on the skill of the writer and the art director.

Just as with television, the creative team can choose from a wide range of possible treatments – humour, demonstration, shock, emotion, celebrity – and the decision as to which of these is used will probably be made by the copy-writer. Furthermore, it is the copy-writer who will pore over the product literature, reading the consumer research and looking for a creative concept that will meet the brief.

This research element of the job can be very demanding, particularly when the ad is intended for a specialist audience such as hi-fi buffs, financial experts or car enthusiasts. Such ads call for more detailed information and persuasion than ads aimed at a general audience, and the copy-writer must learn the subject inside out before trying to convince people who have been steeped in the topic for years. The copy-writer must talk to the client's own technical staff, to the retailers and to customers, to find out how the product and the market are perceived. Much of this work will already have been done by the agency's planners in devising the advertising strategy, and it may be that the copy-writer can borrow their findings and incorporate them. The art director will be there too, but for ads of any complexity it is the writer whose understanding of the product is more important.

During this process, one fact may leap out and become the headline (as was the case in David Ogilvy's Rolls Royce ad). Many of the greatest ads are based on such discoveries – sometimes they do not concern the product itself, but are nevertheless of great relevance to it. For example, Crisan shampoo grabbed attention for one of its ads with the headline: 'Seventy of your hairs will drop out today. How are you looking after the rest of them?' The famous 'Fresh food is now flying in to Biafra' ad for Christian Aid was conceived when the copy-writer talked to a journalist who had just come back from Biafra, and was told that mothers were catching flies to feed to their children.

Another key decision that will generally be taken by the copy-writer rather than the art director is the length of the copy that will appear. The number of words in an ad can vary from none at all, in the case of the surrealist Benson & Hedges ads (unless you include the statutory Government health warning, which was not the work of the copy-writer), to well over a thousand. Some ads (such as those for Heineken) have a headline and no body-copy, while others (such as those for Volvo) consist of a thousand words of body-copy and no headline.

These days there are comparatively few 'long copy' ads, certainly in those countries where television advertising is a major force. This is often thought to be because the craft of copy-writing has been allowed to lapse since the coming of television, with few writers having the skill to write lengthy copy and maintain the reader's – or even their own – interest. An alternative view is simply that since the coming of television people have learned to react differently to advertising, and images are now seen to be more powerful than words. The ads with few words tend to be those in which image – rather than argument and reason – has been chosen as the main creative element. Indeed, some press ads which have little or no body-copy can run perfectly well as posters, and often do.

The length of copy depends very much on the job to be done, and the product or service concerned. Generally speaking, the more complex and expensive the product, the longer the copy the reader is prepared to take in. Car advertisements tend to be among the longest, and are often filled with performance specifications of the model and its rivals. Financial ads, too, often use long copy to explain the details of a new investment scheme. By contrast, ads for food and household items, which are relatively cheap and are bought frequently, tend to be shorter since there is seldom a great deal to be said about them.

However, like all generalizations about the creative process, this one has numerous exceptions. The Volkswagen car ads never used reams of copy, and occasionally used one- or two-word headlines (such as 'Lemon' or 'Think small'). The Perdue chicken ads in the United States ('It takes a tough man to make a tender chicken') used long copy and so do many food ads that feature recipes. The Crisan shampoo ads, as well as sometimes carrying 17-word headlines ('Seventy of your hairs . . .'), also contained a great deal of body copy – and no picture of a girl with shining hair, either.

The Crisan ad was written by David Abbott of Abbott Mead Vickers/SMS, who has shown what can be done with long copy for a wide variety of advertisers, including Sainsbury, Volvo and Books for Children. For example, the copy for one series of Volvo ads filled almost a whole page of a broadsheet newspaper, without a headline, yet it made compulsive reading.

Financial Times

"It was a bitterly cold morning and I was thankful for the Volvo's efficient heating system.

I had slipped Mozart's clarinet concerto into the stereo and was looking forward to a pleasant drive when I saw the hitchhiker. His placard intrigued me and breaking the habit of a lifetime, I stopped."

He slipped into the passenger seat, placing his bag carefully at his feet.

"Thank you very much sir, for stopping."

"I was intrigued by your sign; flattered I suppose," I replied.

"Oh, I admire Volvos very much. I'm reading engineering and I know what goes into them."

Perhaps only praise of my family or possibly my garden could have brought a swifter flush of pleasure to my cheeks.

"What exactly is it that you admire?"

It is rare enough these days to have one's judgement confirmed by youth and I was determined to enjoy every minute of it.

"It's the little things. Do you know what happens when one of your tail lights fails?"

"Yes, a light flashes on the dashboard to tell me."

"That's true, but did you know you can replace the bulb from inside the boot?"

I confessed that I didn't and made the point that such news was hardly likely to start a rush on 6-cylinder Volvos.

"Ah, but it should. If a company is so thoughtful about the little things, think how efficient the big things will be."

I muttered something about preaching to the converted and turned the stereo down – my passenger

evidently wanted to talk.

"Tell me, do you ever drive really fast? I hope you don't mind me asking?" He grinned like a boy.

"Well, since you're reading engineering and not law, I confess that there have been times when I have gone over 70 mph. On the Continent, of course, and in the presence of a trained nurse."

He looked chastened.

"Oh, I didn't mean that, I just meant it's a great engine at speed; the V6 is very smooth, don't you think?"

I agreed that it was, but not to let him completely off the hook stressed that at the ripe old age of 38, I found the Volvo's top speed not the only attraction.

"Have your studies of the Volvo 264 GLE revealed the presence of air-conditioning, automatic gearbox, power steering, central locking, metallic paint and electric windows?" I asked.

"Yes indeed, all included in the price of £9,995."

He was, it seemed, a student who always did his homework.

By now the early sun had won its battle with the clouds and I asked my passenger if he'd mind if I opened the sun roof. There are few things more pleasant to my mind than to feel the crisp air around one's head whilst one's feet remain comfortably warm.

"Tell me," I said, "how long do you have to wait normally for a Volvo to give you a lift? It's not exactly a common car."

"Ah," he said, "well to be absolutely honest, I don't always wait for a Volvo."

He reached into his bag and showed me four different placards, each expressing a preference for a particular car.

"I always stand at that exact point in the road, where I can see the car before the driver sees me and I whip out the appropriate card. It always works."

I found his honesty disarming and thought here was a young man who would go far, placard or no.

"But I do genuinely prefer to ride in a Volvo."

"You don't have to say that."

"I mean it. You see everyone asks me about the placards and when I tell them, some drivers get really ratty and if I'm going to be in a car with a ratty driver, I'd rather be in a car that's as safe as the Volvo."

I smiled. He was, after all, a true fan.

The Volvo 264 GLE.

In this Volvo ad the reverse technique is demonstrated (*above*). The picture is in fact merely a headline for the very long – but very readable – body-copy.
Agency: Abbott Mead Vickers.

While researching the product copy-writers often look for one fact that may leap out and become the headline. This ad for Rolls Royce by David Ogilvy

(*below*) is a famous example of this technique.
Agency: Ogilvy & Mather.

The Rolls-Royce Silver Cloud—$13,550.

"At 60 miles an hour the loudest noise in this new Rolls-Royce comes from the electric clock"

What makes Rolls-Royce the best car in the world? "There is really no magic about it—it is merely patient attention to detail," says an eminent Rolls-Royce engineer.

Sainsbury ads have an unmistakable style – a double-page spread, black and white headline, a lot of copy on one page and a colour photograph filling the other (*right*). The 'look' of an ad can say as much about the advertiser as the copy.
Agency: Abbott Mead Vickers.

A fickle fungus makes these wines remarkable. A fickle public keeps them reasonable.

In certain parts of Bordeaux the humid autumn weather encourages a particular kind of fungus to attack the grapes.

What might appear to be a catastrophe is, in fact, a blessing.

The fungus is called by the locals 'la pourriture noble' (the noble rot) and they watch its progress through the vineyard like anxious parents.

Anxious lest it should stop.

For the bizarre fact is, the fungus causes a wonderful concentration of the grapes' juices that gives the wines of Sauternes and Barsac a unique, rich texture and aroma.

Unfortunately, the fungus is fickle and doesn't attack all the grapes in the vineyard at the same time.

Some grapes may be ready for picking in September, others may not be graced with the 'noble rot' until October or even November.

In a long, fine autumn it can take as many as seven pickings to complete the harvest. In a severe autumn, the grapes can be ruined before the fungus does its work.

Small wonder that the production of these sweet Bordeaux wines is a hazardous and costly business.

Why then can you find Appellation Contrôlée wines from these regions sitting on Sainsbury's shelves for around £2 or £3 a bottle?

We'd like to claim it's because of our excellent buying powers – and that's largely true – but it's also due to the fickleness of public taste.

Many people still think it unsophisticated to enjoy a sweet wine.

Others don't quite know when to drink a Sauternes and consequently ignore it.

In the face of such prejudice the wines haven't yet been able to command the prices they deserve; but the picture is changing.

More and more wine experts are writing about these neglected wines.

Some recommend you drink your Sauternes with fruit – perhaps a fresh peach, strawberries or nectarine.

Others favour it accompanied by a biscuit or a bowl of nuts.

Many believe you should enjoy it on its own. All believe you should drink it chilled.

As for Sainsbury's, we merely suggest you buy in a bottle or two while prices are still something of a bargain.

After all, with publicity such as this, the public could be fickle once more and cause quite a demand.

Good wine costs less at Sainsbury's.

The role of the art director

The reason the Volvo ads worked was due not just to the skill of the copy-writer, but also to that of the art director – in this case Ron Brown, who has worked with Abbott over many years. Whereas at one time the writer used to produce the copy and then hand it over to an art director (who would often have to lay it out according to strict rules – say, a squared-up half-tone illustration, with a headline above and body-copy beneath), today writer and art director work together as a team. Words and pictures are married, with the copy often heavily dependent on the picture.

In these Volvo ads, the copy is set in two columns, indented to let in a single picture, and the style is instantly recognizable. The picture is not the usual large, glossy, heavily retouched photograph that is customary in car ads. In one case, the car was not pictured at all, the photograph being of a hitch-hiker

The layout of this ad for Land Rover encapsulates the message it is putting across (*right*). It is almost impossible to look at the ad without turning the magazine round to see the picture the other way. The graphics along the bottom add 13 strong sales points in a highly original way.
Agency: TBWA

with a sign saying 'Cambridge. Volvo preferred.', and even when the car was shown it was almost an incidental feature of the photograph.

Abbott and Brown's work for Sainsbury also has a particular style – double-page spreads in colour magazines, with a colour photograph filling one page, and black and white headline and copy on the other. If the word 'Sainsbury' was deleted throughout the ad, you would still know instantly who the ad was for.

The 'look' of a press ad can say as much about the advertiser as the copy, and many companies try to establish a style that is uniquely theirs through a combination of illustration, typography and layout. Volkswagen was one of the first to establish this principle, and Doyle Dane Bernbach's campaign, created by art director Helmut Krone and copy-writer Julian Koenig, was the inspiration for hundreds of creative teams to change both the look and the content of their ads.

The art director's job is as complex as that of the writer, and can often take a good deal longer. The art director must decide whether to use photography or illustration, who to commission for the job, which type face to use, how prominent to make the headline and a dozen other artistic matters that will affect the look and impact of the ad. The copy-writer will make suggestions, just as the art director will contribute to the copy, but in the end there is no doubt whose the responsibility is.

Roughs

Whatever the final form of the ad, whether it is humorous or hard-hitting, long copy or short, illustration or photograph, it will first appear in the form of a rough design – known as a rough or a scamp – by the art director. This will almost certainly include the headline (though even this may be tidied up or reworked later), but not the body-copy, which will be indicated by a few wavy lines. The main feature of the illustration will be apparent, as will its position on the page, so the rough should convey the eventual look of the ad, if not its detail and polish. It is in this form that it will be shown to the creative director and then the account group.

Such roughs are sometimes shown to the client for approval before being turned into a more finished form, but many clients insist on seeing only 'finished' roughs in order to judge the likely result better. It is possible that, as with animatics, an ad will go through several stages of roughs before being approved. Most press ads are researched at the rough stage, to ensure that they are on the right lines. Finished roughs are generally drawn by illustrators in the art department.

Unlike TV ads, most press ads do not have to be submitted for approval by the regulatory authorities. One of the main differences between ads on TV and radio and those in other media is that the broadcast ads have to be pre-vetted. Press ads are occasionally turned down by a media owner because of objections to their content – and if there is any doubt the rough should be submitted for approval first – but this is comparatively rare. However, in some countries, a handful of categories do have to be approved in advance. For example, the UK's Advertising Standards Authority insists on pre-vetting cigarette ads.

All press ads are first shown to the client in the form of a 'rough' or 'scamp', as in this ad for Aristoc tights (*above*).

An outstanding series of photographs by Lester Bookbinder for White Horse whisky used visual puns incorporating a white horse (*far right*). Unfortunately, the client felt the message was too subtle and that a shot of the bottle was needed in the ad: the agency disagreed and they parted company.
Agency: FCO.

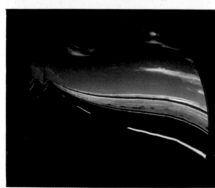

These three photographs (*right*) were retouched and put together by Gilchrist Studios to produce the photograph below.

The following is an extract from the instructions given to the retoucher: '*5 × 4 dupe of reflection for wheel* Ret 5 × 4 trans of reflection to cut curved section out of spare 5 × 4 and physically strip into 5 × 4 to step repeat reflection of road for outer rim of wheel. Black up to continue shape.'

Photography and illustration

Once the rough and the copy have been approved, the production of the ad can begin, and one of the key elements is the decision whether to use illustrations or photographs. This may well have been decided already, when the ad was conceived, but often the decision cannot be made until various executions have been tested.

The choice can depend as much on practical issues as on artistic ones. Two of the most important factors are whether the ad is intended to be in colour or black and white, and whether it will appear in a magazine or a newspaper. Many newspapers are printed on such poor quality paper ('newsprint' as it is known) that a complex photograph, with lots of detail and varying degrees of light and shade, will not reproduce well. While there are ways around this, many art directors decide that the best answer is not to use a photograph at all, but a line drawing. This can also be the solution if an ad has to be produced very quickly, since a simple line drawing or cartoon is usually quicker than a photograph.

Normally, the main influence on the decision between illustration and photography is the straightforward one as to which will achieve the purpose of the ad better. To this extent, some of the considerations that influence the choice between film and animation in television commercials will come into play. It might be thought that, for ads using fantasy, illustration would be better, since it has none of the constraints of realism that photography has, but in fact special effects and retouching mean that photographs can be altered to show almost anything. Similarly, it might be thought that photography would always be used where realism was necessary, but in fact an illustrator can often produce just as realistic a picture as a photographer can. Indeed, often in advertisements it is hard to tell whether it is a photograph or an illustration that has been used.

Photography tends to be the more expensive, though obviously much depends on the calibre of the photographer and the illustrator, and hence their comparative market rates. In a photograph, all the 'ingredients' generally have to be paid for: models, if people are to be depicted; a home economist, if food needs to be prepared; travel to the location, if the shot is to be taken outside the studio; special effects, if they are needed; a make-up artist, and so on. By contrast, an illustrator can produce work entirely from imagination, though it is true that sometimes, in a complex job, photographs will be used for reference. In other words, the comparative cost depends on the job to be done.

Many advertisers insist on a photograph of their product in the ad – the 'pack shot' as it is known in the case of packaged goods. This fulfils the basic task of ensuring that the reader knows what to look for on the supermarket shelf. Nevertheless, it can have a restrictive influence on the 'creativity' of the ad, and many creative teams only put it in on sufferance. One of the best-known disagreements between a client and agency on this issue was that over White Horse whisky in the United Kingdom. The agency had produced a very striking series of press ads and posters using photographs by Lester Bookbinder, using visual puns incorporating a white horse. One showed a basketball player with the horse and the headline 'Scotch and American',

SCOTCH AND AMERICAN

This Ralph Steadman illustration, 'Hitting The Wall', was used by sports shoe firm Nike as a poster, with the company's logo in the bottom right hand corner as the only 'selling' message (*above*).
Agency: FCO.

A famous 1930s poster for Dubonnet by Cassandre which ran for 20 years (*below*).

another showed the horse being groomed under the headline 'Neat Scotch'. The presence of the white horse was intended to be enough to convey the name of the brand in a subtle but instantly recognizable way – there was not a shot of the bottle in sight. However, after one series of ads, the client decided that a pack shot was needed – but the agency disagreed and there was a parting of the ways.

In the case of cars, the 'pack shot' – ie the picture of the car itself – can be a highly technical business, with very complex lighting and retouching to ensure that the model looks at its best, and indeed almost all advertising photography requires great attention to such detail.

Often it is not the product itself that is the main focus of attention but the consumer benefit – the sun-tan (in the case of a sun-tan oil) or the smooth legs (in the case of a lady's razor). Here too the photography has to be perfect in every detail.

Much depends on the skill of the photographer or illustrator, and some specialize in a particular type of work, as do film directors. It is up to the agency's art buyer (if it has one) together with the art director to know who are the photographers or illustrators best suited to a particular job. Some photographers specialize in food shots, cars or fashion. Illustrators too can be chosen for particular techniques, but they are more likely to be chosen for their style – whether it is line drawing (such as Ralph Steadman) or airbrush (such as Philip Castle).

Photographers and illustrators must be briefed at length and in detail by the art director, just as film production companies must, to ensure that the work they produce is what is required. The briefing will include such details as the type of model required, the location and the layout of the photograph or illustration. Very occasionally, the main feature of the ad will be the fact that the picture is by a celebrity, in which case he or she will be given virtually a free hand. Daimler some years ago used pictures of the car by famous photogra-

ROBIN SENSED IT WAS A BOLD PLAN
TO REMOVE THE LEMON FROM HIS GILBEY'S

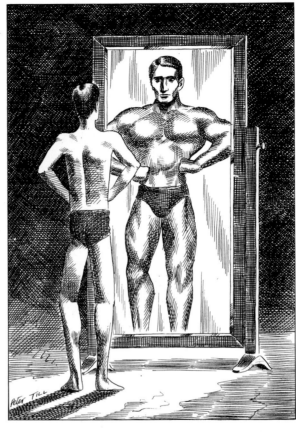

Line drawing can be just as effective as full-colour illustration as Glen Baxter (*far left*) and Peter Till (*left*) have demonstrated. Baxter's ad is one of a series for Gilbey's Gin. Till's drawing is one of a series for the Advertising Standards Authority.
Agencies: Gilbey's Gin – Collett Dickenson Pearce; ASA – Davidson Pearce.

phers, and Alençon more recently featured photographs of famous women wearing their clothes, again by well-known photographers. Once the briefing has been completed, the agency will ask for an estimate, and once this has been approved the work can begin.

The form in which the picture arrives at the agency varies. In the case of an illustration, it is quite straightforward and the artist simply hands over the artwork, whether it is a black and white line drawing or a colour painting. In the case of a photograph, it generally depends on whether it is to be reproduced in black and white or colour. A black and white photo will normally arrive in the form of a large print – as large or larger than the size at which it is to be reproduced – whereas a colour photograph will be delivered as a transparency. A photographer will usually bring in a selection of shots for the art director to choose from – this is less usual in the case of an illustrator, for obvious reasons.

Adrian George's Hockneyesque style is much in demand from advertisers, and is, in turn, much imitated. This illustration (*left*) is for Basildon Bond writing paper.
Agency: Hedger Mitchell Stark.

Futura
Franklin Gothic
Bembo
Garamond
Goudy

Roughly a third of all advertising in the United Kingdom uses one of these five type-faces *(above)*.

The anarchic style of the typography in this Sharp ad *(top far right)* is designed to appeal to its product's target group, the young, and appeared in the music paper, *Melody Maker*.
Agency: Ayer Barker.

This type style *(bottom far right)* harks back to the days of Long John Macdonald, and it has won many awards for typography in the process.
Agency: Collett Dickenson Pearce.

Typography

Not all press ads use a picture. Some rely totally on the layout of the type, the type-face itself and, occasionally, a technique such as 'reversing out' (white type on a black background), to attract the reader's attention. Whether or not there is a picture, typography will have a major impact on the look of an ad – through both the type-face chosen and the manner in which it is laid out. By maintaining a consistent 'look' in its advertising, a company establishes a house style, and the type-face is one of the most important elements.

There are hundreds of different faces from which a typographer and art director can choose, yet advertising tends to use only a few. One UK type expert estimates that about a third of all advertising uses just five faces – Futura, Franklin Gothic, Bembo, Garamond and Goudy. In addition to choosing the face, the typographer has to select the size of type to be used, and the form in which it will appear. Type sizes are measured in points, with the body-copy of an ad probably being set in 10 or 12 point type, and the headline in 24 point, 30 point or larger. Headlines can be set in 'upper case' (all capitals) or upper and lower case, but body-copy is generally always set in the latter as it is easier to read. A further variation comes from the fact that most faces are available in a number of different forms – light, bold, italic, condensed, extra light and so on.

A type-face must be easy to read, and with most faces this is virtually taken for granted. However, typography is subject to the vagaries of fashion and sometimes this basic requirement is forgotten in the art director's eagerness to create a new look. Much research has been done into the legibility of type-faces, and inevitably David Ogilvy has rules on the subject, stating that type should never be reversed out, or set in capitals or a sanserif face, because these are all hard to read. Equally inevitably, many agencies break these rules – often with successful results.

A sanserif face is one without the cross-lines at the ends of each letter, and this is a key element in typographic fashion. Until recently, sanserif faces were very popular for advertising headlines, but many more serif headlines are now appearing. Similarly, italic headlines, which once looked dreadfully old-fashioned, are now coming back into vogue. Occasionally, art directors use type to form part of the illustration in the ad. This is not simply a question of indenting the type to fit round the picture – though that is another popular device – but actually laying out the type in the form of a picture. In one Land Rover ad, for example, the list of dealers at the bottom of the page was transformed into bits of mud clinging to a farmer's boots. In another instance, a picture of a glass and a bottle of Johnnie Walker Black Label whisky were made up entirely of type.

Once the type has been chosen, the copy will be set at a typesetting house. This is usually done these days by means of photo-setting, through a machine that will project any one of hundreds of different faces, letter by letter, onto adhesive film. The typesetters will work to a type mark-up, produced by the typographer, showing the size of type required and the space to be filled. A proof of the copy is sent back for checking by the typographer, and once approved it is passed on to the art studio for incorporation into the 'mechanical' artwork.

It is commonly known that Her Majesty Queen Victoria had a particular affection for Scotland.

She loved the wildness and ruggedness of our countryside.

She loved the folk who lived here, descendants of the clansmen who were every bit as wild and rugged as the landscape.

And we, in turn, had great respect for, her. Because she was a Highlander at heart.

She fished for trout and learnt to stalk.

She dried the Prince of Wales' scarlet socks by peat fires.

She ate bannock. And loved to hear the ghillies playing the pipes.

She was also a wee bit partial to our whisky.

How much of this was due to the influence of her faithful Highland servant, the famous John Brown, we cannot tell.

But it was a fact that one of Her Majesty's pleasures while in the Highlands would be a visit to a local distillery.

One day, while the Queen was in Fort William, she visited the Ben Nevis distillery.

For the proprietor, 'Long John' Macdonald, it was a great honour.

love of Scotland, and of her taste for fine scotch whisky.

One wonders what impression Long John formed of the Queen during her brief visit and just how much the canny gentleman discovered about her.

But whatever he thought, he was not a man to blether about it.

In fact, he himself was very secretive.

To this day, it is not known in the family exactly when or where he was born.

Or even what he looked like.

(With no portrait or photograph to refer to, the picture of Long John on our bottle is purely from an artist's imagination.)

All that is certain is that he did make fine scotch whisky.

It's as if that was all he wished folk to remember about him.

Her Majesty Queen Victoria was certainly impressed with his distillery.

And at the end of the visit Long John presented her with a cask.

A clipping, which we have discovered, reveals that the story was told in the Illustrated London News:

"Mr Macdonald has presented a cask of whisky

WHAT DID LONG JOHN MACDONALD KNOW OF QUEEN VICTORIA'S LOVE AFFAIR WITH SCOTLAND?

Family and friends nicknamed him 'Long John' because of his magnificent stature.

He was a giant of a man standing six feet four inches in his stockings.

His whisky, too, was head and shoulders above the rest.

So special was Long John's dram that it became known far and wide not by the name of the distillery, as was the usual practice, but by the gentleman's own name.

It was certainly fit for a Queen.

Particularly the discerning palate of Queen Victoria.

The story goes that as Long John escorted Her Majesty around the distillery, she spoke of her great

to Her Majesty, and an order has been sent to the Treasury to permit the spirits to be removed, free of duty, and deposited in the cellars of Buckingham

Ben Nevis Distillery in the 19th Century.

Palace. A request has been made that it shall not be opened until His Royal Highness the Prince of Wales attains his majority, which will give it a rest

of fourteen years."

By the time the Prince reached his majority the whisky in the cask would have been finely matured.

One imagines that when the Queen tasted the perfectly matured fourteen year old scotch, she looked back and admired Long John not only for his generosity, but also for his perfect sense of timing.

LONG JOHN.

Yellow, magenta, cyan and black are the process colours employed in colour printing. They initially print as tiny dots of colour which are eventually combined to give the colour of the original. The reproduction is broken down into many stages (*right*) before the colour negative can be made. The original is photographed four times through coloured filters to produce a separation negative for each colour. Once the colour separation process has been carried out, positives are made from the separation negatives. All the positive images are combined in printing to produce a full-colour image. Black is nearly always added at the end.

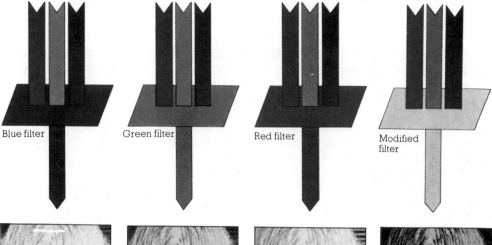

Blue filter   Green filter   Red filter   Modified filter

Yellow printer negative   Magenta printer negative   Cyan printer negative   Black printer negative

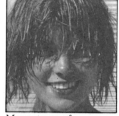  

Yellow proof   Magenta proof   Cyan proof   Black proof

Yellow proof   Yellow plus magenta   Yellow, magenta plus cyan   Yellow, magenta, cyan plus black

A screen is used to reproduce a halftone original (*above*). If this is enlarged (*top*) the halftone dots become clearly visible. The lightest areas are black dots on white, and the shaded parts are white on a black background.

Producing the ad

The ad has been written and designed, the finished rough and copy have been approved by the client, the illustration or photographic work has been completed and the type has been set. How do all these various elements get put together in a form in which they can be reproduced in a newspaper or magazine?

Some agencies have their own art studio, others put the work out to specialist companies, but either way it is in the art studio that the press ad is physically put together, emerging as mechanical artwork, which can then be turned into either a printing 'block' or 'plate', depending on the method of printing to be used.

The artwork consists of a high quality paper board on which the type is pasted, exactly in the form in which it is to appear in the press. This job is done by a paste-up artist in the studio, and is highly skilled work. The illustrative material may also be pasted down if it is to be reproduced in black and white, but it may well come separately, in which case it will be accompanied by a tracing guide showing how the various pieces of artwork are to be assembled.

The type-face presents no problem for reproduction, and neither does a straightforward line drawing, because in each case the printing ink has a clear shape to reproduce. However, a photograph or an illustration has to be 'screened' for printing purposes. This is done by taking a photograph of the original artwork through a fine screen, which turns the picture into a great many small dots, varying in light and shade. The greater the number of dots, the more detailed the picture will be, thus the screen size will vary depending largely on the quality of the paper to be used. Coarse paper, such as that used by most popular newspapers, demands a coarse screen of, say 65 dots to the inch, while coated magazine paper will successfully reproduce twice that many. The resulting picture is called a half-tone, and can be incorporated into any of the various printing processes.

Colour pictures demand a more complicated version of this process. The transparency will almost certainly have to be retouched and the colour balance altered to produce the correct colours on reproduction, and this is a highly-skilled process carried out by specialist companies. Most colour reproduction is 'four colour' and the effect is achieved by separating the picture out into its constituent colours – blue, yellow, red and black – from a combination of which all the other colours can be reproduced. A separate plate or block is made for each of these colours, with each colour being separated from the others photographically through the use of filters. The paper thus has to go through the printing machines four times for colour pages, compared with just once for black and white ones.

Up to the point at which plates or blocks are made, the production process is virtually the same whichever method of printing is to be used. From here on, however, there are several different ways of getting the ad reproduced, and the choice lies not with the agency or the art studio, but with the medium in which the ad is to appear, since different publications are printed in different ways.

Printing processes

Three main forms of printing are used by magazines and newspapers. The original method (which is still used by newspapers in Fleet Street and many papers elsewhere), is called letterpress. It involves the relief principle used by Gutenberg and Caxton, whereby the surface to be printed is raised, covered with ink and then pressed onto the paper. Some papers and small jobbing printers still use a flatbed press in which the type is brought down flat onto each sheet of paper, and this requires blocks to be made for both illustrations and advertisements. Most letterpress printing is now done on rotary or cylinder presses, which roll the ink onto the paper. These machines use thin metal plates, onto which the design from the flat forme has been transferred. Either way, it is now possible to make blocks for an advertisement straight from mechanical artwork.

The second process is called litho or lithography, and it has rapidly become the most popular form of printing for most magazines and newspapers. It works on the principle that grease and water repel each other. A photographic plate is made of the page to be reproduced, but instead of raising the surface that is to be printed (as happens in letterpress printing) it is treated with a greasy substance which makes it receptive to the ink. The plate is dampened with water before it comes into contact with the ink, so that only the areas to be printed – from which the water has been repelled by the grease – take the ink up. In most litho printing, the plate does not come directly into contact with the paper. Instead it prints onto a rubber blanket, which in turn prints onto the paper. This method is known as 'offset' litho printing, and it protects the litho plate from wear or damage. A further variation is 'web offset' printing, in which the machine prints onto a reel of paper instead of individual sheets.

The third process is called photogravure, and it works on the opposite principle to that of letterpress relief printing, in that the image is etched into the printing plate, using various depths to produce the variations in light and shade. This process, known as intaglio, requires much more careful preparation of the

Four ways of making prints (*above*). In relief printing (1) paper is pressed on to inked raised areas of wood or metal. For intaglio printing (2) lines are incised into a block and the paper absorbs the ink in the crevices. In planographic printing (3) the design is drawn in grease which retains the ink. Screen prints (4) use stencils attached to a screen or mesh.

plates than the litho system does, and it is generally used for magazines with high circulations and hence long print runs, for which it is more economical than litho. However, the quality of reproduction is generally less good.

In both litho and gravure publications, agencies have simply to provide the mechanical and the transparencies for the advertisement, which the publication will then turn into a plate for printing. For letterpress publications, the agency must supply a block of the ad, which will be made by a specialist firm of block-makers from the agency's mechanical and transparencies. The block must be made to exactly the right size – as must the mechanical for gravure printing – but this is not vital for litho printing.

It is the job of the agency's print production department to ensure that all these various stages of the print process are co-ordinated and take place at the right time, and in particular that the ad reaches each publication in the right form by the stated copy date. Every publication has to receive a block or a mechanical, and this adds a fair amount to the cost of the overall process if a number of different publications are being used. However, because this can be a considerable disin-

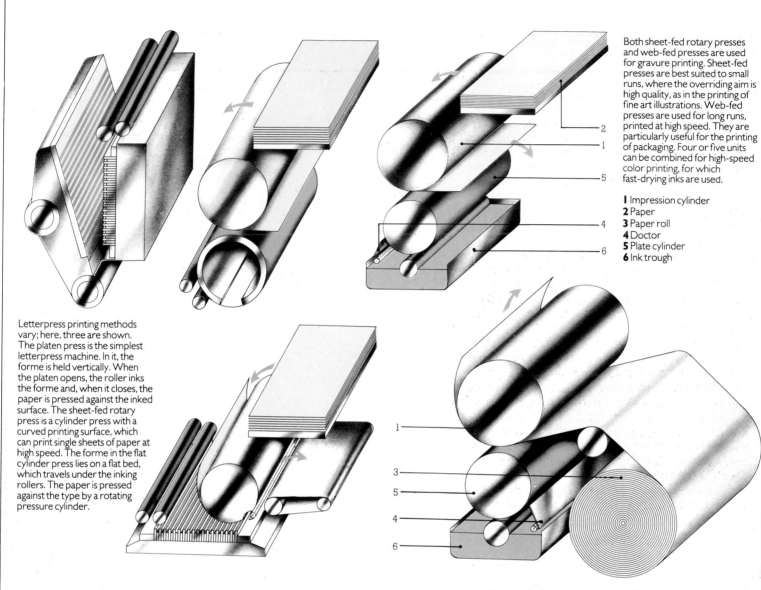

Letterpress printing methods vary; here, three are shown. The platen press is the simplest letterpress machine. In it, the forme is held vertically. When the platen opens, the roller inks the forme and, when it closes, the paper is pressed against the inked surface. The sheet-fed rotary press is a cylinder press with a curved printing surface, which can print single sheets of paper at high speed. The forme in the flat cylinder press lies on a flat bed, which travels under the inking rollers. The paper is pressed against the type by a rotating pressure cylinder.

Both sheet-fed rotary presses and web-fed presses are used for gravure printing. Sheet-fed presses are best suited to small runs, where the overriding aim is high quality, as in the printing of fine art illustrations. Web-fed presses are used for long runs, printed at high speed. They are particularly useful for the printing of packaging. Four or five units can be combined for high-speed color printing, for which fast-drying inks are used.

1 Impression cylinder
2 Paper
3 Paper roll
4 Doctor
5 Plate cylinder
6 Ink trough

Offset lithography works on the same principle as planographic printing. The ink is offset from the plate to a rubber blanket and then transferred to the paper.

1 Ink Rollers
2 Plate cylinder
3 Blanket cylinder
4 Printed image
5 Sheet transfer cylinder
6 Impression cylinder
7 Paper
8 Dampening rollers

centive to advertisers to use publications, some regional publishing companies have grouped together to offer advertisers a centralized service, requiring just a single invoice payment for the media space, and a single set of mechanicals. New technology is making this concept easier to operate. The Regional Newspaper Advertising Bureau in the United Kingdom has a machine which can 'squeeze' or expand an advertisement to fit into different-size spaces, without distortion, to cope with the fact that many newspapers have different column widths.

Is there a simpler way?

There is an alternative method of production for advertisers who do not want to go through these complexities. Most publications are happy to set the words and pictures for advertisers, but this means they have no influence over the way the ad looks, which can make all the difference between an ad's success or failure. Almost all classified advertising is typeset by the publications concerned, the only exceptions being some semi-display ads placed by large organizations who prefer to pay extra to have their ads looking well-designed, even though they are comparatively small and appear on the classified pages.

POSTERS

Creating and preparing a poster for production is very similar in many ways to producing a press advertisement. Indeed, a number of advertisers use the same artwork for both print media. Nevertheless, there are several important differences between the two, and these will affect the way the creative team treats posters.

Posters have been described as an art director's rather than a copy-writer's medium. They are large, colourful and very public. In most cases, they have to be absorbed quickly and from a long way away, which means that they must be simple and easy to read. For once, a snappy headline can be all that is needed in the way of copy, because there simply is not time for the audience to take in anything more. A single headline and a picture will generally carry the most impact, and it often helps if the words are at the top of the poster, because they are less likely to be obscured by trees and buses.

However, there are exceptions, the most notable of which is transport advertising, where posters inside buses and trains or at bus stops and on station platforms can be stared at for many minutes at a time, and quite long copy absorbed. One of the most extreme examples of this is a recent campaign by the UK's Advertising Standards Authority, which is running press ads with extremely long and detailed copy as 16-sheet posters on the opposite side of the tracks at London Underground stations. Very few people will read the ad in one go (they would have to miss several trains if they did), but the fact that most commuters stand at the same point on the

This striking Persil poster (*Left*) set a totally new style and is extremely visible on 4-sheet sites in shopping centres.
Agency: J. Walter Thompson

This poster for Banks's & Hansons beer recreates the feeling of yesteryear through the use of a picture made of tiles (*below*). The poster is not an illustration but a photograph of a specially made ceramic model.
Agency: TBWA.

Perrier is an example of a brand with a very small advertising budget that built itself – and the whole bottled water market – into a large business solely through the poster medium. The 'Eau' puns and the distinctive style and photography of the posters (*this page*) meant that the brand built an awareness far higher than its budget could have been expected to generate.
Agency: Leo Burnett.

platform every day means that they will be able to read it over a period of time. Such posters would get totally lost in a busy high street or shopping centre (where people are on the move either on foot or in cars), but on sites where people have to stop for any length of time they work well.

The vast majority of posters use a single phrase or sentence, and it is here that the wit of the copy-writer must be at its sharpest, since any extraneous words must be sliced away. It is often said that headlines in press ads should be straightforward and should not tease the reader. With posters, however, a witty headline, marrying text and picture succinctly, can often have the greatest impact. Many people see the same posters day after day (if only for a moment each time), and a straightforward 'selling' headline may very quickly lose their attention, whereas a witty one often becomes a topic for conversation. Posters are a prime repository for puns.

One of the most talked-about posters in recent years was for the London Rubber Company's Durex contraceptive. Durex was at that time sponsoring a Formula One racing car, and the poster simply showed a picture of the car with the word Durex emblazoned on the side, under the headline, 'The small family car'.

Another equally witty poster was developed into a whole campaign, with spectacular sales results for the brand concerned. Perrier, the French sparkling water, was advised to use posters as its main advertising medium in the United Kingdom by its agency Leo Burnett, and one of the lines the creative department came up with was 'Eau la la'. As Perrier established a market for bottled water in the United Kingdom, a number of competitors emerged, and the company decided it needed a long-term property for the brand, and so the 'Eau' theme was developed as the creative platform for all the posters.

'Eau' provided a shorthand way of saying 'unique, distinctive, French and fun', says the agency. Puns such as 'H_2Eau', 'Eauasis' and 'Bistreau' not only amused people but flattered the understanding of the Perrier drinker, while the platform could also be adapted to convey specific benefits on a tactical basis, through the use of lines such as 'N'eau Calories'. The headlines were generally backed by simple photographs of the distinctive green bottle or a sparkling glass of Perrier, thus concentrating visually on the physical attributes of the brand.

Posters such as those for Durex and Perrier made the medium a favourite for creative teams in the United Kingdom who realized that here was a wonderful outlet for the witticisms that normally never got further than the creative department or the pub. This opportunity was exploited to the full by London Weekend Television and its advertising agency Gold Greenlees Trott, which started the first weekly poster campaign promoting a different programme every week, usually with a jokey headline and picture. Some of the posters were extremely irreverent, particularly one showing Margaret Thatcher spanking the Archbishop of Canterbury and another showing her husband Denis doing the washing-up in a pinafore. However, they were not as irreverent as some of the posters that got turned down.

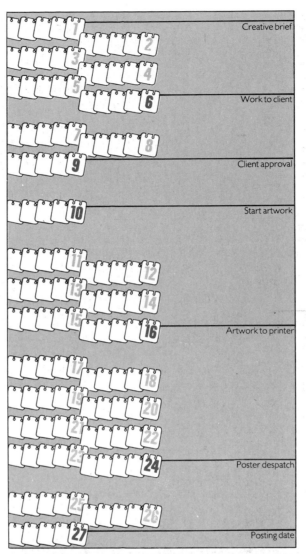

Creative brief
Work to client
Client approval
Start artwork
Artwork to printer
Poster despatch
Posting date

This chart (*left*) shows the maximum recommended time-scale for the preparation of a poster campaign, in order to ensure that each stage receives proper attention. Very few campaigns get this amount of time. However, Harrison Salinson (the poster-buying company that produced this timetable for its clients) also points out that – if necessary – it is possible to accomplish the process extremely quickly. In one recent campaign, the posters were printed and posted six days after the agency gave its approval.

The small family car.

This poster for Durex (*left*) with its brilliantly witty headline was one of the most talked-about ads of its day.
Agency: Benton & Bowles.

The art of irreverence was taken into new territory by this outrageous poster for LWT (*below*).
Agency: Gold Greenlees Trott.

ITV Sunday 6·00pm. Credo.
The Government and the Church.

A poster within a poster for Johnnie Walker Black Label whisky (*above*) in which the text does all the work.
Agency: TBWA.

Hassall's classic Skegness poster (*right*), produced for the London and North Eastern Railway, was created in the age when illustration dominated the poster hoardings.

Illustration or photography

Posters like those for Durex and Perrier show that the outdoors can be a copy-writer's medium, but there is no doubt that it is art directors who are most stimulated by it because of the impact it can give their designs. Even the smallest posters – 4-sheets, which are 40 in wide by 60 in high – are 25 times the size of the average magazine, and the 48-sheet, which is the most popular size with creative teams, is a massive 20 ft by 10ft. The 48-sheet is the poster equivalent of the double-page colour spread, and owes much of its popularity to agencies such as Collett Dickenson Pearce, who devised the dramatic campaigns for Benson & Hedges, Pretty Polly tights, Heineken and Fiat.

In the early days of posters, and indeed until quite recently, the vast majority used illustrations featuring such immortal images as Toulouse Lautrec's Paris, Gilroy's Guinness zoo and Hassall's Skegness. Nowadays, most posters feature photographs, with a few notable exceptions such as Heineken. Even some of the Benson & Hedges posters that look like illustrations are in fact cleverly edited photographs.

However, in some posters these days, art directors are using no illustration or photography at all. This is not just in cases where the text does all the work, such as TBWA's 48-sheet poster for Johnnie Walker Black Label situated at the mouth of an Underground tunnel, which consisted simply of the words in white on a black background: 'You are about to enter the longest whisky advertisement in the world.' Ciba-Geigy (which makes the adhesive Araldite), and its agency FCO, created a huge stir in the UK by actually gluing a Ford Cortina onto a poster site, to illustrate the strength of the product. In fact, the car was glued to a bracket, which then had to be screwed to the hoarding with the help of a crane, but the demonstration was genuine. The copy

When was the last time a man said you had a great pair of jeans?

Pretty Polly brings back lovely legs

line read, 'It also sticks handles to teapots,' and the ad won a number of creative awards.

There are other examples of 'one-off' posters, though most are less dramatic, being hand-painted on site. Nevertheless, they can create real impact by the use of extra pieces which make the image look as though it is breaking out of the confines of the rectangular hoarding. A White Horse whisky poster has the head of the horse protruding round the edge of the site, and in some states of America, where planning regulations are less restrictive than in some parts of the world, there are some spectacular outdoor 'effects'.

Producing the poster

Such one-offs have to be produced in whatever way is appropriate for the site concerned. Most outdoor advertising is in the form of printed paper posters which have to be stuck onto each site by a bill poster, though on many new hoardings the poster is now held in position by glass or perspex.

Most posters are printed by the litho method, and the production process is exactly the same as that of a press ad. The difference comes at the printing stage, since this part of the process is the responsibility of the advertiser and the agency, unlike in press advertising, where it is done by the publication. The agency has to print sufficient copies of each poster to provide one for each site, together with spares in case of damage by weather or vandals. Large posters are printed in several sheets, which are put together by the staff of the poster contractor when the poster is being put up. It is the agency's job to make sure that the contractor has put up each poster correctly, but this is obviously a time-consuming and expensive job, and so in the United Kingdom the poster industry has set up a Poster Audit Bureau to oversee the whole operation.

The Pretty Polly tights posters (*above*) helped rebuild the popularity of the medium with art directors and helped bring photography to the fore. *Agency: Collett Dickenson Pearce.*

'One-off' posters like this (*below*) can create a stunning impact in the right location.

YOU CAN TA

THE LEAGAS DELANEY PARTNERSHIP
22, Endell Street, London WC2H 9AD. Telephone 01-836 0661.

Client   PHILIPS
Product   VIDEO RECORDERS
Date Typed   20th January, 1982

Title   'FIRIPS'
Ref No.

T.V. ☐ Cinema ☐ Radio ☐
Length   60 seconds
I.T.C.A.   Submitted ☐ Approved ☐

CUSTOMER : Morning Squire.

SALESMAN : Morning Sir.

CUSTOMER : I'd like a video caster please.

SALESMAN : A video recorder, anyone in particular.

CUSTOMER : I'd like to have some specifications.

SALESMAN : Yes.

CUSTOMER : And functions. I must have some functions.

SALESMAN : I see did you have any model in mind.

CUSTOMER : Well a friend mentioned the Harry-keri-caboogie-
           casoonni-whatchamacallit you know the Japanese
           one the 2000 'cause I'm very technically minded
           you see.

SALESMAN : I can see that Sir.

CUSTOMER : So I want one with all the bits on it, all the
           Japanese bits you know the 2000.

SALESMAN : What system?

CUSTOMER : Oh aah electrical I think 'cause I'd like to be
           able to plug it in to the television you see -
           I've got a Japanese television.

SALESMAN : Have you?

CUSTOMER : Yeah, I though you'd be impressed, yeah the 2000
           the Hoki-Koki 2000.

SALESMAN : Well Sir there is this model.

CUSTOMER : It looks smart.

SALESMAN : Eight hours per cassette all the functions that
           the others have and I know this will be of interest
           a lot of scientific research has gone in to making
           it easy to operate even by a complete fool like you.

CUSTOMER : Pardon?

SALESMAN : It's a Philips.

CUSTOMER : Doesn't sound very Japanese.

SALESMAN : No Firips, it's a Firips.

CUSTOMER : Well, aaa it's a 2000 is it.

SALESMAN : Well in fact it's a 2022.

CUSTOMER : Mmmm no, no it hasn't got enough knobs on it no.
           What's that one over there?

SALESMAN : That's a washing machine.

CUSTOMER : What sort - Japanese?...

MVO   : The VR2022 video you can understand from Firips.

This Philips ad (above) was largely written by the performers, comedians Mel Smith and Griff Rhys-Jones, and as a result their delivery and timing are perfect. The creative director involved, Tim Delaney, had given similar freedom to John Cleese when working on Sony with equally successful results. The campaign has won numerous awards. *Agency: Leagas Delaney.*

RADIO

Producing radio advertising is similar in many ways to producing television commercials. Both rely on actors, composers and musicians, and both need to conjure up images that will linger in the mind. Furthermore, both need to do this in very short periods of time – generally 30 seconds. Indeed, the soundtracks of some television commercials have made very effective radio commercials, as 'reminders' of the TV campaign.

The similarities between radio and television commercials must not, however, be over-emphasized. The differences between creating ads for the two media are substantial, and many advertising people maintain that radio is the more problematical of the two. This is partly because it is relatively easy to improve a poor television script by hiring a top director and adding glossy 'production values' which make the commercial look wonderful. On radio, if the script is no good, no amount of production – except, perhaps, a very strong music track – can save it. The other reason it is more difficult is the absence of any visual image, which means that everything the ad has to convey – name, price, stockists, functions, varieties (size, colour, flavour) or whatever – has to be on the soundtrack: in television, much of this information can be given on the screen, without being spoken at all.

Writing the script

The first decision, as with any medium, is deciding which sort of treatment should be used, and more often than not in radio it comes down to a choice between humour and music. This is largely because these are the two most effective ways of stimulating a reaction from radio listeners, and of getting them involved in the commercial.

A radio script looks very similar to a television script, with the obvious difference being that there is no column for the visual half of the commercial. (Nevertheless, the writer should still have a strong visual image of what is going on.) The script is generally written by the agency creative team, but sometimes the agency – or occasionally the client – calls in a radio production company to create the commercial from start to finish. Many of the most successful radio commercials have been made in this way.

An award-winning series of commercials for the electrical giant, Philips (featuring comedy stars Mel Smith and Griff Rhys Jones) was largely written by the performers themselves – indeed, many of the best lines emerged from improvisations in the recording studio. It is rare for an advertiser or agency to give its performers such freedom, and it is no coincidence that the agency creative director on the Philips account, Tim Delaney of Leagas Delaney, had used a similar technique with John Cleese on the Sony business some 10 years before, when the account was at BBDO.

At some stage the script has to be approved, first by the client and then by the advertising control body, in exactly the same way as TV scripts. In the case of an ad where improvisation in the studio is permitted, the client can only approve the ad after it has been made.

Several Philips commercials – some of them very funny – were never run because the client turned them down. Such a system might be regarded as very risky, not to say wasteful, were there not a very high strike rate of good commercials as well.

Producing the commercial

Having written the commercial and had it approved, the agency must appoint a production company (assuming one has not already been involved before this stage). It is possible for an agency creative team to cast its own actors, hire a studio and produce the ads itself, but this rarely happens since the results tend to be less good than when a specialist radio production company is involved.

The casting is important and is generally seen as part of the production company's job, unless the agency script has been written specifically with someone in mind (or unless the agency has appointed a writer/ performer, such as Cleese, to do both jobs). In a follow-up ad to 'How to write a great radio ad', Tony Hertz examines the production side of radio, and rule four is concerned with casting: 'The dozen or so people who seem to do most of the radio ads are skilled, reliable and numbingly over-used. One way to make your commercial sound fresh is to find fresh performers. This means auditioning; relying on a voice agent to do your casting for you is like asking a publication to select your type-face.'

It is at the production stage that the use of writer/ performers comes into its own, since they can make the script sound natural and achieve the best possible timing; this can make all the difference between a very good commercial and a poor one. 'The timing in most radio commercials is wrong because they are written by copy-writers and performed by voice-over artists', says Tim Delaney. 'I prefer to use comics.'

Even with professional comics, however, good timing is not something that can be taken for granted. Sometimes a commercial is exactly right the first time round: this was the case with the Philips ad that has received the most acclaim, 'Firips' (a supposedly Japanese rendering of the company name), which was produced as a demonstration commercial and helped Leagas Delaney win the account. 'It came out of the first session we did round the microphone on day one', says Griff Rhys Jones. 'It's funny how the one you just knock off first works so well, and then you spend ages trying to get the rest up to the same standard.' Others are worked on at great length, with the script being altered and improvised to see which way it works best. 'A surprisingly good number of things come up simply by having an idea and then being committed to sitting in front of microphones for several hours', says Mel Smith.

This technique of hiring a studio for a good length of time, with a commitment to having to produce several commercials by the end of it, is unconventional – most ads are produced in as short a studio time as possible. Nevertheless, even with an agency-written script performed by voice-over artists it is possible to improvise. One Hertz rule says: 'Don't be rigid. Allow for inspiration and improvisation and "magic" moments which can really lift a production. You can help this happen by creating a studio environment in which it can.'

When a music track is required, sufficient time in the studio is equally important to ensure the best possible performance. Recording music is a far more complex technical operation than recording speech, and there are specialist companies both composing and producing music for commercials.

Post-production

Commercials can be put onto either cassette or cartridge tapes for delivery to the radio stations, or they can be played to stations via landline from a central studio. Either way, the commercial will be transferred to cartridge by the station itself – the cartridge holds a self-contained 'loop' of tape that can be started at the touch of a button by the station presenter at the beginning of a commercial break.

This advice for advertisers (*above*) appeared in the trade press as an ad for the Radio Operators production company. It was written by award-winning producer Tony Hertz. A follow-up ad was headed, 'How to produce a great radio ad.'

7 PLANNING AND BUYING THE MEDIA

INTRODUCTION

In straight cash terms, the media planning and buying process is the most important element of the campaign, since this is the stage at which the major proportion of the budget is spent. A saving of 10 per cent on a budget of $10 million is well worth having, and such savings are perfectly possible by skilful planning and negotiating – in most countries at least.

The media is the area in which countries differ most from each other, and it is only possible to generalize about the way media space and time are bought. Quite apart from the fact that some countries have TV advertising and others do not, there are some countries where very little negotiation with the media owners is possible, such as Austria and Denmark, and others where every rate is subject to negotiation, such as the United Kingdom.

THE MEDIA PLANNER

The media planner's job is to determine how the advertiser's media budget should be distributed in order to reach the target market most effectively. It involves not just the decision as to whether to use press or television, posters or radio (which is a decision taken more or less jointly by the client, the agency account man, the creative team and the media planner), but which TV stations and publications, what size and length of space or airtime should be booked, what times of day or days of the week the ad should appear, and so on.

Let us assume that the agency account group – having been advised by the media planner – has already decided, with the client, on the target market for the campaign and that there should be a 'mixed media' schedule, consisting of television, women's magazines and posters. The planner must decide how to split the budget between the three media, and must produce an outline schedule showing when and where the campaign will run and how much each element will cost. As at every other stage of the campaign planning process, much will depend on market research – in this case, particularly media research showing which publications are heavily read by the target audience, how many people are likely to watch a particular television programme, which poster sites are passed by the most people, and so on.

In determining the optimum media schedule, the planner must think in terms of three factors – coverage, frequency and cost-per-thousand. Coverage (or reach) is defined as the percentage of the target market that will see the campaign at least once. Frequency is the number of times each person will have an opportunity to see (OTS), or hear (OTH), the campaign. Cost-per-thousand (CPT) means the cost of reaching 1,000 of the target audience, whether it is men, housewives with children or, in the case of some TV campaigns, not people at all, but homes. Every media schedule will be summarized in terms of these three factors, so that the advertiser knows the potential impact of its campaign. Ideally, of course, the advertiser would like the shedule to show a coverage of 100 per cent of its target market, but

this is impracticable. It is virtually impossible to reach the whole of a target group, and the last few per cent would be far too costly to reach. As for frequency, the number of OTSs is simply a factor of the budget – the more the ads appear, the more OTSs will be generated.

For a television campaign, there is another form of measurement that is regarded as a legitimate media target in itself, namely television rating points (TVRs), or, in the United States, gross rating points (GRPs). This is the product of detailed audience research, and a rating point is defined as the percentage of the target audience viewing (or at least having the set on during) a particular spot. Thus the media target for a particular campaign might be 1,500 men TVRs or 2,400 housewife TVRs – the aggregate of all the TVRs built up during the campaign. However, TVRs are not a direct measure of coverage and frequency, since some people watch television far more heavily than others – it may be that some viewers have seen the commercial 10 times while others of the target group have not seen it at all. In the media plan, therefore, the TVR target is often supplemented by the figures for target coverage (say 87 per cent of men) and frequency (say 6 OTSs).

It is customary to aim for as high a proportion of the target market as possible, but it is not essential if there are good reasons for going for a restricted section of the market. In any product category there will be heavy and light users, with the heavy users accounting for a high proportion of the total sales (for example, 8 per cent of Guinness drinkers account for 35 per cent of all Guinness sold). If it can be shown that a particular medium reaches a high proportion of the heavy users, it may not matter if the light users are missed by the campaign. The Target Group Index (TGI) provides just this sort of information, showing how many heavy petrol purchasers or dog food buyers are reached by each publication.

While coverage is a major consideration, it has also to be balanced by cost, and the media planner will have a copy of the rate-card of every TV station, publication, outdoor contractor and radio station. From these, and the circulation, readership and viewing figures, the planner can work out the cost-per-thousand for each medium against the target audience. In most agencies nowadays, such work is done with the aid of computers which will produce cost-ranking analyses, listing the publications in order of their cost-per-thousand with, naturally, the lowest cost at the top. However, quantitative data is not sufficient on its own. It may be that a certain publication has a higher cost-per-thousand than the others, but justifies this in ways other than sheer audience size, perhaps because of its editorial authority and quality, or because it has a particular affinity with a section of the target audience.

Other factors that need to be considered are seasonal timing and regional placements. Does the campaign need to run at particular times of the year? If not, there is better media value to be had during the off-peak advertising seasons after Christmas and in mid-summer. Does the advertising need to be seen throughout the country? It might make better sense to advertise only in the key regions with large populations, so that by concentrating the budget the impact will be greater.

There are other decisions on timing to be made.

When planning the media schedule it is important that there is a high degree of cooperation between all the groups involved in the campaign. Planning meetings (*left*) are held at regular intervals so that the media planner can collate all the individual group's input and produce the optimum media schedule in terms of coverage, frequency and cost-per-thousand.

Assuming the product is not seasonally-oriented – in other words, it does not have to be advertised at the beginning of summer, say, like sun-glasses and ice cream – and that it does not have a sufficiently large budget to permit it to be advertised all the year round, the planner must decide whether to stretch the campaign out over a long period, or whether to put all the money behind a quick campaign that will have greater impact. This debate – 'drip' versus 'burst' – is endlessly argued among advertising economists, but for most companies the burst technique, using, say, two three-week bursts of advertising in a three-month period, is the more usual.

Being a relatively scientific area of the advertising process, such media debates occur a great deal, and there is a large amount of accumulated wisdom and research as to the best way in which to distribute the budget. How many times does an advertisement need to be seen to produce the maximum impact – once, twice, four times? How soon does an ad start to irritate people, particularly on radio, where the high frequency of commercials is necessary because so many listeners dip in and dip out? (Such questions must be borne in mind when the planner is deciding how many OTSs to plan for.) Which is more effective, a double-page spread (DPS) or a single-page ad in a magazine? Even if the DPS costs less than twice the price of the single page (in general, the longer the spot and larger the space, the lower the price is proportionately), the planner has to decide whether the DPS will be nearly twice as effective as the full-page ad. Would it not be better to spend the money on two single pages in separate titles? It is here that the element of 'creative' media buying comes in. At one time, double-page spreads were relatively uncommon – not surprisingly given that they cost nearly twice as much as a full-page, and hence virtually halve the frequency of the campaign. Yet the impact they can

have, with the use of strong creative work, can be enormous, not least because there is no editorial matter on the spread to distract the reader.

One agency, Collett Dickenson Pearce, spotted the opportunity when the UK's first Sunday colour supplement was launched in the 1960s, and started buying double-page spreads for its clients, securing a very good deal with the publisher because of the trail-blazing nature of its work. Very quickly, other agencies and advertisers discovered the benefits of the double-page spread, but they had to pay the market rate. Colletts pulled off the same trick in the 1970s with the 48-sheet poster. The very large, landscape-shaped posters suddenly became extremely popular with advertisers (not to mention art directors), and were booked for months ahead. Once again, the agency received very good media value from the contractors.

It is not always necessary to look for bigger spaces, and many advertisers cannot afford to. Similar impact can be generated by the novel use of small spaces on particular pages of a newspaper, provided the creative work is strong enough. As with so many other elements of the media planning process, this is an area where judgement, rather than the computer's cost-ranking expertise, has to be used.

All these factors will be taken into account by the media planner when the media schedule is being laid out. The media schedule is an outline plan for the whole year, showing which months the campaign will run in, which TV areas and what publications have been chosen, what length of commercial and what size of press ad will be used, and showing the cost of each element of the campaign and its intended coverage and frequency. Once the proposed schedule has been approved by the account executive and/or the client, it is passed to the buyer (unless the planner is also the buyer), to start negotiating and booking space.

Television is the primary medium for Impulse because of its creative advantages of vision, colour, movement and sound. However, it does not cover the target market sufficiently cost-effectively on its own, so cinema and the teenage press are used as well. The press ad (*above*) reflects the TV campaign, to the extent of using a still from the commercial (*top right*). *Agency: Lintas.*

Impulse is an international Unilever brand, a body spray that is sold on virtually the same strategy in over 50 countries. In the United Kingdom it is marketed by Elida Gibbs, the Unilever toiletries subsidiary, and its advertising is handled by the agency SSC&B: Lintas Worldwide.

The Impulse television commercials show handsome young men chasing attractive young women with bunches of flowers. 'Men can't help acting on Impulse', runs the copy-line. Television alone is not sufficient, however, to cover the target market cost-effectively, as the agency's media strategy document makes clear:

'Target Market
Primary: 13- to 24-year-old women.
Secondary: 25- to 44-year-old C2D women.
Budget
£892,000.
Seasonality
Minor sales increase during summer months.
Media Strategy
1. Television
   Mandatory to use television:
   a) 'Live' medium, with vision, sound, movement – creatively, best able to portray Impulse scenario;
   b) TV has built brand to current success;
   c) Virtually all major brands use TV;
   d) Important for brand leader to emphasize own importance, to both trade and consumer, by continuing use of TV;
   e) Likelihood of increased competitive activity on TV;
   f) Gradual broadening of age range of users requires medium giving broad coverage of 25- to 44-year-olds as well as 13- to 24-year-olds.
   However, ITV viewing by 13- to 24-year-olds is relatively low – for every 100 'all women' TVRs there are only about 70 '15- to 24-year-old women' TVRs. There is therefore a need to use other media to upweight the prime target market.
2. Cinema
   a) Cinema's main strength is among 15- to 24-year-olds – against women of this age, its coverage compares favourably with television's in many months of the year;
   b) Like television, cinema is a 'live' medium and can thus convey the Impulse scenario effectively – unlike television, it offers 100 per cent colour reception;
   c) Cinema has considerably greater impact than TV – research has shown that awareness figures in day-after recall tests can be nearly 70 per cent higher for a commercial shown in cinemas than for the same commercial shown on television.
   Though there is a strong need to continue with 'live' media – TV and cinema – both are expensive against young women. There is also, therefore, a need for the use of a relatively 'cheap' medium, even though limited in its message, to provide additional frequency economically.

3. Teenage Press
   a) Teenage magazines reach 15- to 24-year-old women at only 15 per cent of the cost of cinema, thus providing very cheap exposure with reasonably high coverage levels;
   b) They fulfil an educative and personal role in young girls' lives during the 'growing-up' years;
   c) They provide 100 per cent colour.

Summary
1. Use of television during cheaper months and prior to start of spring/summer sales period provides coverage of total market.
2. Use of cinema during more expensive TV period provides upweight coverage of prime target market.
3. Use of teenage press during expensive TV period provides cheap frequency and cover against prime target market.'

In drawing up the detailed media proposals, the Lintas media planners decided to use television for three weeks in January and three weeks in March in the London and South TV regions, and for four weeks in January and March/April in the other TV regions. The cost of the two London and South bursts was £117,000 and the ratings target was 415 'all women' TVRs (290 '15- to 24-year-old women' TVRs). The cost of the bursts on the rest of the network was £244,000 and the target 570 'all women' TVRs (400 '15- to 24-year-old' TVRs). The length of the commercials to be used in these bursts was 20 seconds. The planners also proposed a burst of four weeks in August throughout the ITV network. The cost was to be £646,000, the target 340 'all women' TVRs (240 '15- to 24-year-old women' TVRs) and the commercials were to be 30 seconds long.

By advertising in January and August, considerable savings could be made compared with the peak demand months of October and November. In January, TV airtime was calculated to have cost 40 per cent less than it would have in November; August's airtime cost 30 per cent less and March's 20 per cent less.

A national cinema campaign was proposed for the second half of the year. The six month campaign would cost £172,000 and deliver 104 '15- to 24-year-old women' coverage points. A further campaign would run from May to September in 30 holiday centres at a cost of £4,000.

The press campaign would run from the second half of August until the end of November – the most expensive months for TV advertising. The media planners prepared a cost-ranking chart of the likely magazines to be considered for the schedule. This listed the magazines in order of the lowest cost per 'coverage point' (calculated by dividing the cost of the advertisement by the percentage coverage the magazine delivers – the cost of the 'My Guy' advertisement £1,400, its percentage coverage 10 per cent, so its cost per coverage point was £140).

From this analysis, seven separate press schedules were drawn up, involving 15 magazines and different

SCHEDULE EVALUATION

Publication	Schedules - Nos. of insertions						
	1	2	3	4	5	6	7
Oh Boy	3	3	-	-	-	2	2
My Guy	3	5	3	5	3	3	3
Blue Jeans	3	5	3	5	3	3	3
Patches	3	5	3	5	3	3	3
Jackie	3	5	3	5	3	3	3
Hers	3	3	3	-	-	2	2
Nineteen	3	3	3	3	3	2	2
Look Now	3	3	3	-	3	2	2
Over 21	3	3	3	-	-	2	2
Argus 3	3	3	3	3	3	2	2
Womans World	3	2	2	3	3	2	2
Options	2	-	-	-	3	2	2
Honey	2	-	-	-	-	2	2
Cosmo	-	-	3	3	3	2	2
Company	-	-	-	-	-	2	-

	1	2	3	4	5	6	7
% Cov. 15-24 Women	62.3	63.1	65.6	65.4	65.3	66.0	65.8
Ave. OTS	5.5	6.0	5.2	5.5	5.0	4.9	5.1
Gross OTS	14572	16017	14514	15193	14002	13869	14271
3+% Cov. 15-24 Women	41.6	40.0	44.8	43.8	44.5	40.9	41.3
% Cov. 15-19 Women	76.2	77.5	76.7	77.8	77.3	79.5	78.9
% Cov. 20-24 Women	50.0	46.9	53.7	51.9	54.3	55.6	54.0

Schedule 4 was recommended as it performed well in terms of coverage and cost efficiency

In order to decide which magazines to use, the media planners prepare a schedule evaluation chart (*left*) listing 15 potential titles and their coverage of the target market, including the average number of OTS (opportunities to see) generated by different combinations. Seven separate schedules were prepared, and Schedule 4 was recommended to the client as being the best in terms of coverage and cost efficiency.

numbers of insertions in each. The coverage and the number of 'opportunities to see' offered by each schedule was calculated, and the planners recommended schedule number four. This involved five insertions in four weekly titles and three insertions in four monthlies and gave a coverage of 65.4 per cent of women between the ages of 15 and 24, each of whom, on average, would see the ad five and a half times.

The complete media proposal was put to the client and accepted, at which point it was given to the agency media buyers who had to negotiate the purchase of the media time and space. In the case of cinema and the magazines, the negotiation was done by the planners themselves, but for television, agencies have specialist buyers.

SSC&B:LINTAS WORLDWIDE
London
Proposed Media Plan 1983

Client   Elida Gibbs Ltd

Product   Impulse   Date   6.12.82   Key   Press - colour pages

	DEC	JAN	FEB	MAR	APR	MAY	JUNE	JULY	AUG	SEPT	OCT	NOV	DEC
W/C Monday	27	3 10 17 24 31	7 14 21 28	7 14 21 28	4 11 18 25	2 9 16 23 30	6 13 20 27	4 11 18 25	1 8 15 22 29	5 12 19 26	3 10 17 24 31	7 14 21 28	5 12 19 26

TELEVISION

LONDON AND SOUTH

415 Women TVRs
(290 15-24 women TVRs)   JAN 20 secs 190   MAR 20 secs 225

Budget £117,000   JAN £49,000   MAR £68,000

REST OF NETWORK
570 women TVRs
(400 15-24 women TVRs)   JAN 300   MAR 270

Budget £244,000   JAN £115,000   MAR £129,000

NETWORK
340 women TVRs
(240 15-24 women TVRs)   AUG 30 Secs (240) 340 £285,000

TOTAL TV BUDGET £646,000

PRESS
350 15-24 Cover pts £70,000

CINEMA   - 30 seconds
Nat.

104 15-24 women cover pts £172,000
(45% at 2.3)

78 (15-34 women cover pts
(36% at 2.1)

Butlins :

30 holiday centres £4,000

TOTAL BUDGET £892,000

The media plan (*left*) prepared by the agency for its client shows at a glance the year's proposed campaign, month by month, medium by medium, burst by burst. The figures for TVRs (television rating points) are targets to ensure sufficient coverage of the target market. After the campaign has run, the actual performance in terms of TVRs will also be measured.

```
                                          T.V. BUYING SCHEDULE                         PAGE 1        REQUESTOR KIRSTY

                                                                                       STATION GROUP    YORKS
  ME26 RUN ON 22MAY84 AT 22.49                                                          STATION          YORKS1
                                          PERIOD 1 AUG 83 - 31 AUG 83                   UNIVERSES        2355,2266
  AGENCY    LI    LINTAS ADVERTISING LIMITED
  CLIENT    E25   ELIDA GIBBS LTD
  PRODUCT   7     IMPULSE
  CAMPAIGN  6     IMPULSE
                                                                                       ---ALL WOMEN---     ----HOMES----
  SERIAL  GI DAY DATE TIME    SEC D   GROSS      NET      30SEC REMARKS                 TVR  IMPS  CPT      TVR  IMPS  CPT
  NUMBER                          P   COST      COST      COST -------

  WEEK=32                                                                               121  495  1.72]     7   150  1.06
  T1788939 GE W/C 1AUG DP     30 2   851.00    851.00    851.00 30HMS/G1                  4   93  1.71       6   140  1.37
  A9824004    MON 1AUG 1557   30 1   159.65    159.65    159.65                           5  113  1.71       5   110  1.26
  A9823999    FRI 5AUG 1616   30 2   192.64    192.64    192.64                           3   81  1.71       3    67  1.21
  A9823998    SUN 7AUG 1314   30 1   138.35    138.35    138.35                           2   48  1.71       8   180  1.55
  A9823093    TUE 9AUG 1529   30 1    81.65     81.65     81.65                           7  163  1.71      29   648  1.31
  A9822087    FRI 19AUG 1541  30 1   278.71    278.71    278.71                          21  498  1.71
                                     851.00    851.00    851.00
       GHI TOTALS     5 SPOTS                                                            [7  165  4.76]      6   130  6.02
                                                                                          4   91  8.65
  T1788829    MON 1AUG 2358   30 4   784.00    784.00    784.00 HILLST/RC               124  565  6.44]     37   832  4.37
  A9824003    MON 1AUG 2356   30 4   784.00    784.00    784.00                          33  767  4.75

  T1788818    TUE 2AUG 1845   30 3  3640.00   3640.00   3640.00 XRDS/RC                   15  118  3.75]      8   190  2.32
  A9824002    TUE 2AUG 1845   30 3  3640.00   3640.00   3640.00                            7  158  2.79

  T1788839    WED 3AUG 1328   30 1   442.00    442.00    442.00 NEWS/RC                  114  330  4.59]     20   451  3.35
  A9824001    WED 3AUG 1328   30 1   442.00    442.00    442.00                           15  342  4.42

  T1788851    THU 4AUG 1742   30 3  1512.00   1512.00   1512.00 BENSON/RC                 79 1856  3.89      99  2252  3.21
  A9824000    THU 4AUG 1743   30 3  1512.00   1512.00   1512.00                            9  206  3.89      11   250  3.21

       WEEK TOTAL     9 SPOTS       7229.00   7229.00   7229.00
       WEEK AVERAGE                  803.22    803.22    803.22                          124  565  6.44]     33   742  4.90
                                                                                         30  708  5.14
  WEEK=33
  T1788840    MON 8AUG 1957   30 3  3640.00   3640.00   3640.00 CORDST/RC                124  565  6.44]
  A9823094    MON 8AUG 1958   30 3  3640.00   3640.00   3640.00                           30  708  5.14

  T1788949 GE W/C 8AUG DP     30 2   880.00    880.00    880.00 30HMS/G1                 121  495  1.78]      5   106  1.12
  A9823095    MON 8AUG 1612   30 2   118.91    118.91    118.91                            3   76  1.56       5   120  1.28
  A9822088    THU 18AUG 1558  30 1   154.13    154.13    154.13                            4   99  1.56       8   180  1.74
  A9822084    SAT 20AUG 1515  30 2   205.13    205.13    205.13                            6  132  1.56       4   100  1.74
  A9822082    SUN 21AUG 1623  30 2   173.95    173.95    173.95                            5  112  1.56       5   117  1.18
  A9820557    TUE 23AUG 1357  30 1   137.61    137.61    137.61                            4   88  1.56       3    78  1.16
  A9820554    FRI 26AUG 1559  30 1    90.27     90.27     90.27                            2   58  1.56      31   701  1.26
                                     880.00    880.00    880.00                           24  565  1.56
       GHI TOTALS     6 SPOTS
                                                                                        117  400  9.09]     37   848  4.29
  T1842773    FRI 12AUG 2010  30 3  3640.00   3640.00   3640.00 RC/ATEAM                  31  727  5.01
  A9823092    FRI 12AUG 2010  30 3  3640.00   3640.00   3640.00
```

This computer print-out shows the ratings performance during two weeks of the Impulse TV campaign in one ITV region, Yorkshire, which covers some 10 per cent of the country. The print-out may look daunting but much of the detail is explained along the top – day, date, time of transmission and so on.

THE MEDIA BUYER

One reason why many agencies prefer to have both the planning and the buying of a campaign done by the same person is that a good deal of the negotiation can be done at the planning stage, where it will influence the way the schedule has been drafted. As in the case of the larger sizes of ads in magazines and on posters, it is also possible to negotiate an advantageous rate with newspaper owners who may, for example, want to attract food advertisers onto their papers. If it is known that a certain space can be bought for half the published rate, it will have a major impact on the schedule as a whole, either ensuring that the paper offering the cheap rate gets far more insertions than another or, alternatively, allowing more of the budget to be spent elsewhere.

Why should a newspaper want to offer advertising space at half price? The answer lies in the competitive nature of advertising, and the need for media owners to offer incentives to advertisers. While the newspaper owner may lose some money by accepting the food advertiser at half price, the hope is that other food advertisers will follow suit (advertisers are always copying their competitors), in which case they will be charged the full rate. The television stations in the United Kingdom have been particularly successful with this strategy, attracting new categories of advertiser onto television with special low rates, thus enabling them to test the power of the new medium.

All of this means that a skilful media buyer can gain enormous savings for clients by playing one media owner off against the other. In this respect, buying advertising space and airtime is not different from the buying and selling of any other commodity. For example, people who buy media in large quantities qualify for discounts. In newspapers there are 'series discounts' offering advertisers, say, nine insertions for the price of eight. On television, there are 'volume discount' incentives on some stations for advertisers who spend over a certain sum during the course of the year. However, size is not everything, and some agencies and media independents claim – with justification – to buy more effectively than other agencies twice and three times their size (the one thing that is certain is that every agency in town maintains that it buys media more cost-effectively than any other).

The media planning and buying element of advertising has grown remarkably in importance in the last few years, and the opportunities for savings of millions of dollars cannot be ignored by any company. Some large advertisers now have media co-ordinators, whose job is to ensure that their agencies get the best possible deal out of the media owners. They measure the buying performance of each of their agencies in terms of costs-per-thousand and other variables, and the internal 'league tables' of such multi-agency clients generate fierce competition between the agencies' media buyers.

By saving money for their clients, agencies could well be reducing their own income, since they generally get a commission on the advertiser's expenditure. However, this does not prevent them from buying as well as they can. In the first place, such money as they do save may well get spent on an extra burst of advertising, while the better they are seen to buy, the better their chance of winning more business from the client.

8 MEASURING THE RESULTS

Once the compaign has run its course, all that remains to be done is to try to find out whether it has worked. Advertisers spend almost as much time and effort agonizing over whether a campaign has achieved its aims as they do putting the advertising together – and quite rightly, considering the large sums of money involved and the lack of any tangible returns.

Lord Leverhulme, founder of the Unilever empire, once said that he knew half of the money he spent on advertising was wasted, but he did not know which half: advertisers face much the same problem today. Has the campaign achieved its stated objectives? If it has, the advertiser might be perfectly satisfied, but will nonetheless want to know whether those results could have been achieved using less advertising, or none at all. If it has not, the advertiser will want to find out why. Was the creative work at fault, or did too few people see the advertising? Was the product or service itself wrong, or was the lack of success due to outside factors such as a distribution problem or the launch of a new competitor? Most important of all, how can better results be achieved next time?

Market research is used throughout the campaign process to help companies formulate their decisions: in the conception of a new product, in the pinpointing of a target market, in the selection of the media and in the creation of the advertisements. Its final task is to measure whether the process has worked.

MARKET RESEARCH

The underlying principle of market research is that it is possible to determine what a great many people have done or are likely to do from the actions of a relatively small number. The key lies in the selection of the sample to be researched: it must be representative of the target market in the important respects of age, sex, social group and purchasing behaviour. The size of the sample is also an important factor. Obviously the ultimate sample would be a complete census of all the members of a target group, but this is impractical in most cases. Failing that, the larger the sample is, the more precise the research will tend to be, though the cost will inevitably be higher too.

The selection of a sample is done in two ways: *quota sampling* and *random probability*. With quota sampling, the research firm determines the profile of the client's target group in terms of demographic and geographical characteristics, and then finds people who match this profile; in the case of random probability, it selects particular people within the target group at random from a complete list such as the electoral register, and then makes every effort to interview them, even if it means going back many times until they can be interviewed at home.

A large proportion of market research is conducted on a *continuous* basis, either through panels of consumers who keep a record of all their purchases in particular product fields every week, or through audits in which interviewers record sales levels, prices and other information at a selected sample of stores. Such research is only available to subscribers, who buy reports on a monthly or quarterly basis. In addition, many companies commission *ad hoc* research which is designed to find out specific information about their brands that is not available in other ways. Most of these surveys are conducted through face-to-face interviews, though telephone interviewing is becoming more common. Usage and attitude surveys are among the most widely used *ad hoc* projects, giving companies such information as the awareness of brands and frequency of purchase, information that is unlikely to emerge from the continuous research surveys.

A half-way house between continuous and *ad hoc* research is provided by *omnibus* surveys: these are conducted regularly, every week or fortnight, by certain research firms, and the questions asked are aimed at finding out specific information for clients. In this way, several clients can share the costs of *ad hoc* research in the same way that the costs of panels or retail audits are shared.

In addition to such *quantitative* research (which uses specific questionnaires to generate figures that are statistically valid and directly comparable) many advertisers also use *qualitative* research. This involves less formal questioning, with far smaller samples, more highly trained interviewers and longer interviews than quantitative research. Instead of statistics, qualitative research generates quotations taken from the transcript of the taped interviews.

Qualitative research is done in one of two ways: *group discussions* or *semi-structured interviews*. Group discussions (which are by far the more widely used) generally take place either in the interviewer's home or in a hotel room, and last between one and two hours. They usually involve between four and a dozen people in the client's target market – for example, young beer drinkers, business men or housewives – and the interviewer leads the discussion, making sure that what is said is relevant to the matter in hand and that the client's questions are answered, but without necessarily betraying who the client is or exactly what the purpose of the discussion is, since this could conceivably influence the group's remarks. Such research is likely to use several different groups in a range of locations. However, sometimes a group discussion can be inhibiting, particularly when the subject is a sensitive one, such as contraception, and in these cases the semi-structured – or 'depth' – interview with one person is often a better method.

All these methods are used by advertisers at various stages of the campaign. Both quantitative and qualitative research is used in devising the marketing and advertising strategies and in developing the creative treatment and pre-testing advertisements. In addition, many advertisers use *tracking studies* – surveys on a continuous or regular basis that track awareness of products and advertising, attitudes to brands, and claimed purchasing behaviour. This enables them to monitor changes over time and relate this to their own advertising and to the activity of their competitors in the relevant fields.

HAS THE CAMPAIGN WORKED?

Perhaps the most thorough attempt – certainly in public – to prove that advertising works has been that made by the Institute of Practitioners in Advertising in the United Kingdom, which now gives awards for campaigns that have been proved to be effective. One of the organizers of the scheme, Dr Simon Broadbent, vice-chairman of Leo Burnett in London, has analysed the methods used in evaluating the campaigns in the IPA's book, *Advertising Works*, and he points out some of the problems: 'Sales are affected by many factors other than advertising: the quality of the product, its price, distribution and promotions, total consumers' spending, seasonality, competitive activity and so on. In a proper evaluation of advertising, these factors must be measured and taken into account.' In addition, the profitability of a campaign, he says, can only really be measured in the short term. 'The longer term contribution of advertising may be greater than in the current year – and this is particularly likely for a new brand, for which a one- or even two-year payoff cannot often be expected. It is hard to imagine some of the most famous brands reaching their present positions without the help of past advertising in positioning them, explaining their use and giving them a personality, yet few if any people have techniques which they trust to evaluate advertising's results over several years.'

The trap not to fall into when evaluating advertising is, according to Dr Broadbent, that of simple association: we did this, sales or consumer measures did that. 'It is obvious that half the brand shares in any one year will increase (ignoring own label, launches and so on),

In both the Krona and John Smith's case histories, the advertising agencies were able to demonstrate to their clients' satisfaction and to outside observers that advertising had played a fundamental part in the sales success. To do this, they used many of the research methods described in this chapter.

KRONA

In the case of Krona, the sales data came from three sources: Van den Berghs' own delivery figures; TCA (standing for Television Consumer Audit), a panel of 6,600 households, based on television company transmission areas, whose grocery purchases are measured continuously by the research company, AGB; and a distribution check conducted in grocers every two months by the research firm, Stats MR.

The distribution of Krona in the test areas of HTV and Westward was monitored for a year from October/November 1978 by Stats MR, rising from 78 per cent to 93 per cent. Krona's share of volume sales was measured during the same period by TCA and rose from nothing to 16 per cent within a year.

The consumer data on the launch of Krona came from several separate quantitative and qualitative surveys during the first year. The first check on awareness of the brand was conducted through a series of quantitative studies based on the Quick Reading method developed by the Unilever Marketing Division. The research was conducted among margarine users in the test areas, who had been categorized by age and class. It showed that within five weeks of the advertising beginning 20 per cent of the market were aware of the brand spontaneously, 79 per cent were aware of it when prompted and 24 per cent had tried it. (These figures rose in succeeding months.)

The Quick Reading Monitors also provided data on how consumers first found out about Krona, what made them try it, whether they had seen the TV advertising and whether they were likely to buy it again. A separate survey of 187 housewives who had ever bought Krona was also conducted, in their homes, in November 1978 and showed that already over 50 per cent had bought more than one pack and felt they had stopped buying other brands or cut down on them.

A Market Monitor was conducted in the HTV and Westward areas in March and April 1979 by the research firm, Taylor Nelson & Associates. Its objects were to evaluate Krona's success in terms of awareness and penetration, to investigate its likelihood of repurchase or trial, and to evaluate the product's perceived acceptability and positioning. From a quota sample of 945 housewives, three sub-groups were identified who were taken through an extended interview: those who had bought Krona and would definitely or probably buy it again (acceptors); those who had bought it but were unlikely to buy it again, or did not know (rejectors); and those who were aware of Krona and had seen a pack in a store (aware non-buyers). This showed that 50 per cent of buyers said they would definitely buy Krona again, and a further 29 per cent would probably buy it again. Nearly half the acceptors had switched to Krona from butter rather than margarine.

There were also two qualitative research surveys. One, conducted by Quicksearch, was designed to evaluate response to the launch campaign after four months' exposure and to elicit response to a likely follow-up campaign. This consisted of 30 individual interviews – 15 trialists and 15 non-trialists, all of whom were aware of the Krona advertising.

The second, conducted by Gregory Langmaid Associates in March 1979, consisted of four group discussions and 16 depth interviews in Swansea and Bristol. All the respondents were from the B, C1 and C2 social grades, and were aged between 20 and 55. Half were users of Krona (who had bought the brand twice or more), the other half were non-users and non-rejectors of the brand (housewives who had heard of the brand but had not tried it). The object of the survey was to examine attitudes to Krona in order to test the acceptability and comprehension of two new Krona commercials, and to probe the suitability and effectiveness of Rene Cutforth as a presenter.

and in those markets where there is volume growth, a high proportion of marketing activity is always associated with sales success in some form', he says. 'This is hardly proof of cause and effect.' Similarly, the fact that a campaign is admired in the business for its creative work or liked by the advertiser's sales force or board is not evidence of sales effectiveness – though these unmeasured benefits may well be valuable.

There are four main advertising elements that can be evaluated, says Dr Broadbent: a single campaign idea (as in a launch, or when a brand has had consistent advertising for some time); a change in the advertising strategy; a change in the amount spent on advertising; and changes in the media used. There is no universal method for evaluating a campaign since there can be many different advertising objectives and ways in which the advertising is expected to work, but the most common combination of methods is that of a single sales-based measure (change on last year, or an area test or statistical analysis) plus consumer usage and attitude data which can help show how advertising affected people and why a sales change may be credible.

Of the sales measures, area tests or test markets are widely used by advertisers to try out new products and new advertising treatments. A few companies, such as Beecham, make allowance statistically for factors other than advertising that could have affected sales in the area test. Beecham's Area Marketing Test Evaluation System (AMTES) involves studying the measurable factors that affect sales before the area test actually starts, so that these can be taken into account accurately. However, most area tests do not go to such lengths, though a careful eye is kept on such factors to make sure that nothing distorts the test. The best single measure of success is that of direct response – coupons cut from press ads, telephone calls to special numbers or, simply, letters responding to an offer made in the body-copy of an ad. This is a cast-iron method of judging an advertisement's effectiveness.

When it comes to usage and attitude data, it is important to separate consumers' responses about the product from those about the advertising so that awareness of the advertising is not confused with awareness of the product: there are many campaigns which people remember well in every respect except the most important – the name of the brand.

JOHN SMITH'S BITTER

The sales data for the John Smith's Bitter analyses came from three main sources: Courage Sales' record of ex-brewery production; the Beer Market Survey (BMS), a census of major brewers' sales to which each brewer contributes its own sales figures confidentially, so that each can monitor market trends and its own share; and the Wyman-Harris Licensed Trade Monitor (LTM), a quarterly audit of retail trade sales carried out by auditor observation in pubs (over 300 pubs in the Northern England sample used for John Smith's).

The consumer data came from two sources. The quantitative research came from the Marplan Usage and Attitude Survey, a regular consumer study commissioned by the brewer, Courage, covering drinking behaviour and brand imagery. It is structured to represent the universe of men drinking bitter once a week or more, with regional upweights of specific groups, including the 18- to 24-year-olds. It was used to find out how many drinkers claimed to drink John Smith's 'most often' as compared with other beers; how many had ever tried it; and how many felt it was 'good value for a bitter', or was 'for knowledgeable drinkers' or had 'lots of flavour'. All these ratings improved markedly after the first burst of the 'Big John' campaign.

The qualitative research was handled by the agency itself, Boase Massimi Pollitt, in keeping with its belief in the importance of the 'planning' function within agencies. Forty group discussions were held in Yorkshire over a period of two years. The first stage was intended to help the agency and advertiser understand the reason for the brand's sales decline. Ten group discussions were held: the sample consisted of regular drinkers of both John Smith's and competitive bitters, in five Yorkshire towns covering strong and weak John Smith's trading areas. Three further stages were carried out during the creation of the advertising to confirm the relevance and appeal of the strategy, and to develop the execution. Post-campaign qualitative research showed that the desired message was getting across and that there was an improvement in the brand's status.

Verbatim quotations from the taped discussions illustrate the point: 'It's a masculine ad, all macho' (man from York, 25-40 age group); 'They're aimed at a big lad who's been knocking down a tree and wants to get down to tap room' (Leeds, 18-30); 'It shows that John Smith's are still in business, still as good as ever was, as traditional as ever was' (Leeds, 30-45).

In addition to the sales and consumer data, BMP also looked at advertising expenditure data. This came from a firm called Media Expenditure Analysis Ltd (MEAL) which monitors all advertising on television and in major newspapers and magazines, calculating the expenditure of every brand on the basis of the rate-card price for the space or airtime. The MEAL data showed that John Smith's share of beer advertising in the Yorkshire region had declined from 26 per cent in 1977 to 12 per cent in 1980. In 1981, its share of advertising expenditure rose to 26 per cent again.

The cases of Krona and John Smith's illustrate the lengths to which advertisers and agencies go to check on the development and progress of their advertising campaigns. By no means all campaigns are as successful as these – indeed, many campaigns and many new products fail altogether. Nevertheless, provided the research is conducted thoroughly lessons can be learned from such failures that can be put to good use in the development of other products and future campaigns.

A

A4 Standard paper size: 11¾ × 8¼in (297 × 210mm) . *Note:* A5 is the size of a folded A4 sheet 18¼ × 5⅞in (210 × 148mm).

ABC Audit Bureau of Circulations. Audits total number of copies of a given publication actually sold.

AB/C1/C2/DE The four most commonly used definitions of socio-economic class (upper and professional middle class/white collar class/skilled working class/unskilled working class and others, including pensioners).

Acknowledgement Any statement expressing thanks for contributions to a work by organizations or individuals.

ACORN A Classification of Residential Neighbourhoods. Classifies people according to the area in which they live on the basis that similar neighbourhoods attract similar types of people with similar spending patterns.

Acrylic A polymer based on synthetic resin. Most paints with an acrylic emulsion base can be mixed and diluted with water. They dry to a tough, flexible, waterproof finish.

Adaptation ('Adapt') An advertisement modified to a different format.

Ad hoc survey Survey of particular topic at a specified time; one-off research.

Adshel (1) A poster contractor. (2) A 4-sheet poster in a shopping precinct or High Street.

Advance Money paid to an author or other contributor in advance of publication, chargeable against subsequent royalty payments.

Advance (Early) Booking Discount Rate A reduced rate for advertising booked in advance, either by a specified number of weeks or by a given date in the month preceding transmission. Usually given as a fixed percentage off the rate-card but occasionally separate advance booking rates are offered.

Advertiser The person or company on whose behalf an advertisement is placed.

ASA Advertising Standards Authority. (1) The organization which handles public complaints about advertising (other than TV and radio) and is also responsible for administrating the application of the British Code of Advertising Practice. (2) American Standards Association. An ASA number appears on film stock to provide a basic quantity from which the length and f number of exposure can be calculated.

Agate (US) Type size of 5½ points.

Agate line (US) Measurement of space in newspaper advertising, denoting ¼in depth by one column width.

Agency fee Remuneration based on a negotiated fee as opposed to commission.

Aided recall An interviewing technique where subjects are asked to select the responses to questions from a list of suggested answers.

Air (US) A large amount of white space in a layout.

Airbrush, Airbrushing A mechanical painting tool producing a fine spray of paint or ink, used in illustration, design and photographic retouching.

AIRC Association of Independent Radio Contractors. The Trade organization which represents independent local radio stations.

Air date The broadcast date of a TV or radio commercial.

Airtime The time available for transmission of programmes and commercials in a contractor's area. Thus, an agency buys airtime comprising individual spots for an advertising campaign.

Alignment The arrangement of type or other graphic material to level up at one horizontal or vertical line.

All in hand A typesetting job when it is in the hands of the compositors.

Alterations Changes made to the body of a text after proofing.

Analysis In market research, the summarising of data in a form that is understandable — in *quantitative* research this is usually *tabulation*, and in *qualitative* research by re-organizing the data in some way.

Animatic A moving, animated element within a TV commercial.

Animation A method of film-making that produces movement by rapid projection of a series of sequential still images, usually drawings or cartoons.

Annotation A type label used on an illustration.

Answerprint The final stage in the production of a TV film, at which colour grading is achieved and from which final copies for distribution are obtained.

Apron (US) Extra white space allowed at the margins of text and illustrations forming a foldout.

Aquatint An intaglio process that allows reproduction of even or graded tones.

Art (paper) Paper with a smooth glossy surface produced by a coating of china clay compound on one or both sides.

Artwork Matter other than text prepared for reproduction such as illustrations, diagrams and photographs.

Ascender The section of a lower case letter rising above the x-height, eg., the upper part of an h or d.

Assembled negative Negative of line and halftone copy used in preparing a printing plate for photolithography.

Attention factors Research-based factors applied to the BARB-reported audience to allow for distractions or breaks in viewing.

Attitude The opinions and responses of individuals or groups towards other people, things or institutions which predispose them to a certain type of behaviour. (see *Behaviour*).

Audience research See Media research.

Audit (1) See *Retail audit*. (2) *Home audit*. A count of consumer goods or consumer durables in the home.

Availability Applies to a media space or slot which is available for advertising, or the date when a site is free for advertising.

Average issue readership The number of people who have looked at a publication during the period in which it is current.

B

Background In an illustration or photograph, the part of the image that appears furthest from the viewer, or on which the main subject is superimposed.

Balance In a layout or design, an arrangement that is visually pleasing, eg an equal relationship between text and illustrations on facing pages.

Balloon (1) A circle enclosing copy in an illustration. (2) In cartoons, the areas containing dialogue.

Banded Pack On-pack premium attached by tape or similar means to product package. Also used when several units are banded together.

Banner A main headline across the full width of a page.

BARB Broadcaster Audience Research Board, responsible for the television rating research reports for BBC and ITV.

Bar code A pattern of vertical lines identifying details of a product, such as country of origin, manufacturer and type of product, conforming to the universal product code. The pattern is read by a computer-controlled sensor for stock control purposes.

Base artwork Artwork requiring the addition of other elements, eg halftone positives, before reproduction.

Base film The basic material for contact film in platemaking for photomechanical reproduction, to which film positives are stripped.

Base line The imaginary line on which the bases of capitals rest.

Basic Rates The price for spots bought according to day and time of transmission.

Bastard size Not conforming to one of the usual sizes.

Batters Damaged or broken letters in print-work.

BDMA British Direct Marketing Association. The representative organization of advertisers, agencies and suppliers in the direct marketing business.

Bed The steel table of a printing press on which the *forme* is placed for printing.

Behaviour The things people do, like, buy, read, view etc as opposed to their attitudes or what they think. Behavioural research covers buying and consuming data but excludes *attitude* data.

Below-the-Line Also known as sales promotion. Publicity other than direct advertising, eg displays in stores, consumer competitions and give-aways.

Bevel The sloping surface of a type rising from the shoulder to the face.

Bias A sample which is inaccurate because of irregularities in sampling procedure, eg *interviewer* bias or bias in the construction of the sample.

Billboard (US) Outdoor advertising sign or poster, often large-scale.

Blank (US) Thick paper used for posters and advertising display.

Blanket The sheet used to cover the

impression cylinder of a printing machine, usually made of rexine or rubber. Also the sheet used to cover the flong when making a stereo mould from a *forme*.

Blanket cylinder The cylinder of an offset press that transfers the ink image to the paper.

Blanket to blanket press *(US)* An offset printing press in which paper is fed between two blanket cylinders to print both sides at once.

Bleed That part of the image which extends beyond the trim-marks of the page. Illustrations which spread to the edge of the page allowing no margins are described as bled-off.

Block (1) Halftone or line illustration engraved or etched on a zinc or copper plate, for use in letterpress printing. (2) A metal stamp used to impress a design on a book cover. The verb to block means to emboss a book cover. (3) *(US)* Metal or wood base on which a plate is mounted to type height.

Block in To sketch in the main areas and reference points on an image as preparation for a drawing or design.

Blockmaker A person producing plates for letterpress printing by the technique of photograving.

Blues, blueprints Low quality proofs for initial checking, printed as white lines on a blue ground. See *ozalid*.

Blue sensitive Quality of film that is sensitive to blue or ultra-violet light.

Board Stiff paper (cardboard) used in printing, especially for covers.

Body copy/matter/type (1) Printed matter forming the main part of a work, but not including headings etc. (2) *(US)* Body type refers to the actual type used in setting a text.

Body matter The text of an advertisement etc.

Bold, bold face Type with a conspicuously heavy, black appearance. It is based on the same design as medium weight type in the fount.

Bonus spot/airtime A free spot given when a TV contractor makes a mistake in a previous transmission. Sometimes allowed for in rate-cards at times of low demand to supplement a booked campaign.

Border A decorative design or rule around matter on a page.

Bounce-Back Further premium offer made to consumer when he gets give-away or self-liquidator.

Bounce lighting Using reflected light from walls, the ceiling or a suitable reflector when lighting a subject in studio photography.

Box Type within an enclosed frame of rules or border.

Bracketed type Type in which the serif is joined to the main stem in an unbroken curve.

BRAD British Rate and Data, a monthly publication giving advertising costs and technical information for all UK media.

Break (Commercial Break or Commercial Slot). Period during which commercials are transmitted between programmes and at intervals during programmes.

Break(down) An *analysis* group. Data is often broken (or broken down) by age, sex, user group or other category.

Broad (segment) spot A spot booked in a given time segment. The contractor usually negotiates in which particular commercial break the spot is transmitted.

Broadsheets Publications measuring 22in (56cm) or less in width but more than 14in (36cm) in depth. See Tabloids.

Broadside/broadsheet Old term for a sheet of paper printed on one side only.

Bromide (1) A photographic print on bromide paper. (2) A proof from photocomposition, made on paper rather than on film.

Bubble-pack Bubble of rigid transparent plastic to hold and protect a product.

Burst — see Campaign.

Bus sides The long strip between decks on a double-decker bus. Other sites available on buses are double-fronts and double-backs.

Buyer — see Time Buyer.

Buying Brief — see Media Plan.

B/W Black and white.

C

C type A term for a photographic colour print produced directly from a negative. It refers to a method of processing developed by Kodak.

C(C1, C2) A socio-economic group comprising the skilled working class (C2) and lower middle class (C1), about 22% and 31% of the population respectively.

Cable A system whereby TV signals are fed to homes from a central source by wire. Existing systems are simple and carry six to ten channels.

CAD Computer aided design. See *Computer Graphics*.

Callback (1) A repeat call to a previous *informant* to ask further questions after leaving a *sample* of the product. (2) A repeat call on an informant who was not at home earlier.

Camera Ready A term applied to artwork, copy or paste up that is ready for reproduction.

Campaign Advertising campaign. **Burst campaign** advertising is concentrated into a limited time period and usually repeated at intervals through a year.

Cancellation Cancellation of bookings, which is normally permitted without penalty up to six or eight weeks in advance of transmission. Thereafter different sliding scales of penalties apply.

Canvass (1) A poll or *census* in which everyone is questioned instead of just a *sample*. (2) The *filtering* procedure whereby the target audience in a particular group is located and the rest discarded.

CAP Code of Advertising Practice Committee which lays down guidelines for the control of advertising content.

Capital, cap The term for upper case letters, deriving from the style of inscription at the head, or capital, of a Roman column.

Caps and smalls Type consisting of capitals for initials and small caps in place of lower case letters.

Caption Strictly speaking, the descriptive matter printed as a headline above an illustration, but also generally used to refer to information printed underneath or beside a picture.

Caption Board Artwork for film titles or studio use when making videotape titles.

Card Rates Quoted rates for advertising. The negotiated cost of a commercial spot may be subject to one or more discounts.

Carriage (1) The part of a printing machine on which the forme moves backwards and forwards during printing. (2) The similar part on a typewriter.

Cartridge (1) Taped copy of a radio commercial sent to radio stations. (2) A type of rough surfaced paper.

Casting-off Calculating how much space manuscript copy will take up when printed in a given typeface.

Catchline Word put at the top of a page or over a piece of type to indicate its place in the whole.

Cathode ray tube Vacuum tube producing information display electrostatically.

Cel (1) Cellulose acetate. (2) In animation, a transparent sheet in the proportion of the film frame on which one stage of the sequence is drawn.

Cell (1) A recessed dot in a photogravure plate forming part of the image for inking. (2) *(US)* see *Cel*. (3) *(US)* A mask used in photographic methods of reproduction.

Census The enumeration of all people or groups involved in a survey.

Centre fold/spread The centre opening of a section (two pages) where one plate may be used to print facing pages with following page numbers. Centre spreads are also called 'naturals'.

Centred Type which is placed in the centre of a sheet or type measure.

Certificate of Insertion Certificate issued by publishers or their printers to confirm that loose inserts have been included.

Character (1) An individual item cast in type, eg a letter, figure, punctuation mark, sign or space. (2) A set of symbols in data processing which represents a figure, letter etc.

Character count The number of characters in a piece of copy.

Character merchandising The use of well-known characters, usually from the cinema, TV or comics for product promotion

Chase A metal frame into which type and blocks are fitted to make one page. The type is held in place by furniture and quoins.

Chroma copy Colour print made without a negative.

Chromolithography Lithographic printing in several colours by traditional techniques.

Chromo-paper Paper which is more heavily coated than art paper. The surface can be dull or glazed. It is used for colour lithography.

CI Copy instruction issued to a publication for placing an advertisement.

Cibachrome print High quality colour print from a transparency.

Circulars Printed advertising in any form, including printed matter sent out by direct mail.

Circulation The number of copies sold per issue of a publication.

Classified ad Newspaper or magazine advertisement without illustration, sold by the line.

Cleaning The process of correcting or removing a name and address from a mailing list or shifting it from one category to another.

Clip A shot or sequence of shots from a film.

Cluster analysis A mathematical techinique for grouping data into clusters with similar characteristics.

Collarette Card with hole which fits over the neck of a bottle to which a give-away premium can be attached.

Colour Bars A strip of process colours at the top of proof acting as a guide to colour strengths.

Colour chart Chart used in colour printing to standardize and select or match coloured inks or tints used.

Colour correction The adjustment of colour values in reproduction to obtain a correct image.

Colour filters Thin sheets of coloured glass, plastic or gelatin placed over a camera lens to absorb or allow through particular colours in the light entering the camera.

Colour guide The colour guide is the set of small marginal marks placed on each of the three negatives used in making blocks for colour printing, so that the printer can superimpose them in register when building up the picture. It also refers to the set of progressive proofs supplied by the plate and blockmaker as a guide to the printer.

Colour key A process for reproducing coloured line drawings. A line block is made from the original drawing and pulls are taken from this, printed in light blue ink; on these the colours are drawn and etched, a separate sheet for each printing.

Colour negative film Film which provides a colour image in negative form after processing.

Colour positives A set of screened positive colour separations.

Colour reproduction A blanket term for several reproduction methods in which the use of photographic masks improves the quality of colour.

Colour separation Process used to give two or more colours on one sheet by separating type and blocks from the first setting into one *forme* for each colour.

Colour separations The number of images or pieces (subjects) to be separated in the colour separation process.

Colour sequence The accepted order of letterpress printing. In four colours it is yellow, red, blue, black.

Colour transparency A positive photographic image produced in colour on transparent film.

Column (1) A section of a page divided vertically, containing text or other matter. It is measured by the horizontal width. (2) A vertical section in tabulated work.

Column inch/centimetre A measure of space used to calculate the cost of display advertising in a newspaper or periodical. The measure is one column width by one inch (or one centimetre) depth.

Column rule The light-faced rule used to separate columns in newspaper.

Combination line and half-tone A combined block or plate used to reproduce photographs with superimposed figures, letters, diagrams etc.

Combine A printing plate containing both half-tone and line.

Commercial art A term used to describe artwork intended for use in advertising or promotion, as distinct from fine art.

Commercial Break/Slot — see Break.

Commission A 15% deduction from quoted rates allowed to recognized advertising agencies by ITV. The advertiser may negotiate partial repayment of commission or pay additional fees to the agency.

Commitment Discount — See Discounts.

Competition Test of skill requiring proof-of-purchase for entry. Prizes are offered for correct answers, and tie-breakers ensure the required numer of major prize-winners.

Compilation Break — see Themed Break.

Compose To set copy in type.

Composing room The area of a printing works specifically designated for typesetting and make up.

Composite artwork Artwork combining a number of different elements.

Composition Type which has been set in a form ready for reproduction by letterpress printing or photolithography.

Compositor The person responsible for setting type, whether by hand or machine process.

Computer An electronic device for the high-speed processing of information.

Computer graphics The use of computers to generate an output of information in graphic form, eg as a picture, diagram or printed characters.

Computerized composition/computer typesetting The use of computers to control various aspects of photocomposition such as character assembly. The computer can be programmed with details of format, tabulation, rules of punctuation, type sizes, measure etc.

Concept Board Illustrations and words used for research purposes to describe creative concepts.

Condensed A typeface with an elongated, narrow appearance.

Consumer Buyer, potential buyer or nonbuyer of product, brand or service.

Consumer Research Research into the numbers, characteristics, preferences and behaviour of consumers.

Contact print, contacts Photographic print or prints made by direct contact with an original positive or negative at same size.

Contact screen A half-tone screen made in a film base which has a graded dot pattern. It is used in direct contact with a film or plate to obtain a half-tone negative from a continuous tone original. Contact screens give better definition than the conventional glass screen.

Container premium A special re-usable container in which a product is packed.

Continuous Research Research in which data is collected on a continuing basis to reflect changing trends and conditions.

Continuous tone This term is used to refer to photographs or coloured originals in which the subject contains shades between the lightest and the darkest tones.

Contones Four-colour continuous tone separations produced by a camera using colour filters.

Contrast The degree of separation of tones in a photograph in the range from black to white.

Controlled Circulation Publications, usually of a trade or specialist nature, with a pre-selected circulation and sent direct to target audience.

Copperplate printing An Intaglio process used in short run printing, producing a sharp, but very black image.

Copy (1) A facsimile, such as a carbon copy. (2) The words of an advertisement or text as distinct from the pictures. (3) A manuscript supplied to a printer. (4) A complete advertisement supplied in any form.

Copy Control Copy restrictions applying to ILR which are laid down by the IBA.

Copy Date The date by which copy must be submitted to the publication.

Copy Test A test of advertising copy, either before or after the advertisement is published which aims to discover *consumers'* reactions to the advertisement.

Copy-writing A term applied to writing of copy specifically for use in advertising.

Corporate identity/housestyle The elements of design by which a company or other institution establishes a consistent and recognizable identity through communication, promotion and distribution material. See also Letterhead, Logotype.

Correction overlay A translucent overlay, registered to artwork, on which corrections are made.

Correlation Statistical degree of relationship between fators. A correlation of 1.0 is perfect agreement; − 1.0 is perfect disagreement, and 0.0 no relationship at all. A score of 0.8 or more shows very close agreement.

Cost/Rank Order The ranking of publications in order of cost of advertising space and readership.

CPI Cost per Inquiry. Total cost of mailing or advertisement divided by the number of inquiries received.

CPO Cost per Order. Similar to Cost per

Inquiry but based on actual orders.

Cost per Thousand (CPT) The cost to the advertiser of reaching 1,000 homes or people in the target audience. Each exposure to the commercial is one impact or impression.

Coupon Part of an advertisement which is completed by the reader to request information or samples from the advertiser.

Coupon Offer Coupons or vouchers given to consumers allowing them a discount on the product being promoted.

Cover The number of times an advertisement is seen or heard. **Gross cover** is the total number of times. **Net cover** is the percentage of the target audience who receive at least one exposure to a spot. **Four Plus Cover** is the percentage who get at least four exposures.

Coverage Also known as *net coverage* or reach. The number of people in a particular target group who have the opportunity to see or hear an advertisement at least once. It is expressed as a percentage, or sometimes in thousands.

Cover Date The date of publication shown on the cover although the publication may be available earlier.

Credit/courtesy line A line of text accompanying an illustration giving the name of an organization or individual supplying the picture or artwork.

Cromalin A substitute proof for a conventional four-colour proof.

Crop To trim a photograph or illustration. The crop or cropmark is the part of the photograph or illustration to be eliminated.

Cross-head Subsection paragraph heading or numeral printed in the body of text, usually marking the first subdivision of a chapter.

Crown A paper and poster size = 15in × 10in (381cm × 254cm). Double-crown = 30in × 20in (162 × 508cm).

Cumulative Cover The cumulative build up of readership of a publication.

Curved plate A plate used in a rotary press that curves around the plate cylinder.

Cut-Out An illustration in which the background is cut away.

Cutting Copy First version of a TV commercial.

Cyan A shade of blue used in four-colour printing.

Cylinder press A printing press in which the forme is carried on a flat bed under a paper-bearing cylinder for an impression to be made at the point of contact.

D

D(DE) The lowest socio-economic group, containing the unskilled working class (D) and those living at the lowest levels of subsistence (E), about 24% and 9% of the population respectively.

DBS — see Direct Broadcast Satellite.

D/C or D.C. Shorthand for double-column.

Daguerreotype A method of making and fixing a photographic image. It was invented in 1833 by L.J.M. Daguerre.

Date-plan Plan showing when and where the advertisements in a campaign will appear.

Day-part Parts into which days are divided for purposes of TV advertising (eg day-time, pre-peak, peak-time, post-peak).

Daytime A day-part, usually until 1600 hours on weekdays.

Deadline The final date set for completion of a particular job.

Dealer Incentive Any incentive aimed specifically at the retailer or wholesaler, sometimes known as a dealer loader.

Deep-etch Half-tone A half-tone plate with unwanted screen dots removed, leaving areas of plain paper on the printed sheet.

Demographics The division of an audience by age, sex, social status and other characteristics.

Density Of type, the amount and compactness of type set within a given area or page. Of a transparency or printed image, the measure of tonal values.

Depth of field The area in front of or behind the point of focus in a photographic image at which other details remain in acceptable focus.

Depth interview Unstructured, informal interview designed to uncover attitudes and motivation.

Descender That part of a lower case letter that falls below the X-height.

Desk Research Research using published data, past research and other existing material, without recourse to field work.

Diary Record of items bought or other specified behaviour, kept by informants in consumer panels and other surveys.

Didot point The continental unit for type. It measures 0.0148in whereas an English point is 0.013837 in.

Die stamping A form of printing where all the characters are in relief.

Digitize To convert an image into a form that can be processed, stored and electronically reconstructed.

Digitizing pad/tablet An input device that translates freehand drawing into digitized form for computer use.

DIN Deutsche Industrie Norm. A code of standards published in Germany, still used in rating film speeds.

DBS Direct Broadcast Satellite. A space satellite which can transmit broadcast signals to ground receivers within its range. Large numbers of channels can be transmitted.

Direct colour separation Colour separation in which a halftone screen is used in the original separation to produce screened negative directly.

Direct Mail Advertising A promotional effort using direct delivery (usually by mail) to distribute advertising material.

Direct Response Advertising Advertising through any medium designed to generate a direct response by mail, telephone, or other measurable means.

Discrimination test Test to show how

many people can detect the difference between products tested. The most common form is the triadic test, in which informants test three products (two of which are the same) and are asked to pick the odd one out.

Display advertisement Advertising matter designed to a size or quality to attract immediate attention.

Display matter/type Larger typefaces designed for headings etc, usually above 14pt in bookwork.

Display size The size of type used for headings, advertising matter etc. It is always greater than 12 point so clearly distinguishable from body type.

Distribution (1) Retail distribution, recorded in terms of percentages of outlets stocking a product; 50% distribution means that half the stockists hold the product. (2) Shorthand for frequency distribution, a statistical term describing the spread of data along a *scale* or parameter.

Dot The smallest basic element of a halftone.

Dot for dot reproduction A direct method of producing printing film by photographing a previously screened image. A maximum of 10 percent enlargement of reduction can be achieved.

Double column Two columns across each page.

Double-spread Two facing pages on which matter is continued directly across as if they were one page.

Down Stroke A heavy stroke in a type character, originally the downward stroke of a pen in calligraphy.

Draft To compose copy or an illustration in a basic form to be refined, or an item so prepared. A final draft is copy that is ready for printing.

Drip — see Campaign

Drive and housewife time Time periods with specific audiences. Drive time tends to be morning and evening rush hour, housewife time the hours in between.

Dry Mounting The use of heat-sensitive adhesives.

Dry Transfer Lettering Characters transferred to the page by rubbing them off the back of the sheet.

Dupe *abb* duplicate.

Duplicate A copy of an original (transparency, block, film etc.) that is exact in every way and at exactly the same size.

Duplication Overlap of readership between different publications.

Dustbin check Also known as a home audit. A form of retail audit in which brand consumption is determined by asking informants to discard empty packs into a special dustbin.

E

Ear, Ear-piece The advertising space or spaces beside the front-page title-line of a newspaper.

Early booking — see Advance booking.
Early (Off-Peak) — see Peak time.
Early payment discount Discount offered by contractors for settling an invoice by the first working day of the month following transmission.
Electro A printing plate duplicated electrolytically from the original.
Em A unit of linear measurement, usually 12 points or 4.5mm.
En A measurement half the width of the em, used in *casting off*.
Equal impacts A system whereby the same number of rating points is set as a target in each area and the budget in a campaign is allocated to achieve this.
Establishment survey Large-scale survey of homes conducted on behalf of BARB to establish demographic profiles in each ITV region so that representative panel homes can be recruited.
Estimate Calculation of the cost of work on a printing order.
Exploded view Drawing of an object showing its parts separately but arranged in such a way as to indicate their relationships within the object when assembled.
Extra origination charges Charges made by publishers for four-colour work which require more than one transparency.

F

Face (1) The printing surface of any type *character*. (2) The group or *family* to which any particular type design belongs, as in *typeface*.
Factor analysis A mathematical procedure for reducing data used in *attitude* research (see *cluster analysis*).
Fat face A *typeface* with extreme contrast in the widths of thin and thick strokes.
Filler An extra figure or piece of *copy* in a magazine or newspaper put in to fill space in a page or *column*.
Film make-up Assembling the elements of a photostat advertisement.
Film master A complete film positive of an advertisement used to make duplicates.
Filter A gelatin, glass or plastic sheet which may be placed over or in front of a camera lens to alter the colour or quality of light passed through to the film.
Finished artwork — see *Artwork*.
Finished Rough See *Presentation Visual*.
Fish eye lens A wide angle lens that produces a distorted image with a pronounced apparent curve.
Fix To spray a drawing or other artwork with a fixative so that it cannot smudge.
Fixative A clear varnish sprayed over *artwork* to protect it.
Flat-bed Describes a press which has the printing forme on a plane surface, as distinct from a press with a curved printing surface. In a flat-bed cylinder press the forme is placed and moved to and fro under the cylinder,

while the flat-bed web press prints from a flat forme on to an endless roll of paper.
Flip-charts A presentation in which the pages can be turned.
Flip-Charts A presentation prepared in a ring binder or similar form so that the 'pages' can be turned.
F/M Facing matter. Indicates that the advertisement will face editorial matter.
Foolscap Standard size printing paper, 13½ × 17in (343 × 432mm).
Foot (1) The margin at the bottom of a page or the bottom edge of a book. (2) The undersurface of a piece of type.
Format Size, make-up and general appearance of a publication.
Forme Type matter and illustration blocks assembled into pages ready for letterpress printing.
Forty-eight Sheet Standard poster size 20 × 10ft.
Fount or Font A complete set of type for a given type face.
Four-colour process A method of printing in full colour by colour separation, using four plates in cyan, yellow, magenta and black.
Four-colour Scans Set of colour-separated screened positives made by scanning a transparency.
Four Plus (4+) Cover See *Cover and Frequency*.
Four-sheet A poster size 40in × 60in.
Free-fall Insert A promotional piece included in a newspaper or magazine.
Freephone Free telephone facility to allow readers or direct mail recipients to enquire or order by phone.
Freepost Postage-paid address or envelope for use at no cost to the sender.
Frequency The number of times an individual viewer sees a commercial in a campaign. See *cover*.
Frequency distribution Describes how many people saw how many ads, in the campaign. Expressed as *opportunities to see* (OTS).
Full out Instruction to typesetter to set copy across a full measure, ie not indented.

G

Galley (1) Long shallow tray in which type is kept. (2) Common usage: galley proof. Form in which text comes from the typesetter before copy is arranged into pages.
Gatefold An extra leaf folded in to extend a page. Often part of the front cover.
GHI Guaranteed Homes Impressions. TV airtime where the contractor guarantees to deliver a number of homes impressions.
Give-away Low-cost premium given away free.
Grading A laboratory process whereby uniform colour quality is ensured throughout a film or video tape.
g/m², or **gsm**. grams per square metre A unit of measurement for paper used in printing.

Grant Apparatus used by artists and typographers to enlarge or reduce drawings.
Graphic-design Design involving two-dimensional processes, for example, illustration, typography, photography and printing methods.
Gravure A printing process in which the image is etched onto a plate. The plate is inked, then wiped clean, leaving the ink in the image. It then prints off onto the paper.
Grid A measuring guide used by designers to ensure consistency in layouts. The grid shows type widths, picture areas and specified trim sizes, etc.
Gross costs — see Cost per Thousand
Gross cover — see Cover
Gross OTS The total coverage of a campaign plan, adding together the coverages achieved by each single advertisement. Expressed in thousands.
Group discussion Research technique used to survey social habits and attitudes, in which a number of people discuss a topic under the direction of a researcher.
G-spool A copy of a videotape commercial sent to TV stations. Also referred to as a DUB.
Guard Book (1) A book containing copies of all advertisements published for a client. (2) A book which contains the essential information of a client's advertising activities.
Gutter (1) In imposition, the space made up of fore-edges of pages plus the trim. (2) Common usage: the channel down the centre of a page.

H

Half-tone Process by which *continuous tone* is simulated by a pattern of dots of varying size. A half-tone block is a zinc or copper printing plate prepared by this process.
Half-tone blow up The enlargement of a half-tone negative to coarsen the screened dot pattern.
Hall test Research conducted at a central location, for example a hall in a shopping precinct, particularly useful when home visits are impracticable.
Handling house A specialized service dealing with checking, packaging and mailing of premiums, etc.
Hanging punctuation Punctuation marks allowed to fall outside the measure of a piece of text.
Hardware A term for equipment. It generally applies to the apparatus in a computer.
Head-on site Poster panel facing aproaching traffic.
Heavy (*typ*) An alternative term for *bold*.
Highlight The lightest tones of a photograph or illustration.
Hoarding A series of posters fronting the street and running along the pavement.
Hologram/holograph (1) An image with the illusion of three dimensions created by lasers. (2) In publishing, a manuscript hand-written by the author.

Hot metal General term for composing machines casting single pieces of type from molten metal.

House style The style of spelling, punctuation and spacing used in a printing or publishing house to ensure consistent copy during typesetting.

I

IFC Inside front cover.

Illustration (1) A drawing, painting, diagram or photograph reproduced in a publication to explain or supplement the text. (2) A term used to distinguish a drawn image from one that is photographed.

Image (1) The subject to be reproduced as an illustration on a printing press. (2) The way a product, shop or operation is perceived, which may or may not reflect reality. **Brand image:** a brand's identity in the eyes of the consumer.

Impact/Impression — see Cost per Thousand.

Imperial A size of printing and drawing paper, 22 × 30in.

Incentive (1) Any premium offered in return for performing a specified task and normally used in the context of salesmen and dealer incentives. (2) Alternative word for premium.

In charge date The date from which an advertiser starts to pay for his poster, ie the date the campaign starts. Posters are usually posted within five working days of the in charge date.

ISBA Incorporated Society of British Advertisers.The representative organization which voices the opinion of advertisers.

Indent To begin a line (or lines) with a space.

IBA Independent Broadcasting Authority. The controlling body for commercial television and radio.

Informant The person giving information or answering questions. Also called respondent or interviewee.

In-home placement Product testing in the home.

In-house (Of a process or service) Carried out within a company, not bought in.

Inkers The rollers on a printing press which apply ink to the type and block surfaces.

In-pack Give away premium inside product package.

In pro In proportion. A term used to direct the enlargement or reduction of photographic material.

Inserts See insets.

Insets Also called inserts. Advertising material added to or bound into a publication after it has been printed.

Inspection Report Detailed description of poster sites prepared by qualified inspectors.

Intaglio A printing image below the surface of the plate.

IPA Institute of Practitioners in Advertising. The representative organization of the advertising agency business in the UK.

Island site A press which is surrounded on at least three sides by editorial matter.

ISP Institute of Sales Promotion. The professional body of the promotion business.

Issue date/cover date The official publication date of a magazine or newspaper, which may differ from the on-sale-date when it appears on bookstalls.

Italics Typeface with *slanting letters*.

ITCA The Independent Television Companies Association Ltd. A trade association for programme companies or contractors.

ITV Independent Television. Commercial TV, as distinct from the publicly funded BBC.

J

JICPAS Joint Industry Committee for Poster Advertising Surveys.

JICRAR Joint Industry Committee for Radio Audience Research.

JICNARS — NRS The Joint Industry Committee for National Readership Surveys. The definitive and comprehensive readership survey for UK publications.

Justification Spacing of words and letters so that each line of text finishes at the same point.

Justify To even up left and right hand sides of a column of type.

Juxtaposition The placing of competing posters next to each other.

K

Key Code in advertisement coupon to indicate the publication from which replies have been sent.

Key lines Lines on artwork to indicate position of elements on areas for tint laying or painting up solids etc.

Key number A code in a corner of a reply coupon to check response.

Key size Unit of photosetting type size measurement.

Kodatrace A clean film overlay on artwork that carries additional instructions for printers or blockers.

L

Laminate To protect paper or card and give it a glossy surface by applying a transparent plastic coating through heat or pressure.

Landscape/horizontal format A format for illustrations, press ads, posters etc in which the width is greater than the height.

Layout An outline or sketch which gives the general appearance of the printed page, indicating the relationship between text and illustration.

Leaders Dots or dashes set in line to link figures or words.

Leads Thin strips of metal used to increase space between lines of metal type.

Leaf Two pages.

Legend Another name for a caption.

Letraset Trade name for dry transfer lettering on a plastic sheet that is rubbed down on paper or board in preparing artwork.

Letterpress (1) The process of printing from a raised image (as in typewriting). (2) The text of a book, including line illustrations.

Library shot/pic A picture or illustration taken from an existing source.

Light pen A device used with a VDU to retrieve information from a computer, using a drawn symbol rather than keyboard instructions.

Line and half-tone An illustration process in which line and half-tone negatives are combined then printed on to a plate and etched.

Line block A printing plate, usually from a drawing, with no graduations of tone.

Line by line The buying of position sites on an individual basis to suit specific needs.

Linefeed The photosetting equivalent of leading.

Lip-sync Synchronization of sound in films to match movement of speaker's lips.

List (Mailing list) Names and addresses of individuals or companies having a common characteristic or interest

List Broker A specialist who arranges for one company to make use of another's list.

List Cleaning — see Cleaning.

List Owner A person who has developed or purchased a list of names having something in common.

Literal A spelling mistake in printed matter.

Litho — see Offset Lithography

Litho negatives or postives Screened film supplied to publications.

Lithography Printing from a dampened, flat surface using greasy ink, based on the principle that oil and water do not mix.

Logo, Logotype (1) The distinguishing emblem of a company or organization. (2) A word or several letters cast as one unit.

Lower case Small letters, as distinct from capitals. See also Upper case.

Loyalty A measure of brand allegiance determined by consumer panels or attitude research.

M

Machine proof The final proof, taken when the publication is ready for printing.

Magenta The shade of red established as one of the standard four-colour letterpress printing inks.

Mail-in A premium for which the consumer has to write in.

MPS Mail Preference Service. A service of the BDMA where consumers can have their names removed from or added to mailing lists.

Make ready The work done by the printer on the press to achieve the best possible reproduction.

Make-up (1) The general arrangement of a paper or book. (2) The actual assembling of a page ready for printing.

Margins The blank areas on a printed page which surround the matter.

Marked proof The proof, usually on galleys, supplied to the author for correction. It contains the corrections and queries made by the printer's reader.

Mark up To specify every detail needed for the compositor to set the copy. The mark up is copy with instructions on it.

Market segmentation The process of identifying different groups of buyers in a particular market according to age, sex, class etc.

Married print (Combined print) Film with picture and sound correctly synchronized.

Masking (1) Applying a protective layer to an illustration to cover an area while other parts are painted or airbrushed. (2) Blocking out part of an image with opaque material to prevent reproduction or to allow for alteration in copy. (3) A technical method of adjusting values of colour and tone in photomechanical reproduction.

Master proof A printer's proof read and marked with corrections and queries.

Masthead (1) The individual style of the name/title of a newspaper or magazine. (2) Details of a publisher and staff printed on the editorial or contents page of a newspaper or periodical.

Matrix (plural, **Matrices**) Mould from which type is cast.

Mats Papier mâché matrices used in newspaper printing.

Matter Either manuscript or copy to be printed, or type that is composed.

MEAL (figures) Media Expenditure Analysis Ltd, a company which monitors advertising expenditure.

Mechanicals The material supplied to a publication, already assembled, for the reproduction of an advertisement, ie headlines, pictures, text etc. (See Paste-up.)

Media Plural term referring to information sources, eg radio, television, publishing.

Media Independent An organization specializing in buying airtime and press space etc and perhaps planning campaigns. It is an alternative to the media department of a large advertising agency. Also called a buying house or shop.

Media owner A company which owns and operates commercially a media organization in television, press, or other media.

Media plan Plan by advertising agency showing proposed distribution of the client's budget and rationale for choices made.

Media research The study of media audiences or readers concerned with estimating numbers or types of people who see or hear the advertising appearing in these media, and how they react to it.

Media schedule A computer record of the bookings made for a campaign.

Media systems A comprehensive system for recording bookings and transmissions and invoicing advertisers by computer.

Merchandising Facet of marketing concerned with achieving maximum product movement at retail level.

Metric spot length TV commercials in lengths of 10, 20, 30 seconds instead of the former 7, 15, 45 seconds.

Mini-page A press space, usually about three-quarters of the width and depth of a page, surrounded by editorial matter. A premium applies.

Mix — see Dub.

Mock Up The rough visualization of a publication or packaging design.

Moiré A printing fault where half-tones appear as a mechanical pattern of dots.

Mono (Monochrome) Black and white printing, as distinct from colour.

Monotype (1) The trade name for composing machines which cast single types. (2) The process of making a painting on glass or metal and then taking an impression on paper.

Motivation research A form of media research which seeks to establish relationships between people's behaviour and their underlying motives, desires or emotions.

Multiple exposure In photography, stages of the same subject or separate images superimposed to form one image.

MVO — see Voice Over

N

Narrowcast All uses of a TV other than receiving a signal through an aerial (broadcast), eg local cable programmes, video games, pay TV.

Natural Break — see Break

Negative/Neg Photographic image fixed in reverse tones or colours from which positive prints can be obtained.

Net cost — see Cost per Thousand

Net cover — see Cover

Net coverage/reach The total unduplicated coverage of a campaign plan. It describes the number of people covered at least once, either in thousands or as a percentage.

News proof A proof on newsprint-type paper to simulate newspaper.

Newsprint The paper used for printing newspapers, characteristically absorbent because it is unsized.

N/M Next matter. A press space which appears next to editorial.

NRS National Readership Survey

NS The Newspaper Society. Trade association for provincial newspaper publishers.

NPA Newspaper Publishers Association. Trade association for national newspaper publishers.

O

Octavo (1) A sheet of paper folded in half three times, to make eight or sixteen pages. (2) A standard broadside divided into eight parts.

Off-pack Premium not attached to product package but given away at point-of-sale.

Off-peak — see Peak-time

Offset (1) In letterpress printing an unwanted transfer of ink from a printed page to another sheet. (2) Offset lithography.

Offset lithography A method of lithography by which the image is not printed direct from the plate but 'offset' first on to a rubber-covered cylinder, the blanket, which performs the printing operation. For offset litho publications, the agency supplies artwork, not a block.

On-line Interconnected functions in computer work under the direct control of a central computer.

On-pack Give-away premium attached to outside of product package.

On-sale date The date on which a publication goes on sale on bookstalls. May differ from issue/cover date, especially with monthly magazines.

Opinions What people think; their views on particular subjects. Sometimes distinguished from attitudes in being more changeable.

Optical A trick effect achieved mechanically by combining two or more film pictures into one by superimposition.

OCR Optical character recognition. Device for the electronic scanning of copy and its conversion into photoset matter without keyboard operation.

Optical titles Titles superimposed on film. Sometimes called opticals.

Option An option to book a TV spot.

Oracle — see Teletext

Original Any matter or image intended for reproduction.

OTH Opportunities to hear. The number of times a person in the target audience is exposed to the radio station airing the advertisement. The size of a radio campaign is often described by average OTH for all members of the target audience. (See Cover)

OTS Opportunities to see. The number of times a member of the audience is exposed to the TV station screening the commercial. The size of a TV campaign is often described by average OTS for all members of the target audience. Also used in press coverage. (See Cover)

Outdoor advertising Posters, signs, facias and all forms of advertisement appearing out of doors.

OBC Outside Back Cover. The outside back cover of a publication.

Out-takes Film sequences shot but discarded in the edited version.

Overlap area An area where two or more ITV stations can be received.

Overlay (1) A transparent sheet used in the preparation of multicolour artwork. (2) A translucent sheet covering a piece of original artwork, on which instructions may be written.

Overmatter Matter set which does not fit into the appropriate space.

Overprint Printing over an already printed area.

Over-runs — see Discounted Airtime (Guaranteed Audience Packages)

Ozalid A trade name referring to a method of copying page proofs by the diazo process.

P

Page make-up — (1) see Make-up. (2) In photocomposition, a display showing copy as it will appear on a page.

Page proofs Proofs of type which have been paginated. They are the secondary stage in proofing, after galley proofs and before machine proofs.

Pagination (1)The arrangement of pages. (2) Printing the page numbers.

Panel A sample of shops or people used for regular periodic research. The panel provides continuous measurement as distinct from the survey, which goes back to different people to ask the same question.

Pantone Range of colour guides in paper in self-adhesive form.

Paper-set An advertisement set up in type by the publication instead of being reproduced from a block or mechanicals.

Paste-up A layout of a number of pages used to plan the positioning of illustrations, captions and text.

Patch To change one element of a layout or printing plate.

Pay-TV A system whereby homes connected to cable may choose programmes such as first-run films and pay for them when they are viewed.

Peak time The evening period when audiences would normally be at their highest and consequently with the highest rates on the rate-card. All other time is called off-peak.

PE plate The method of etching letterpress plates in one operation with a powderless etch.

Penetration A measure of usage in consumer research, representing the proportion of homes or individuals to whom a particular product has penetrated in terms of either purchase or consumption.

Perfect binding A binding method in which the leaves of a publication are trimmed at the back and glued, but not sewn.

Perfect register Colour advertisements which appear on one page of a newspaper without cutting the design as happens with wallpaper colour.

Personality promotion Representatives call on homes, awarding cash or goods if consumers can show proof of buying a product and will answer questions about product.

Photocomposition The production of display line and text by photographic means on film or paper. Photocomposing machines assemble lines or letters from various forms of photo matrix.

Photograph A representational image formed by the action of light on a sensitized material.

Photogravure The process of printing from a photomechanically prepared surface, which holds the ink in recessed cells.

Photolithography A method of printing in which the image is transferred to the plate photographically and printed on a lithographic printing machine. Sometimes known as offset.

PMT Photomechanical transfer. A mechanical method of quickly producing photoprints from flat originals for use in paste up and presentation.

Photomontage The use of images from different photographs combined to produce a new composite image.

Photo-polymer A printing process requiring bromides.

Photoprint A copy made by photocopying the original and making a print from the negative. Of better quality than a photostat.

Photo-set Also called film-set. Headlines and text composed photographically instead of using metal letters.

Photostat A copy made directly from the original, by, eg, a Xerox machine.

Pica (1) The old name for 12-point, a unit of measure used in setting. (2) One of the typefaces commonly used in typewriters.

Pilot A small test survey, the aim of which is to establish whether the main survey is feasible.

Planner The person who puts together the media plan for presentation to the client.

Planographic Used of methods of printing from a flat surface, as in lithography.

Plate (1) An electro or stereo of set-up type. (2) A sheet of metal bearing a design, from which an impression is printed. (3) A full page book illustration, printed separately from the text often on different paper. (4) A photographic plate.

Plate press A printing press in which a flat plate, or platen, is lowered and pressed against a horizontal forme.

Point Standard unit of type size. In the British-American system there are 72 points to the inch. See also Didot points.

Point-of-Sale display Also called point-of-purchase display. Display material used in retail outlet to draw attention to product.

POP Post Office preferred. Standard envelope sizes.

Portrait pages Alternative name for mini-pages.

Portrait A picture or page with the vertical dimensions greater than the horizontal.

Positive (1) An image made photographically on paper or film, usually derived from a negative. (2) A photographic colour transparency of film with a positive image, used in platemaking.

Poster A large-scale display or advertising sign on card or heavy paper.

PPA Periodical Publishers Association. Trade association for magazines and periodicals publishers.

Pre-empt structure The theory of the pre-empt system for TV buyers is that the final cost will be governed by demand. If a buyer books a spot at a low rate but another is prepared to pay a higher rate for it, the former can be pre-empted and he loses the spot.

Premium An item offered to a buyer, usually free or at a nominal price, as an inducement to purchase or try out a product or service.

Presence factor — see Attention Factor

Presentation visual Also called a finished rough. Material prepared as a sample of the proposed appearance of a printed work.

Press date The date on which a publication is printed.

Press proof The last proof to be read before giving authorization for printing.

Press run The total number of copies produced in one printing.

Pre-testing Research to test advertising before it is used as part of a campaign.

Primary colours Pure colours from which all other colours can be mixed. In subtractive colour mixing, used in printing, they are magenta, cyan and yellow. The primary colours of light, or additive colours, are red, blue and green.

Print origination In printing, all preparatory work completed prior to proofing.

Print run The number of copies required from a printer and the process of printing the copies.

Printing processes The main classes of printing processes are intaglio, planographic, relief, stencil. All these rely on the contact of surfaces under pressure.

Printout (1) Record of information made by printing device attached to a computer. (2) An enlarged copy made from a microform.

Process colours Cyan, Magenta, yellow.

Profile More usually *consumer* profile. Description of a group of consumers in terms of their buying habits, attitudes, or personal characteristics. Often expressed in percentage form.

Programme schedule A schedule of programme plans usually issued four times a year by the TV contractor, which the TV buyer can use to estimate audiences when deciding which spots to book.

Progressive proofs The proofs taken in colour printing as a guide to shade and registration. Each colour is shown separately and also imposed on the preceding colour.

Projection The representation of a three-dimensional object or a line or figure from a given viewpoint or by graphic conventions. The main types of projections are axonometric, conical, cylindrical, isometric, orthographic, parallel and perspective.

Projective techniques A range of research techniques which allow the respondent to express his views on a sensitive topic indirectly by attributing them to an imaginary third party.

Promotion Presentation and advertising intended to encourage the production and marketing of a product.

Prompt This is a device used deliberately to influence an informant's answer, such as using a list of pre-coded answers.

Prompted recall — see Recall

Proof An impression obtained from an inked plate, stone, screen, block or type in order to check the progress and accuracy of the work. Also called a pull.

Proof-of-purchase Token from product package, such as label or box-top, enabling consumer to qualify for a premium.

Proof reader A person who reads proofs to correct and revise copy where necessary.

Proof-reading Marks The established way of marking corrections on printers' proofs.

Psychographics The study of characteristics or qualities which denote the lifestyle or attitude of consumers.

Pull A proof or print from a block or type.

Pull-out section Pages of a periodical that can be detached together.

Q

Quad Four times the normal paper size — 35 × 45in (890 × 143mm).

Qualitative research Research techniques which are not designed to produce quantifiable results for statistical analysis.

Quantitive Research Research techniques designed to produce quantifiable results for statistical analysis.

Quartertone The most commonly used photo-mechanical process after the half-tone. Continuous tone is converted back into line and some of the tones are omitted. The sharp, bold effect is enhanced by retouching the negative or print.

Quarto A piece of paper folded in half twice, making quarters or eight pages.

Questionnaire A precise research instrument. Respondents are asked set questions in a fixed order so that their answers can be quantified.

Quota The number and type of people one interviewer is required to interview as his or her contribution to the total quota sample.

Quota sample A sample in which interviewers are required to collect information from a predetermined number of people with specific, observable characteristics. Age, sex and class are the features most often controlled for. Quota sampling aims to get a cross-section without resorting to the more complex random sampling.

R

R-type A direct process of producing photographic colour prints, developed by Kodak. R19 is the production of a print from artwork, R14 from a transparency.

Random sample A sample in which each item or member has an equal probability of being selected. A common method is to pick every name from an electoral roll or other such list.

Range left/right A form of setting in which lines of unequal length form a vertical either on the left-hand side of the column or on the right.

Ranking In research, the placing of items in order of preference.

Rate-card Document issued by a publisher or contractor setting out advertising rates.

Rate protection The practice of allowing existing bookings to remain at previous rates when a new rate-card is issued at short notice.

Rating (point) — see TVR

Reader A person who reads and corrects the printer's proofs against the original manuscript.

Readership The number of people reading or looking at a copy of a publication.

Recall Memory, act of remembering. Term used in interviewing, as in spontaneous recall, prompted recall.

Reduced price offer Price reduction printed on-pack.

Regional adviser — see Local, Dealer or Regional Rates

Register (1) The correct alignment of pages with the margins in order. (2) The correct positioning of one colour on another in colour printing.

Register marks Marks or devices used in colour printing to position the paper correctly.

Release (form) A form signed by models or anyone being photographed or filmed, giving permission for the picture to be used for advertisement purposes.

Relief printing Printing methods in which the image is obtained from a raised surface.

Repetition The effect of repeated presentation of an advertisement so that the same people have frequent opportunities to see it.

Reproduction proof/repro High quality proofs on art paper. They are used to prepare finished material for printing and can be used as artwork.

Resolution The efficiency of a photomechanical or computer graphics system in reproducing fine detail.

Respondent The consumer being interviewed.

Response (1) The number of consumers who respond to a promotional activity. (2) The behaviour evoked by a stimulus, for instance, the answer to a question, or the choice made from a selection.

Response function A subjective value given to a campaign to determine the probable value to the advertiser.

Retail audit Continuous specialized research using a sample of retail distributors to study stock levels and the sales performance of specific products. The most widely used Retail Audit is carried out by Nielsen.

Retouching Correction or alteration of photographs by an artist.

Reverse Print in opposite way to normal, as when a picture left becomes right or when black becomes white.

Reverse B to W Reverse black to white. An instruction to the printer to reverse the tones of an image.

Reversed out (of type matter). Having the appearance of being cut out of solid colour.

Revise proof or Revise A proof which incorporates corrections or revisions marked on an earlier proof.

RNAB Regional Newspaper Advertising Bureau. Promotes advertising in the regional press.

ROM Run of month. There is no guarantee as to which day the advertisement will appear.

Roman (1) Upright typesetting face (as opposed to italics). (2) Light typesetting face (as opposed to bold).

ROP See Run of press, Run of paper.

Rotary Press A newspaper press which uses a cylindrical printing surface. Papers are delivered folded and counted, ready for dispatch.

Rotogravure Intaglio printing performed on a rotary press.

Rough A sketch showing a proposed design.

ROW Run of week. The advertisement appears or not, at the media owner's discretion. A lower tariff applies.

ROY Run of year. There is no guarantee as to which month the advertisement will appear.

Rules Metal strips, of type height, in various widths and lengths, used for printing lines in letterpress (hot metal) printing.

Run The number of impressions taken from a forme at one time. A short run means few copies, a long run, a large number of copies.

Run-of-paper (1) The advertisement is placed at the media owner's discretion. Standard rates apply. (2) An advertising position which gives no display advantages.

Run of press Colour printing included as a standard feature of printing for publications.

Run on (1) Typography to continue without starting a new paragraph. (2) Printing to produce additional copies at the same time as the original requirement.

Run over To carry over words from one line to the next.

Rushes The first prints of the film before editing.

S

Saddle-stitch A method of fastening the sheets of a publication by stitching mechanically through the middle fold.

Sales In retail audit, the level of retail sales, expressed either in volume or monetary value.

Sales incentive Any incentive offered to salesmen.

Sample A fraction of the whole taken to represent the whole. In market research, a sample of the population taken to represent the whole. Generally the larger the sample, the greater its accuracy.

Sanserif A typeface without serifs and usually without stroke contrast, eg, the typeface in which this glossary is set.

Scaling, Scaling up To determine the degree of enlargement or reduction necessary to reproduce an original image within a given area of a design. The scaling may be represented as a percentage of the image area or in figures proportionate to the dimensions of the original, using a diagonal bisection of the image to govern the increased or reduced measurements.

Scamp A rough sketch of an advertisement.

Scatter Proofs Proofs for checking the quality of illustrations in photomechanical reproduction. To reduce proofing costs, as many images as possible are proofed altogether, with no reference to correct positions in a layout.

SCC Single-column Centimetre. The basic unit of measurment in newspaper advertising.

Schedule Details of advertising proposed or booked showing the media, nature of space, size, dates, costs etc.

Scraperboard Prepared board with a surface of gesso. It is first inked over and then scratched or scraped with a point or blade to give the effect of a white line engraving.

Screen Also called the half-tone screen. The number of dots per square inch on a half-tone process block; the lower the number, the coarser the reproduction will be.

Screen clash A disruptive pattern in an image produced when two or more half-tone screens have been positioned at incorrect angles.

Screen printing Printing method used for small runs. Ink is forced through the fine mesh of a fabric or metal screen. The image is formed by a stencil made photographically on the screen or a cut stencil that adheres to the screen fabric.

Segment — see Time Segment

Self-liquidator/Self-liquidating premium Any incentive the charge for which covers cost of premium, handling charges and postage.

Separation — see Colour separation.

Separation artwork Artwork in which a separate layer is created for each colour to be printed, usually by means of translucent overlay.

Series discount A discount saved by booking a series of advertisements in a publication.

Serif The small terminal stroke at the end of the main stroke of a letter.

Set (1) The width of a type body. (2) Used as an instruction to typesetters, as in 'set to 12 picas' or as a description, ie 'hand-set'. (3) The proportions of the Em of a size of type.

Share Percentage of the market, or of any total.

Sheet A single piece of paper.

Sheet fed A printing machine into which sheets are fed singly.

Shelf-talker A small self-service point-of-sale display attached to shelving.

Show-through A fault in which a printed impression on one side of the paper is visible on the other side.

Shrink-wrap Flexible plastic film covering product, applied by heat shrinking process.

Site Location where posters are displayed.

Site Classification The grading of poster sites according to position, traffic volume, proximity to sales outlets etc.

Sixteen-sheet A standard poster size measuring 120 × 80in (305 × 203cm).

Slot — see Break

SLP — see Self-liquidator.

Social grades Also called socio-economic grades. Social class (A, B, C₁, C₂, D, E), usually determined by the occupation of the head of household.

Soft focus A photographic effect in which the image is slightly diffused to soften the lines and edges of a shape without distorting the true focus. There are different ways of achieving the effect, such as with a specially made filter or shooting through a glass plate smeared with petroleum jelly.

Software A term used for computer programs and general items. It also refers to paper and magnetic tape.

Solus position The position of an advertisement on a page where there is no other advertising matter.

Spectacular A large display with cut-outs, lighting and sometimes moving parts.

Split transmission Simultaneous transmission of different TV programmes or commercials to two areas within one contractor region.

Sponsorship Financing of sports or cultural activities, usually by commercial companies.

Spot A booking or transmission of a television commercial. Each spot is a multiple of 10 seconds.

Spot rate Quoted rate for an individual booking as opposed to packages of airtime.

Spread — see Double Spread

Squared-up Half-tone A half-tone image confined to a rectangular shape.

Strap A subheading that appears above the main headline of a newspaper or magazine story.

Stripping (1) Assembling two or more images to produce a composite or multiple image for photomechanical reproduction. (2) The removal of photographic emulsion from a support to assemble with others on another support.

Supersite A very large poster site, usually about 30 × 10ft (9 × 3m) and hand-painted.

Supplement Material added to a publication separately or included in a reprint that supplies added detail to the text.

T

Tabloids A newspaper with small pages (half the size of a broadsheet).

Tailor-made Promotion A promotion specifically designed for one retailer. Also known as One chain.

Takes Different versions of each shot of a photograph, film or sound recording.

TAP Total Audience Package. A package of radio airtime.

Target audience Segments of the population to whom an advertising campaign is directed.

TC (1) (Of advertisement) Till countermanded: to run until further notice. (2) (Of editorial matter) To come, ie, will be sent to printers later.

TCA The Television Consumer Audit. A regular panel survey of grocery purchases by consumers.

Tear sheet (1) Page or item torn from a periodical and filed as reference material. (2) Page containing an advertisement torn from a periodical in lieu of a proof or a complete copy of the publication.

Telecopier A means by which facsimiles of typed matter, layouts etc, can be transmitted and received over telephone lines.

Telephoto lens A camera lens for use at long range.

Teletext Systems whereby data, messages and still pictures can be received and decoded by a TV set and the viewer can select pages by using a keypad.

Template Shape or sheet with cutout forms used as a drawing aid.

Terminal A device for receiving information from and/or sending information to, a computer. May be a VDU or a printer linked to the computer by cable or via the telephone.

Test market area A defined area which has the specified characteristics of the country for use in testing a product or campaign.

TGI The Target Group Index. Gives product data and media exposure reports on a wide range of products.

Thirty-two sheet A poster size measuring 120 × 160in (3 × 1.5m).

Themed break A break where two or more spots are booked together by an advertiser and the total time period used for different products.

Tie-breaker Device used in competitions to ensure that only a certain number of people win prizes. Usually involves writing a slogan or completing a sentence.

Time buyer The person with a brief to buy airtime from contractors. In some agencies the buyer is also the planner.

Time segment Segments of time for which different advertising rates apply, depending on the time in the week.

Time-sharing Also called multi-programming. Use of a computer by several independent programmers simultaneously.

Tip-in An insert usually smaller in size than the publication and not bound into it.

TMU Type mark up). Copy on which a typographer has marked instructions for the compositor indicating typeface, size, arrangement, etc.

Trade mark A word or symbol identifying a product or service and linking it to the manufacturer or supplier.

Trading stamps Tokens given to customers at retail outlets, according to the value of their purchase. Customers fill special books and exchange these for gifts or cash at redemption centres.

Traffic builder Store promotion designed to encourage movement through the store.

Tranny Short for transparency.

Transmission certificate A certificate confirming that a particular TV commercial has been transmitted.

Transparency A full-colour positive image on photographic transparent film which can be viewed through a projector.

Transpose To correct the wrong order of characters, words, lines or images on a manuscript or proof.

Triadic test See *Discrimination test*.

Tri-colour A standard prime colour used by a publication, such as Tri-red, Tri-blue, Tri-yellow.

Tube cards Card advertisments displayed in carriages on Underground systems.

Turnaround The length of time elapsing between the start and the finish of a particular job.

TV contractors Companies which have a contract with the IBA to operate in a specified franchise area, providing ITV programmes and selling advertising time.

TVR Television rating. A unit of measurement indicating the percentage of the total audience viewing a particular spot, expressed in terms of a target audience, e.g., 30% men TVRs or 40% housewife TVRs. The total of all TVRs is an index of a campaign's effectiveness.

Twelve-sheet Made up of several sheets posted side by side to form one advertisement. 10 × 5ft (3 × 1.5m).

Two Pages Facing Bleed into Gutter The full designation for a double-page spread split in the centre.

Type, typeface The raised image of a character cast on a rectangular piece of metal used in letterpress printing.

Type mark up see TM.

Typography The art, general design and appearance of printed matter using type.

Type scale/gauge A rule marked with a scale of type measurements, points, ems, picas, compositors etc, used by designers

Typesetting Methods of assembling type for printing, by hand, machine or photographic techniques.

Typo *(US)* Typographic error. An error in typewritten or typeset copy. See also Literal.

Typographer The person who designs and plans the typographical layout of a proposed printed work. This may include designing typefaces.

U

Underlay Colour, tone or pattern effect laid in underneath artwork, a photograph or illustration.

Universe Group of persons which is being investigated and from which a sample is taken (e.g., 'homes universe' or 'housewives universe').

Unjustified With lines which are centred or which align only at one margin, instead of being spaced to fill the measure of the line.

Upper case The capital letters in a fount of type.

Usage Number and type of people using or consuming (as opposed to buying) a product.

USP Unique Selling Proposition. The feature of a brand which distinguishes it form the competition.

U & A User and awareness study.

UHF Ultra High Frequency, the standard transmission mode for television signals world-wide. (See also VHF).

V

Variance (analysis of) A statistical procedure to establish the relative importance of different factors, e.g., region, age and sex.
VCR Video Cassette Recording. A method of transferring TV signals onto tape. Viewers with recorders may record their own programmes from the TV or buy pre-recorded cassettes.
VDU/VDT Visual display unit/terminal. A device with a TV screen for displaying information from a computer, and a keyboard for feeding information into the computer.
VHF Very High Frequency, the transmission mode for, eg, high-quality radio reception.
Video Videotape recording or VTR. A method of recording visual images on tape with sound, with facility for viewing the recording as it is being made. The image monitor is a TV set. TV programmes and commercials may be made on video instead of film.
Video cassette Philips, VCR or Sony-Umatic

are generally used for reference or research purposes.
Viewdata Any system which links TV sceens to central computers by means of telephone lines. The user can call up different computers, select pages of data and send messages back to the computer.
Vignette (1) A story or lifestyle encapsulated in a few lines. (2) A small illustration or decoration without a border.
Visibility The maximum distance from which the potential audience can see and read an advertisement.
Visual A mock-up of the proposed appearance of a design or layout presented as a rough drawing, or if more highly finished, as a presentation visuaL.
VO Voice Over. Initials used in radio/TV/ film script to indicate the opening of spoken words in relation to the picture. (MVO = male voice over, FVO = female voice over).
Volume Discount — see Discounts
Voucher Copy of a publication given by publishers as proof that an advertisement has appeared.

W

Web A continuous roll of paper which feeds a printing press.
Web-fed A printing press supplied with paper from a web, rather than in separate sheets.
Web-set Offset press working from a web or reel of paper
Weight test — see Discounts.
Weighting The adjustment of data by assigning different values to various parts of the results according to importance.
Wide-angle lens A camera lens giving an unusually wide angle of view without distortion. See also Fish eye lens.
Widow A single word standing as the last line of a paragraph in typeset copy. To be avoided if possible.
Word processor Equipment usually linked to a computer, so that input copy can be stored and automatically printed out at high speed and stored information can be quickly corrected.

The author would like to thank the following individuals and institutions for their kind assistance in the production of this book:

Advertising Age
Advertising Association
Advertising Standards Authority
Allen Brady & Marsh
Association of Media Independents
Ayer Barker

BMW (GB)
Bartle Bogle Hegarty
Diane Basapa
Beecham Products
Stephen Benson
James Best
Martin Boase
Boase Massimi Pollitt
Bowater-Scott
Simon Broadbent
Jeremy Bullmore

Campaign
Capital Radio
Cato Johnson

Central Office of Information
Chiat/Day
Paul Clark
Rita Clifton
Miles Colebrook
Communication Advertising and Education Foundation
Courage
Mike Cozens
Creative Review

Ken Dampier
Davidson Pearce
Tim Delaney
Rex Dobinson

Elida Gibbs

Winston Fletcher
Nick Fulford

Michael Gilmour
Lionel Godfrey
Granada Television
Arthur Guinness & Son

Tony Hertz
History of Advertising Trust
Michael Hook
Kirsty Hutton

Incorporated Society of British Advertisers
Independent Broadcasting Authority
Institute of Practitioners in Advertising

Bernadette Johnson

Stephen King

Lever Brothers
Levi Strauss
Tim Lindsay
Lintas
Alban Lloyd
Frank Lowe
Mike Luckwell

Marketing Week
McCann-Erickson
Ken Miles
Mirror Group of Newspapers
More O'Ferrall
News International
A. C. Nielsen

Ogilvy & Mather
Nick Phillips
Gerry Postlethwaite

Anthony Rau
Griff Rhys Jones
Rowntree-Mackintosh

Saatchi & Saatchi
Tony Scott
Mel Smith
Toby Syfret

The Times
J. Walter Thompson

Unilever

Van den Berghs

Watney Mann & Truman Brewers
Mike Waterson
Graham Watson
John Webster
Robin Wight
Wight Collins Rutherford Scott
John Wigram
F. W. Woolworth

plus the individual agencies and advertisers — and the unnamed creative teams — whose work is reproduced in these pages.